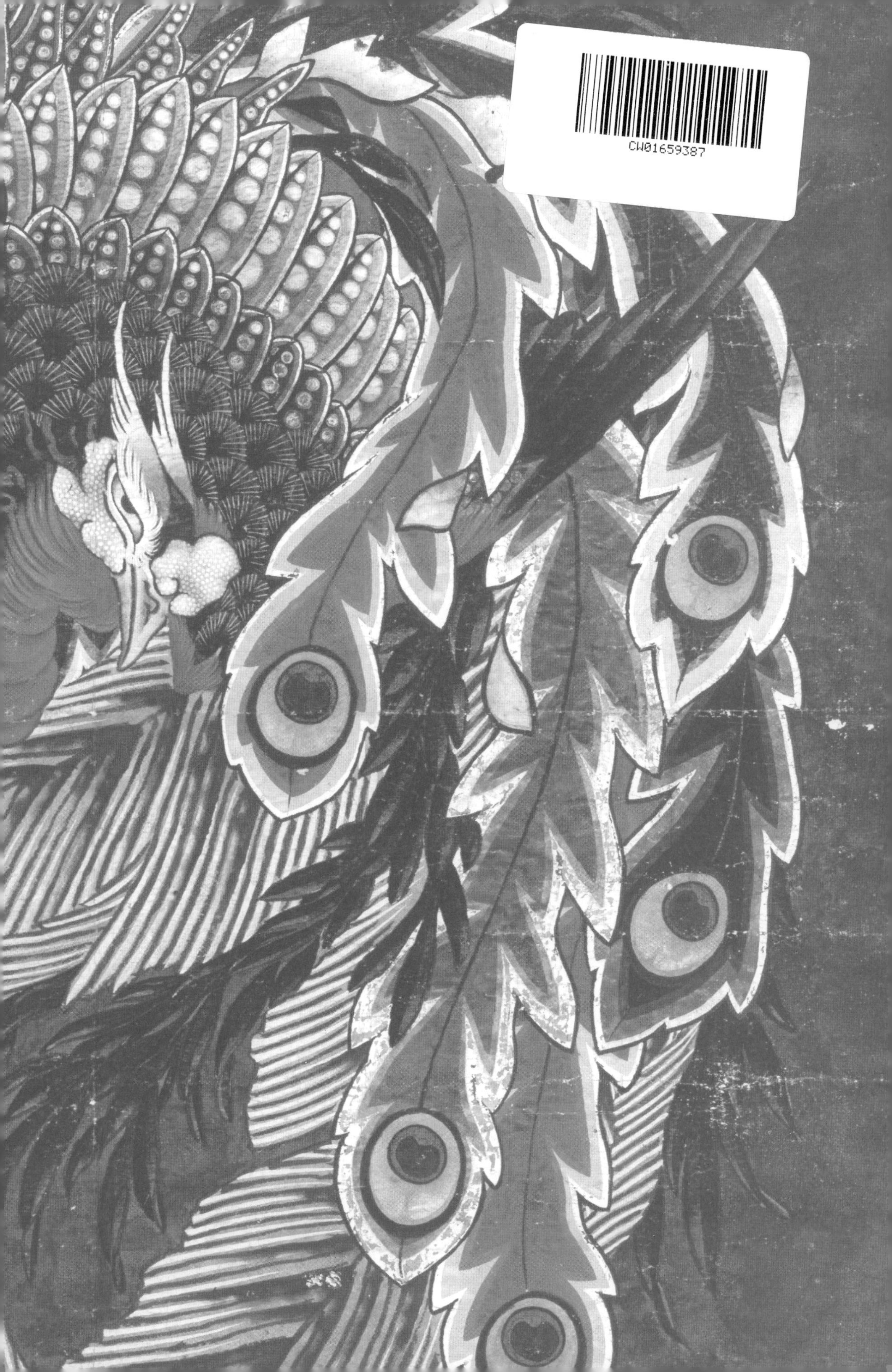

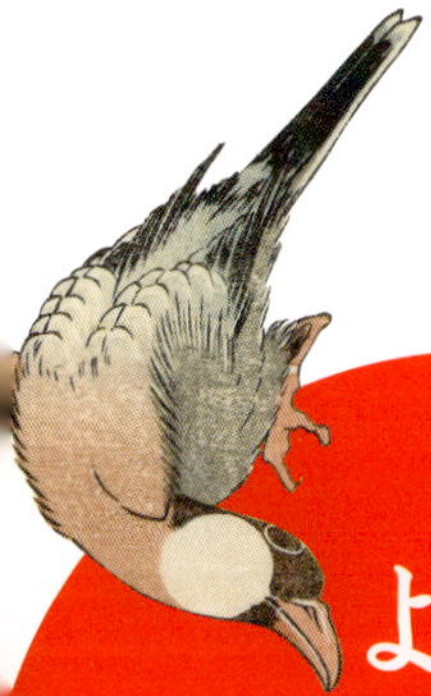

ようこそ

北斎の世界へ

〈英訳付〉

日野原健司［著］

東京美術

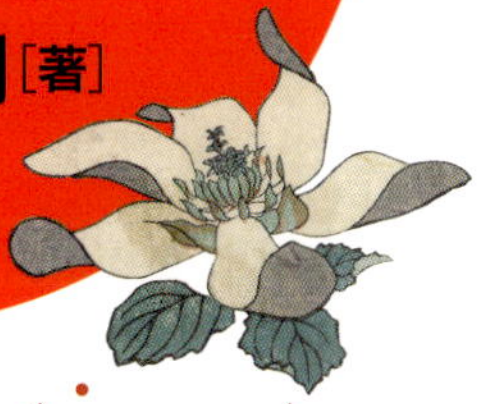

An Introduction to HOKUSAI

(in English and Japanese)

Anecdotes about the Renowned *Ukiyo-e* Artist

Text by **Hinohara Kenji**

Tokyo Bijutsu

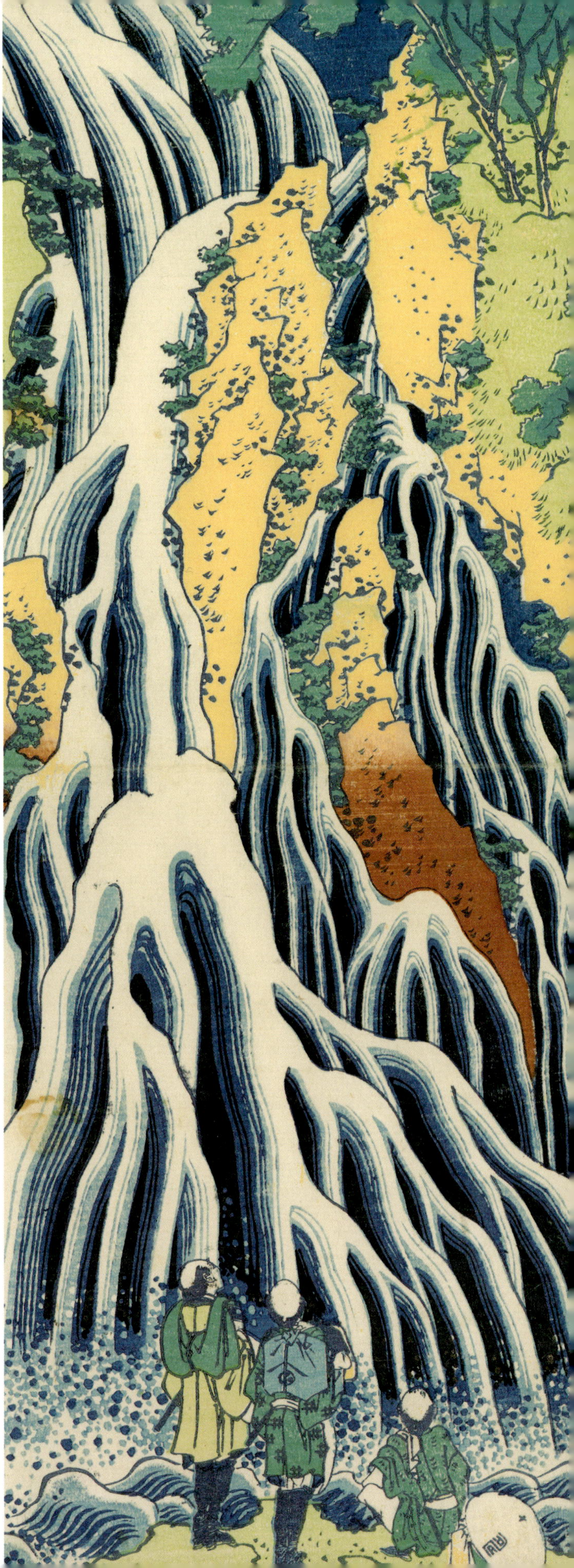

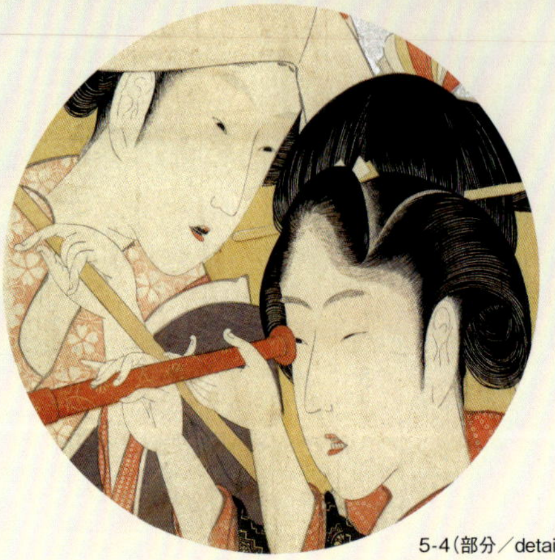
5-4（部分／detail）

ようこそ、北斎の世界へ！
Welcome to the world of Hokusai!

はじめに

葛飾北斎（1760~1849）は、江戸時代の庶民に愛された浮世絵師です。多岐に渡るジャンルで活躍し、90歳で亡くなるまで絵筆をとり続けました。巨大な波を描いた代表作「冨嶽三十六景　神奈川沖浪裏」は、パスポートや紙幣のデザインに採用されるなど、現在の日本でも高い人気を誇っています。また、日本を代表する芸術家の一人として、世界中にその名前が知れ渡っているといえるでしょう。

本書は、葛飾北斎について、浮世絵師としてどのような活躍をしていたのかはもちろんのこと、その人となりや暮らし方といった人物像についても紹介した入門書です。北斎のことを詳しく知りたいという人のために、様々な視点からの情報を簡潔にまとめました。本書をお読みいただければ、北斎の素晴らしい世界を、より一層深く楽しむことができるでしょう。

日本語と英語を併記していますので、英語圏の方々に北斎の入門書として利用していただきたいのはもちろんのこと、日本の読者にも北斎の魅力を海外に発信する際に役立てていただければ幸いです。

Introduction

Katsushika Hokusai (1760-1849) was an *ukiyo-e* artist loved by the people of the Edo period. He was active in wide-ranging genres and continued working with paintbrush in hand until he died at the age of 90. His popularity continues in present-day Japan with, for example, his masterpiece *Thirty-six Views of Mount Fuji: Great Wave off the Coast of Kanagawa* being used as designs for Japanese passports and banknotes. Moreover, his name is known globally as a leading artist of Japan.

This book is intended as an introduction not only to the achievements of Katsushika Hokusai as an *ukiyo-e* artist, but his personality including his disposition and lifestyle. Information from various viewpoints is provided concisely for those of you who would like to learn about Hokusai in detail. By reading it, you should be able to enjoy the wonderful world of Hokusai in further depth.

As the text is written in Japanese and English, hopefully English-speaking readers will find it helpful as an introduction to Hokusai and Japanese readers as an aid to share the fascination of Hokusai with people all over the world.

［凡例］
1　作品情報は原則として、作者名、作品名、制作年代、判型・材質・技法、所蔵、指定の順に記している。
2　作者名、作品名は、所蔵者の定めたものや慣例を参考にし、著者の判断に基づいている。
3　英訳は概ね対訳としているが、より理解しやすいように一部手を加えた箇所がある。また註に対する参考文献の英訳は省略した。
4　本文中の年齢は、生まれたときを1歳とする数え年で表している。

[Notes]
1. In principle, data on the works are listed in the following order: artist, title, date, format (size)/medium/technique, collection, designation.
2. The artists' names and the titles of the works are based on the author's judgment with due consideration of details provided by the owners and conventions.
3. The text is generally bilingual with some adjustments made to facilitate the understanding. Bibliographic details provided as footnotes have not been translated into English.
4. Ages are given in the traditional Japanese system, which counts a person's age as one year old during his or her year of birth, with one year added at the start of every new year.
5. Years are cited according to the Gregorian calendar, with the Japanese era name omitted in the English text. As the Gregorian calendar was not adopted in Japan until 1872, days and months before that are referred to in ordinal numbers.

目次

Contents

ノンブル脇のカットは葛飾北斎『北斎漫画』三編（メトロポリタン美術館蔵）より作成。
The illustrations beside the page numbers were taken from *Houkusai’s Sketches*, part 3 (The Metropolitan Museum of Art)

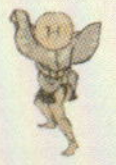

●北斎の生涯　The Life of Hokusai

年号	西暦 Year	年齢 Age	出来事 Incident
宝暦10年	1760	1歳 Age 1	9月23日、本所割下水に生まれる。 Born in Honjo Warigesui on the twenty-third day of the ninth month.
明和2年	1765	6歳 Age 6	この頃から好んで物の形を写すという。 Said to have enjoyed drawing the shapes of things from around this age.
安永2年	1773	14歳 Age 14	この頃、木版彫りの技術を学ぶ。 Learns woodblock carving techniques around this time.
安永7年	1778	19歳 Age 19	この頃、勝川春章に入門する。 Becomes a pupil of Katsukawa Shunshō around this time.
安永8年	1779	20歳 Age 20	勝川春朗と号して錦絵を発表し始める。「三代目瀬川菊之丞の正宗娘おれん」(図3-1)。 Assumes the name Katsukawa Shunrō and begins presenting *nishiki-e* (polychrome prints). *Segawa Kikunojō III as Oren, the Daughter of Masamune* (fig. 3-1).
寛政4年	1792	33歳 Age 33	12月8日、師匠の勝川春章が没する。 His teacher, Katsukawa Shunshō, dies on the eighth day of the twelfth month.
寛政6年	1794	35歳 Age 35	この頃、勝川派を離脱して、宗理号を襲名する。 Secedes from the Katsukawa school and assumes the name Sōri around this time.
			東洲斎写楽、5月から翌年にかけて役者絵を発表。 Tōshūsai Sharaku presents actor prints from the fifth month of 1794 to the following year.
寛政9年	1797	38歳 Age 38	狂歌絵本『柳の絲』(図4-1)。 *Kyōka* picture book, *Willow Tresses* (fig. 4-1).
			蔦屋重三郎が没する。 Tsutaya Jūzaburō dies.
寛政10年	1798	39歳 Age 39	宗理号を門人の宗二に譲り、北斎辰政を名乗る。 Transfers the Sōri name to his dsiciple Sōji and takes the name Hokusai Tokimasa.
			狂歌絵本『男踏歌』(図4-2)。 *Kyōka* picture book, *The Stamping Song of Men* (fig. 4-2).
寛政12年	1800	41歳 Age 41	狂歌絵本『東都名所一覧』(図4-3)。黄表紙『竈将軍勘略之巻』(図15-1)。 *Kyōka* picture book, *Famous Places in Edo at a Glance* (fig. 4-3). *Kibyōshi, The Book of Tactics of General Oven* (fig. 15-1).
享和元年	1801	42歳 Age 42	この頃、美人画「風流無くてなゝくせ」(図5-4)。 Produces the *bijinga*, *Seven Fashionable Habits* (fig. 5-4) around this time.
享和2年	1802	43歳 Age 43	狂歌絵本『美やことり』(図4-4)。 *Kyōka* picture book, *The Bird of the Capital* (fig. 4-4).
文化元年	1804	45歳 Age 45	4月13日、音羽護国寺の開帳において120畳大の達磨半身像を描く。 Paints a 120-*tatami*-mat-large half-length portrait of Bodhidharma at an opening ceremony at Otowa Gokoku-ji on the thirteenth day of the fourth month.

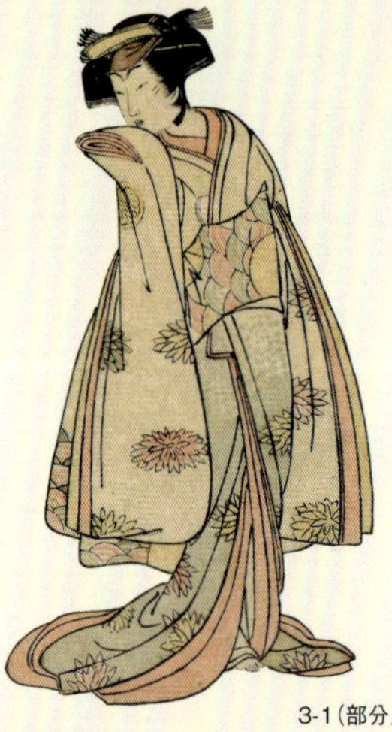
3-1（部分／detail）

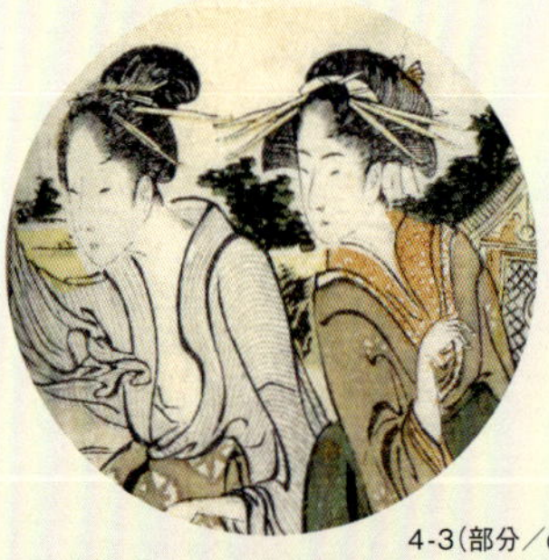
4-3（部分／detail）

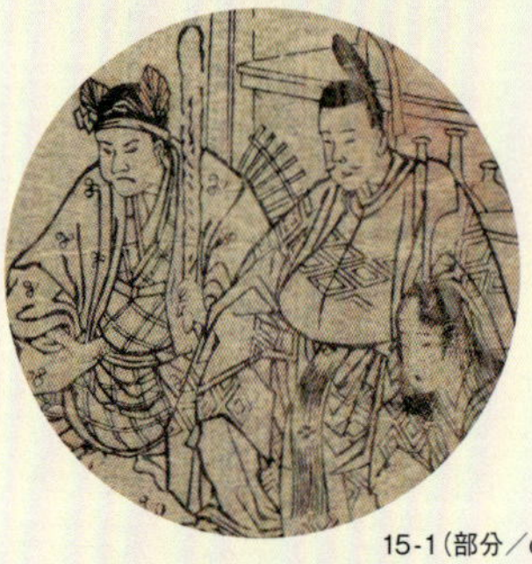
15-1（部分／detail）

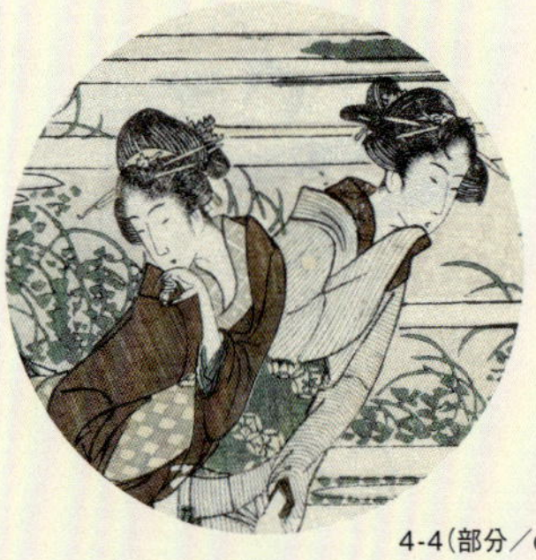
4-4（部分／detail）

年号	西暦 Year	年齢 Age	出来事 Incident
文化2年	1805	46歳 Age 46	読本挿絵『新編水滸画伝』初編（図6-1）。 *Yomihon* illustrations, *New Illustrated Edition of the Water Margin*, part 1 (fig. 6-1).
文化3年	1806	47歳 Age 47	春から夏頃、曲亭馬琴宅に寄宿する。 Lodges at Kyokutei Bakin's house from around spring to summer.
			6月頃、木更津へ旅行する。絵馬「富士の巻狩り図」（図39-1）。 Travels to Kisarazu around the sixth month. Votive tablet, *Boar Hunt at the Foot of Mount Fuji* (fig. 39-1).
			喜多川歌麿が没する。 Kitagawa Utamaro dies.
文化4年	1807	48歳 Age 48	読本挿絵『椿説弓張月』前編（図6-2～3）。この頃、肉筆画「酔余美人図」（図5-5）。 *Yomihon* illustrations, *Strange Tales of the Bow Moon*, part 1 (figs. 6-2~3). Produces the original painting, *Drunken Beauty* (fig. 5-5) around this time.
文化6年	1819	50歳 Age 50	読本挿絵『総角物語』後編（図32-1）。 *Yomihon* illustrations, *Agemaki monogatari*, part 2 (fig.32-1).
文化7年	1810	51歳 Age 51	この頃から戴斗号を用いるか。 Begins using the name Taito from around this time?
			絵手本『己痴羣夢多字画尽』前編（図8-1）。 Drawing manual, *Collection of the Pictures Formed by the Character*, part 1 (fig. 8-1).
文化9年	1812	53歳 Age 53	秋頃、名古屋に滞在し、『北斎漫画』の下絵を描く。 Stays in Nagoya around autumn and does the underdrawings for *Hokusai's Sketches*.
			読本挿絵『占夢南柯後記』（図31-1）。絵手本『略画早指南』前編（図8-2）。 *Yomihon* illustrations, *Yumeawase nanka kōki* (fig. 31-1). Drawing manual, *Quick Lesson in Simplified Drawings*, part 1 (fig. 8-2).
			この頃、春画『絵本つひの雛形』（図9-3）。 Produces the *shunga*, *Picture-book Models of Couples* (fig. 9-3) around this time.
			兄弟子であった勝川春好、没する。 Katsukawa Shunkō, a senior disciple of Shunshō, dies.
文化11年	1814	55歳 Age 55	絵手本『北斎漫画』初編（図8-3）。春画『喜能会之故真通』（図9-1～2）。 Drawing manual, *Hokusai's Sketches*, part 1 (fig. 8-3). *Shunga*, *Pine Seedlings on the First Rat Day* (figs. 9-1~2).
文化13年	1816	57歳 Age 57	この頃、長男の富之助が没する。 His eldest son Tominosuke dies around this time.
文化14年	1817	58歳 Age 58	春頃から名古屋に滞在。10月5日、名古屋の西掛所境内にて、120畳大の達磨半身像を描く Stays in Nagoya from around spring. Does a 120-*tatami*-mat-large half-length portrait of Bodhidharma within the precincts of Nishikake-sho, Nagoya on the fifth day of the tenth month.
文化15年／文政元年	1818	59歳 Age 59	大坂へ旅行するか。雪花亭北洲、春陽斎北敬が入門。 Travels to Osaka? Sekkatei Hokushū and Shun'yōsai Hokkei become his disciples.

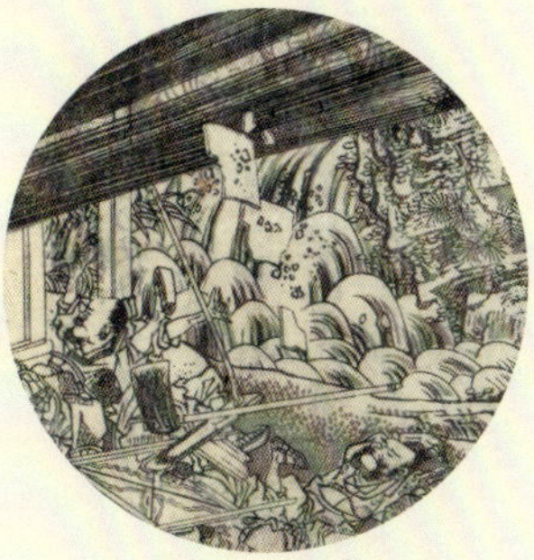
6-1（部分／detail）

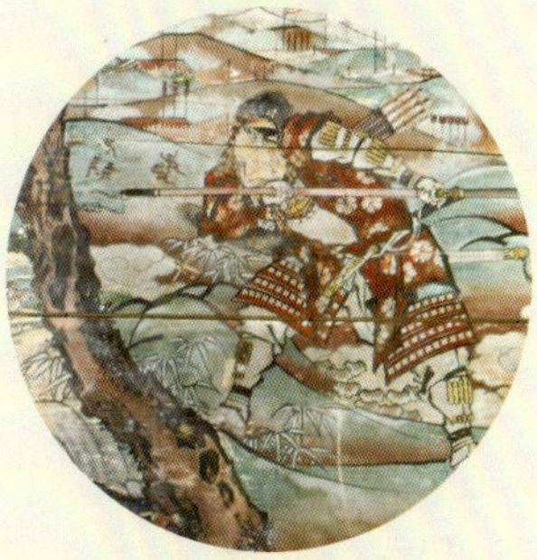
39-1（部分／detail）

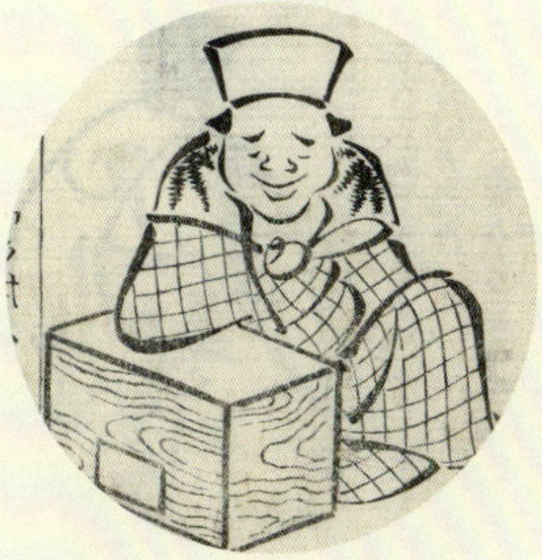
8-1（部分／detail）

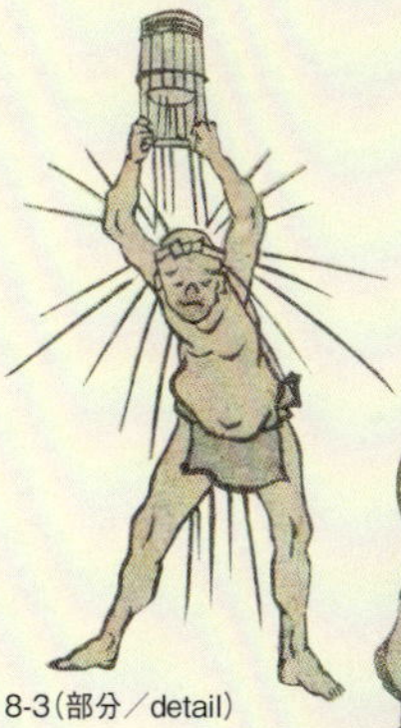
8-3（部分／detail）

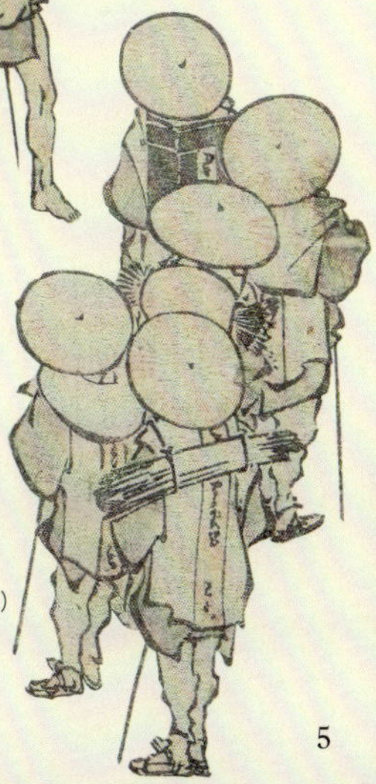
8-3（部分／detail）

年号	西暦 Year	年齢 Age	出来事 Incident
文政2年	1819	60歳 Age 60	戴斗号を門人の斗円楼北泉に譲るか。絵手本『北斎画式』(図41-1)。 Transfers the Taito name to his disciple Toenrō Hokusen? Drawing manual, *The Form of Paintings of Hokusai* (fig. 41-1).
文政3年	1820	61歳 Age 61	為一号を用いる。 Uses the name Iitsu.
文政4年	1821	62歳 Age 62	春画『万福和合神』(図9-6)。 *Shunga, God of Myriad Conjugal Delights* (fig. 9-6).
文政6年	1823	64歳 Age 64	この頃より、川柳に卍の号を用いる From around this time, begins using the name 卍 when he composes *senryū*.
			絵手本『今様櫛𥻨雛形』(図8-5)。 Drawing manual, *Modern Designs for Combs and Tobacco Pipes* (fig. 8-5).
文政7年	1824	65歳 Age 65	絵手本『新形小紋帳』(図8-6)。 Drawing manual, *The Book of New Patterns for Kimono Fabrics* (fig. 8-6)
文政9年	1826	67歳 Age 67	カピタンのデ・ステューレルが北斎の肉筆画(図38-1～2)を受け取る。 *Kapitan* J. W. de Sturler collects original paintings (figs. 38-1~2) from Hokusai.
文政10年	1827	68歳 Age 68	この頃、中風を患うが、自家製の薬で回復する。 Suffers paralysis, but recovers with homemade remedies around this time.
文政11年	1828	69歳 Age 69	6月5日、妻こと、没する。 His wife Koto dies on the fifth day of the sixth month.
文政12年	1829	70歳 Age 70	孫の放蕩に苦しむ。 Troubled with his grandson's prodigality.
天保元年	1830	71歳 Age 71	この頃から天保4年(1833)頃にかけて、風景画「冨嶽三十六景」(図1-1~2, 2-1, 12-1~4, 40-2)。 From around this time to c. 1833, he produces *Thirty-six Views of Mount Fuji* (figs. 1-1~2, 2-1, 12-1~4, 40-2).
天保2年	1831	72歳 Age 72	この頃、妖怪画「百物語」(図10-3~5)、花鳥画「芥子」(図13-1)。 Produces pictures of ghosts, *One Hundred Ghost Stories* (figs.10-3~5); pictures of flowers and birds, *Poppies* (fig. 13-1) around this time.
天保3年	1832	73歳 Age 73	閏11月28日、長女の元夫・柳川重信が没する。 His eldest daughter's ex-husband, Yanagawa Shigenobu, dies on the intercalary twenty-eighth day of the eleventh month.
天保4年	1833	74歳 Age 74	この頃、風景画「諸国瀧廻り」(図11-3)。 Produces landscapes, *Tour of Waterfalls in Various Provinces* (fig. 11-3) around this time.
天保5年	1834	75歳 Age 75	絵本『富嶽百景』初編。この頃、風景画「諸国名橋奇覧」(図11-4)、花鳥画「文鳥 辛夷花」(図13-2)。 Picture book, *One Hundred Views of Mount Fuji*, part 1. Produces landscapes, *Wondrous Views of Famous Bridges in Various Provinces* (fig. 11-4); pictures of flowers and birds, *Java Sparrow and Magnolia* (fig. 13-2) around this time.
			この頃、浦賀に潜居するといわれる。 Said to have lived in hiding in Uraga around this time.

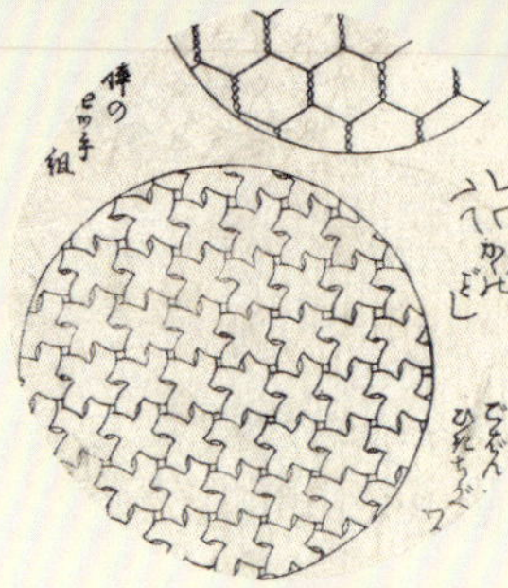
8-6(部分/detail)

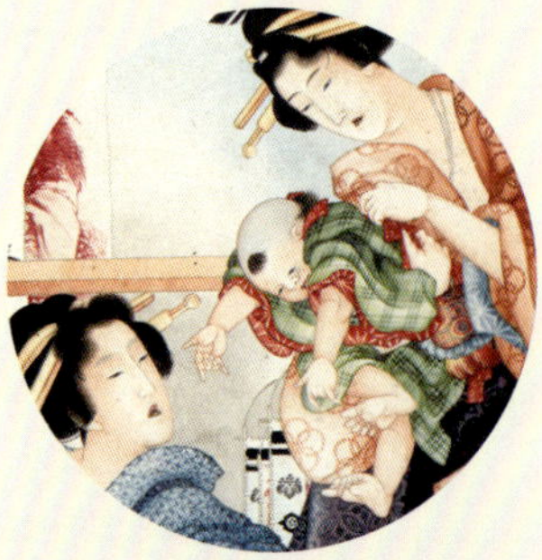
38-1(部分/detail)

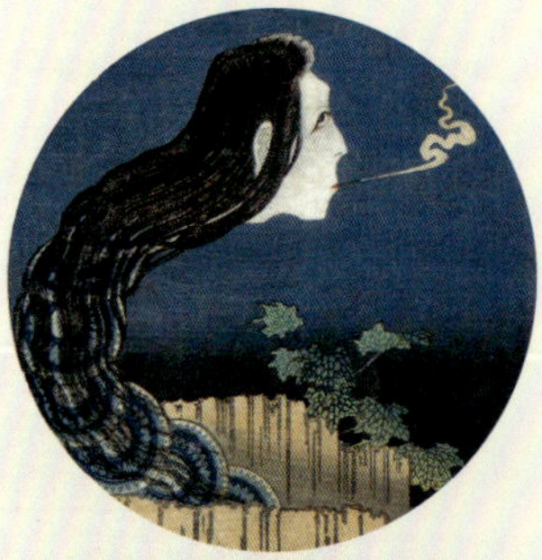
10-4(部分/detail)

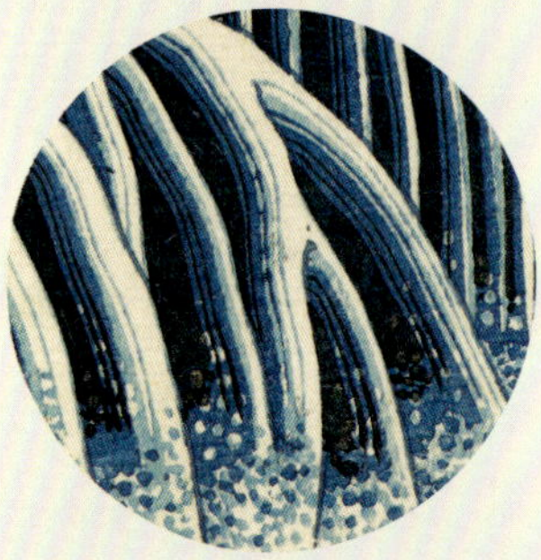
11-3(部分/detail)

13-2(部分/detail)

年号	西暦 Year	年齢 Age	出来事 Incident
天保6年	1835	76歳 Age 76	相州、豆州へ旅行する。この頃房総方面へ旅行するか？ Travels to Sōshū and Zushū. Travels to the Bōsō area around this time?
			絵本『富嶽百景』二編（図12-5～6）。 Picture book, *One Hundred Views of Mount Fuji*, part 2. (fig. 12-5～6)
天保7年	1836	77歳 Age 77	武者絵本『和漢絵本魁』、『絵本武蔵鐙』（図21-2, 36-1）。 Warrior picture books, *Picture Book of Chinese and Japanese Warriors* and *Picture Book, The Stirrups of Musashi* (figs. 21-2, 36-1).
天保10年	1839	80歳 Age 80	肉筆画「西瓜図」（図14-3）。 Original painting, *Watermelon* and *Knife* (fig. 14-3).
天保11年	1840	81歳 Age 81	房総方面へ旅行するか。鳥瞰図「唐土名所之絵」。 Travels to the Bōsō area? Bird's-eye view, *Famous Places in China*.
天保13年	1842	83歳 Age 83	翌年にかけて、「日新除魔図」（図19-1）を日課として描く。 Draws *Daily Exorcisms* (figs. 19-1) as a daily routine until the following year.
			柳亭種彦が没する。 Ryūtei Tanehiko dies.
天保15年／弘化元年	1844	85歳 Age 85	小布施に旅行する。東町祭屋台天井絵「龍図」「鳳凰図」。 Travels to Obuse. Ceiling paintings for the Higashimachi festival float, *Dragon* and *Phoenix*.
弘化2年	1845	86歳 Age 86	小布施に旅行する。上町祭屋台天井絵「男浪図」（図43-3）「女浪図」（図43-4）。 Travels to Obuse. Ceiling paintings for the Kanmachi festival float, *Masuculine Waves* (fig. 43-3) and *Feminine Waves* (fig. 43-4).
			読本挿絵『釈迦御一代記図会』（図6-6）。 *Yomihon* illustrations, *Illustrated Life of Shakamuni* (fig. 6-6).
嘉永元年	1848	89歳 Age 89	曲亭馬琴が没する。 Kyokutei Bakin dies.
嘉永2年	1849	90歳 Age 90	肉筆画「雨中の虎図」（図14-5）、「雲龍図」（図14-6）、「富士越龍図」（図26-1）。 Original paintings; *Tiger in Rain* (fig. 14-5), *Dragon in Rain Clouds* (fig. 14-6), and *Dragon Rising above Mount Fuji* (fig. 26-1).
			4月18日、浅草聖天町の遍照院境内の長屋にて没する。 Dies in a tenement house within the precincts of Henjō-in, a temple in Asakusa Shōdenchō, on the eighteenth day of the fourth month.
			4月19日、誓教寺にて葬儀が執り行われる。 Funeral held at Seikyō-ji on the nineteenth day of the fourth month.

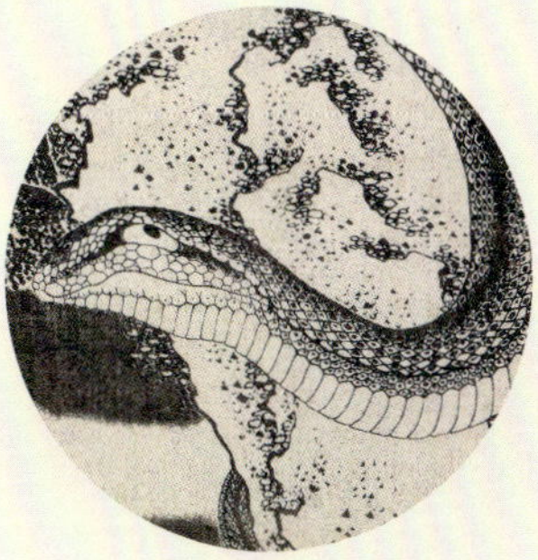
36-1（部分／detail）

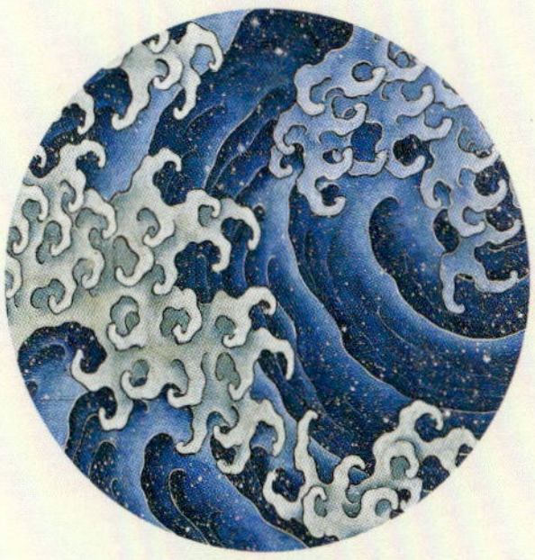
43-3（部分／detail）

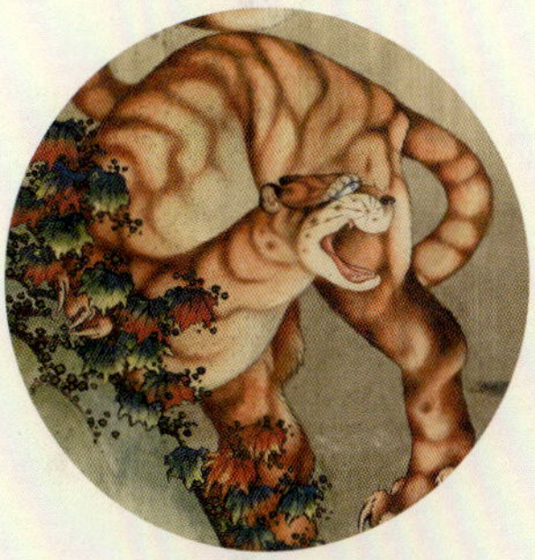
14-5（部分／detail）

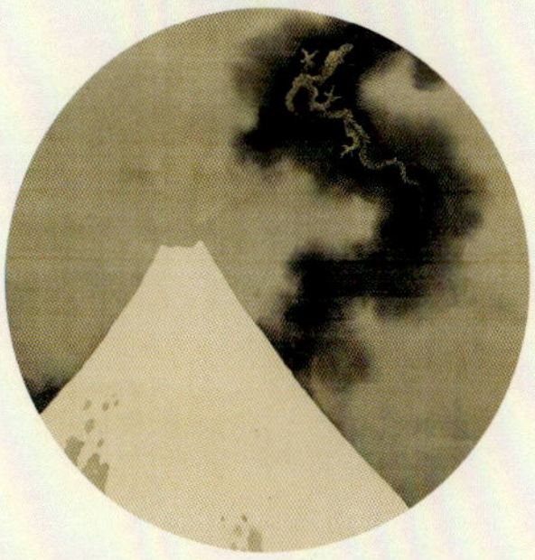
26-1（部分／detail）

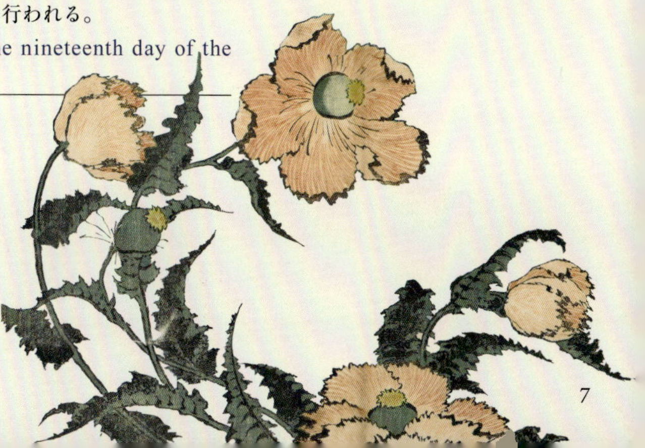
13-1（部分／detail）

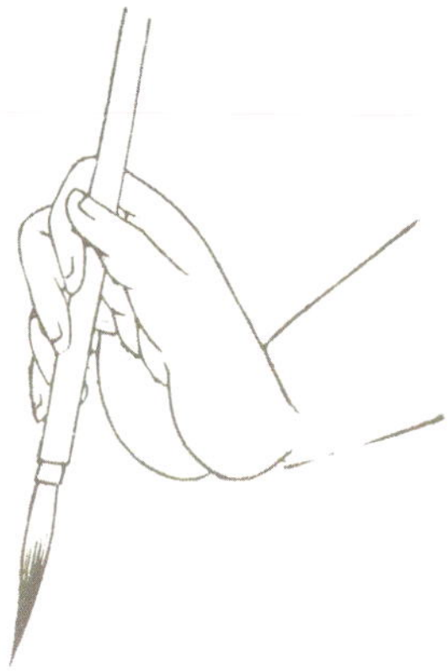

1 Foremost in Range and Numbers
活躍の幅も数もトップクラス

The Number of Works by Hokusai
点　数

北斎は、20歳に浮世絵師としてデビューしてから90歳で亡くなるまで、絵筆を握り続けました。約70年間に渡る画業の中で、膨大な量の作品を残しています。

その点数は、多色摺版画（錦絵と摺物）は約3000点、版本は200点強、肉筆画が1000点近く、さらに素描は何百も確認されていると指摘されています[1)]。錦絵だけに限ってみると、北斎と同時代に活躍していた歌川国貞や歌川広重、歌川国芳たちよりも少ない点数ではあります。しかし、北斎は版本や肉筆画の制作が多いのが特徴です。特に版本は複数巻からなることが多く、作品の点数以上に多くの挿絵が含まれています。例えば、読本34点（後編や続編などは合わせて1点としています）に対して、挿絵の総数は1400図にも達しています[2)]。北斎の作画点数は、浮世絵師の中でもトップクラスであったといえるでしょう。

一方、北斎の版画、例えば有名な「冨嶽三十六景　凱風快晴」（図1-1）が世界に何点残っているかというと、おそらく100点以上あるかと推測されますが、正確な点数を確認するのは難しい状況です。美術館のように所蔵を明らかにしていればいいのですが、個人のコレクターが公表していないケースや所蔵不明になったケースも多くあるからです。また、同じ作品でも、摺りによって絵自体の印象が大きく変化することもあり（図1-2）、北斎の作品の全貌を緻密に整理することは非常に手のかかるものでした。

21世紀に入ってから、世界各国の美術館のコレクションが急速にオンライン化されています。これらの情報とこれまでの研究成果を重ね合わせることによって、北斎の作品の全貌は、今後より明らかになっていくことでしょう。

1)　ロジャー・S・キーズ「北斎、その最晩年」『北斎―富士を越えて―』（展覧会図録）、あべのハルカス美術館、2017年

2)　鈴木重三ほか編『北斎読本挿絵集成』全5巻、美術出版社、1971～73年

Hokusai continued to work with paintbrush in hand from when he debuted as an *ukiyo-e* artist aged 20 to his death at the age of 90. Throughout his approximately seventy-year-long artistic career, he left a colossal number of works.

There are considered to be approximately 3,000 polychrome prints (*nishiki-e* and *surimono*), more than 2,000 *hampon* (woodblock-printed books), close to 1,000 *nikuhitsuga* (original paintings), and several hundred drawings confirmed as works by Hokusai. Looking at *nishiki-e* only, the number of works Hokusai produced is smaller than those produced by his contemporaries Utagawa Kunisada, Utagawa Hiroshige, and Utagawa Kuniyoshi. The distinguishing feature of Hokusai is that he produced many woodblock-printed books and original paintings. Particularly regarding the woodblock-printed books, they often consisted of multiple volumes and contained more illustrations than the number of titles. For example, the total number of illustrations included in 34 *yomihon* (counting sequels as part of one work) amounts to 1,400. Consequently, the number of works Hokusai produced was probably foremost among the *ukiyo-e* artists.

On the other hand, it is difficult to confirm the exact number of prints by Hokusai that remain worldwide. For example, there are probably 100 or more impressions of *Thirty-six Views of Mount Fuji: Mild Breeze on a Fine Day* (fig.1-1) all over the world. Whereas works in museum collections are made public, there are private collectors who do not disclose their possessions and cases in which the ownership is unknown. Furthermore, regarding the same work, depending on the printing, the impression of the picture itself can be altered significantly (fig. 1-2). Therefore, putting the overall aspect of Hokusai's oeuvre in meticulous order was an extremely laborious procedure.

The collections of museums all over the world have rapidly been made available online in the twenty-first century. By accumulating such information and the fruits of studies conducted so far, the totality of Hokusai's oeuvre should become clearer in the future.

※本章のタイトル脇のカットは葛飾北斎『略画早指南』後編（島根県立美術館／永田コレクション蔵）より作成
The title illustrations for this chapter were taken from Katsushika Hokusai, *Quick Lessons in Simplified Drawings*, part 2 (Shimane Art Museum, Nagata Collection).

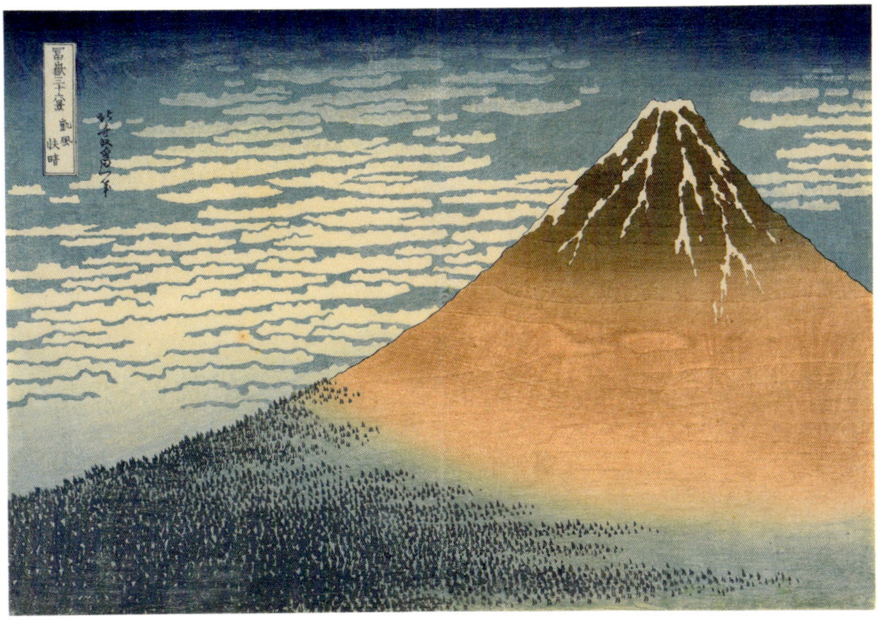

1-1 葛飾北斎 **冨嶽三十六景（ふがくさんじゅうろっけい） 凱風快晴（がいふうかいせい）**

天保元～4年（1830～33） 大判錦絵 島根県立美術館（新庄コレクション）蔵

「赤富士」の通称で知られる北斎の代表作。凱風と呼ばれる初夏の南風によって、辺りの靄が吹き飛ばされ、夏の富士山が赤茶けた地肌を見せています。北斎は、白い雪を被った富士山というステレオタイプなイメージに揺さぶりをかけようとしたとも考えられます。この作品は、摺（ず）りや保存状態の良し悪しはともかく、世界各地の美術館で所蔵されています。

1-1 Katsushika Hokusai

Thirty-six Views of Mount Fuji: Mild Breeze on a Fine Day

1830–1833, *ōban nishiki-e*, Shimane Art Museum (Shinjō Collection)

A representative work by Hokusai commonly known as the "Red Fuji." A mild, early summer wind from the south blows the haze away, exposing the reddish-brown surface of the summer mountain. Here, Hokusai may have been trying to shake up the stereotyped image of Mount Fuji crowned with snow. Although the printing and state of preservation can vary, impressions can be found in museums all over the world.

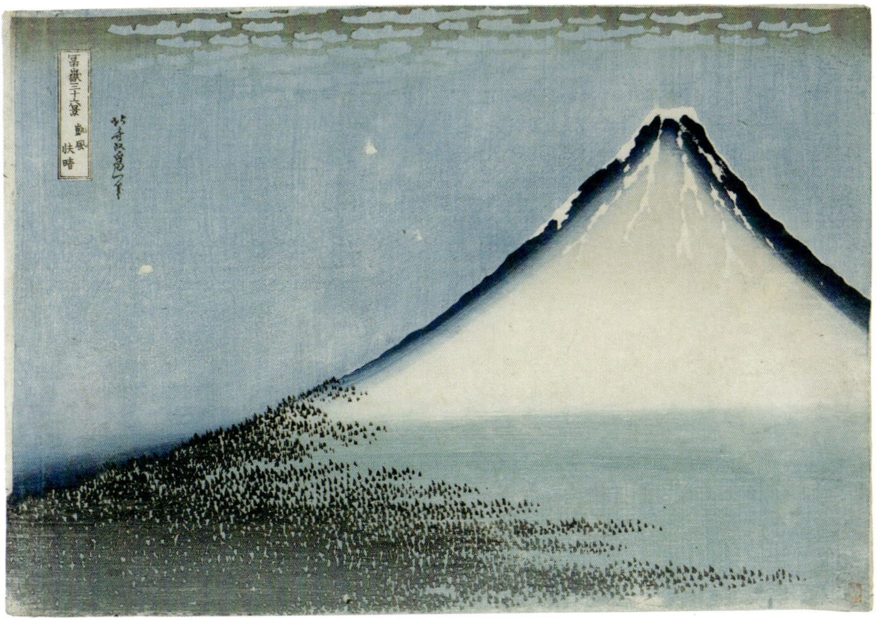

1-2 葛飾北斎 **冨嶽三十六景（ふがくさんじゅうろっけい） 凱風快晴（がいふうかいせい）**

天保元～4年（1830～33） 大判錦絵 茂木本家美術館蔵

「凱風快晴」の後摺として制作された、通称「青富士」です。富士山の稜線の内側を藍色のぼかし摺りにした藍摺の作品で、夏の富士山を描いた「赤富士」とは全く印象の異なる冬の富士山となっています。

1-2 Katsushika Hokusai

Thirty-six Views of Mount Fuji: Mild Breeze on a Fine Day

1830–1833, *ōban nishiki-e*, Mogi-Honke Museum of Art

This is a later edition of *Mild Breeze on a Fine Day* commonly known as the "Blue Fuji." The inside of the ridgeline is printed in Prussian blue gradation. Totally unlike the effect of the "Red Fuji" depicting the mountain in the summer, this is a view of Mount Fuji in the winter.

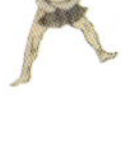

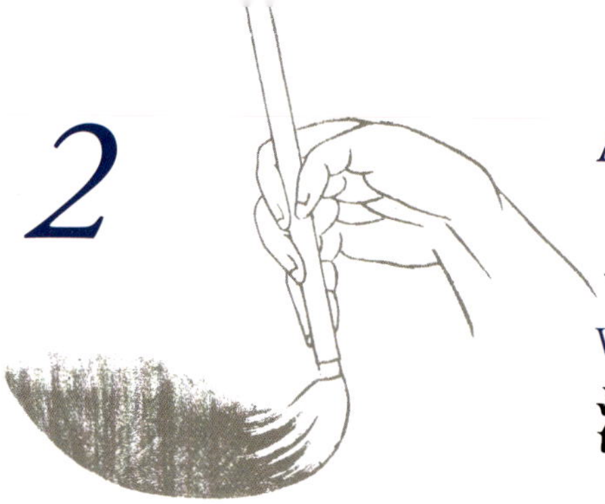

2 A Lifelong Theme
生涯追い続けたテーマ

Waves
波

「冨嶽三十六景　神奈川沖浪裏」(図2-1) は、荒れ狂う巨大な波を描いた傑作として有名です。北斎がこの波を描いたのは70歳を過ぎてからですが、いきなりこの年齢になって波を描くというアイデアが閃いた訳ではありません。

北斎はすでに40代頃から波に対して強い関心を抱いていました。「おしをくりはとうつうせんのづ」(図2-2) や「賀奈川沖本杢之図」といった、「神奈川沖浪裏」のプロトタイプをすでにこの時期に制作しています。ただし、「神奈川沖浪裏」ほどの波の迫力には到達しておらず、未完成だったといえるでしょう。

北斎はその後も生涯を通じて波の表現を試みていきました。40代半ばに手がけた読本挿絵 (→24頁参照、図2-3) や、50代半ば以降の絵手本 (→32頁参照) にその痕跡がいくつも認められます。特に興味深いのが『北斎漫画』二編 (図2-4) でしょう。波打ち際に寄せる波と引いていく波の動きを描写したものですが、北斎が実際に波の動きを海岸で観察していたのではないかと想像させられるのです。

「神奈川沖浪裏」は、北斎が長年に渡って波の表現を試み続けた結果としてたどり着くことができた境地でありました。しかし、北斎の波への関心はそれがゴールではなかったようです。「冨嶽三十六景」のすぐ直後に刊行された『富嶽百景』(→48頁参照) における「海上の不二」(図2-6)、さらに86歳には祭屋台天井図「男浪図」「女波図」(図43-3~4) といったダイナミックな波の描写を試みています。北斎は波というテーマを亡くなる直前まで追い続けたのです。

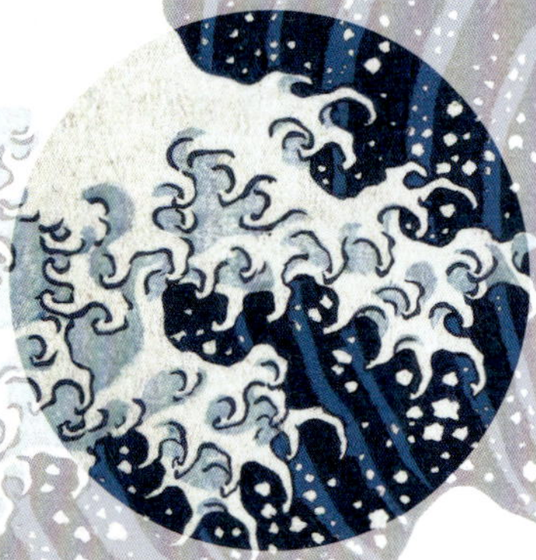

Thirty-six Views of Mount Fuji: Great Wave off the Coast of Kanagawa (fig. 2-1) is a well-known masterpiece depicting a huge raging wave. Hokusai was over 70 when he produced this wave, but it is not as if he hit upon the idea all of a sudden at that age.

Hokusai already had a keen interest in waves from around his forties. Back in those days, he had already produced prototypes of *Great Wave off the Coast of Kanagawa* such as *Fast Skiffs Navigating Large Waves* (fig. 2-2) and *Honmoku off the Coast of Kanagawa*. However, the waves in the earlier works had not attained the impact of *Great Wave off the Coast of Kanagawa*, making them appear unfinished.

Thereafter, throughout his lifetime, Hokusai continued attempts in depicting waves. Evidence of such efforts are provided in *yomihon* illustrations (see p. 24, fig. 2-3) he did in his mid-forties and drawing manuals (see p. 32) he did from his mid-fifties onwards. A particularly interesting example would be one in *Hokusai's Sketches*, part 2 (fig. 2-4). It shows the movement of the waves rolling in toward the water's edge and those receding, suggesting that Hokusai may actually have observed the movement of the waves on the beach.

Great Wave off the Coast of Kanagawa was a state that Hokusai managed to arrive at as a result of continuous attempts at the representation of waves. Nevertheless, that was not the goal of his interest in waves. In *One Hundred Views of Mount Fuji* (see p. 48), which was published immediately after *Thirty-six Views of Mount Fuji*, he ventured on depicting an even more dynamic wave entitled *Mount Fuji above the Sea* (fig. 2-6) and furthermore, at the age of 86, *Masculine Waves* and *Feminine Waves* (figs. 43-3~4), ceiling paintings for a festival float. Hokusai continued to pursue the theme of waves until immediately before his death.

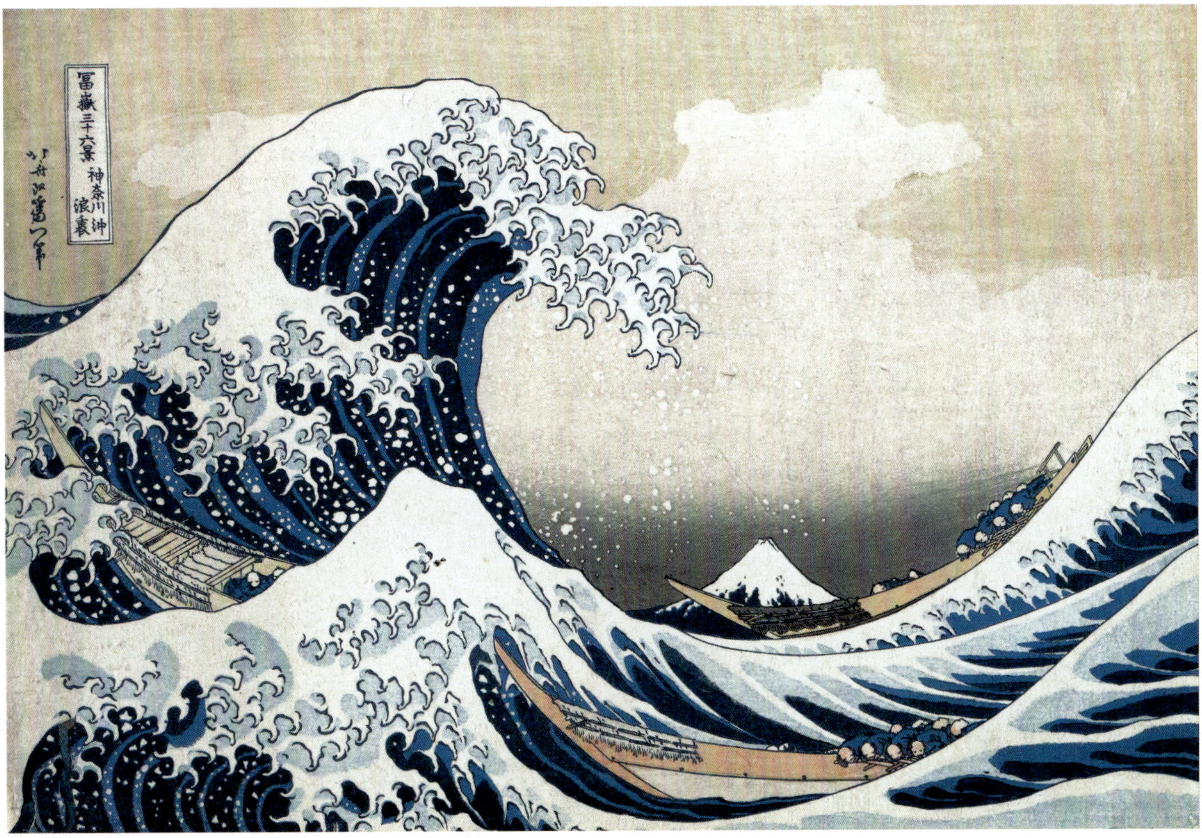

2-1 葛飾北斎 **冨嶽三十六景(ふがくさんじゅうろっけい)　神奈川沖浪裏(かながわおきなみうら)**
天保元～4年(1830～33)頃　大判錦絵　メトロポリタン美術館蔵

濃い藍色と薄い藍色、水色といった海の色がストライプ状に配置されることで、波がせり上がっていく勢いが増していく効果をもたらしています。また、波頭がまるで襲いかかる爪のような形をしているのも、波が崩れていく迫力を高めています。

2-1 Katsushika Hokusai
Thirty-six Views of Mount Fuji: Great Wave off the Coast of Kanagawa
c. 1830–1833, *ōban nishiki-e*, The Metropolitan Museum of Art

The arrangement of the colors of the sea in stripes of dark Prussian blue, pale Prussian blue, and light blue effectively captures the wave gaining momentum as it rises. The claw-like crest of the wave enhances the impact of its break, too.

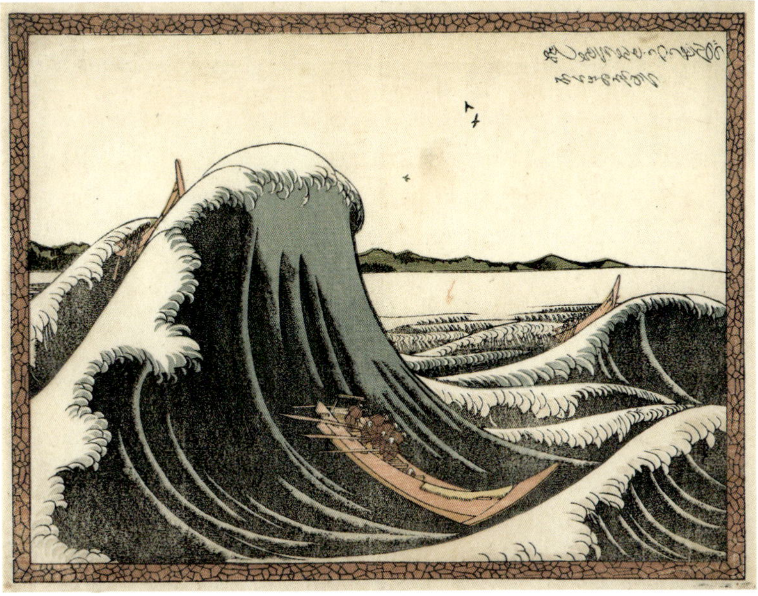

2-2 葛飾北斎
おしをくりはとうつうせんのづ
文化元～3年(1804～06)頃　中判錦絵
名古屋市博物館蔵

「神奈川沖浪裏」の約30年前に制作された、同じ趣向の作品です。西洋画を意識した波の陰影によって、せり上がっていく波の不気味さは出ていますが、舟に襲いかかる波のスピード感や迫力までは十分に表現されていません。

2-2 Katsushika Hokusai
Fast Skiffs Navigating Large Waves
c. 1804–1806, *chūban nishiki-e*, Nagoya City Museum

Produced thirty or so years before the Great Wave, this is a work similar in scheme. The uncanniness of the gradually rising waves is expressed by means of shading influenced by Western painting, but the sense of speed and impact of the waves attacking the skiffs are not yet fully represented.

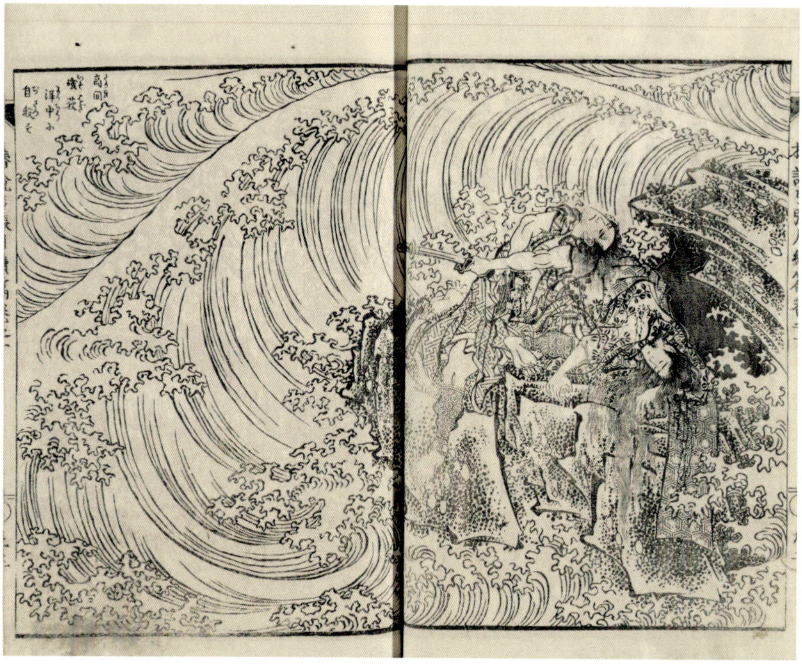

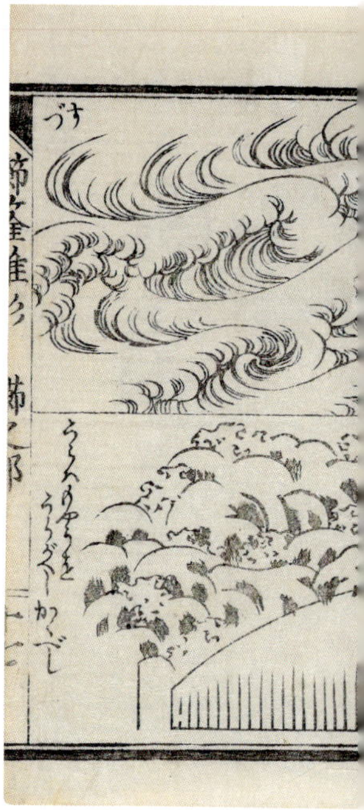

2-3 曲亭馬琴作・葛飾北斎画 『椿説弓張月』続編巻之一

文化5年（1808） 半紙本 国立国会図書館蔵

「神奈川沖浪裏」の約30年前に制作された読本挿絵です。岩場にぶつかって砕け散る波を、墨の線だけで表現しています。波頭の形や、波の動きを示す曲線など、「神奈川沖浪裏」につながる表現の芽生えを確認できます。

2-3 Kyokutei Bakin

***Strange Tales of the Bow Moon*, part 3, vol. 1**

illust. Katsushika Hokusai, 1808, *hanshibon*, National Diet Library, Japan

This is a *yomihon* illustration that was produced thirty or so years before the Great Wave. The waves hitting and breaking on the rocks are depicted in *sumi* ink lines only. The first hints leading to the Great Wave can be identified in the shapes in which Hokusai portrays the wave crests or the curves indicating the undulation.

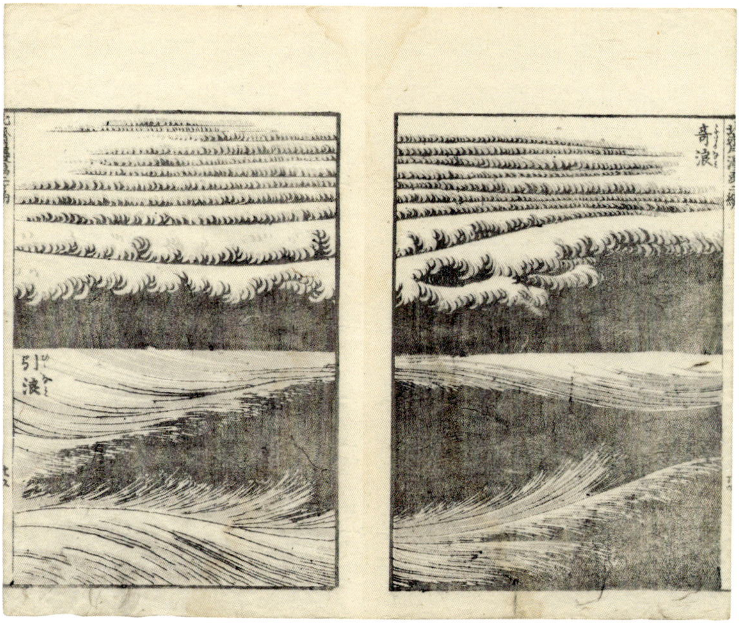

2-4 葛飾北斎 『北斎漫画』二編

文化12年（1815） 半紙本 太田記念美術館蔵

「神奈川沖浪裏」の約15年前に描いた「寄浪」（上）と「引浪」（下）です。北斎は、動いている波をいかに墨の線で描写するかを考えていたことでしょう。このような地道な鍛練の成果が、後の「神奈川沖浪裏」の完成へとつながります。

2-4 Katsushika Hokusai ***Hokusai's Sketches*, part 2**

1815, *hanshibon*, Ōta Memorial Museum of Art

These incoming waves (*top*) and receding waves (*bottom*) were depicted approximately fifteen years before the Great Wave. Hokusai must have been pondering how to depict the waves in motion in *sumi* ink lines only. Such steady discipline was to lead to the achievement of the Great Wave.

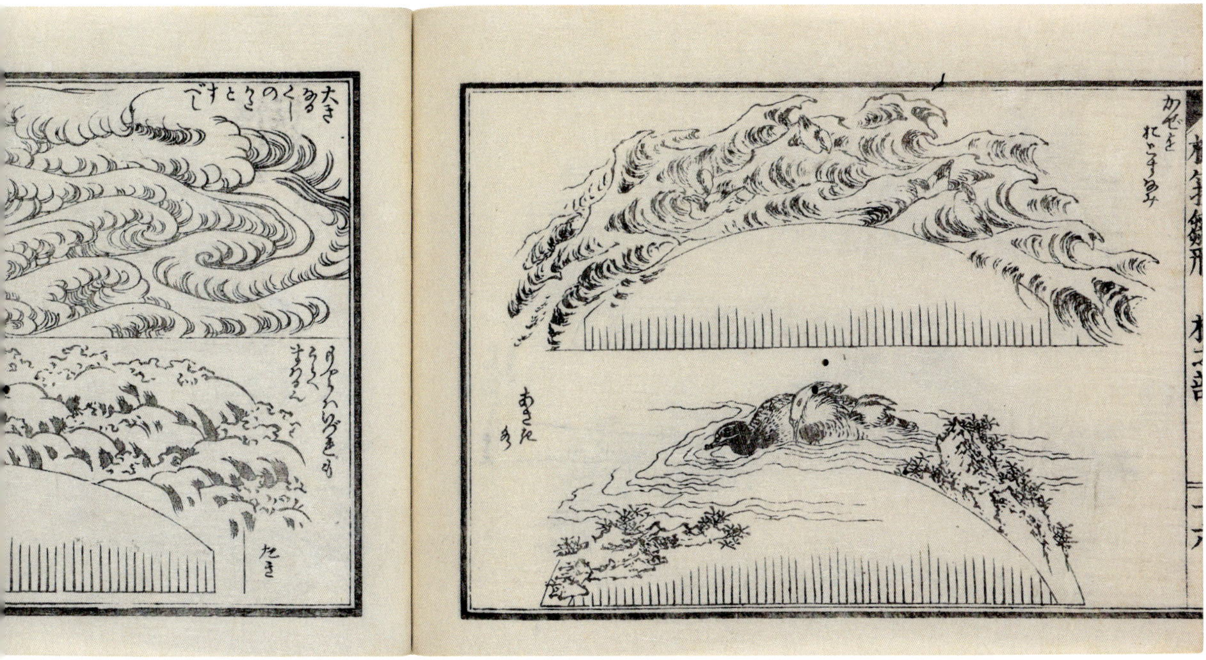

2-5　葛飾北斎　『今様櫛𥶡雛形』
文政6年（1823）　横本　島根県立美術館（永田コレクション）蔵

「神奈川沖浪裏」の約7、8年前頃に描いた絵手本です。櫛の持ち手となる峰の部分のデザインに、北斎は水や波の形を採用しています。水の動きを的確に描写するだけでなく、工芸用のデザインとして簡略化することも同時に考えています。

2-5　Katsushika Hokusai
Modern Designs for Combs and Tobacco Pipes
1823, *yokohon*, Shimane Art Museum (Nagata Collection)

This drawing manual was produced seven or eight years before the Great Wave. Hokusai employs water and waves for the designs on the top of the comb, where it is held. Besides capturing the flow of the water accurately, he also pays attention to simplifying the design for craftwork.

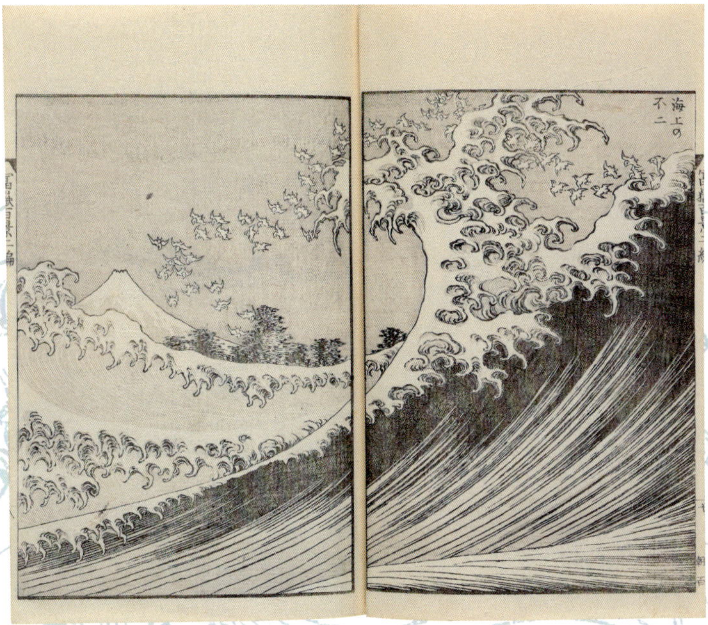

2-6　葛飾北斎　『富嶽百景』二編
天保6年（1835）　半紙本　島根県立美術館（永田コレクション）蔵

「神奈川沖浪裏」の波の表現をさらに推し進めたのが、この「海上の不二」です。波頭の背後に千鳥が飛ぶことで、波の回転力がさらに増し、幻想的な世界に近づいています。この後も北斎の波は「男浪図」「女浪図」（→122、123頁参照）へと進化していきます

2-6　Katsushika Hokusai
***One Hundred Views of Mount Fuji*, part 2**
1835, *hanshibon*, Shimane Art Museum (Nagata Collection)

The Great Wave evolved further into *Mount Fuji above the Sea*. With plovers flying beyond the wave crests, the turning force of the waves gathers further momentum, approaching a phantasmal world. Hokusai's waves went on developing and bore fruit as *Masculine Waves* and *Feminine Waves* (see pp. 122, 123).

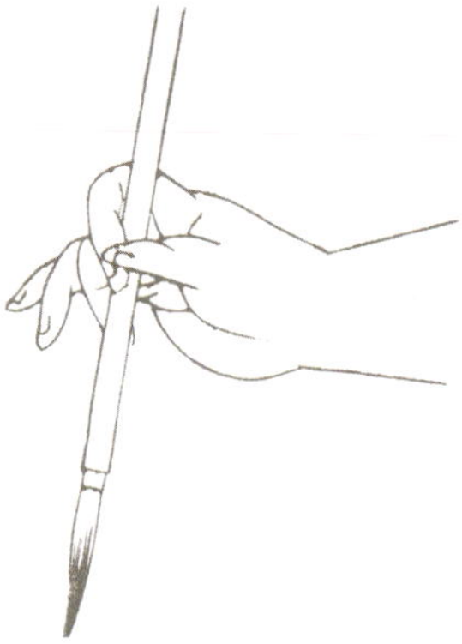

3 The First Step
最初の一歩

Actor Prints
役者絵

北斎は安永7年(1778)、浮世絵師を目指して、勝川春章に入門します。春章は、歌舞伎役者たちの顔をそっくりに描く似顔という新たな表現を確立したことで、当時高い人気を誇っていました(→86頁参照)。北斎は、春章の「春」の字と、春章の別号である旭朗井の「朗」の字を合わせた「春朗」という画号を授けられます。

春章に入門してからわずか1年後、北斎は浮世絵師としてデビューしました。現在確認されている最も古い北斎の一枚摺の錦絵が、安永8年(1779)8月に刊行された4点[1]の役者絵です(図3-1)。北斎は勝川派の一員として、役者絵を描くことからスタートすることになるのです。

寛政6年(1794)、35歳頃に勝川派を離脱するまでの約15年間、北斎は役者絵を描き続けます。しかし、一定の技量には到達しているものの、後の作品に見られるような傑出した個性は感じられません。また、北斎と同時期に春章に入門した勝川春英と比べても制作点数は少なく、抜きん出た評価を得るまでには至らなかったようです。

北斎は、寛政4年(1792)、師匠である春章が没すると、兄弟子の勝川春好との不仲もあり(→86頁参照)、寛政6年(1794)に勝川派を離脱します。勝川派に対しての遠慮があったのか、勝川派を離脱して以降の役者絵はわずかな点数しか確認されていません。

1) 田沢裕賀「作品解説2」『北斎展』(展覧会図録)、東京国立博物館、2005年

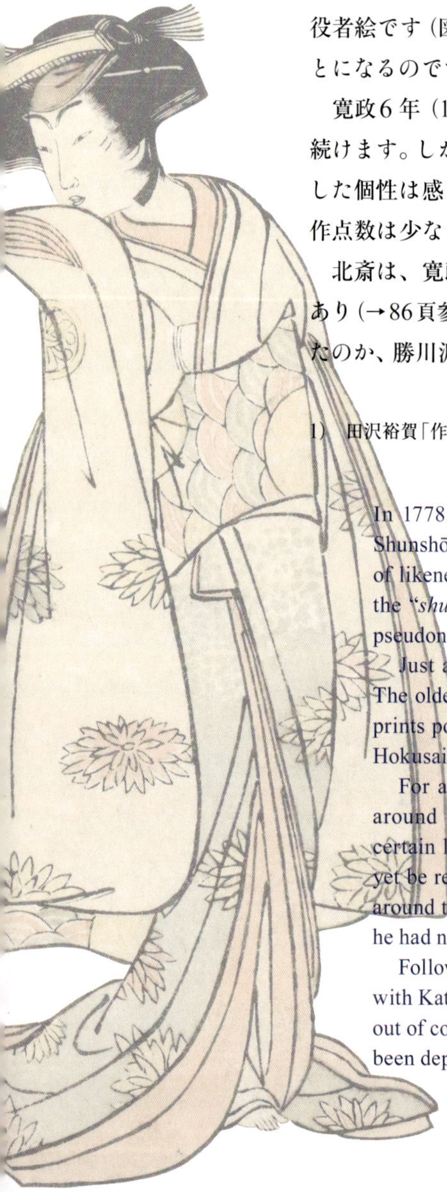

In 1778, aiming to become an *ukiyo-e* artist, Hokusai became a pupil of Katsukawa Shunshō. In those days, Shunshō was immensely popular for having established a new genre of likeness portraits depicting true-to-life images of *kabuki* actors' faces (see p. 86). Taking the "*shun*" character from Shunshō's name and the "*rō*" character from Shunshō's other pseudonym "Kyokurōsei," Hokusai was given the artist name "Shunrō."

Just a year after becoming a pupil of Shunshō, Hokusai debuted as an *ukiyo-e* artist. The oldest single-sheet *nishiki-e* (polychrome prints) confirmed as works by Hokusai are four prints portraying *kabuki* actors, which were published in the eighth month of 1779 (fig. 3-1). Hokusai started out by producing actor prints as a member of the Katsukawa school.

For approximately fifteen years until Hokusai seceded from the Katsukawa school around 1794 aged 35, he continued to depict *kabuki* actors. Although he had attained a certain level of skills, the prominent individuality identifiable in his later works could not yet be recognized there. Compared to Katsukawa Shun'ei, who became a pupil of Shunshō around the same time as Hokusai, the number of works Hokusai produced was smaller and he had not yet been able to achieve outstanding distinction.

Following his master Shunshō's death in 1792, partly because Hokusai did not get on with Katsukawa Shunkō (see p. 86), in 1794, he seceded from the Katsukawa school. Whether out of consideration for the Katsukawa school, only a few actor prints are confirmed to have been depicted by Hokusai after breaking away from them.

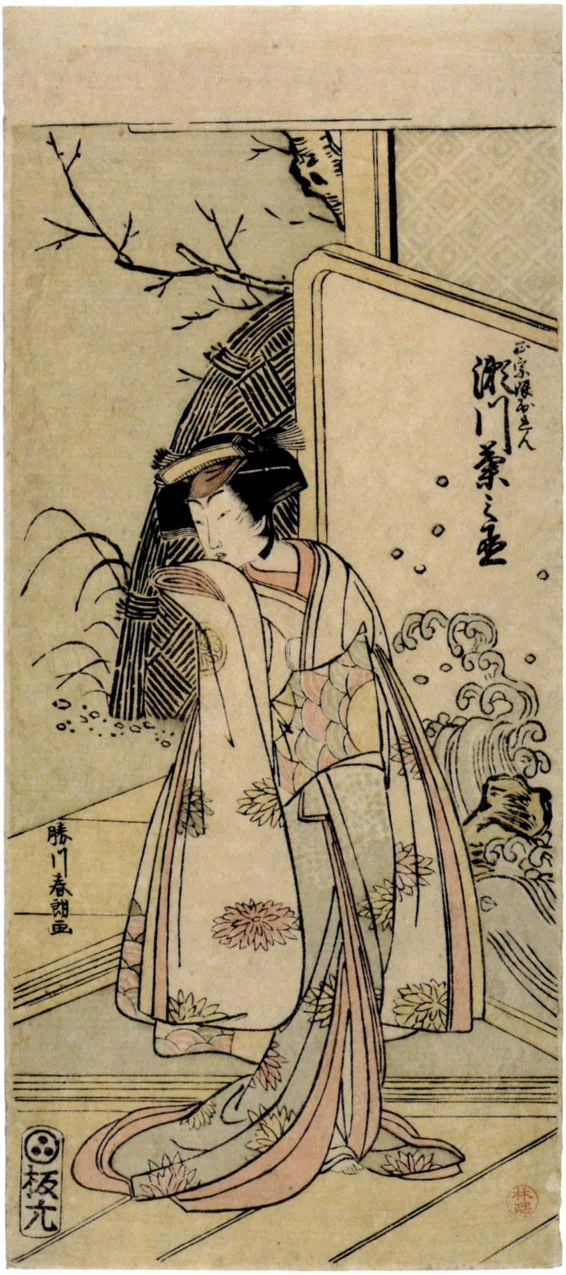

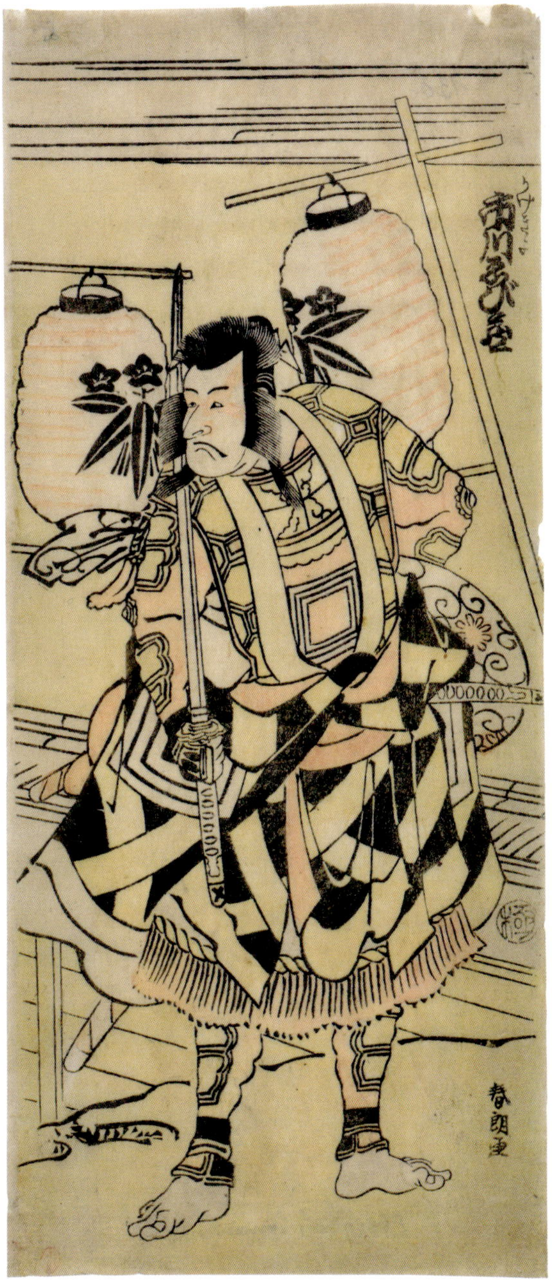

3-1　葛飾北斎
三代目瀬川菊之丞の正宗娘おれん
安永8年(1779)　細判錦絵　島根県立美術館(永田コレクション)蔵

北斎が 20 歳の時に発表した作品。錦絵のデビュー作とされる 4 点のうちの 1 点です。師匠である勝川春章からの影響が色濃いですが、背景の衝立に、北斎の中で最も早い波の描写を確認することができます。

3-2　葛飾北斎　市川蝦像のかげきよ
寛政4年(1792)　細判錦絵　島根県立美術館(永田コレクション)蔵

浮世絵師としてデビューしてから 13 年後、33 歳の時の作品です。一人前の絵師としての技量は備えていますが、勝川派の枠を越えるには至っていません。この年、師匠の勝川春章が亡くなっており、2 年後、北斎は勝川派を離脱することになります。

3-1　Katsushika Hokusai

Segawa Kikunojō III as Oren, the Daughter of Masamune

1779, *hosoban nishiki-e*, Shimane Art Museum (Nagata Collection)

This was presented when Hokusai was 20 years old. It is one of a set of four prints which are considered to be his first attempt at *nishiki-e*. While the influence of his master Katsukawa Shunshō is pronounced, Hokusai's earliest portrayal of waves can be identified on the screen in the background.

3-2　Katsushika Hokusai

Ichikawa Ebizō as Kagekiyo

1792, *hosoban nishiki-e*, Shimane Art Museum (Nagata Collection)

This was produced thirteen years after Hokusai's debut as an *ukiyo-e* artist, when he was 33 years old. While his skills are worthy of a full-fledged artist, he has not yet managed to transcend the framework of the Katsukawa school. Hokusai's master, Katsukawa Shunshō, died the year this print was produced and, two years later, Hokusai seceded from the Katsukawa school.

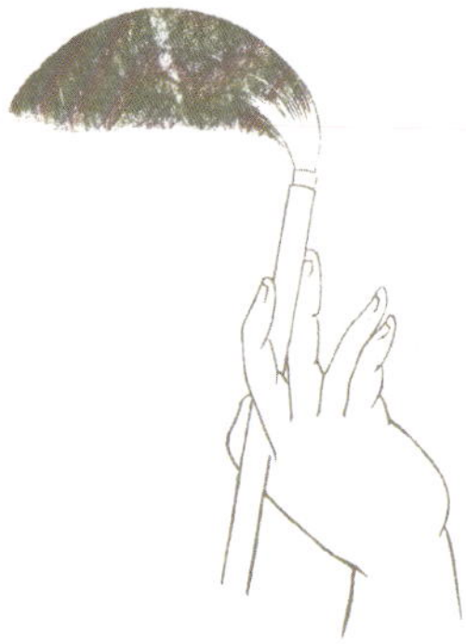

4 In Search of a New Style
新たなスタイルを模索する

Kyōka Picture Books
狂歌絵本

狂歌とは、滑稽な内容を詠んだ和歌のことで、その狂歌を収録した本に挿絵を添えたものを狂歌絵本と呼んでいます。挿絵を制作する技術自体は他の版本と変わりませんが、狂歌絵本は狂歌師たちが資金を負担したり、一定の販売数が見込めたりするため、コストを考えず、高度な彫りや摺りによる豪華な仕立てのものが多く制作されました。また、教養ある狂歌師たちを満足させるような、情緒ある気品に満ちた画風が好まれていました。

北斎が狂歌と関わりを持つようになるのは、勝川派を離れ、琳派の流れを汲む俵屋宗理の画号を継いだ寛政6年（1794）、35歳以降のことです。勝川春朗と名乗っていた時の画風から大きく変化し、瓜実顔ですらりとしたスタイルの美人（→20頁参照）や、自然な奥行き感のある風景などを描くようになり、その人気を確固たるものとします。

はじめは『柳の絲』（図4-1）や『男踏歌』（図4-2）のように、喜多川歌麿や鳥文斎栄之といった有力な絵師と分担して制作することが多くありましたが、『東都名所一覧』（図4-3）、『画本　狂歌　山満多山』（図4-5）、『絵本隅田川　両岸一覧』（図4-6）のように、北斎が単独で挿絵の全てを手がけていくようになりました。このような狂歌絵本の制作は、読本挿絵（→24頁参照）に傾注する文化年間（1804~18）前半頃、40代半ばまで続きます。

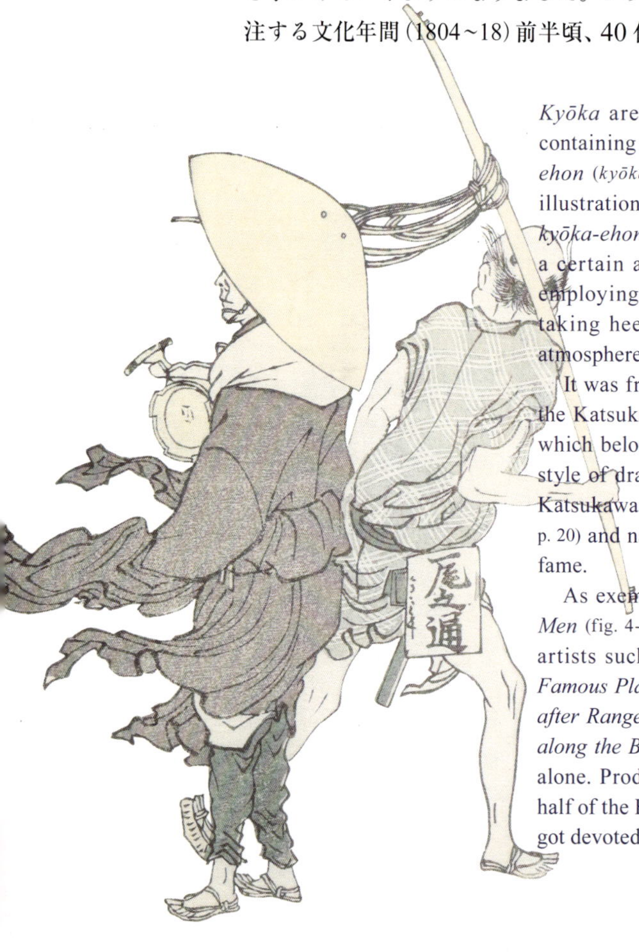

Kyōka are comic, satirical 31-syllable Japanese poems and a book containing *kyōka* accompanied by illustrations is referred to as a *kyōka-ehon* (*kyōka* picture book). Although the techniques required for these illustrations were no different from other picture books, in the case of *kyōka-ehon*, as the picture books were funded by the *kyōka* poets and a certain amount of sales could be estimated, many deluxe versions employing high-level engraving and printing were produced without taking heed of the cost. Furthermore, refined artistic styles full of atmosphere and satisfying to the cultured *kyōka* poets were preferred.

It was from 1794 onwards, after Hokusai had turned 35, seceded from the Katsukawa school, and succeeded to the artist name Tawaraya Sōri, which belonged to Rimpa, that he became involved in *kyōka*. Hokusai's style of drawing changed significantly from the days he bore the name Katsukawa Shunshō and came to depict oval-faced, slender beauties (see p. 20) and natural landscapes with a sense of depth, which established his fame.

As exemplified in *Willow Tresses* (fig. 4-1) and *The Stamping Song of Men* (fig. 4-2), to begin with, he often shared the work with influential artists such as Kitagawa Utamaro and Chōbunsai Eishi. Later on, in *Famous Places in Edo at a Glance* (fig. 4-3), *Picture Book of Kyōka: Range after Range of Mountains* (fig. 4-5), and *Picture Book of Panoramic Views along the Bank of Sumida River* (fig. 4-6), Hokusai did all the illustrations alone. Production of such *kyōka* picture books continued until the first half of the Bunka era (1804–1818), when Hokusai was in his mid-forties and got devoted to *yomihon* illustrations (see p. 24).

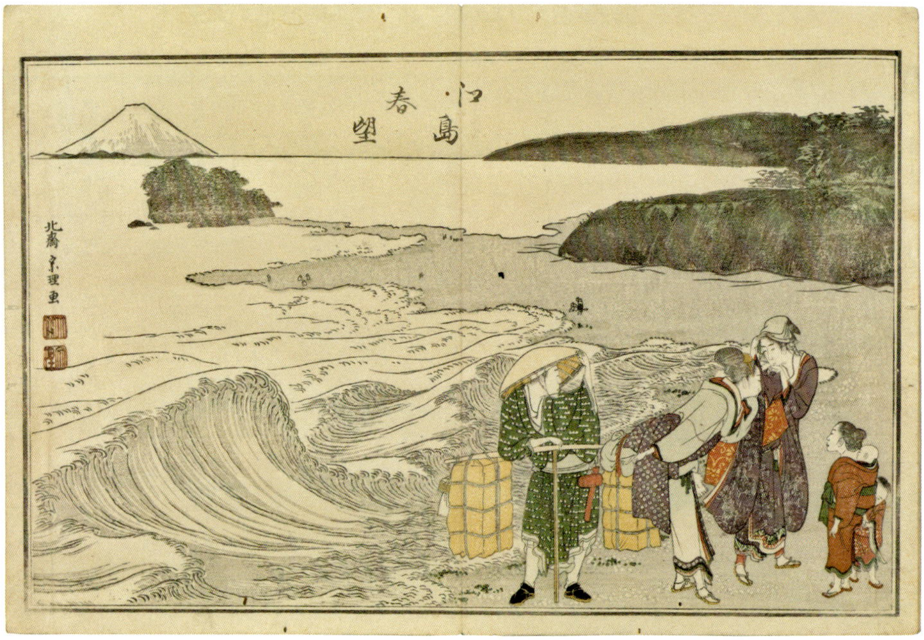

4-1 葛飾北斎ほか画 『柳の絲』

寛政9年(1797) 大本 慶應義塾蔵

「江島春望」と題して、七里ヶ浜から眺めた江の島を描いています。波や富士山といった、北斎が生涯をかけて取り組む画題への関心の萌芽がいち早く認められる点は注目すべきでしょう。本書では他に鳥文斎栄之や北尾重政などが挿絵を描いています。

4-1 ***Willow Tresses***

illust. Katsukawa Hokusai, et al., 1797, *ōhon*, Keio University

Entitled *Spring View of Enoshima*, this is a view of Enoshima seen from Shichirigahama. Note that the first signs of Hokusai's interest in waves and Mount Fuji, subjects that he would continue working on throughout his lifetime, can be identified here. Chōbunsai Eishi, Kitao Shigemasa, and other artists also provided illustrations for this book.

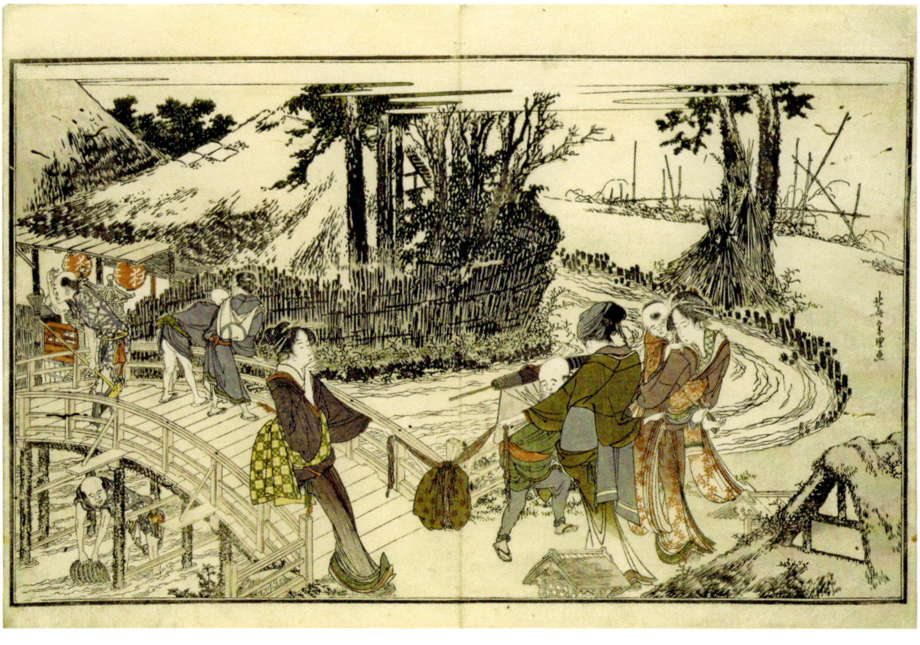

4-2 葛飾北斎ほか画 『男踏歌』

寛政10年(1798) 大本 千葉市美術館蔵

家族連れで江戸近郊の寺社に参詣しているところでしょうか。人物たちは彩色されていますが、背景は墨を基調とした落ち付いた雰囲気となっています。本書では他に喜多川歌麿や鳥文斎栄之などが挿絵を描いています。

4-2 ***The Stamping Song of Men***

illust. Katsushika Hokusai, et al., 1798, *ōhon*, Chiba City Museum of Art

A family appear to be paying a visit to a temple or a shrine in the suburbs of Edo. While the figures are colored, the background is depicted in a calm atmosphere based on *sumi* ink. Artists such as Kitagawa Utamaro and Chōbunsai Eishi also provided illustrations for this book.

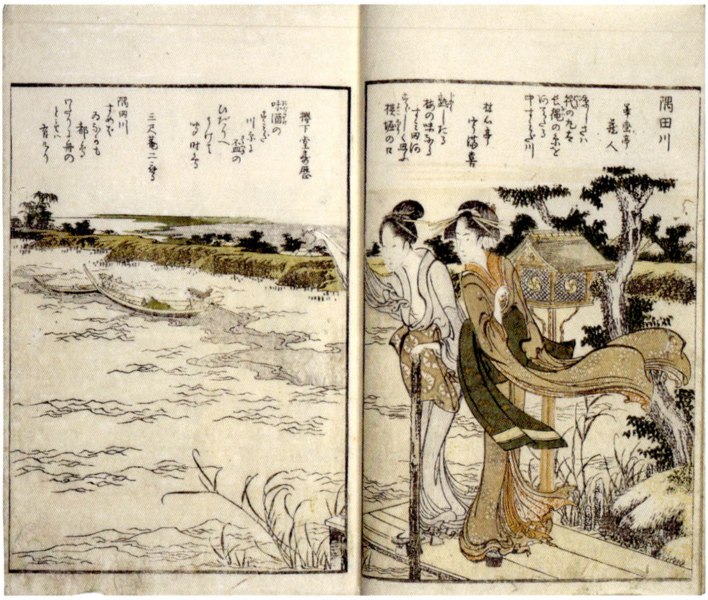

4-3 葛飾北斎 『東都名所一覧』上巻

寛政12年(1800) 大本 千葉市美術館蔵

江戸の町のさまざまな名所を題材にした狂歌絵本です。本図は隅田川の渡し舟の乗り場で舟を待つ２人の女性たち。すらりとしたスタイルの女性の振袖が風にたなびく姿は、この時期の北斎の美人画の特色をよく表しています。

4-3 Katsushika Hokusai

***Famous Places in Edo at a Glance*, vol. 1**

1800, *ōhon*, Chiba City Museum of Art

This is a *kyōka* picture book treating various sights of Edo as the subject matter. In this picture, two women are waiting at a landing stage for a ferryboat to cross Sumida River. The way the long sleeves of the *furisode* the slender women are wearing flutter in the wind is a distinct characteristic of Hokusai's pictures of beauties dating from this period.

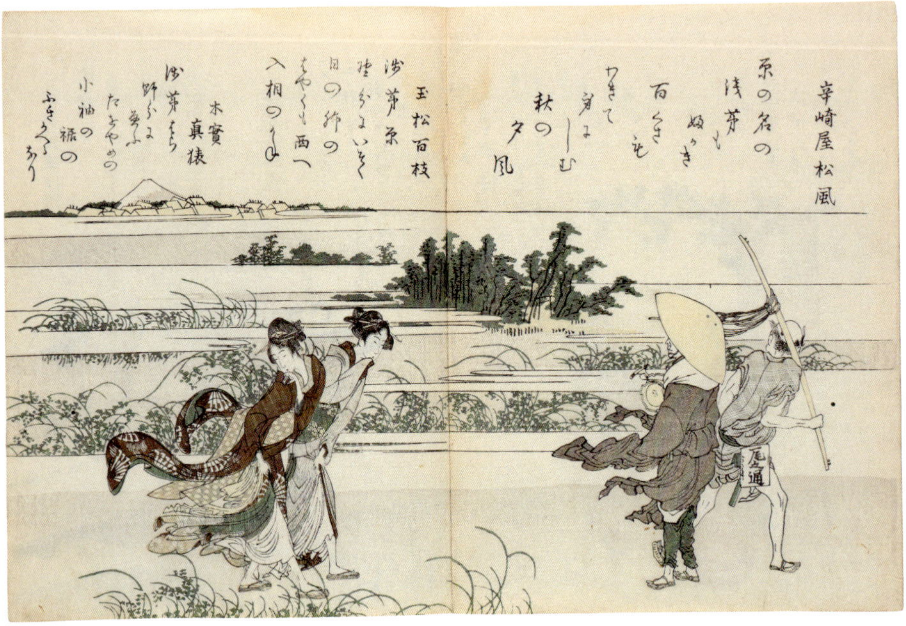

4-4 葛飾北斎 『美やことり』

享和2年(1802) 半紙本 島根県立美術館(永田コレクション)蔵

隅田川沿いの名所を中心とした狂歌絵本です。本図は、浅草の北にある浅茅が原に野分（強い風）が吹きすさんでいる様子を描いています。左奥には富士山の姿が。彩度を落とした色使いが特徴となっています。

4-4 Katsushika Hokusai ***The Bird of the Capital***

1802, *hanshibon*, Shimane Art Museum (Nagata Collection)

This is a *kyōka* picture book focusing on scenic spots along the Sumida River. Here, a fierce autumnal wind raging across Asajigahara, north of Asakusa, is depicted. Mount Fuji can be seen in the left back. The coloring applied in low intensity is distinctive.

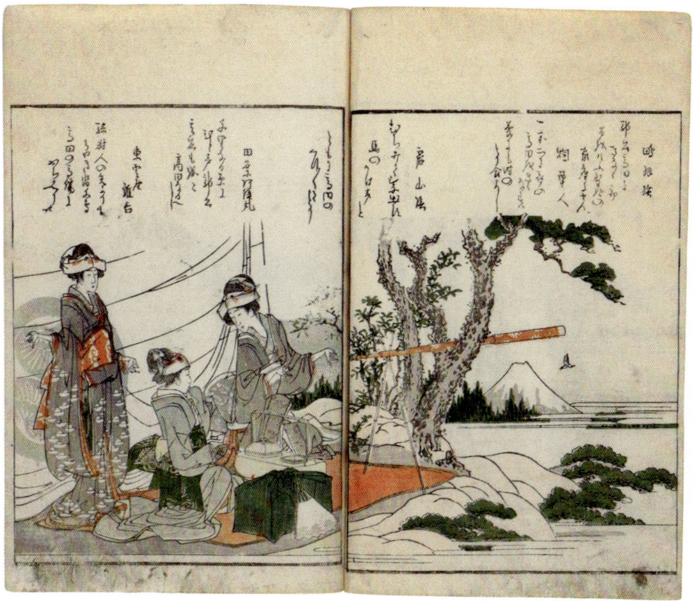

4-5 葛飾北斎『画本狂歌　山満多山』上巻
享和4年(1804)　大本　島根県立美術館(永田コレクション)蔵

山の手の名所を中心とした狂歌絵本です。本図は、高田馬場の高台にピクニックにやって来た女性たち。遠眼鏡を使って、遠くの富士山や空を飛ぶホトトギスを眺めています。

4-5 Katsushika Hokusai
Picture Book of Kyōka: Range after Range of Mountains, Vol.1
1804, *ōhon*, Shimane Art Museum (Nagata Collection)

This is a *kyōka* picture book focusing on scenic spots in uptown Tokyo. Shown here are women who have come for a picnic at a high point in Takadanobaba. Using a telescope, they are looking at Mount Fuji in the distance and a cuckoo flying in the sky.

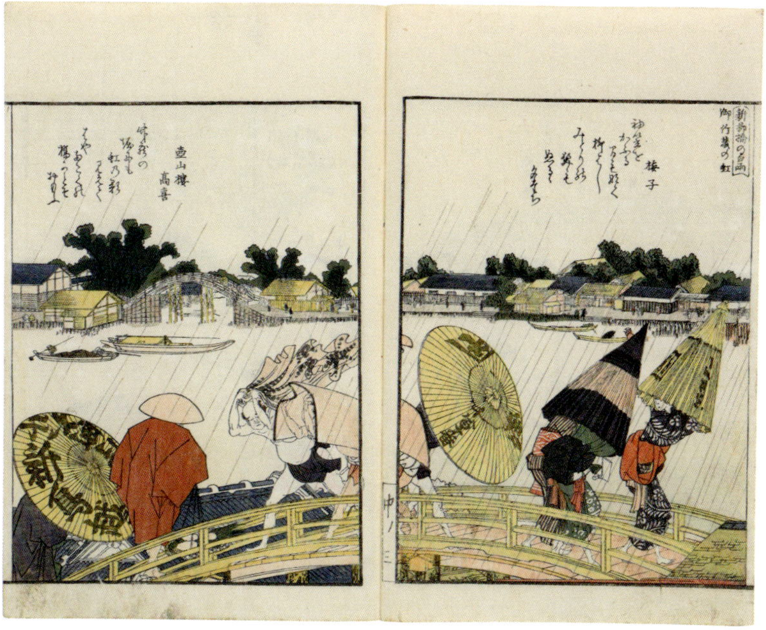

4-6 葛飾北斎『絵本隅田川　両岸一覧』中巻
刊年不詳　大本　島根県立美術館(永田コレクション)蔵

隅田川の河口から上流へとさかのぼっていく狂歌絵本で、ここでは「新柳橋の白雨」を描いています。頁をめくるに従い、春から冬へと季節が移り変わるだけでなく、全ての図が絵巻物のように横につながっているという、北斎らしい計算された仕掛けとなっています。

4-6 Katsushika Hokusai
***Picture Book of Panoramic Views along the Bank of Sumida River*, vol. 2**
n.d., *ōhon*, Shimane Art Museum (Nagata Collection)

This *kyōka* picture book goes upstream along Sumida River from the estuary. Here, we see *A Shower in Shin'yanagibashi*. As you turn the pages, not only do the seasons change from spring to winter but all the pictures are connected sideways in the manner of a picture scroll. It is indeed a carefully calculated device typical of Hokusai.

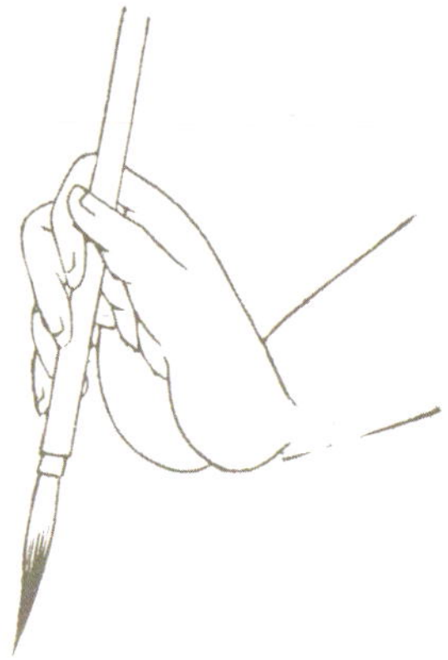

5 Oval Face and Slender Waist
瓜実顔に柳腰
Pictures of Beauties
美人画

北斎は、宗理号を襲名した寛政6年（1794）頃から、本格的に美人画を描き始めます。その特色は、ほっそりとした瓜実顔に、背のすらりとした柳腰の体型といったもので、北斎独自の画風として人気を集めました。その後、為一を名乗る文政3年（1820）頃まで、継続的に美人画を制作し続けました。

まず、版画の作例を見てみると、狂歌絵本（→16頁参照）や狂歌摺物など、狂歌師たちから特別に依頼を受けた作品では、美人の姿がしばしば描かれています。一方、当時の美人画の第一人者であった喜多川歌麿がメインで活躍していた、不特定多数に向けて販売される一枚摺の錦絵においては、その作例がほとんど見受けられません。「風流無くてなゝくせ」（図5-4）が代表作として挙げられる程度です。

肉筆画の作例としては、享和・文化期頃に、脂が乗った力作が多数制作されています。重要文化財に指定されている「二美人図」（図5-1）や「酔余美人図」（図5-5）のように緻密な彩色によるものもあれば、「見立式三番」（図5-3）のように軽やかなタッチと淡い彩色によるものもあり、いずれも肉筆画の絵師としての北斎の力量を見て取れます。なお、北斎の肉筆画の技術を支えるものとして、師匠であり、晩年に肉筆美人画を専らとした勝川春章（→86頁参照）からの学習を見落とすこともできません。

Hokusai began working on *bijinga* (pictures of beauties) on a full scale from around 1794, when he succeeded to the Sōri name. Hokusai's beauties were characterized by their elfin oval face, tall body, and slender waist, which proved popular as an artistic style unique to this artist. From then on, he produced *bijinga* continuously until around 1820, when he assumed the name Iitsu.

Regarding examples of woodblock prints, Hokusai often portrayed beauties in *kyōka* picture books (see p. 16), *kyōka-surimono*, etc., which were specially commissioned by *kyōka* poets. In contrast, while Kitagawa Utamaro, the top-ranking artist of *bijinga* in those days, was busily engaged mainly in single-sheet *nishiki-e* (polychrome prints) sold to an unspecified large number of people, there are hardly any examples of that type by Hokusai. *Seven Fashionable Habits* (fig. 5-4) is about the only work that can be cited as a representative example.

As for examples of original paintings, there are many fine works in the prime of Hokusai's career dating from around the Kyōwa (1801–1804) and Bunka (1804–1818) eras. Whereas *Two Beauties* (fig. 5-1), which is designated as an Important Cultural Property, and *Drunken Beauty* (fig. 5-5) are colored with precision, there are paintings such as *Parody of The Three Ceremonial Pieces* (fig. 5-3) colored in an airy touch. In both cases, Hokusai demonstrates his capability as a master of original paintings. It should not be overlooked that Hokusai's original painting skills were supported by what he learned from Katsukawa Shunshō (see p. 86), his master and an artist who worked exclusively on original paintings of beauties in his final years.

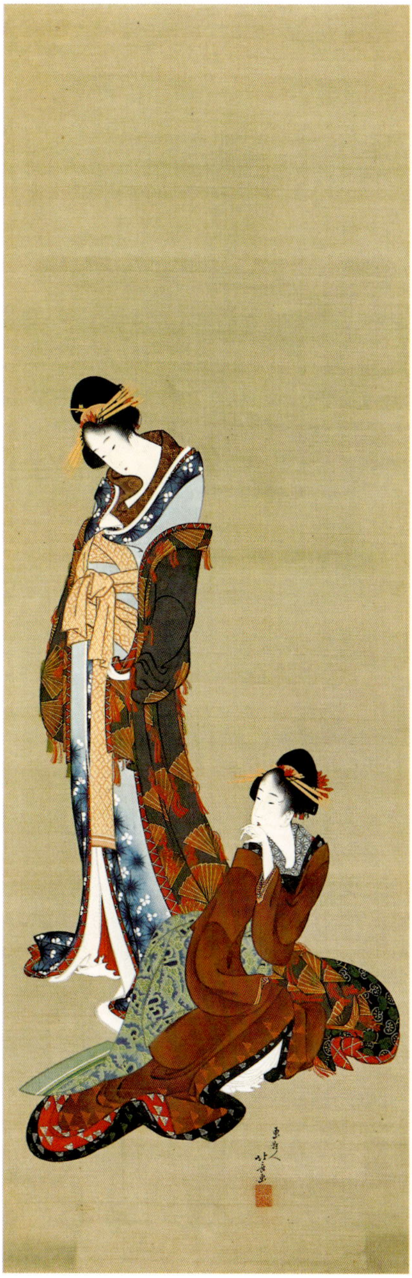

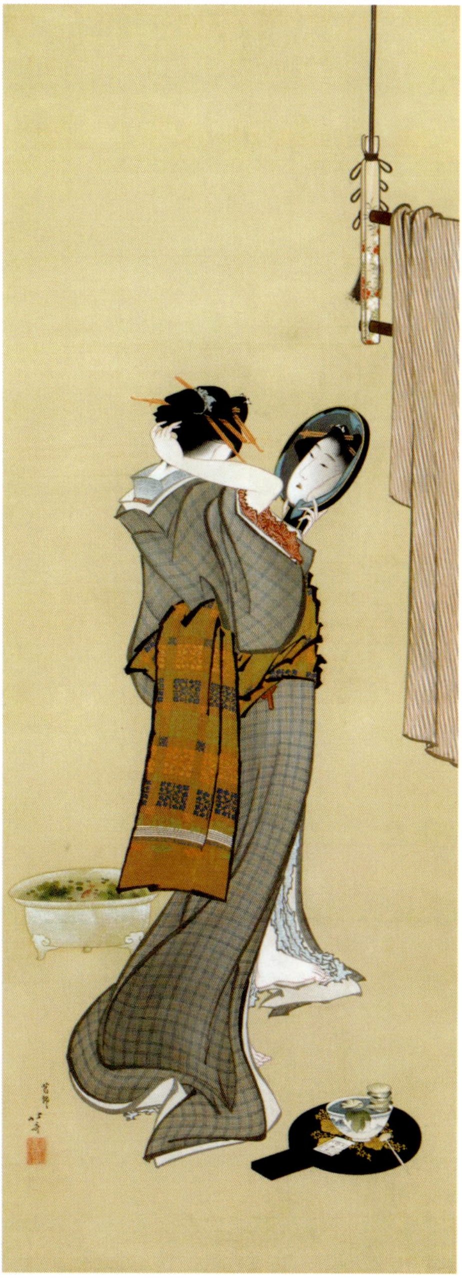

5-1 葛飾北斎 **二美人図**

享和年間(1801～04)頃 絹本着色 MOA美術館蔵 重要文化財

物憂げな表情をして立つ花魁と、口元に手をあてて座る女性のすらりとした体型は、この時期の北斎の美人画の特色をよく表しています。なお、重要文化財に指定されている北斎の作品は、本図の他に、「潮干狩図」（図14-1）と「日新除魔図」（図19-1, 26-2）があります（2020年6月時点）。

5-2 葛飾北斎 **夏の朝**

文化7年(1810)頃 絹本着色 岡田美術館蔵

女性が手鏡をのぞき込みながら髪を整えています。弓なりに伸びた女性の背筋に沿って、着物がなめらかで動きのある曲線で描写されているのが印象的です。足元には金魚が泳ぐ盤や、朝顔の花が浮かぶ鉢が置かれており、夏の季節を感じさせます。

5-1 Katsushika Hokusai ***Two Beauties***

c. 1801–1804, color on silk, MOA Museum of Art, Important Cultural Property

The slender physique of the courtesan standing with a weary look and the woman sitting with her hand over her mouth is distinctive of Hokusai's pictures of beauties dating from this period. In addition to this painting, Hokusai's *Shell Gathering at Low Tide* (fig. 14-1) and *Daily Exorcisms* (fig. 19-1, 26-2) are designated as Important Cultural Property (as of June 2020).

5-2 Katsushika Hokusai

A Summer Morning

c. 1810, color on silk, Okada Museum of Art

A woman is looking into a hand mirror to fix her hair. The way her *kimono* is depicted in smooth, kinetic curves along her body as she leans backward is impressive. There are goldfish swimming in a basin and a bowl garnished with morning glory on the floor, giving hints of summer.

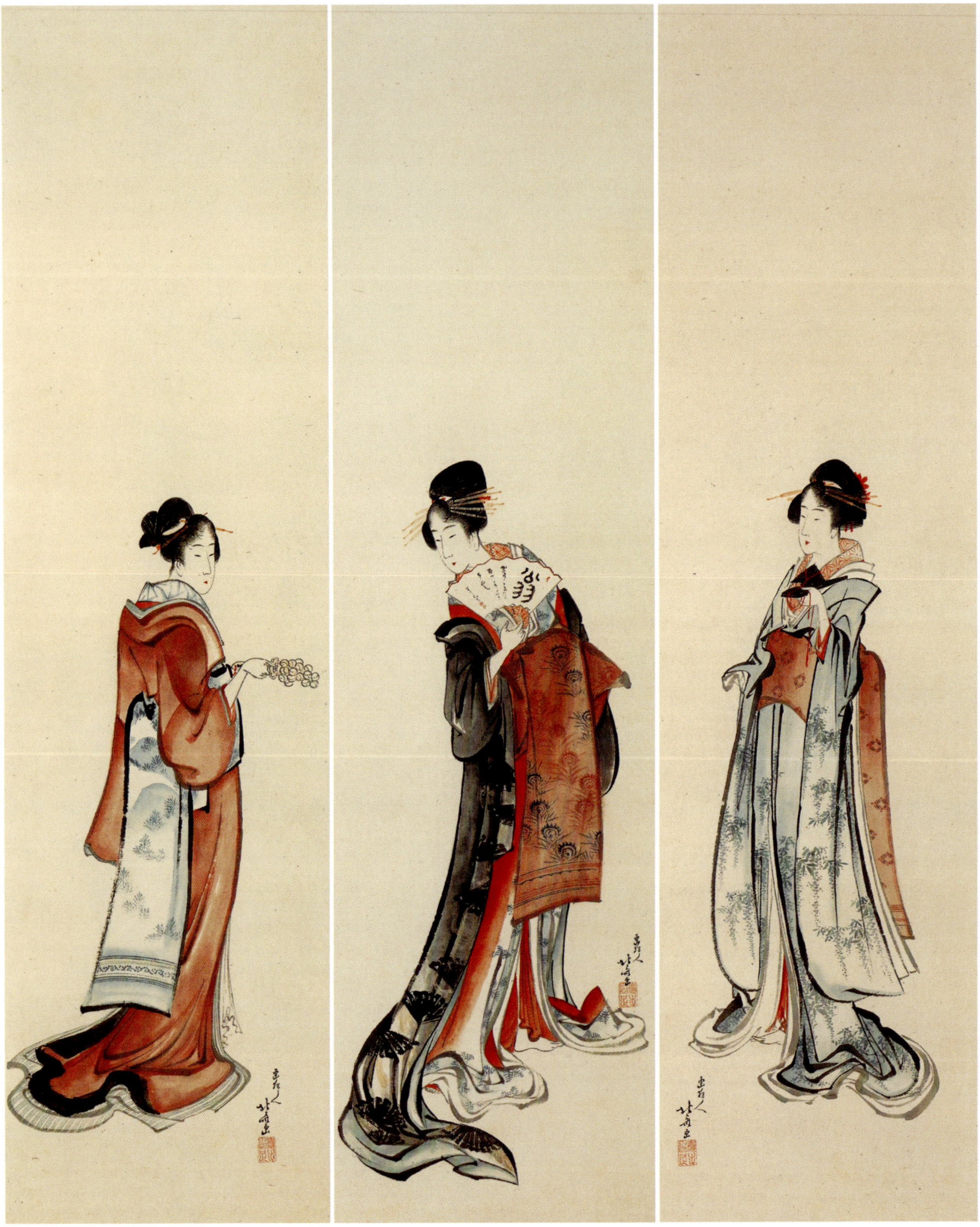

5-3 葛飾北斎 **見立式三番**

享和末～文化初期(1803～07)頃　紙本淡彩　太田記念美術館蔵

能楽の演目である式三番の見立てとなっており、侍烏帽子を持つ右の女性が千歳、翁の文字の入った扇を持つ中央の女性が翁、鈴を持つ左の女性が三番叟をそれぞれ暗示する趣向となっています。短時間で仕上げたと思われる、勢いのある伸びやかな線描が特徴です。

5-3 Katsushika Hokusai

Parody of The Three Ceremonial Pieces

c. 1803–1807, wash on paper, Ōta Memorial Museum of Art

This is a parody of a *noh* performance entitled *The Three Ceremonial Pieces*. The woman on the right holding a *samurai eboshi* (headgear worn with court dress) implies the character Senzai, the woman at the center holding a fan inscribed "*okina* (old man)" Okina, and the woman on the left holding bells Sanbasō. The lively, unconstrained line drawing suggests that these paintings were completed in a short time.

5-4 葛飾北斎 **風流無くてなゝくせ　遠眼鏡**

享和年間(1801～04)　大判錦絵　山口県立萩美術館・浦上記念館蔵

美人大首絵は歌麿が好んで制作していましたが、北斎の美人画の中で、大判錦絵のサイズで制作されたものはこのシリーズしかありません。しかもこのシリーズは「遠眼鏡」のほかに「ほおずき」しか確認されておらず、稀少な作例となっています。

5-4 Katsushika Hokusai
Seven Fashionable Habits: Telescope
1801–1804, *ōban nishiki-e*, Hagi Uragami Museum

Although Utamaro liked producing *ōkubi-e* (half-length portraits) of beauties, this is the only series among Hokusai's pictures of beauties done in the *ōban nishiki-e* size. Moreover, as *Telescope* and *Ground Cherry* are the only two works from this series that are known to exist, this is a rare example.

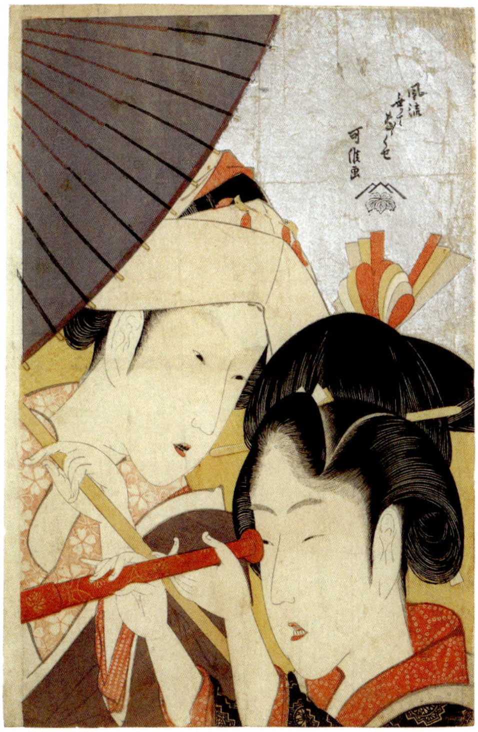

▼5-5 葛飾北斎 **酔余美人図**

文化4年(1807)頃　絹本着色　氏家浮世絵コレクション蔵

酒に酔って三味線箱に伏せている芸者です。物憂げな表情をしており、北斎の美人画の中でも女性の色香を強く感じさせる作例となっています。

▼5-5 Katsushika Hokusai ***Drunken Beauty***
c. 1807, color on silk, Ujiie *Ukiyo-e* Collection

A drunk *geisha* is leaning on her *shamisen* box. She looks weary and her feminine allure stands out among Hokusai's pictures of beauties.

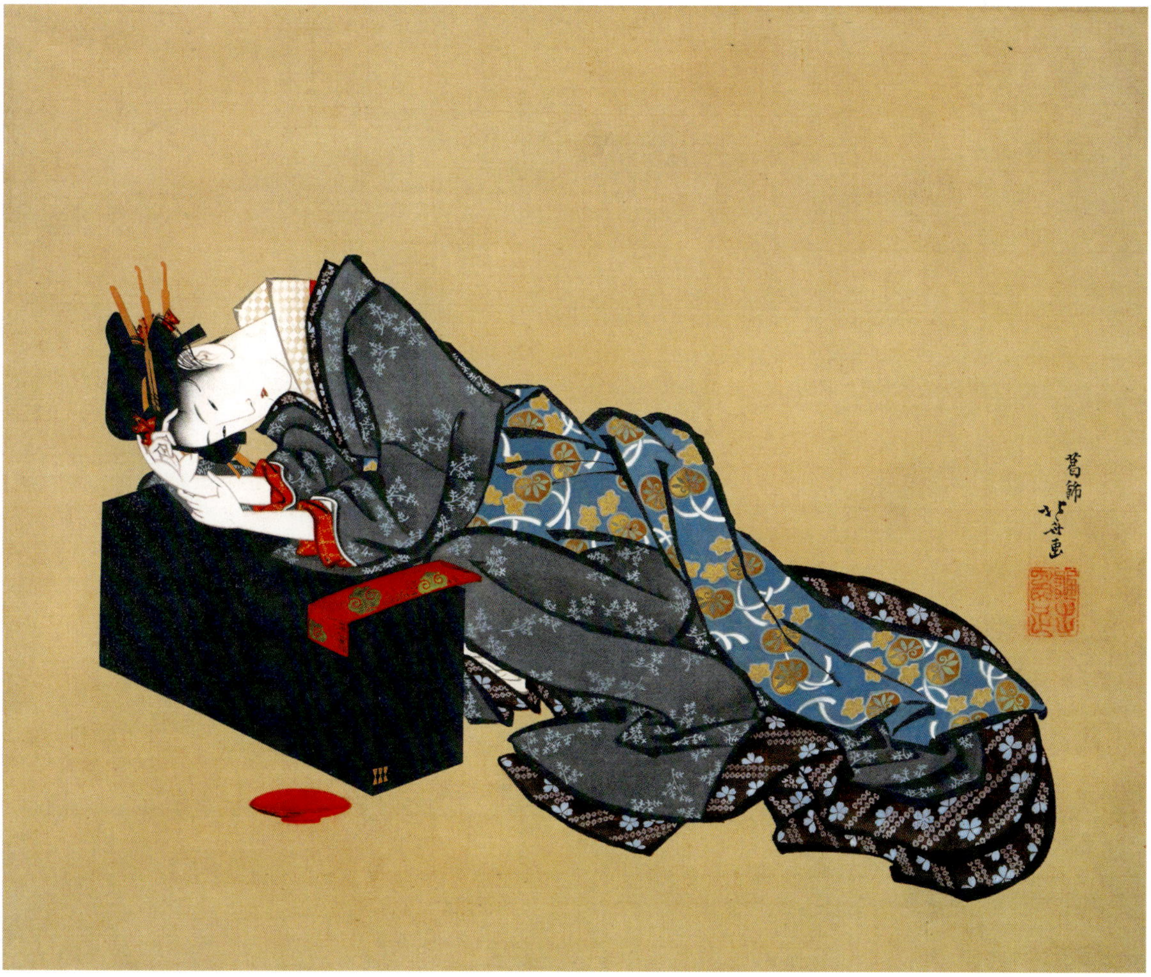

6 Fame for Depictions Full of Impact
その名を轟かせた迫力の描写

Yomihon Illustrations
読本挿絵

読本とは中国の明・清時代の小説の翻案を軸に、日本の伝説や歴史を取り入れた伝奇的要素の強い小説のことで、因果応報や勧善懲悪といった教訓的な内容を多く含んでいます。

読本はページの大半が文章だけで埋められており、挿絵は時折見開きの形で挿し込まれ、一冊当たり数図ある程度にしか過ぎません。しかも、錦絵のように鮮やかな色は付いておらず、墨一色、または薄墨が施されるだけのものでした。しかし、黄表紙（滑稽な内容の大人向けの絵入り小説）や合巻（黄表紙が内容の複雑化に伴って長編化したもの）といった、文字と絵が同じページに含まれた草双紙とは違い、文字とのバランスを気にすることなく、迫力ある構図を画面いっぱいに広げることが可能になったのです。

北斎が読本挿絵を手がけるようになるのは、狂歌絵本を積極的に刊行していた直後、40代半ば以降のことです。享和4年（1804）には曲亭馬琴と『小説比翼文』で初めてタッグを組み、『新編水滸画伝』（図6-1）や『椿説弓張月』（図6-2~4）など、数多くのヒット作を二人三脚で生み出していきました（→92頁参照）。

北斎の読本挿絵で最も目を惹くのが、迫力ある躍動感でしょう。例えば、煙や爆発の表現、あるいは人物や水の動きなど、細部にまで緊張感がみなぎっています。さらに、墨だけという色の制約が、かえってメリハリのある画面を生み、物語の筋が分からなくてもその世界に引き込む効果をもたらしています。溪斎英泉の『無名翁随筆』で「絵入読本此人より大ひにひらけり」と評されたように、北斎の挿絵は文章以上に読者からの人気を集め、その名前は日本全国に轟くことになります。

Yomihon are novels with adaptations of Ming or Qing dynasty Chinese novels at their core, incorporating Japanese legends and history, and containing markedly bizarre elements. They include didactic contents such as reward or punishment for one's past behavior or rewarding good and punishing evil.

The majority of the pages in a *yomihon* were filled with prose only and the illustrations were inserted occasionally as a double spread so that there were only a few illustrations per book. Moreover, they were not printed in bright colors like *nishiki-e* but drawn in monochrome *sumi* ink or highlighted with thin *sumi* ink. However, unlike *kusazōshi* (illustrated storybooks) such as *kibyōshi* (illustrated novels of comical content for adults bound in "yellow covers") and *gōkan* (literally,"bound-together volumes" as a result of the content of *kibyōshi* becoming more complicated), in which the prose and the pictures were included on the same page, in *yomihon*, the artist could deploy impressive compositions across the entire page without paying heed to the balance with the prose.

Hokusai began working on *yomihon* illustrations from his mid-forties, immediately after enthusiastically publishing *kyōka* picture books. He paired up with Kyokutei Bakin for the first time in 1804, when they produced *Shōsetsu hiyokumon*. Thereafter, working closely together, they produced numerous blockbusters (see p. 92) such as *New Illustrated Edition of the Water Margin* (fig. 6-1) and *Strange Tales of the Bow Moon* (figs. 6-2~4).

What is most eye-catching about Hokusai's *yomihon* illustrations is their vigorous sense of energy. For example, his representations of smoke or explosions, the movement of human figures or water, etc. are brimming with tension to the details. Furthermore, the color restriction of *sumi* ink only conversely modulates the image, proving effective in drawing the reader into the story even without understanding the plot. A critique on Hokusai in *Mumei ō zuihitsu* (Essays by an anonymous old man) by Keisai Eisen, reads, "Illustrated *yomihon* developed significantly from this man onwards." Hokusai's illustrations turned out to be even more popular among the *yomihon* readers than the prose, and his name resounded throughout Japan.

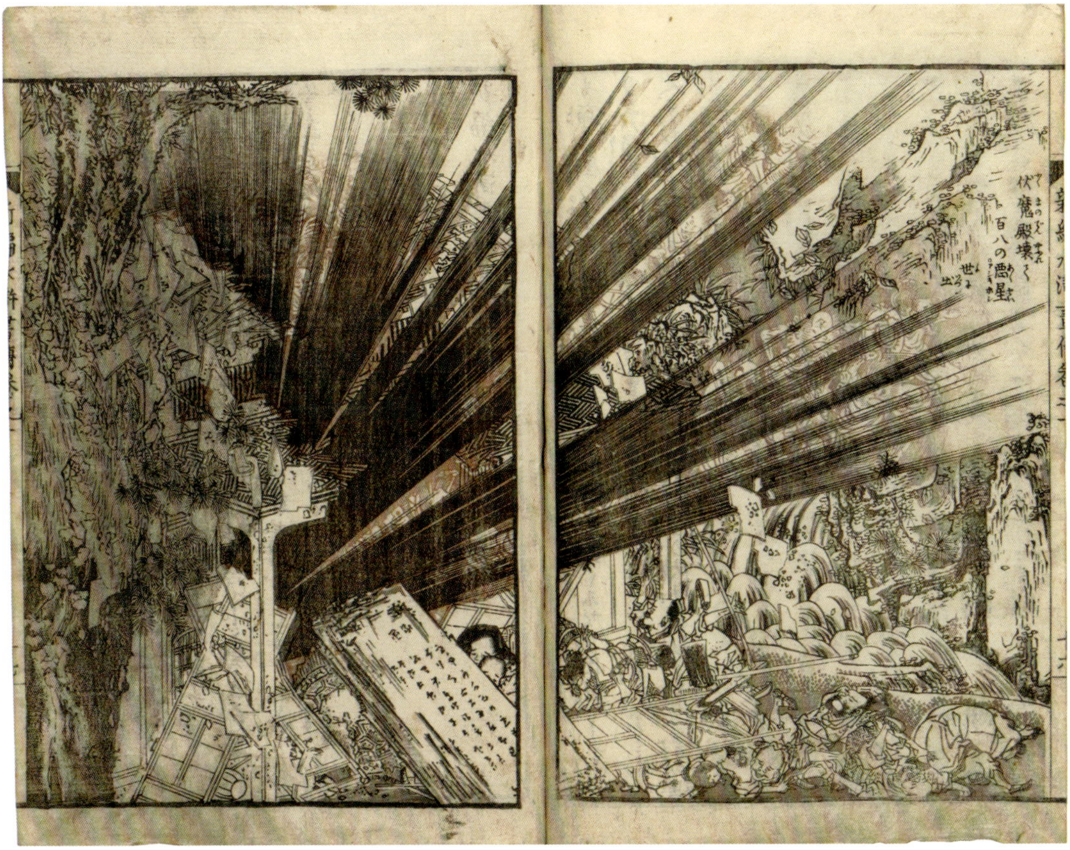

6-1 曲亭馬琴作・葛飾北斎画

『新編水滸画伝』初編巻之一

文化2年（1805）　半紙本　島根県立美術館（永田コレクション）蔵

『水滸伝』の幕開けとなる有名な場面。伏魔之殿から轟音とともに金の光が飛び散り、これが後に梁山泊の108人の豪傑たちとなります。放射状の閃光の間には、白抜きで描かれた魔物たちの姿も見えます。

6-1 Kyokutei Bakin

***New Illustrated Edition of the Water Margin*, part 1, vol. 1**

illust. Katsushika Hokusai, 1805, *hanshibon*, Shimane Art Museum (Nagata Collection)

A famous scene marking the opening of the *Water Margin*. Together with deafening roars, golden rays fly out of the Pandemonium, later to become the 108 heroes of Liangshan Marsh. Demons printed in white can be identified between the radial flashes.

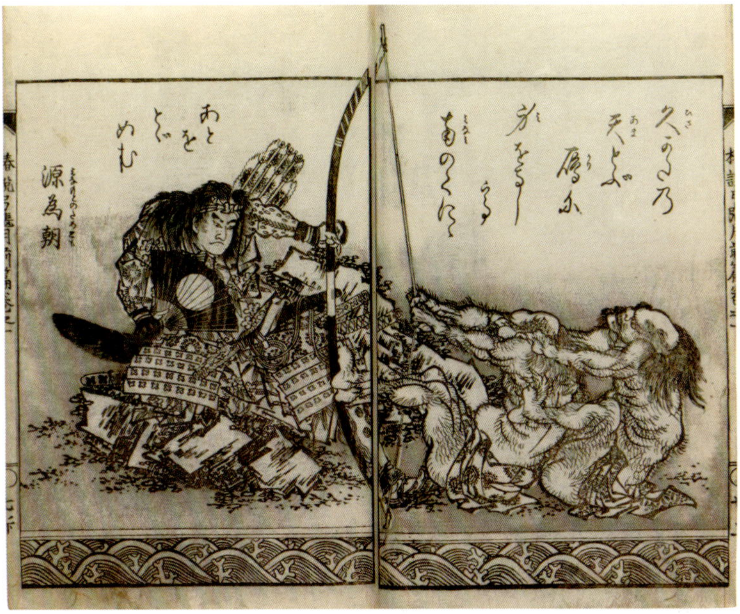

6-2 曲亭馬琴作・葛飾北斎画

『椿説弓張月』前編巻之一

文化4年（1807）　半紙本

島根県立美術館（永田コレクション）蔵

怪力の持ち主である源為朝が、島民たちに自分の使っている弓を引かせようとしています。弓の張りは強く、島民は2人がかりで引っ張ってもびくともしません。

6-2 Kyokutei Bakin

***Strange Tales of the Bow Moon*, part 1, vol. 1**

illust. Katsushika Hokusai, 1807, *hanshibon*, Shimane Art Museum (Nagata Collection)

Minamoto no Tametomo, a man of phenomenal strength, lets the islanders draw his bow, but it is so tight that it does not budge a single inch even with two islanders drawing it.

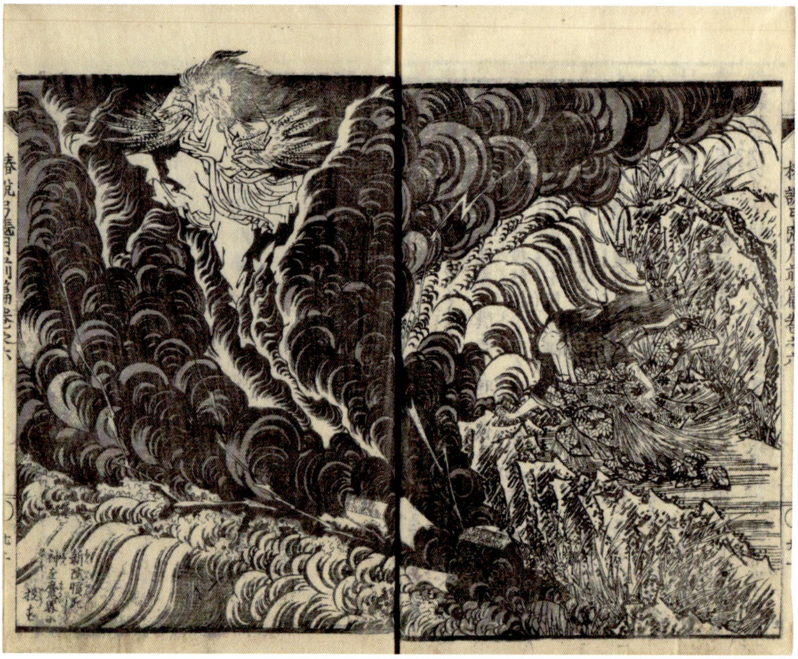

6-3 曲亭馬琴作・葛飾北斎画 『椿説弓張月』前編巻之六
文化4年(1807) 半紙本 国立国会図書館蔵

天狗の姿となった崇徳院。もくもくと湧き立つ黒雲と逆巻く波が画面の大半を覆い、崇徳院が怨霊になった劇的な瞬間を演出しています。

6-3 Kyokutei Bakin
***Strange Tales of the Bow Moon*, part 1, vol. 6**
illust. Katsushika Hokusai, 1807, *hanshibon*, National Diet Library, Japan

Sutoku-in has turned into a mountain spirit. A large proportion of the picture is covered in black clouds billowing up in great volumes and surging waves to stage the dramatic moment that Sutoku-in becomes a vengeful spirit.

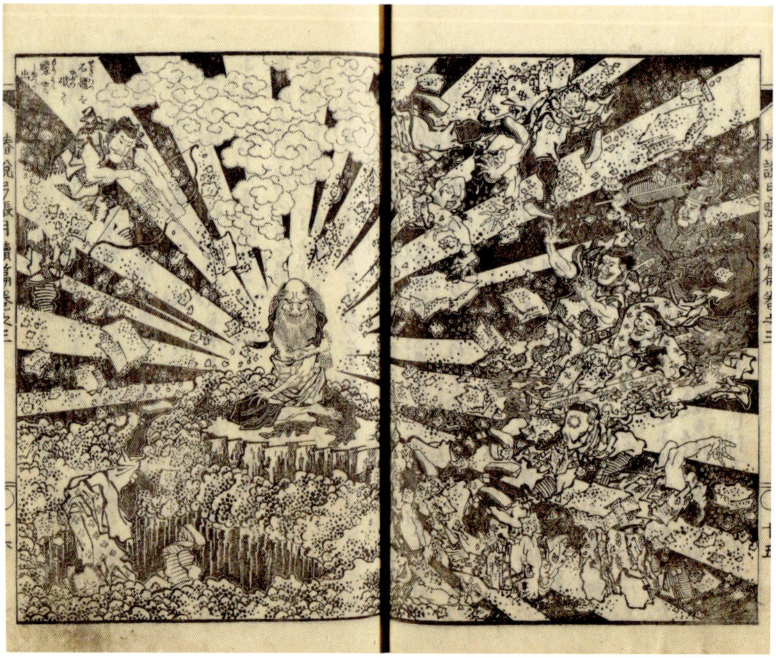

6-4 曲亭馬琴作・葛飾北斎画 『椿説弓張月』続編巻之三
文化5年(1808) 半紙本 国立国会図書館蔵

石棺が砕け散り、中から妖術使いの朦雲が出現した場面です。放射状に延びた白い帯が、現代の漫画を思わせるような迫力ある演出になっています。

6-4 Kyokutei Bakin
***Strange Tales of the Bow Moon*, part 3, vol. 3**
illust. Katsushika Hokusai, 1808, *hanshibon*, National Diet Library, Japan

A sarcophagus is shattered into pieces and from it emerges the sorcerer Mōun. The radiating white strips present an impact suggestive of present-day *manga*.

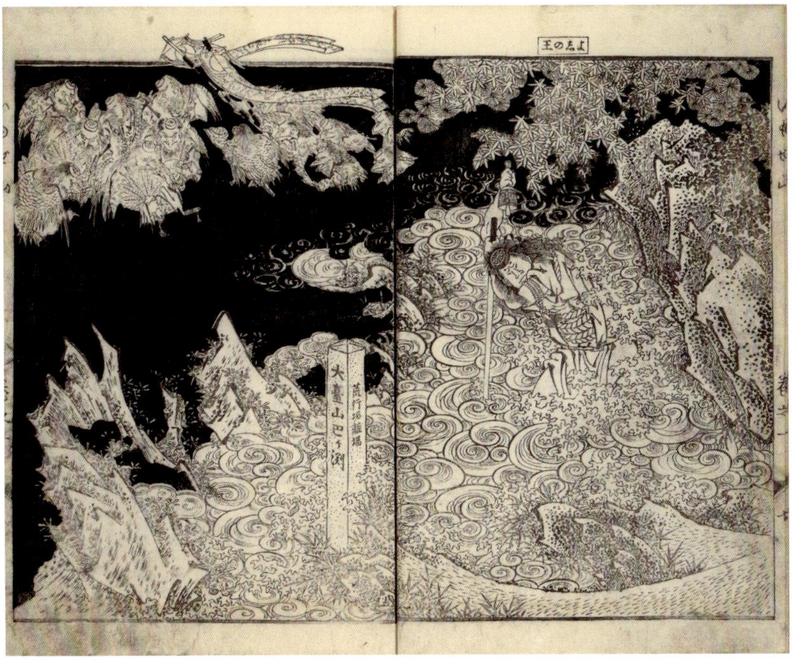

6-5 振鷺亭作・葛飾北斎画 『阸阸妹背山』巻之一
文化7年(1810) 半紙本 メトロポリタン美術館蔵

巴が渕で荒業をする芳野宮。渦を巻くような波によって垢離場（冷水を浴びる行をする場所）の水面が覆われており、非現実的な不気味な空間となっています。

6-5 Shinrotei
***The Mountains of Husband and Wife*, vol. 1**
illust. Katsushika Hokusai, 1810, *hanshibon*, The Metropolitan Museum of Art

Yoshinonomiya undergoes rigorous ascetic exercises at Tomoegafuchi. The surface of the water where the lustration is conducted is covered in swirling waves, presenting an unreal, eerie space.

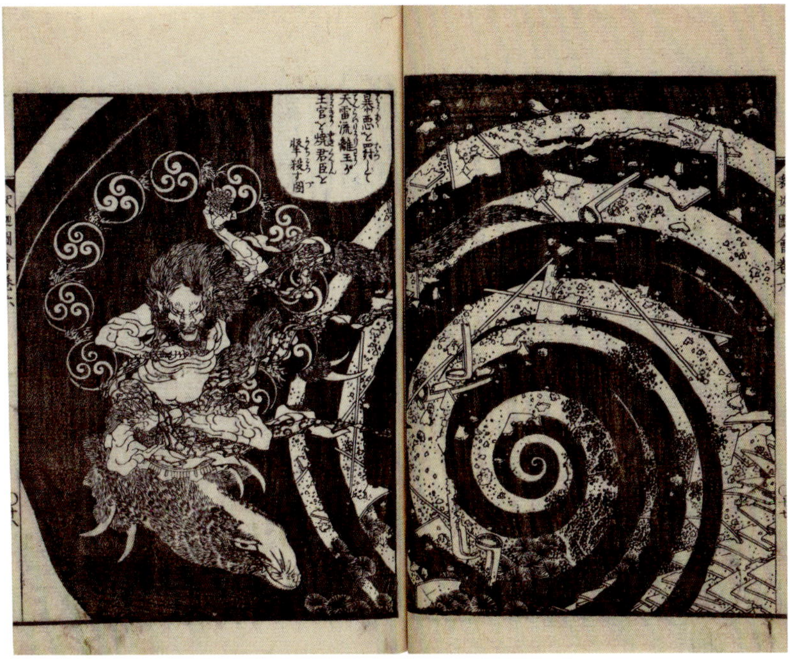

6-6 山田意斎作・葛飾北斎画 『釈迦御一代記図会』巻之六
弘化2年(1845) 半紙本 島根県立美術館(永田コレクション)蔵

暴君の流離王の宮殿に雷が落ち、群臣もろとも地獄へ落ちた場面。北斎は、文中には登場しない雷神の姿を描き、白と黒の渦巻きで被害の甚大さを表現しています。

6-6 Yamada Isai ***Illustrated Life of Shakamuni*, vol. 6**
illust. Katsushika Hokusai,1845, *hanshibon*, Shimane Art Museum (Nagata Collection)

Lightning strikes on the tyrant King Ryūri's palace and he goes together with the whole body of his retainers to Hell. Hokusai portrays the god of thunder, though it does not appear in the story, and conveys the immensity of the damage with a black and white whirlpool.

7

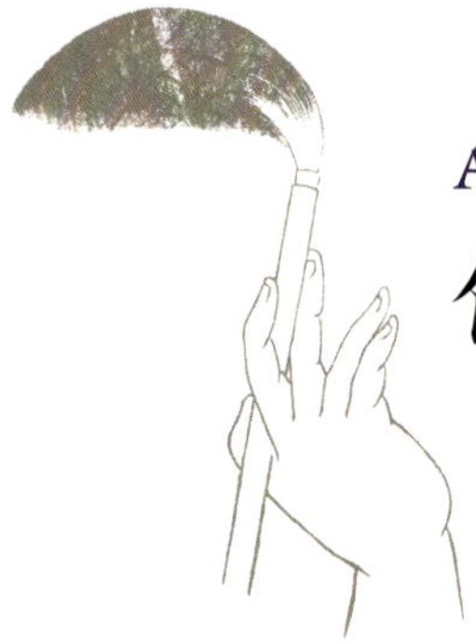

Almighty Master of Bodhidharma
何でもござれの達磨先生

Live Performances
ライブパフォーマンス

絵師は、十分に構想を練って何度も下書きを行うような、入念な準備の上で絵を描くだけでなく、人々が見ている前で、即興で絵筆を動かすということもありました。

その場の求めに応じた題材をすぐさま描いたり、あるいは、題材を逆さまにして描いたり（図7-1）、指を筆にして絵を描いたり、さらには、米粒に2羽の雀を描いたり（飯島虚心『葛飾北斎伝』→124頁参照，以下『北斎伝』）など、その場で見ている人々を楽しませる曲芸のような描き方を北斎は得意としていました。また、真偽のほどは定かではありませんが、11代将軍徳川家斉の御前で絵を描いたというエピソードがあります。長い紙に刷毛で藍を曳き、その上を朱肉を足につけた鶏を歩かせ、竜田川の風景と称したというのです（『北斎伝』）。

さらに、北斎は大勢の人の前で巨大な作品をその場で完成させるパフォーマンスを何度も行っています。文化元年（1804）、護国寺で達磨を描いたほか、本所合羽干場で馬を、回向院で布袋を描きました（『北斎伝』）。中でも有名なのが、文化14年（1817）10月5日、名古屋の西掛所（現在の本願寺名古屋別院）での達磨半身像でしょう。120畳敷（縦18 m×横11 m）の大画面を、大勢の見物人が見守る中、昼過ぎから夕方までかかって完成させました。尾張藩士である高力猿猴庵がその時の様子を挿絵入りで詳細に記録しています（図7-3~5）。北斎はこのパフォーマンスによって、名古屋の人々から「達磨先生」、略して「だるせん」と呼ばれるようになりました（高力猿猴庵『北斎大画即書細図』）。

It was not always that artists underwent elaborate preparation, fully working out the idea and making sketches over and over again. On some occasions, they would draw impromptu in front of an audience.

Hokusai was good at entertaining the people in front of him with acrobatic performances. For example, he would depict a subject matter requested on the spot, draw a subject matter upside down (fig. 7-1), paint with his finger instead of a brush, or paint two sparrows on a grain of rice (Iijima Kyoshin, *Katsushika Hokusai-den* [A biography of Katsushika Hokusai], see p. 124, referred to hereafter as *Hokusai-den*). True or not, there is a well-known anecdote that Hokusai did a painting in the presence of the 11th Tokugawa shogun Ienari. He applied indigo using a wide flat brush on a long piece of paper, made a chicken with its legs covered in red ink walk over it, and called it a view of the Tatsuta River, which is renowned for its autumnal foliage (*Hokusai-den*).

Hokusai also gave numerous performances in which he would complete a huge work in front of a large audience. In 1804, besides painting Bodhidharma at Gokoku-ji, he painted a horse at Honjo Kappa Hoshiba and Hotei, the god of contentment, at Ekō-in (*Hokusai-den*). Among such works, the half-length portrait of Bodhidharma painted at Nishikakesho, Nagoya (the present Hongan-ji Nagoya Betsu-in) on the fifth day of the tenth month of 1817 is famous. On a huge sheet the size of 120 *tatami* mats (18 m by 11 m), it took Hokusai from shortly after noon to early in the evening to complete the portrait in front of a multitude of onlookers. Kōriki Enkōan, a feudal retainer of the Owari domain, kept a detailed record of the occasion with illustrations (figs. 7-3~5). Following this performance, the people in Nagoya called Hokusai "Daruma Sensei (Master of Bodhidharma)" or "Darusen" for short (Kōriki Enkōan, *Details of Hokusai's Performance of Painting a Huge Portrait of the Bodhidharma*).

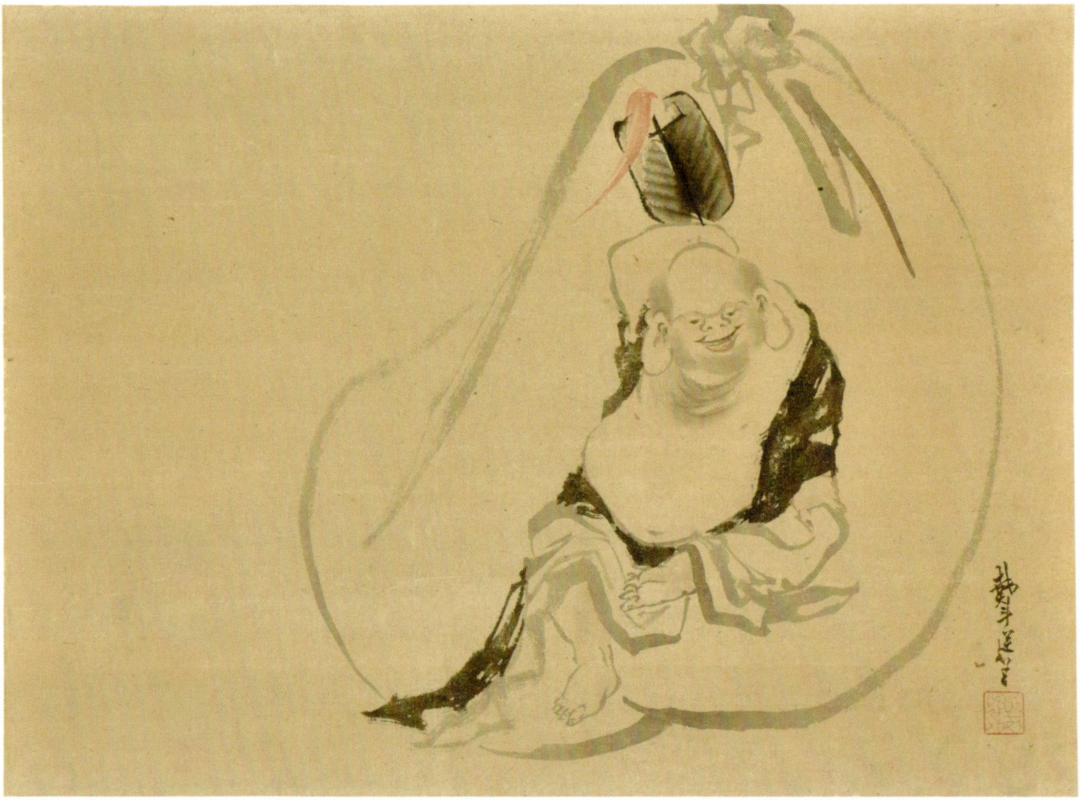

7-1 葛飾北斎 **逆筆布袋図**

文化中期(1810～14)頃　紙本墨画　島根県立美術館(永田コレクション)蔵

「戴斗逆筆」と落款にあるように、袋に腰掛ける布袋を上下逆さに描いた作品です。紙を床に置き、反対側に見物客が座って見ている状態で、即興で描いたのでしょう。

7-1 Katsushika Hokusai

Hotei Painted from Reversed Direction

c. 1810–1814, ink on paper, Shimane Art Museum (Nagata Collection)

As the signature reading "Painted by Taito upside down" indicates, Hotei seated on a bag is painted from the reversed direction. Hokusai probably laid the paper on the floor and painted this impromptu with the audience watching him while seated on the other side.

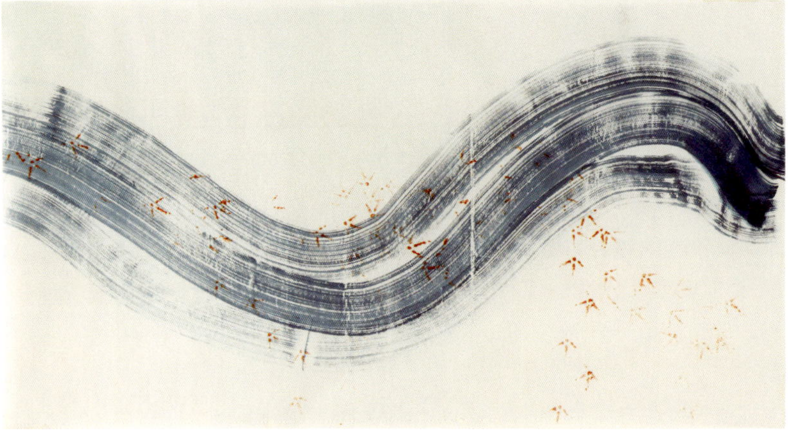

画像提供:すみだ北斎美術館/ DNPartcom (Image: The Sumida Hokusai Museum / DNPartcom)

7-2 向井大祐・勝川ピー **竜田川に紅葉の図**

平成29年(2017)　紙本淡彩　すみだ北斎美術館蔵

将軍の御前で描いたという竜田川図を、文献に基づく想像の元、再現制作した作品です。席上に持ち込むのに手頃な大きさであるチャボ(勝川ピー)の足に朱肉をつけ、実際に紙の上を歩かせています。

7-2 Mukai Daisuke and Katsukawa Pī

Autumn Foliage along the Tatsutagawa River

2017, wash on paper, The Sumida Hokusai Museum

A hypothetical reproduction of the painting of the Tatsuta River, which Hokusai is said to have produced in front of the shogun, was reproduced based on literature and using imagination. A bantam (Katsukawa Pī) was a good size for the occasion. Red ink was applied to its legs before it walked over the paper.

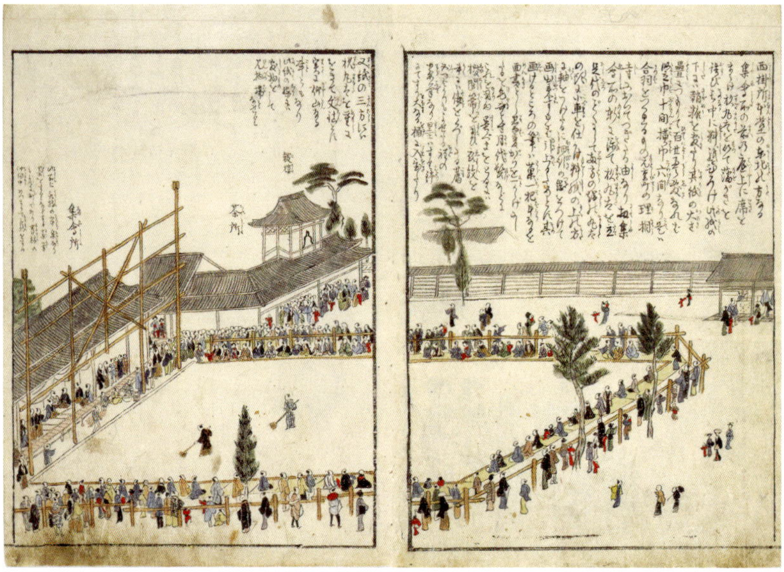

7-3 高力猿猴庵
『北斎大画即書細図』
文化14年(1817)　大本　名古屋市博物館蔵

会場には柵が設けられ、その中に120畳の大きさの紙が敷かれています。左端には完成した達磨図を掛けるための足場もあります。まだ始まっていないにも関わらず、大勢の見物客がすでに集まっています。

7-3 Kōriki Enkōan
Details of Hokusai's Performance of Painting a Huge Portrait of the Bodhidharma
1817, *ōhon*, Nagoya City Museum

The venue is fenced off and, inside, a piece of paper the size of 120 *tatami* mats has been laid out. On the left-hand side, there is a scaffold to hang the portrait of Bodhidharma once it has been completed. There are already many onlookers gathered although the performance has not even started.

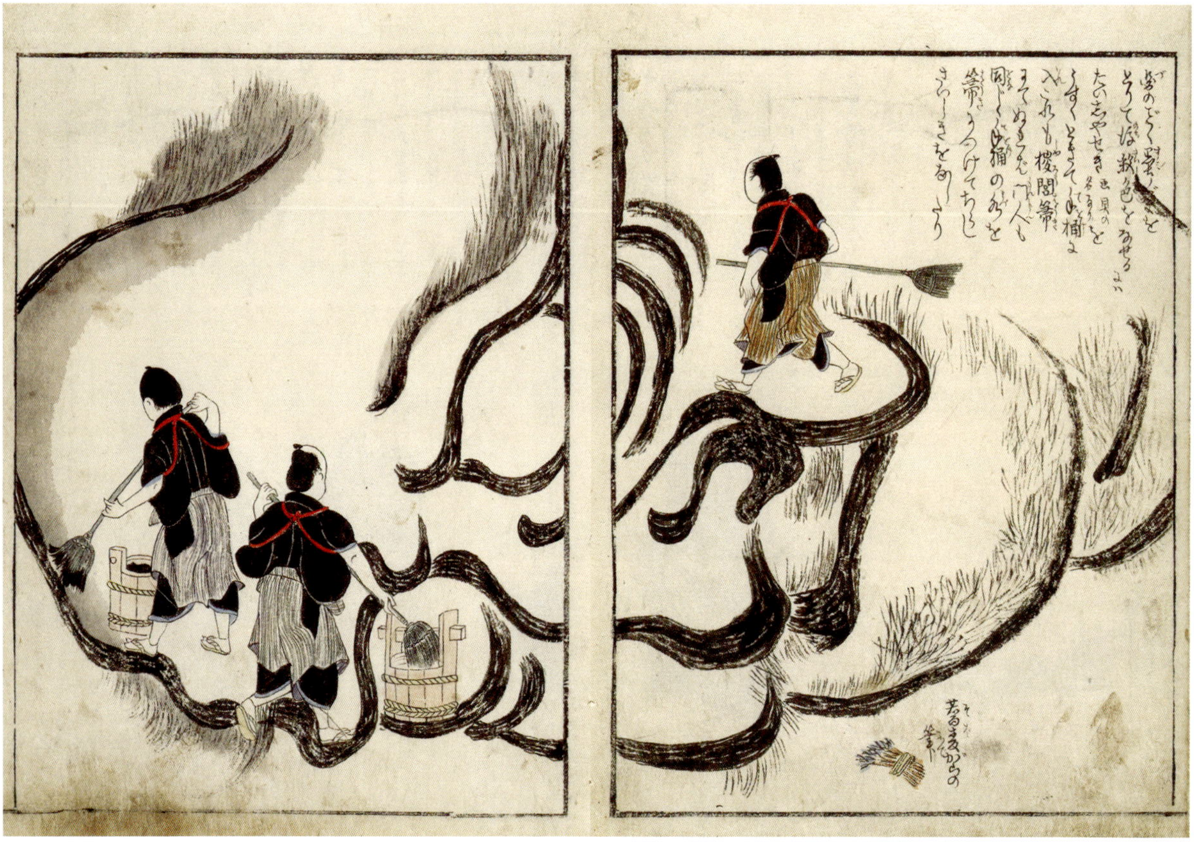

7-4 高力猿猴庵 **『北斎大画即書細図』**
文化14年(1817)　大本　名古屋市博物館蔵

北斎は門人たちに協力してもらいながら、大きな藁筆で達磨を描きました。顔があらかた描き終わり、棕櫚箒を使って薄めの墨で頭部に陰影をつけています。

7-4 Kōriki Enkōan
Details of Hokusai's Performance of Painting a Huge Portrait of the Bodhidharma
1817, *ōhon*, Nagoya City Museum

With his disciples' assistance, Hokusai painted Bodhidharma with a huge straw brush. Having done most of the face, the head is being shaded with thin *sumi* ink using a palm broom.

7-5 高力猿猴庵

『北斎大画即書細図』

文化14年（1817） 大本 名古屋市博物館蔵

達磨図が完成すると足場に引き揚げられました。近くから見ていた見物客たちは、絵の全貌を把握し、その巨大さを実感したことでしょう。翌日には、全体がよく見えるよう、さらに足場を高く組み直して掲げられました。

7-5 Kōriki Enkōan

Details of Hokusai's Performance of Painting a Huge Portrait of the Bodhidharma

1817, *ōhon*, Nagoya City Museum

Once completed, the portrait of Bodhidharma was hauled up to the scaffold. The people who had been watching from close-by would have been able to grasp the full view and get a real feeling of its hugeness. The following day, the scaffolding was reconstructed even higher so that the overall image could be seen better.

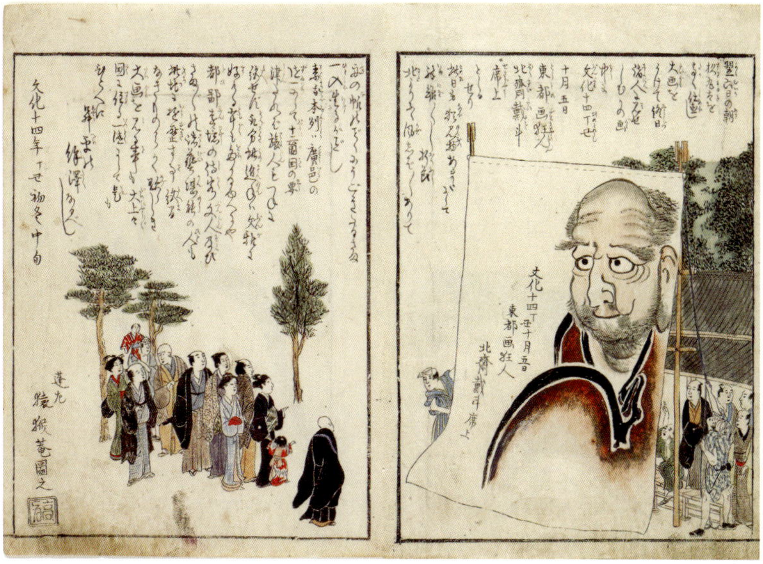

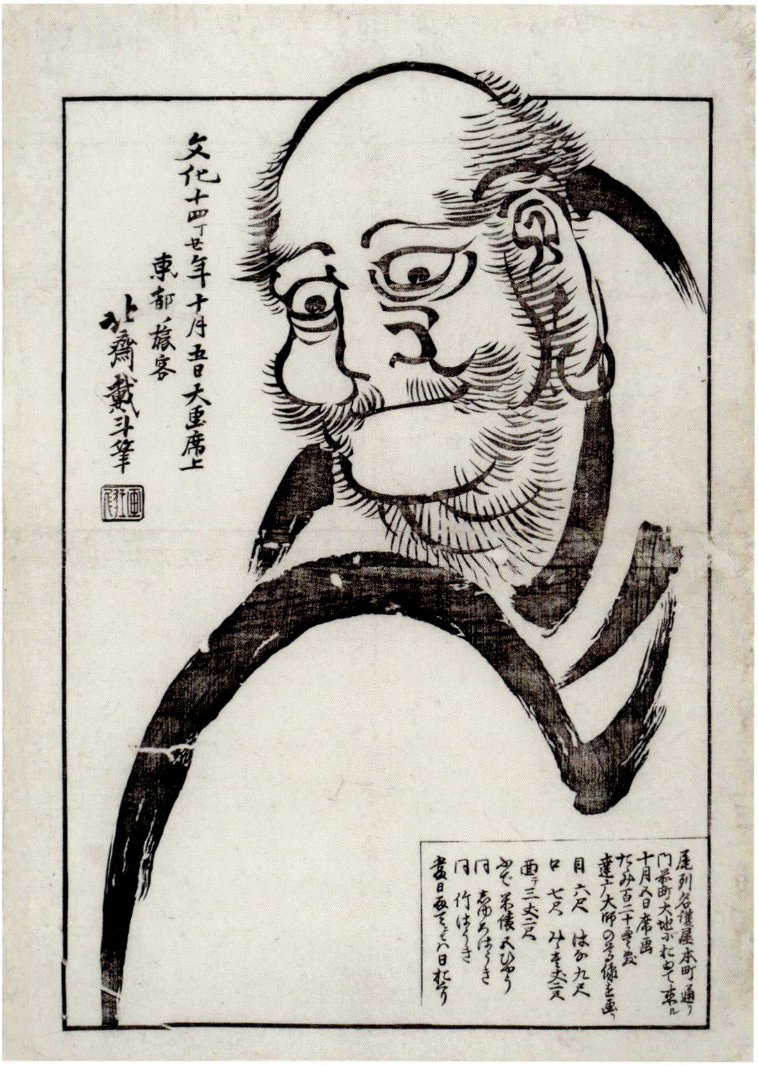

7-6 葛飾北斎

北斎大画即書引札

文化14年（1817） 墨摺絵 名古屋市博物館蔵

達磨図のパフォーマンスを紹介するための引札です。場所と日にち、達磨図の大きさと雨天延期などの情報が記されています。なお、完成した巨大達磨図は、昭和20年（1945）の空襲によって焼失したとされています。

7-6 Katsushika Hokusa

Promotional Handbill for Hokusai's Performance of Painting a Huge Portrait of the Bodhidharma

1817, *sumizuri-e*, Nagoya City Museum

A handbill to promote Hokusai's performance of painting a portrait of Bodhidharma. The venue, date, and size of the portrait are mentioned together with a notice that the performance will be postponed if it rains. The huge portrait of Bodhidharma is considered to have been destroyed in an air raid in 1945.

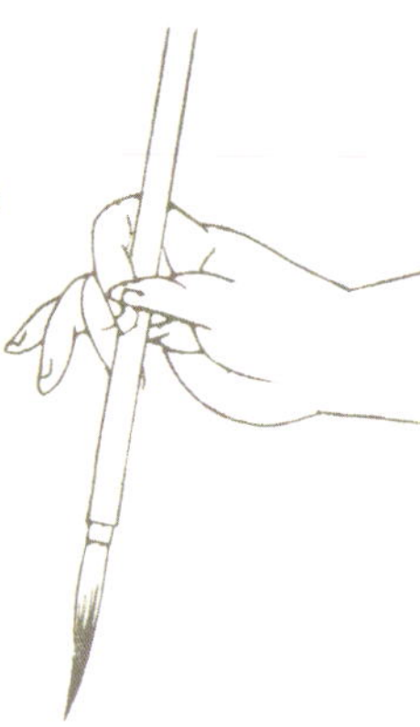

8 With These, Anyone Can Draw
これさえあれば誰でも描ける

Drawing Manuals
絵手本

北斎は、戴斗の画号を用いるようになった文化7年(1810)以降、すなわち51歳以降、絵を学ぶ人に向けた絵手本の制作に傾注します。文字を組み合わせて絵を描く『己痴羣夢多字画尽』前編(図8-1)や、コンパスと定規を使って絵の描き方の手ほどきをした『略画早指南』前編(図8-2)がその皮切りとなります。

そして、文化11年(1814)、ホクサイ・スケッチの名前で世界的に知られる『北斎漫画』初編(図8-3)が刊行されます。「漫画」とありますが、現代のマンガとはまったく異なり、風景や人物、動物などさまざまな事物を描き尽したカット集のようなものです。同時に、絵を学ぶ人たちのための教科書の役割も含んでいました。当初は初編のみの予定でしたが、好評のためにシリーズ化され、最終的に北斎没後の明治11年(1878)に刊行された15編まで続くベストセラーになりました。

さらに、櫛と煙管の図案雛形である『今様櫛𥿻雛形』(図8-5)や、染織家のための図案集である『新形小紋帳』(図8-6)といった職人向けのもの、さらに世を去る前年には『画本彩色通』という彩色の技術を詳細に解説した教科書的な絵手本を刊行しました。

北斎の絵手本は、戯画性の強いものから実用性が強いものまでさまざまです。他の浮世絵師と比べても、制作量や内容の幅は群を抜いており、北斎は絵手本というジャンルを切り開いた第一人者であったといえるでしょう。

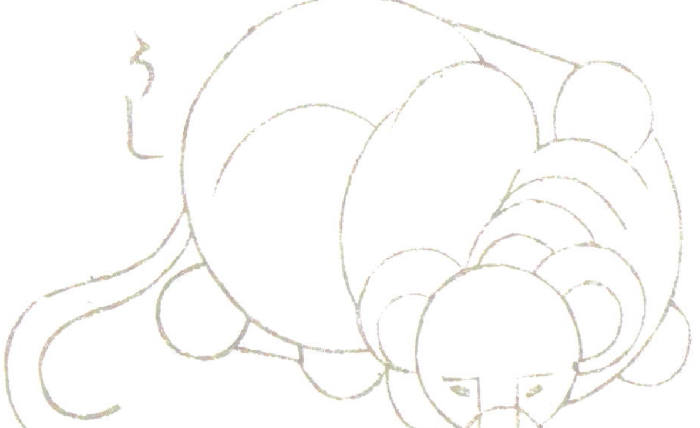

From 1810 onwards, from when Hokusai assumed the artist name Taito and turned 51 years old, he concentrated on *edehon* (drawing manuals) for people learning to draw and paint. He began with *Collection of the Pictures Formed by the Character*, part 1 (fig. 8-1), a book on how to draw by combining letters, and *Quick Lessons in Simplified Drawings*, part 1 (fig. 8-2), which shows how to draw with a compass and ruler.

In 1814, part one of *Hokusai's Sketches* (fig. 8-3), a world-famous collection of sketches by Hokusai, was published. Although it is entitled "*manga*" in Japanese, totally unlike present-day *manga*, it is a collection of sketches depicting a variety of motifs including landscapes, human figures, and animals. At the same time, it also served as a textbook for people learning to draw and paint. Initially only part one was planned, but as it proved popular, it was turned into a series. In the end, it became a best-seller continuing to part fifteen, which was published in 1878, after Hokusai's death.

Hokusai also published manuals for artisans such as *Modern Designs for Combs and Tobacco Pipes* (fig. 8-5) and *The Book of New Patterns for Kimono Fabrics* (fig. 8-6) with designs for dyeing and weaving artisans. The year before his death, he published *Ehon saishikitsū*, a textbook-like drawing manual containing detailed explanations on coloring techniques.

Hokusai's drawing manuals vary from caricature-like works to those highly practical in character. Compared to other *ukiyo-e* artists, both the quantity and range of content are outstanding. Therefore, he can be considered the foremost authority that carved out the genre of drawing manuals.

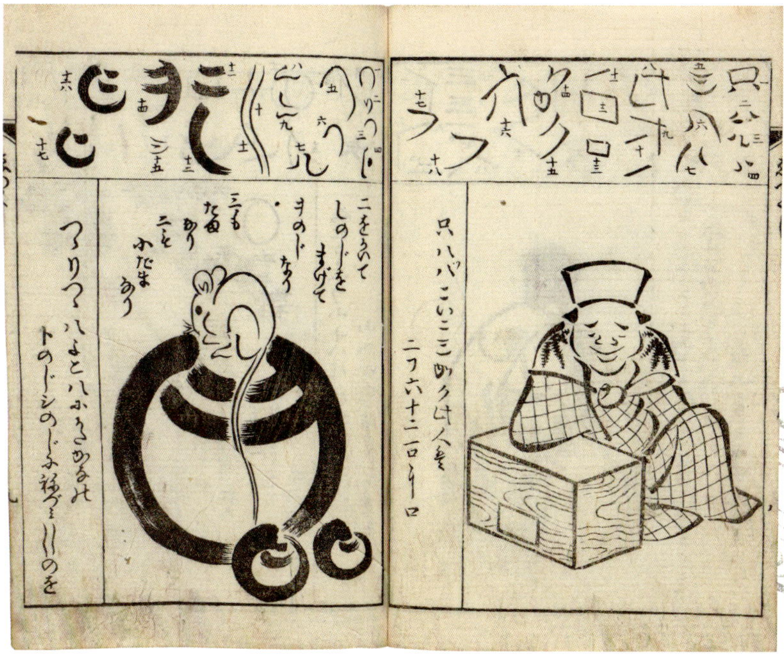

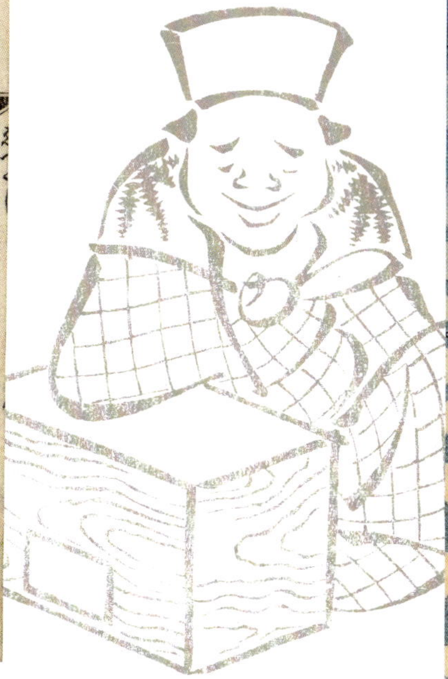

8-1 葛飾北斎『己痴羣夢多字画尽』(おのがばかむらむだじえづくし)前編

文化7年(1810)　中本　島根県立美術館(永田コレクション)蔵

絵描き歌のように、指示どおりに文字を書いていくと絵になるという趣向の絵手本です。職業画家向けというより、絵が好きな素人や子どもたちが楽しめる内容になっています。

8-1 Katsushika Hokusai

***Collection of the Pictures Formed by the Character*, part 1**

1810, *chūhon*, Shimane Art Museum (Nagata Collection)

Like a drawing song, by writing the characters according to the instructions given in the song, you will be able to create a picture. Rather than a drawing manual for professional artists, the content of this book is to be enjoyed by amateurs fond of pictures and children.

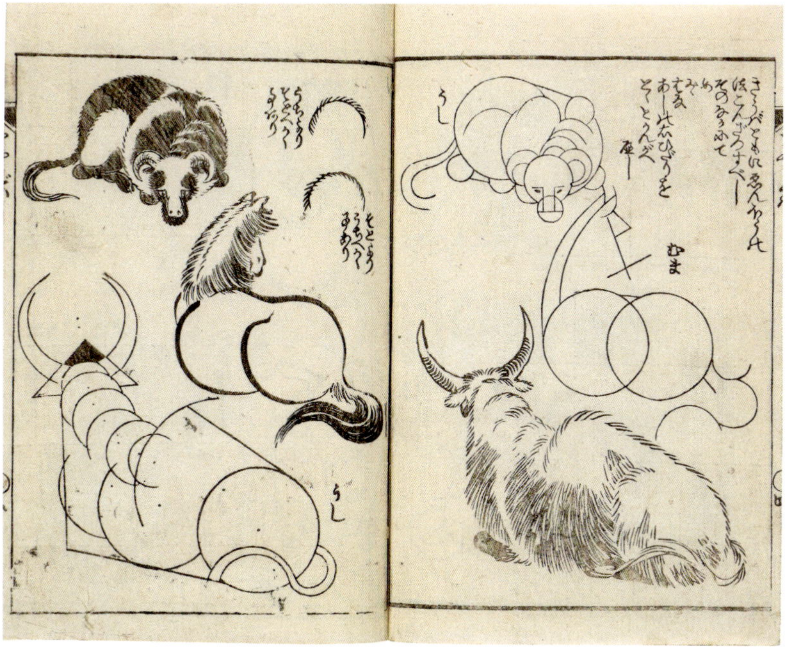

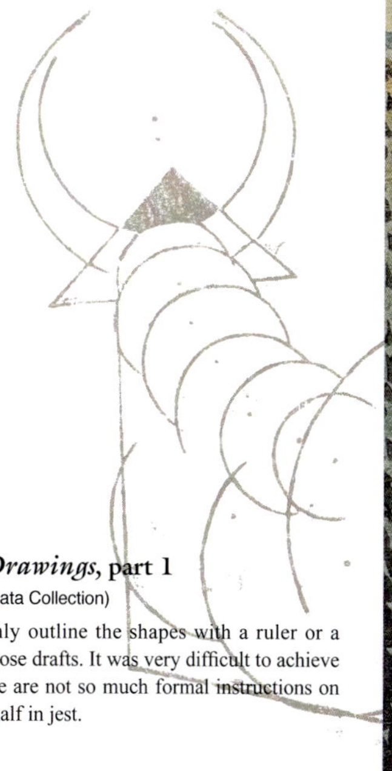

8-2 葛飾北斎『略画早指南』(りゃくがはやおしえ)前編

文化9年(1812)　中本　島根県立美術館(永田コレクション)蔵

定規とコンパスを使って大まかな形を取り、その下絵に基づいて絵を描く方法を指南しています。北斎の完成図に近づけるのはかなり難しく、正式な絵画技法を伝授するというより、面白半分に真似をする戯画の要素が強くなっています。

8-2 Katsushika Hokusai

***Quick Lesson in Simplified Drawings*, part 1**

1812, *chūhon*, Shimane Art Museum (Nagata Collection)

This book teaches you how to roughly outline the shapes with a ruler or a compass and draw pictures based on those drafts. It was very difficult to achieve Hokusai's level of perfection and these are not so much formal instructions on how to paint as cartoons to be copied half in jest.

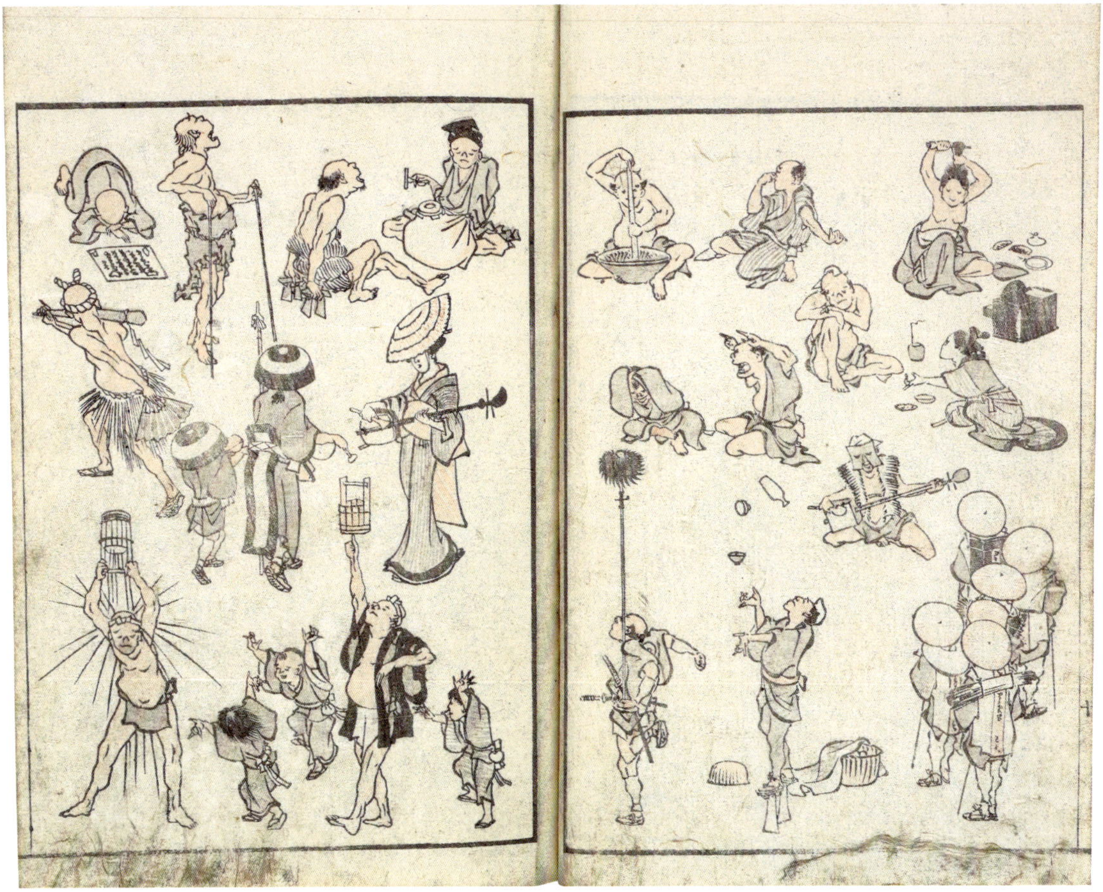

8-3 葛飾北斎 **『北斎漫画』初編**
文化11年(1814) 半紙本 島根県立美術館(永田コレクション)蔵

『北斎漫画』には、老若男女、さまざまな身分や職業の人々が数多く登場します。いずれも生き生きとした動きが的確に捉えられ、ちょっとした動作にも面白味が感じられます。

8-3 Katsushika Hokusai ***Hokusai's Sketches*, part 1**
1814, *hanshibon*, Shimane Art Museum (Nagata Collection)

Men and women of all ages, social status, and occupations appear in *Hokusai's Sketches*. In each case, their lively movements are captured appropriately and even the slightest gesture has its appeal.

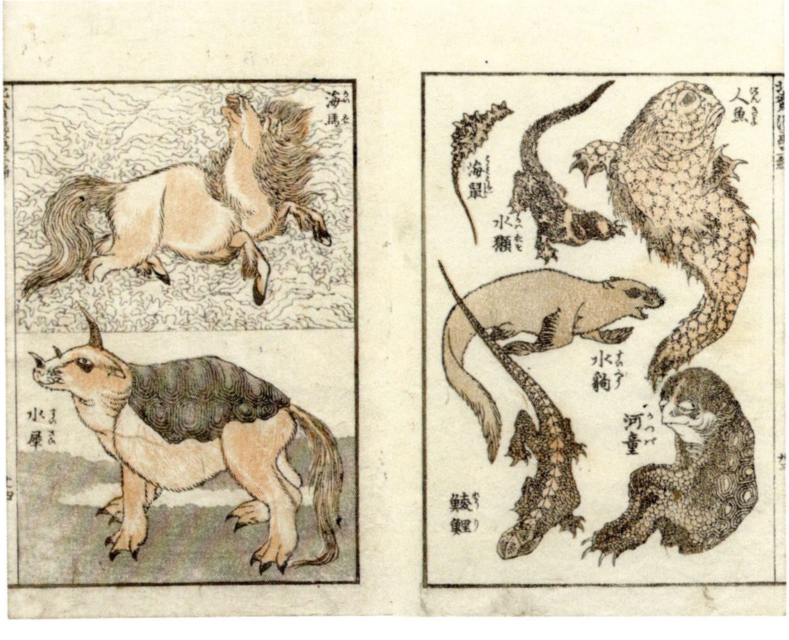

8-4 葛飾北斎
『北斎漫画』三編
文化12年(1815) 半紙本
太田記念美術館蔵蔵

『北斎漫画』では、哺乳類や鳥、魚、昆虫といったさまざまな動物たちも描く対象となっています。どんな動物も形の特徴が細部まで描き込まれており、人魚や河童のような空想の動物でさえもリアリティがあります。

8-4 Katsushika Hokusai
***Hokusai's Sketches*, part 3**
1815, *hanshibon*,
Ōta Memorial Museum of Art

There are also a variety of animals including mammals, birds, fish, and insects portrayed in *Hokusai's Sketches*. The characteristics of the shape of each animal are captured in detail and even imaginary creatures such as mermaids and *kappa* (water sprites) demonstrate a sense of reality.

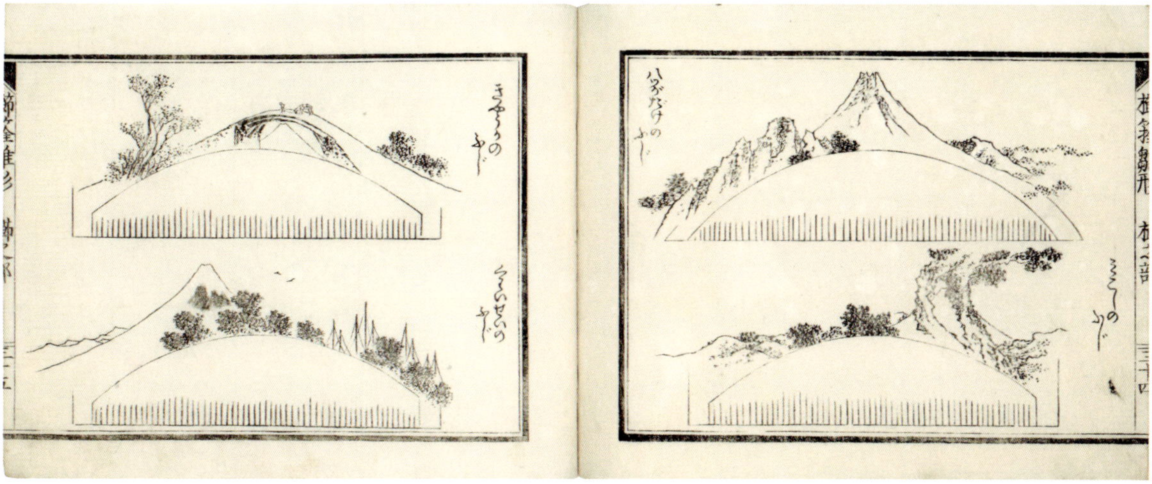

8-5 葛飾北斎 **『今様櫛䉤雛形』（いまようせっきんひながた）中巻**

文政6年（1823） 横本 国文学研究資料館蔵

櫛と煙管（きせる）を作る職人たちのためのデザイン集として制作されたもので、この図案に基づいて制作された工芸品も実在します。ここでは櫛の持ち手となる峰の部分に、さまざまな状況から眺めた富士山の図案が描かれています。

8-5 Katsushika Hokusai

***Modern Designs for Combs and Tobacco Pipes*, vol. 2**

1823, *yokohon*, National Institute of Japanese Literature

This book was produced as a collection of designs for artisans who made combs and tobacco pipes. Craftworks actually produced from these designs exist. Here, Mount Fuji viewed from various situations forms the design for the top of the comb where it is held.

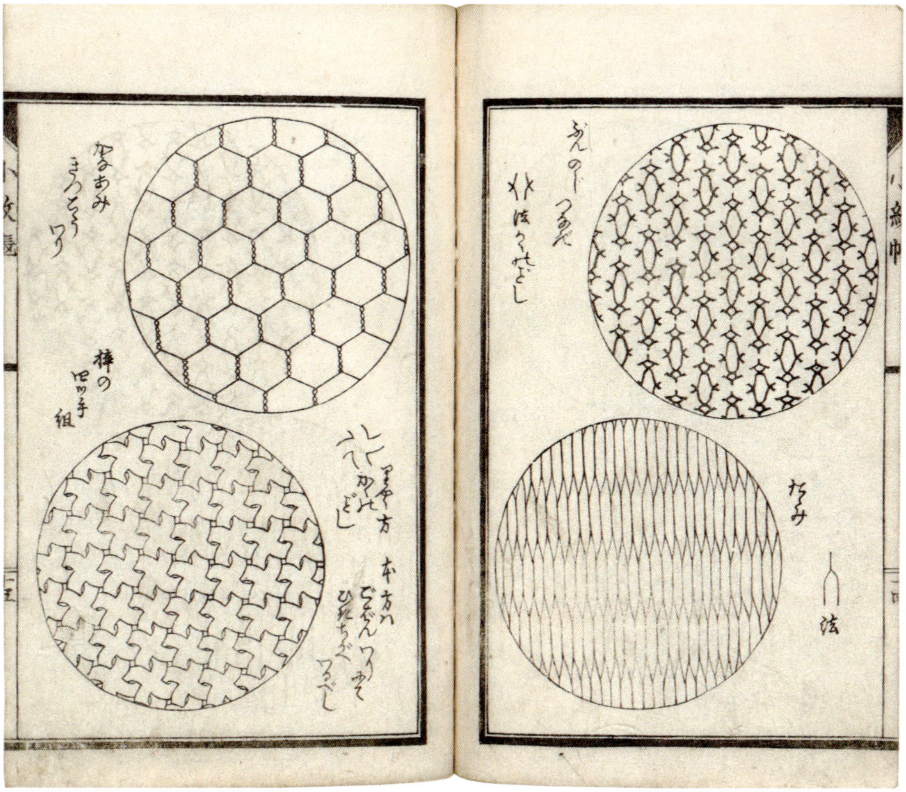

8-6 葛飾北斎 **『新形小紋帳』（しんがたこもんちょう）**

文政7年（1824） 中本 島根県立美術館（永田コレクション）蔵

小紋染のための雛形として制作されたもので、随所に描き方のコツが記されており、実用性が高くなっています。右下は畳の目をデザインしたもの。奇抜なアイデアに基づくデザインも収録されています。

8-6 Katsushika Hokusai

The Book of New Patterns for Kimono Fabrics

1824, *chūhon*, Shimane Art Museum (Nagata Collection)

This was produced as a sample book for fine-patterned *kimono* fabrics. With knacks for drawing provided here and there, it is highly practical. The lower right design is an adaptation of the grains of a *tatami* mat. There are also designs based on eccentric ideas.

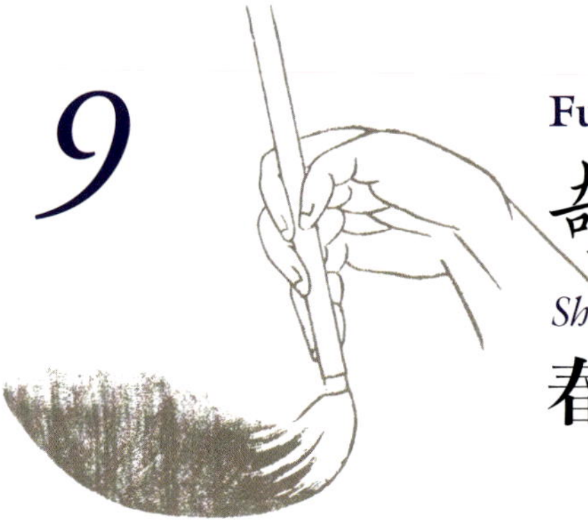

9 Full of Eccentric Ideas
奇抜なアイデア満載

Shunga
春　画

北斎は、浮世絵師たちのほとんどがそうであったように、男女の性行為を描いた春画を制作したとされています。「されています」というのは、春画は他の浮世絵とは異なり、絵師の実名がそのまま署名されているケースがほとんどないからです。北斎も「鉄棒ぬらぬら」という奇妙な隠号を使ったケースがありました。

北斎は、勝川春朗と号していた若い時代から、『笑本股庫嘉里嫁志』や『間女畑』といった墨摺本の春画を手がけています。しかし、北斎が春画を精力的に制作したのは、文化年間後期から文政年間前期、50代から60代はじめにかけての頃です。

北斎の春画として最も印象深いのは、『喜能会之故真通』における海女と蛸の図でしょう（図9-1）。女性の体に蛸の足が執拗にからみつくこの場面は、まさに北斎らしい奇抜なアイデアと独特な官能性に満ちています。美人画（→20頁参照）を得意としていた北斎ですが、その才能は春画においてもいかんなく発揮されているのです。

北斎作とされている春画は10点以上ありますが、北斎の真筆ではないと指摘されているものもあります。すなわち、北斎が門人たちを指揮しただけではないか、あるいは、娘の葛飾応為（→96頁参照）や渓斎英泉といった他の絵師に代作をさせたのではないかといったように、研究者によって見解が分かれているのです。春画の研究は、21世紀に入ってからようやく多くの人たちの関心が集まってきたという段階です。これからの研究の進展によって、北斎の春画についてもさまざまなことが明らかになっていくでしょう。

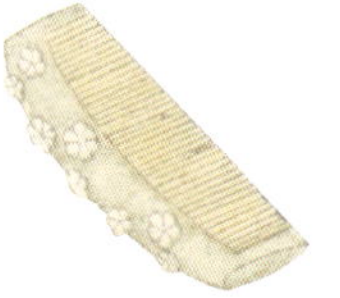

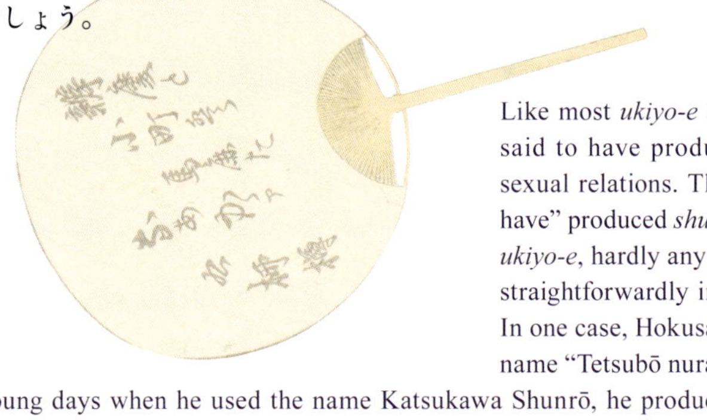

Like most *ukiyo-e* artists, Hokusai, too, is said to have produced *shunga* depicting sexual relations. The reason he is "said to have" produced *shunga* is that, unlike other *ukiyo-e*, hardly any of the works are signed straightforwardly in the artist's real name. In one case, Hokusai used a peculiar secret name "Tetsubō nuranura."

From Hokusai's young days when he used the name Katsukawa Shunrō, he produced *shunga* in the form of *sumizuri-bon* (collections of single-sheet woodblock prints in black and white) such as *Ehon kuragari zōshi* and *Mamebatake*. However, it was from the latter part of the Bunka era (1804–1818) to the early part of the Bunsei era (1818–1830), when Hokusai was in his fifties or early sixties, that he worked vigorously on *shunga*.

The most striking *shunga* by Hokusai is probably *Pine Seedlings on the First Rat Day* (fig. 9-1), a picture of a female diver and octopuses. The scene in which the octopuses' limbs cling persistently to the woman's body is full of eccentric ideas and unique sensuality typical of Hokusai. *Bijinga* (see p.20) were Hokusai's forte, but his talent was amply displayed in *shunga*, too.

There are ten or more *shunga* attributed to Hokusai, but some are doubted as whether they are really by Hokusai. That is to say, opinions among scholars are divided as to whether Hokusai simply supervised his pupils or made other artists such as his daughter Katsushika Ōi (see p. 96) or Keisai Eisen create a work in place of him. Research on *shunga* has finally begun to attract interest in the twenty-first century. Further studies should reveal a variety of details about Hokusai's *shunga*, too.

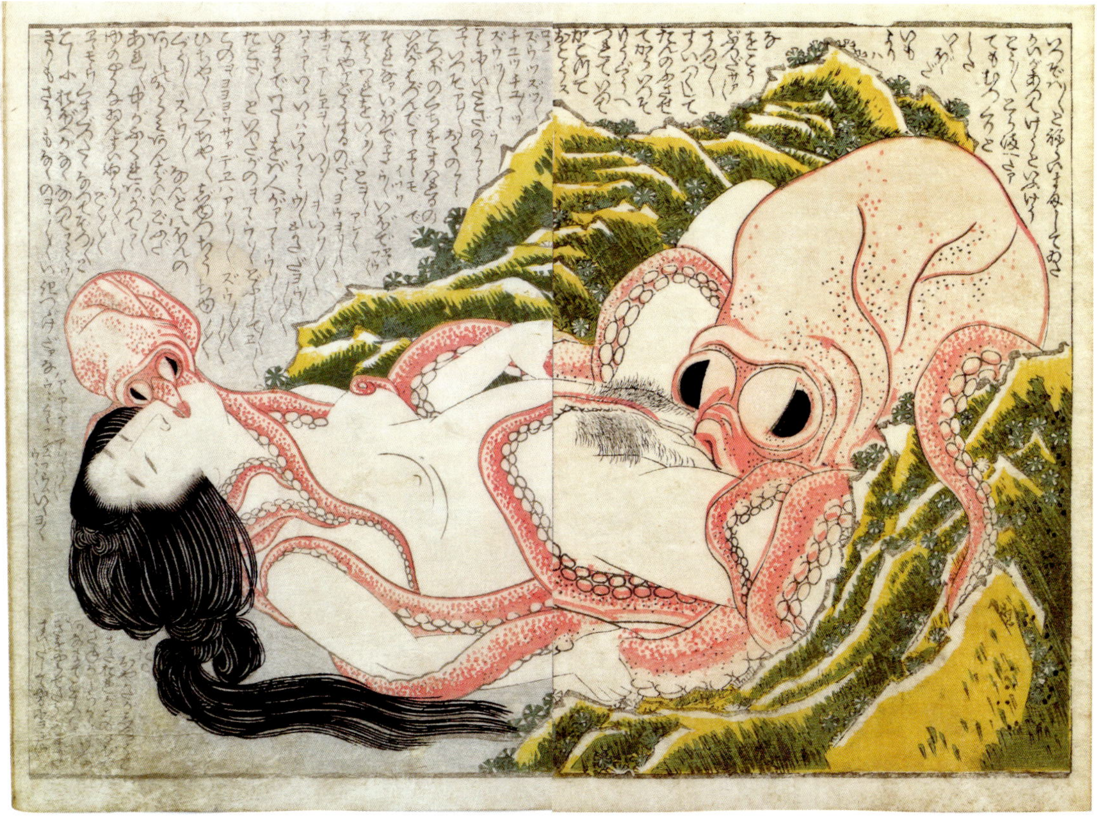

きのえのこまつ
9-1 葛飾北斎『喜能会之故真通』
文化11年(1814)　半紙本　国際日本文化研究センター蔵

海女に襲いかかり、股間と口に吸いつく大蛸と小蛸。体に蛸の足がからまり、海女は絶頂を迎えています。

9-1 Katsushika Hokusai
Pine Seedlings on the First Rat Day
1814, *hanshibon*, International Research Center for Japanese Studies

A large octopus and a small one attack a female diver by sticking to her crotch and mouth. Their limbs are twined around the woman's body as she falls into raptures.

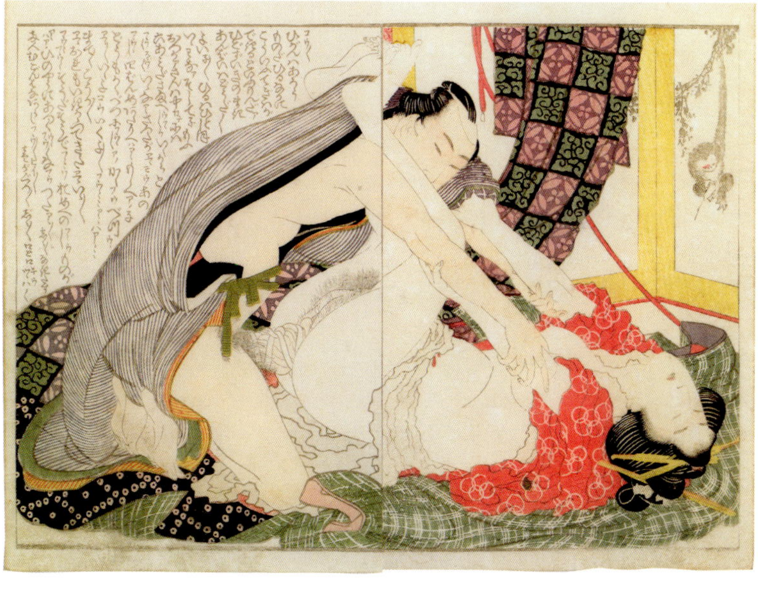

9-2 葛飾北斎
きのえのこまつ
『喜能会之故真通』
文化11年(1814)　半紙本
国際日本文化研究センター蔵

互いに腕と腕を掴み合っている男女の体が三角形を形成し、北斎らしい幾何学的な構図となっています。

9-2 Katsushika Hokusai
Pine Seedlings on the First Rat Day
1814, *hanshibon*, International Research Center for Japanese Studies

Holding each other's arms, the couple's bodies form a triangle, which presents a geometric composition characteristic of Hokusai.

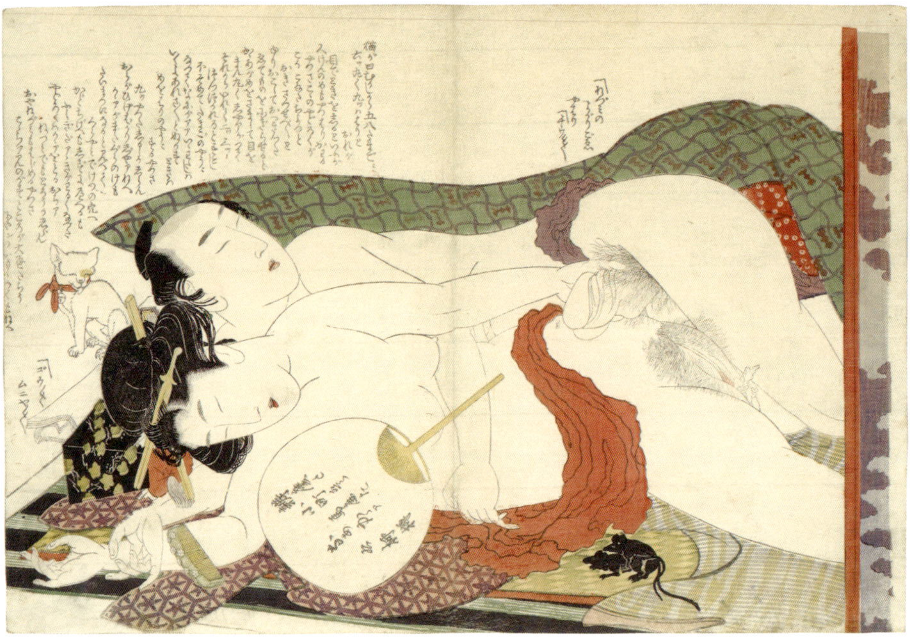

9-3 葛飾北斎 『絵本つひの雛形』
文化9年(1812)頃　大本　国際日本文化研究センター蔵
裸のまま眠ってしまった男女。その様子を猫が冷めたまなざしで眺めています。北斎ではなく娘の応為による作画という説（林美一『艶本研究 お栄と英泉』有光書房、1967年）もあります。

9-3 Katsushika Hokusai
Picture-book Models of Couples
c. 1812, *ōhon*, International Research Center for Japanese Studies
The couple have fallen asleep undressed. A cat watches over them with a chilly look. Some say that this is not by Hokusai but by his daughter Ōi.

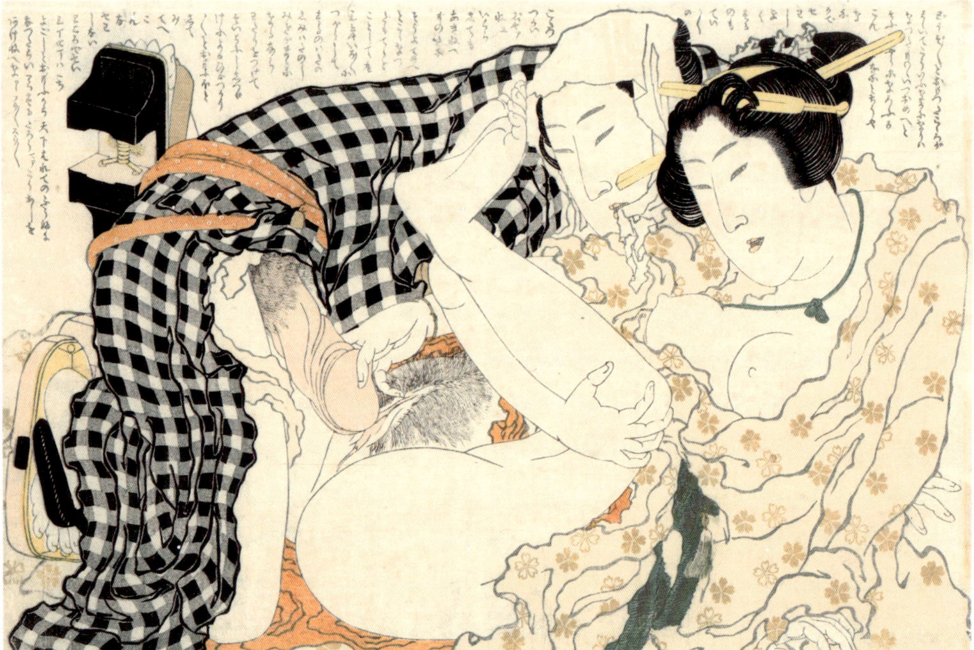

9-4 葛飾北斎 『富久寿楚宇』
文化12〜文政3年(1815〜20)頃　大本　ミカエル・フォーニッツコレクション蔵
恋中の男女が屋外でせわしなく情交を結んでいます。付き合って3年経つのですが、訳あって夫婦になれないことが周囲の文章からわかります。

9-4 Katsushika Hokusai ***Adonis Flower***
c. 1815–1820, *ōhon*, Michael Fornitz Collection
The lovers are hurriedly having an affair outdoors. They have gone together for three years, but the narrative reveals that for certain reasons, they cannot get married.

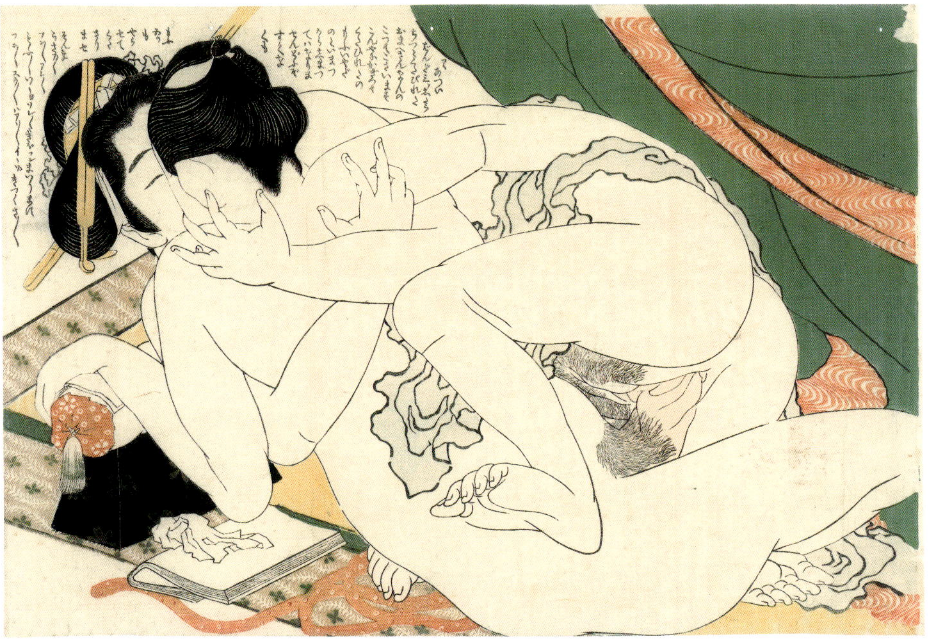

9-5 葛飾北斎 『富久寿楚宇(ふくじゅそう)』
文化12～文政3年(1815～20)頃　大本　ミカエル・フォーニッツコレクション蔵

夏の夜の夫婦の営み。疲れのみえる夫に対し、妻は積極的です。女性の顔半分を男性の後頭部で隠すという構図でキスシーンを描写しています。

9-5 Katsushika Hokusai ***Adonis Flower***
c. 1815–1820, *ōhon*, Michael Fornitz Collection

A husband and wife are making love on a summer night. The husband looks tired, but the wife takes the initiative. The kissing scene is depicted in a composition in which half of the woman's face is concealed with the back of the man's head.

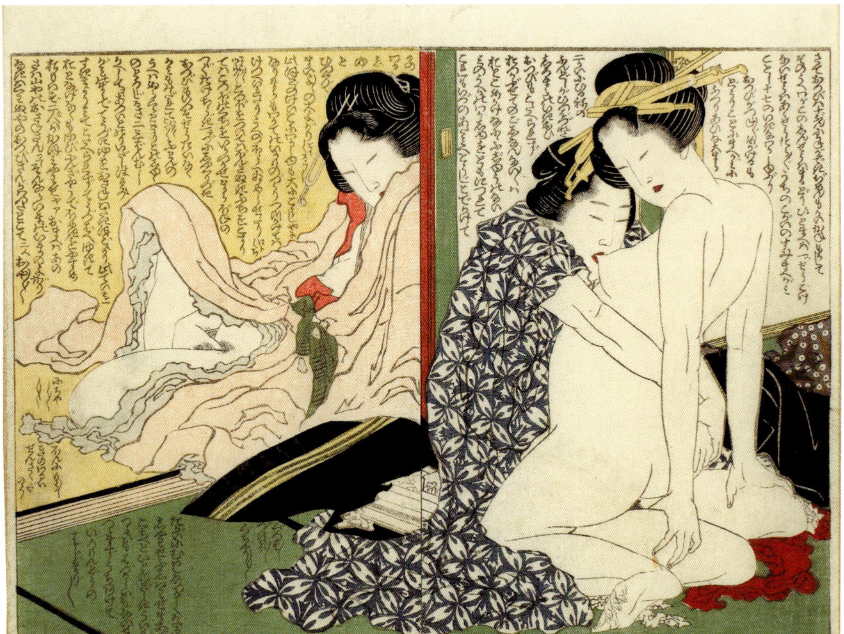

9-6 葛飾北斎 『万福和合神(まんぷくわごうじん)』
文政4年(1821)　半紙本　国際日本文化研究センター蔵

金持ちの家に生まれたおさねと、貧しい家に生まれたおつびという、2人の女性の性の遍歴を描いた波瀾万丈(はらんばんじょう)の物語。物語自体も北斎が執筆したと考えられています。

9-6 Katsushika Hokusai
God of Myriad Conjugal Delights
1821, *hanshibon*, International Research Center for Japanese Studies

A story full of ups and downs about the love affairs of two women, Osane, who was born into a rich family, and Otsubi, who was born into a poor family. Hokusai is considered to have written the story, too.

10

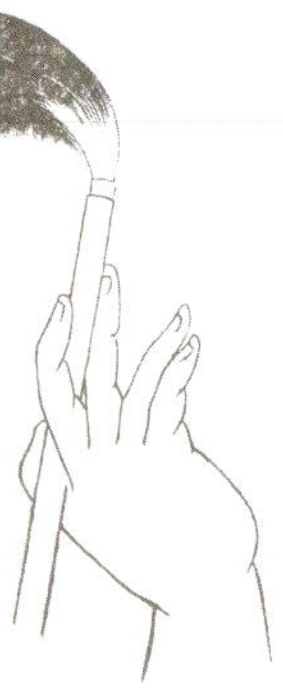

Vibrant Imagination
躍動する想像力

Monsters and Ghosts
妖怪・幽霊画

北斎は、勝川春朗と号していた若い頃、「新板浮絵化物屋鋪百物語の図」（図10-1）において、不気味でありながらもどこか愛嬌のある妖怪たちを描いています。早くから化け物に対して関心があったものと推測されます。

しかし、北斎ならではの卓越した妖怪や幽霊の表現が見られるのには、40代後半まで待たねばなりません。北斎は文化年間前半、読本挿絵（→24頁参照）の制作で人気を集めていました。読本の中には、『新累解脱物語』（しんかさねげだつものがたり）や『霜夜星』（しもよのほし）（図10-2）、『恋夢艋』（ゆめのうきはし）などのように、この世に怨みを持った怨霊や幽霊が登場する物語が数多くあります。北斎は、陰惨でおどろおどろしい怨霊たちが登場する場面を、迫力あるモノクロームの画面で盛り上げています。

それから20年ほど経った天保2~3年（1831~32）頃、「冨嶽三十六景」（→48頁参照）を刊行していたのとほぼ同時期に、「百物語」（図10-3~5）という妖怪や幽霊をテーマとした錦絵を発表しました。「百物語」という題名でありながら、100点どころか5点しか刊行が確認されていないため、当時の人気はそれほど高くなかったようです。しかし、妖怪画・幽霊画の歴史における傑作に仕上がっていることは注目すべきでしょう。特に「お岩さん」（図10-3）や「さらやしき」（図10-4）といった幽霊を描く場合、普通は足のない人間の姿で描かれることがほとんどですが、北斎は人間の形を留めていない妖怪のような形にアレンジしています。北斎の豊かな発想力が遺憾なく発揮されているのです。

During his young days when Hokusai used the name Katsukawa Shunrō, in *Newly Published Perspective Picture: One Hundred Ghost Stories in a Haunted House* (fig. 10-1), he depicted eerie yet somewhat cute *yōkai* (monsters). Hokusai is presumed to have had an interest in inanimate beings from early on.

However, it took Hokusai until he was in his late forties to come up with the distinguished representations of monsters or ghosts so characteristic of Hokusai. During the first half of the Bunka era (1804–1818), Hokusai won popularity for his *yomihon* illustrations (see p. 24). There are many stories among such *yomihon* in which vengeful spirits with a grudge against the world or ghosts appear. Look, for example, at *Shinkasane gedatsu monogatari* (New tale of the deliverance of the woman ghost Kasane), *Stars on a Frosty Night* (fig. 10-2), or *Yume no ukihashi* (Floating bridge of dreams of love). Hokusai livens up a scene in which horrific, spine-chilling spirits appear with a powerful, monochrome image.

Twenty or so years later, circa 1831–1832, around the same time as the publication of *Thirty-six Views of Mount Fuji* (see p. 48), Hokusai presented a series of *nishiki-e* (polychrome prints) entitled *One Hundred Ghost Stories* and treating monsters and ghosts as its theme. Despite being entitled “One Hundred Stories,” far from 100, the publication of only five have been confirmed. It seems that they were not popular in those days.

Nevertheless, it is worth noting that they are masterworks in the history of monster or ghost pictures. Particularly in the case of apparitions like *the Ghost of Oiwa* (fig. 10-3) and *The Mansion of the Plates* (fig. 10-4), conventional portraits depict them mostly as human beings with no legs. However, Hokusai transforms them into ghost-like forms that no longer retain the shape of a human being. Here, Hokusai gives full play to his innovative ideas.

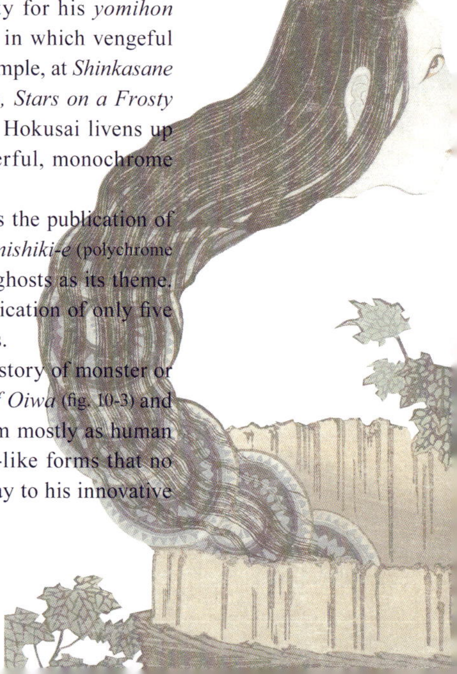

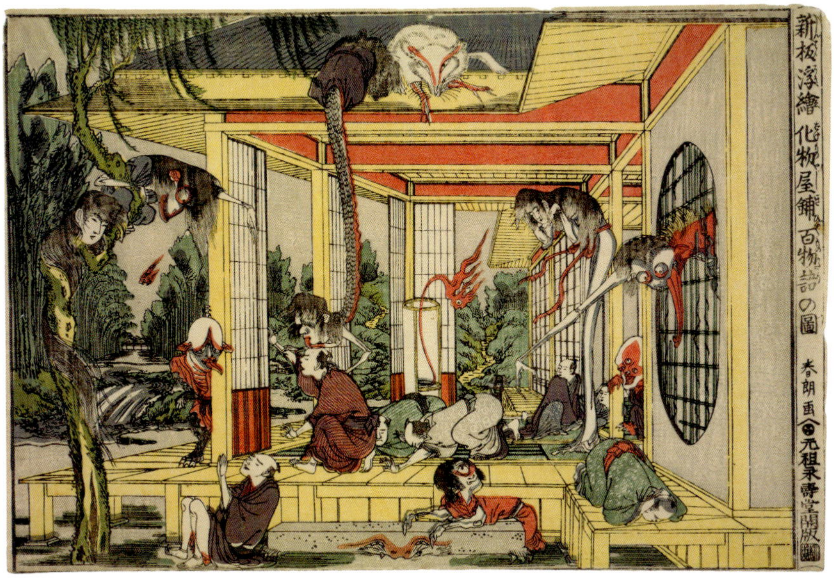

しんばんうきえばけものやしきひゃくものがたり ず

10-1 葛飾北斎 **新板浮絵化物屋鋪百物語の図**

天明年間(1781～89) 大判錦絵 ボストン美術館蔵

北斎が20代後半という若かりし頃に描いた妖怪画です。百物語とは、参加者が怪談を話し終わるごとに灯心をひとつずつ消していく遊びのことで、最後の100本目が消えた時に妖怪が出現するとされていました。

10-1 Katsushika Hokusai

Newly Published Perspective Picture: One Hundred Ghost Stories in a Haunted House

1781–1789, *ōban nishiki-e*, Museum of Fine Arts, Boston

These *yōkai* (monsters) were depicted by the young Hokusai in his late twenties. One Hundred Ghost Stories is a game in which each player tells a ghost story, after which one lampwick is blown out. It was believed that when the last 100th one went out, monsters would appear.

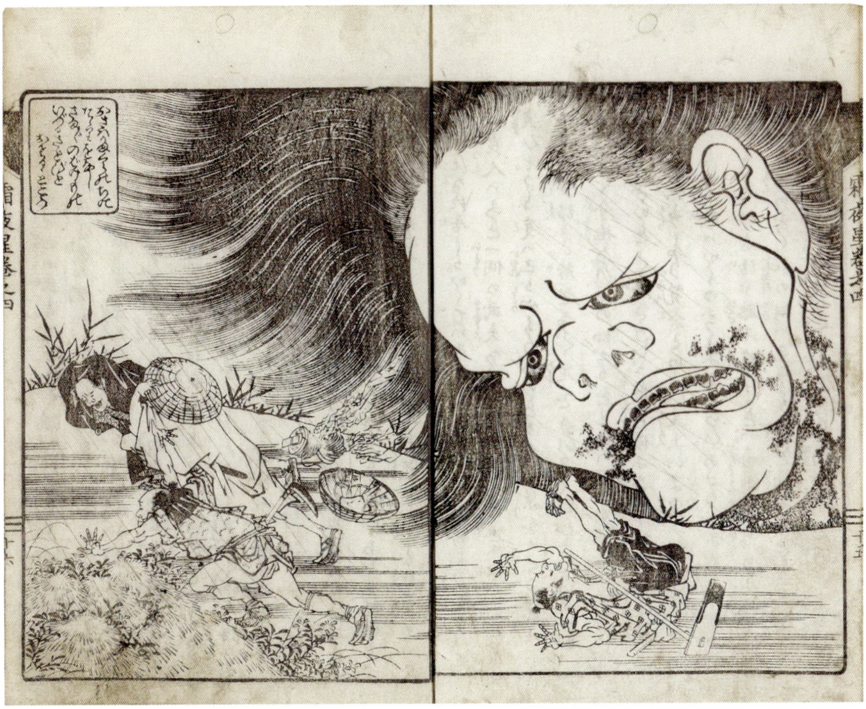

しもよのほし

10-2 柳亭種彦作・葛飾北斎画 **『霜夜星』巻之四**

文化5年(1808)頃 半紙本 名古屋市蓬左文庫蔵

沢子という女性の亡霊が、巨大な顔をして村人たちを驚かしている場面です。この読本を読んでいた読者は、頁をめくった瞬間に目に飛び込んできた亡霊の不気味な顔に強烈な印象を覚えたことでしょう。

10-2 Ryūtei Tanehiko

***Stars on a Frosty Night*, vol. 4**

illust. Katsushika Hokusai, 1808, *hanshibon*, Hosa Library, City of Nagoya

The apparition of a woman called Sawako startles the villagers with her huge face. The moment the reader of this *yomihon* turned the page, the apparition's unearthly face would leap into his or her eyes, having a decisive effect.

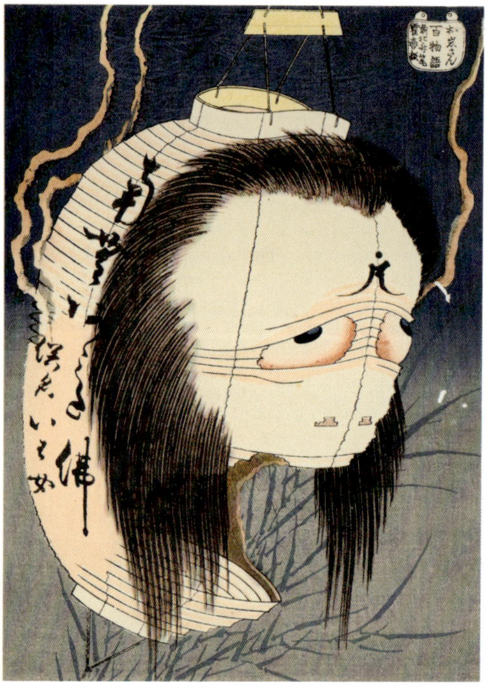

10-3 葛飾北斎　**百物語　お岩さん**

天保2〜3年(1831〜32)頃　中判錦絵
島根県立美術館(永田コレクション)蔵

夫の民谷伊右衛門に毒殺されたお岩が亡霊となって復讐する「東海道四谷怪談」の一場面。本来は人間の姿をしたお岩の亡霊を、提灯と合体させてしまうところに、北斎の発想の飛躍があります。

10-3 Katsushika Hokusai
One Hundred Ghost Stories: The Ghost of Oiwa
c. 1831–1832, *chūban nishiki-e*, Shimane Art Museum (Nagata Collection)

This is a scene from *The Ghost Story of Tōkaidō Yotsuya*, in which Oiwa, as an apparition, takes revenge on her husband Tamiya Iemon, who killed her with poison. Oiwa's apparition was originally in the form of a human being, but Hokusai ingeniously combines her body with a paper lantern.

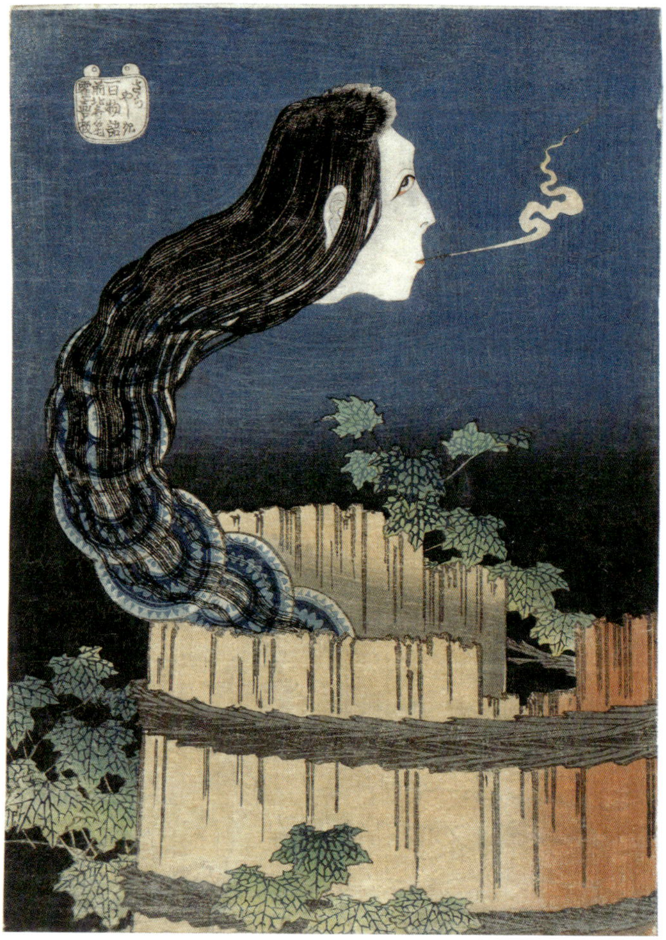

10-4 葛飾北斎　**百物語　さらやしき**

天保2〜3年(1831〜32)頃　中判錦絵　山口県立萩美術館・浦上記念館

主人が大事にしている皿を割った罪で殺されたお菊は、亡霊となって、夜な夜な井戸で怨めしそうに皿を数えるという怪談話です。お菊は本来人間の姿のはずが、皿をつなげたろくろ首の妖怪のようにして描いているところに、北斎ならではの造形センスが光ります。

10-4 Katsushika Hokusai
One Hundred Ghost Stories: The Mansion of the Plates
c. 1831–1832, *chūban nishiki-e*, Hagi Uragami Museum

This is a ghost story about Okiku, a maid who was killed for having broken a plate that her master treasured. Night after night, she becomes an apparition and counts plates at the well. Note Hokusai's creativity in the way he portrays Okiku not as a human being but as a ghost with a long neck composed of plates.

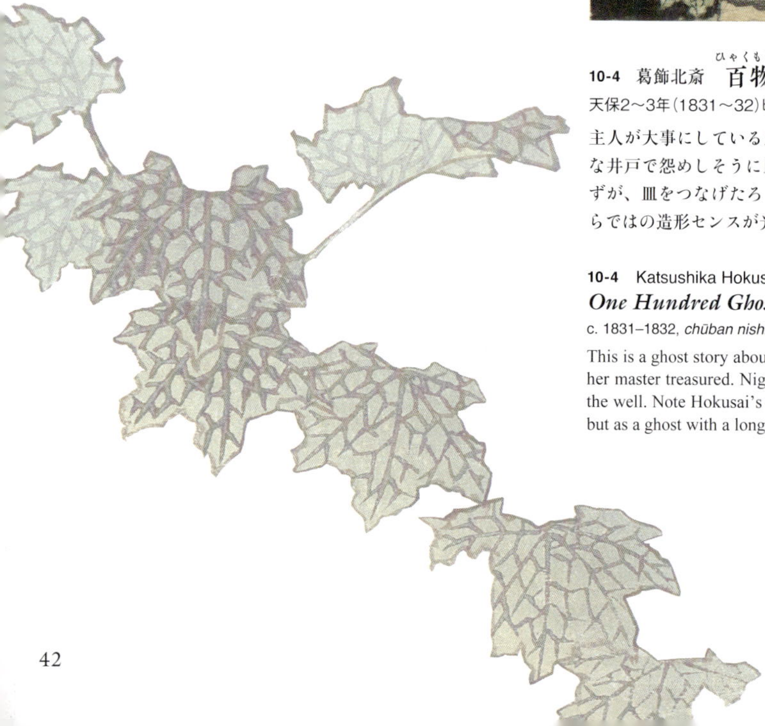

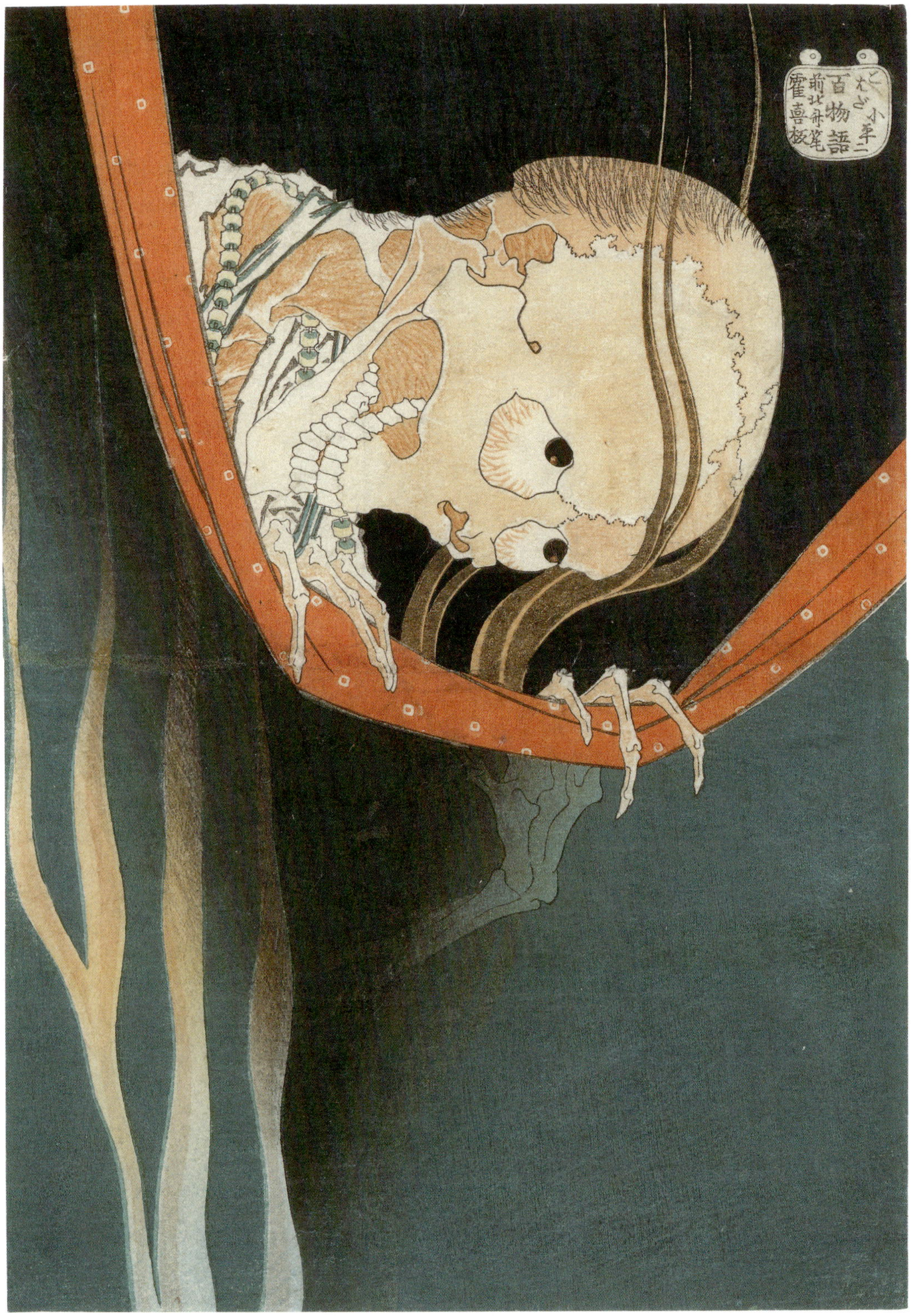

10-5 葛飾北斎　**百物語　こはだ小平二**

天保2～3年(1831～32)頃　中判錦絵　山口県立萩美術館・浦上記念館

妻の情夫に殺された小幡小平次（二）が幽霊となり、妻と情夫への怨みを晴らすという怪談話。小平次の亡霊が、蚊帳の上から２人の寝ている姿を覗き込んでいます。皮膚が剥がれて骸骨のような姿になった小平次の眼には、強い怨みの情念が込められています。

10-5 Katsushika Hokusai

One Hundred Ghost Stories: The Ghost of Kohada Koheiji

c. 1831–1832, *chūban nishiki-e*, Hagi Uragami Museum

This is a ghost story in which Kohada Koheiji, killed by his wife's lover, becomes a ghost and takes revenge on his wife and her lover. Koheiji's apparition peeks at the sleeping couple from above the mosquito net. With his skin stripped off, he looks like a skeleton, but his eyes are glaring with a deep-seated grudge.

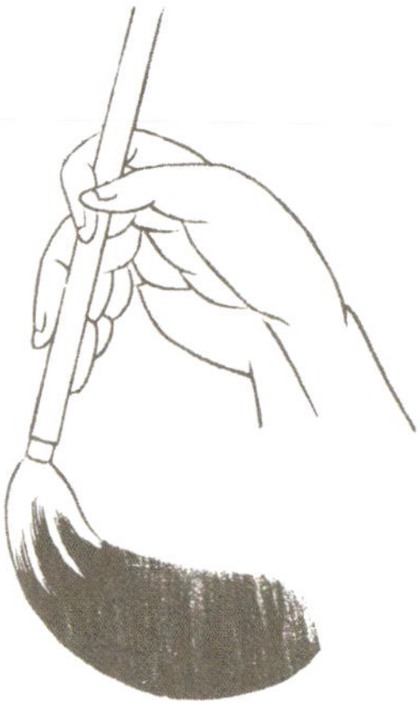

11 Proficient Even in Western Painting
西洋画も我が物に

Landscapes
風景画

北斎は、勝川春朗と号していた若い頃から、風景を描くことに関心を示していました。浅草寺や両国橋（図11-1）、あるいは芝居小屋の室内といった風景を、西洋の透視図法を取り入れて奥行きを強調した「浮絵」と呼ばれる技法で描いています。

40代半ばの文化年間頃になると、西洋の油絵を模したかのような、いわゆる「洋風風景画」に取り組むようになります。「くだんうしがふち」（図11-2）や「おしをくりはとうつうせんのづ」（図2-2）など、画面の周囲を石垣模様の額縁風に囲ったり、題名や落款を横に寝かせて書くことでアルファベット風に見せたりなど、西洋絵画を意識していることは確実です。もちろん、自然な奥行き感やモチーフの立体感を示す陰影表現の導入などの工夫も認めることができます。

50代半ばからは『北斎漫画』を中心とした絵手本（→32頁参照）において、日本各地のさまざまな風景を取り上げていましたが（特に『北斎漫画』七編）、70代に入った頃からは、錦絵による風景画を集中的に発表するようになります。代表作としてあまりに著名な「冨嶽三十六景」（→48頁参照）を筆頭に、滝を題材とした「諸国瀧廻り」（図11-3）や橋を題材とした「諸国名橋奇覧」（図11-4）、海を題材とした「千絵の海」（図11-5）など、日本各地の風景を鮮やかな色彩で描き出しました。晩年になっても制作意欲を衰えさせることなく、新しい風景表現を生み出そうとし続けた北斎の気概を感じることができるでしょう。

Hokusai was interested in painting landscapes from his young days when he went under the name Katsukawa Shunrō. He portrayed views of Asakusa Temple, Ryōgoku Bridge (fig. 11-1), or the inside of a theater employing a technique called *uki-e*, in which Western perspective was incorporated to emphasize the depth.

Around the Bunka era (1804–1818), when Hokusai reached his mid-forties, he began working on so-called "Western-style landscape paintings" as if copying Western oil paintings. In, for example, *Ushigafuchi at Kudan* (fig. 11-2) or *Fast Skiffs Navigating Large Waves* (fig.2-2), the way the borders are surrounded in a frame-like manner with a stone-wall pattern, the way the title or signature and seal are written sideways to make them look like the Roman alphabet, etc. indicate that he was definitely conscious of Western painting. Of course, there are also signs of his efforts to incorporate shading to present a natural sense of depth and the three-dimensionality of the motifs.

From when Hokusai was in his mid-fifties, in *Hokusai's Sketches* and other drawing manuals (see p. 32), he featured landscapes of various parts of Japan (especially in *Hokusai's Sketches*, part 7). Once he reached his seventies, he intensively presented *nishiki-e* (polychrome print) landscapes, of which the best-known example would be *Thirty-six Views of Mount Fuji* (see p. 48). There are also *Tour of Waterfalls in Various Provinces* (fig. 11-3), *Wondrous Views of Famous Bridges in Various Provinces* (fig. 11-4), *One Thousand Pictures of the Sea* (fig. 11-5), etc., which depict views of different parts of Japan in brilliant colors. Hokusai's enthusiasm to paint never declined even late in life and his mettle to continue creating new expressions in landscape can be felt.

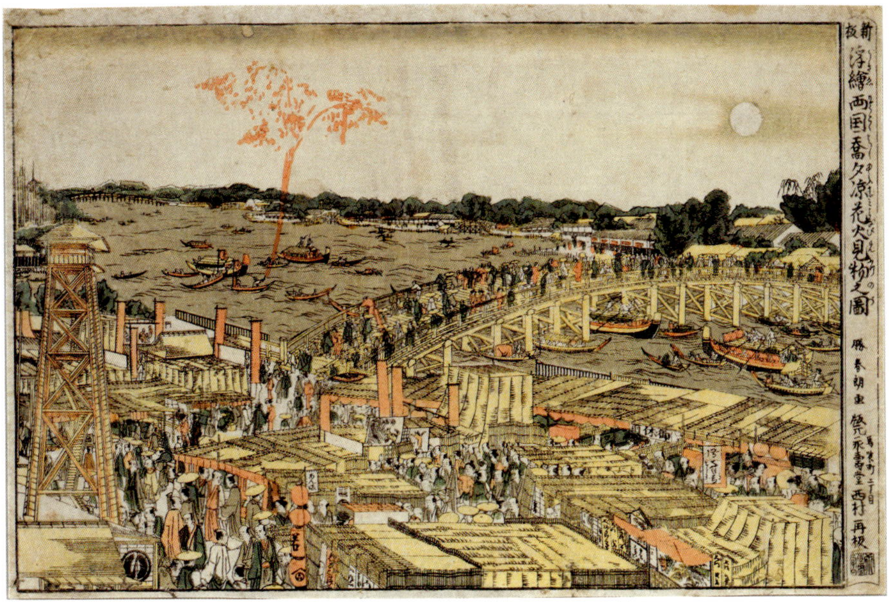

画像提供:すみだ北斎美術館 / DNPartcom (Image: The Sumida Hokusai Museum / DNPartcom)

11-1 葛飾北斎

新板浮絵両国橋夕涼花火見物之図（しんぱんうきえりょうごくばしゆうすずみはなびけんぶつのず）

天明年間(1781-89)頃　大判錦絵　すみだ北斎美術館蔵

西洋の透視図法を取り入れた浮絵。北斎も最初は表現がぎこちないものでしたが、この作品では、表現がこなれ、両国橋周辺の空間の広がりが自然になってきています。

11-1 Katsushika Hokusai

Newly Published Perspective Picture: Enjoying the Evening Cool Viewing Fireworks at Ryōgoku Bridge

c. 1781–1789, *ōban nishiki-e*, The Sumida Hokusai Museum

An *uki-e* incorporating Western perspective. Although Hokusai's rendition was awkward at the beginning, here, he has mastered the technique and the space around Ryōgoku Bridge expands more naturally.

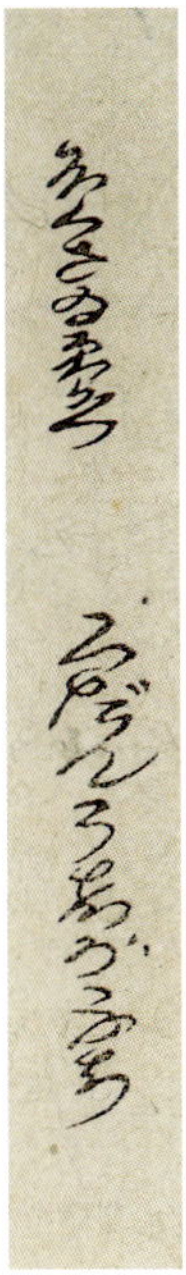

「ほくさゐゑかく　くだんうしがふち」

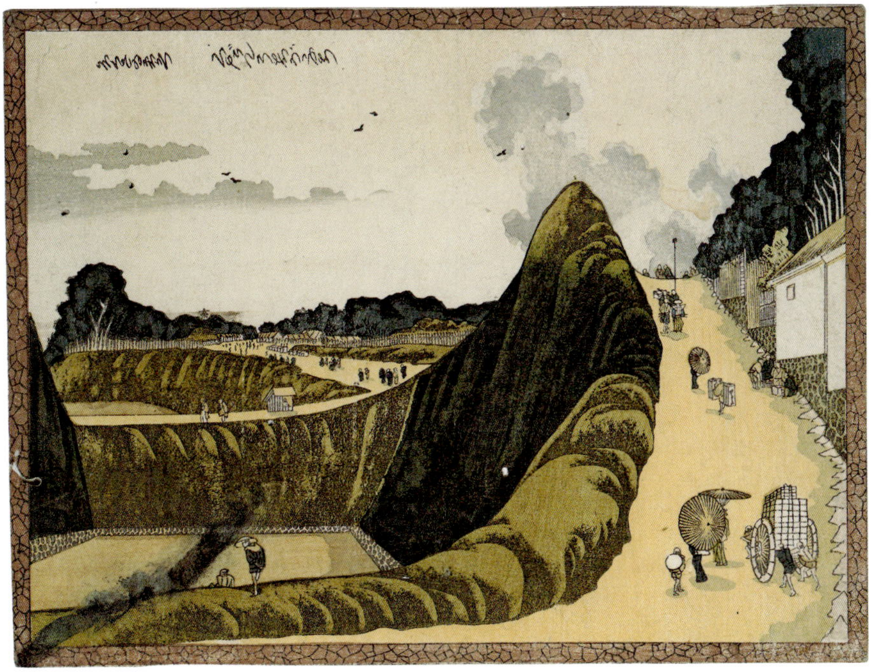

11-2 葛飾北斎　**くだんうしがふち**

文化初期(1804〜06)頃　中判錦絵　中右コレクション蔵

土坡（どは）の陰影の付け方や輪郭線のない入道雲の形、また、坂道を登る人々の足元に影が映っていることなどにも、西洋絵画の表現を取り込もうとする北斎の姿勢を読み取れます。左上にある文字を90度回転させると「ほくさゐゑかく　くだんうしがふち」と読めます。

11-2 Katsushika Hokusai ***Ushigafuchi at Kudan***

c. 1804–1806, *chūban nishiki-e*, Nakau Collection

Hokusai's inclination to incorporate Western painting techniques is visible in the shading of the mound, the thunderhead configured without contours, the shadows depicted at the feet of the people going uphill, etc. When rotated 90 degrees clockwise, the inscription in the upper left reads "Hokusai e kaku [drawn by], Kudan Ushigafuchi."

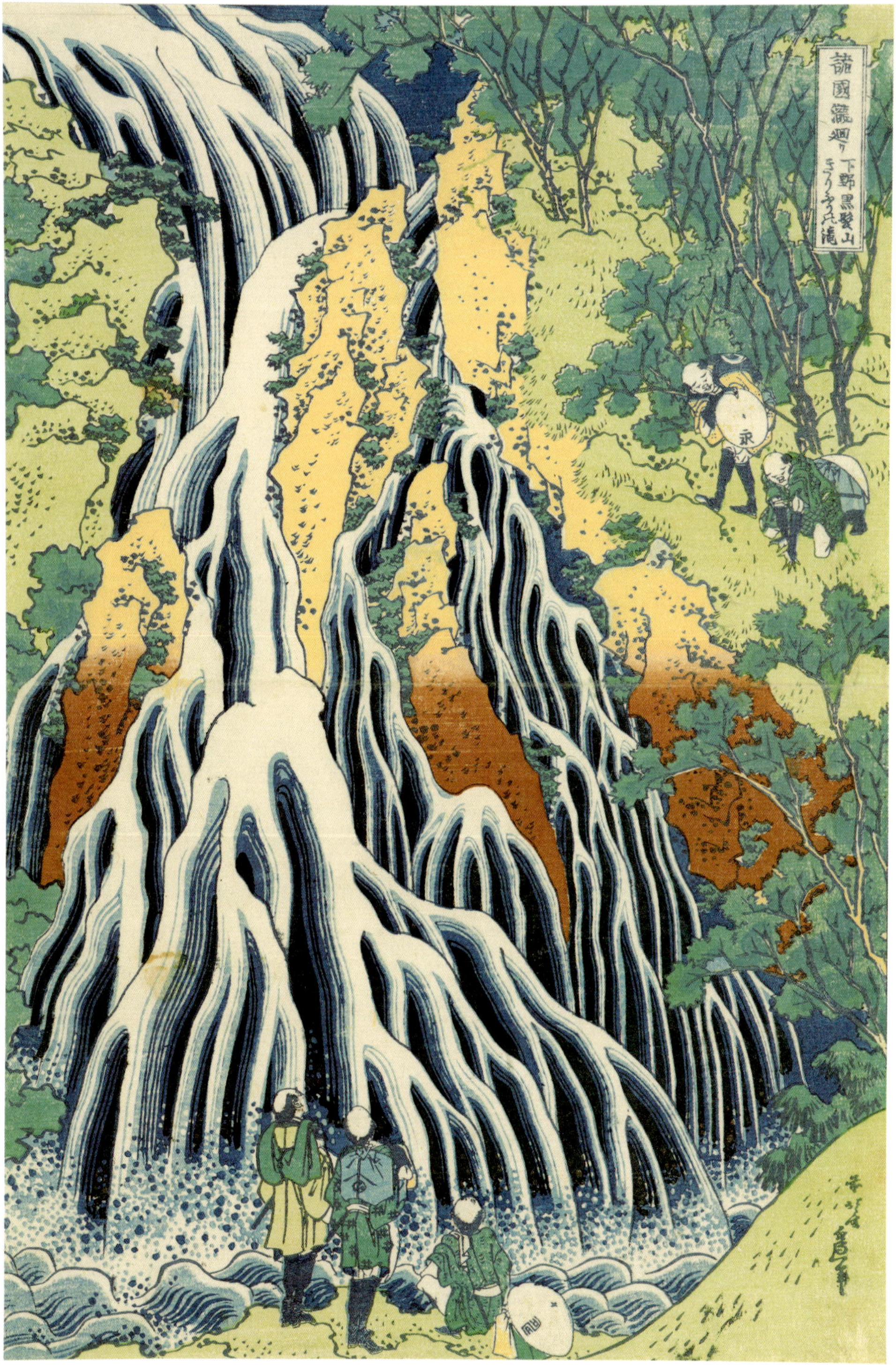

11-3 葛飾北斎
諸国瀧巡り　下野黒髪山きりふりの滝
天保4年(1833)頃　大判錦絵　太田記念美術館蔵

日本各地の滝を題材とした全8点からなるシリーズです。幾筋にも枝分かれして流れる霧降の滝を描いていますが、実際の景色をそのまま描くことよりも、水の動きの面白さをいかに表現するかの方に北斎の関心は向けられています。

11-3 Katsushika Hokusai
Tour of Waterfalls in Various Provinces: The Kirifuri Waterfall at Mount Kurokami in Shimotsuke Province
c. 1833, *ōban nishikie*, Ōta Memorial Museum of Art

A series of altogether eight prints depicting waterfalls in various parts of Japan. This is the Kirifuri Waterfall, which branches out into countless streaks. Rather than depicting a true-to-life view of the actual scene, Hokusai turns his interest to how he can represent the appeal of the water flow.

11-4　葛飾北斎

諸国名橋奇覧　足利行道山くものかけはし

天保5年(1834)頃　大判錦絵　山口県立萩美術館・浦上記念館蔵

日本各地の橋を題材とした全11点からなるシリーズです。切り立った岩の上に建つ清心亭に架かる橋を描いていますが、実際の景色を正確に写し取ったものではなく、幻想的な風景に仕上げています。

11-4　Katsushika Hokusai

Wondrous Views of Famous Bridges in Various Provinces: The Hanging-cloud Bridge at Mount Gyōdō near Ashikaga

c. 1834, *ōban nishiki-e*, Hagi Uragami Museum

A series of altogether eleven prints depicting bridges in various parts of Japan. This is the bridge that leads to Seishintei, a tea hut standing on a precipice. Instead of accurately reproducing the view, Hokusai finishes it off as an illusory landscape.

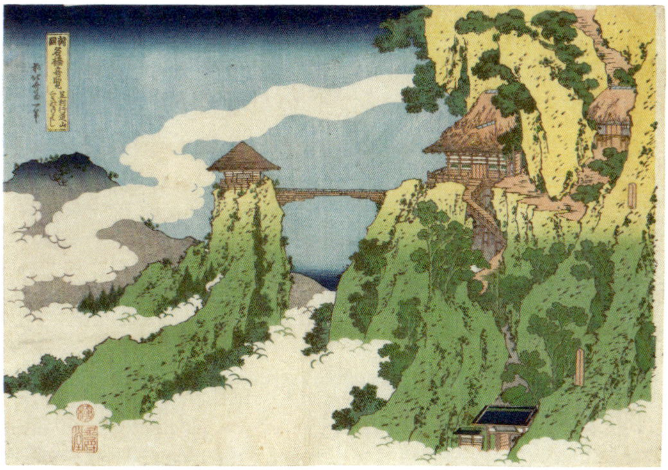

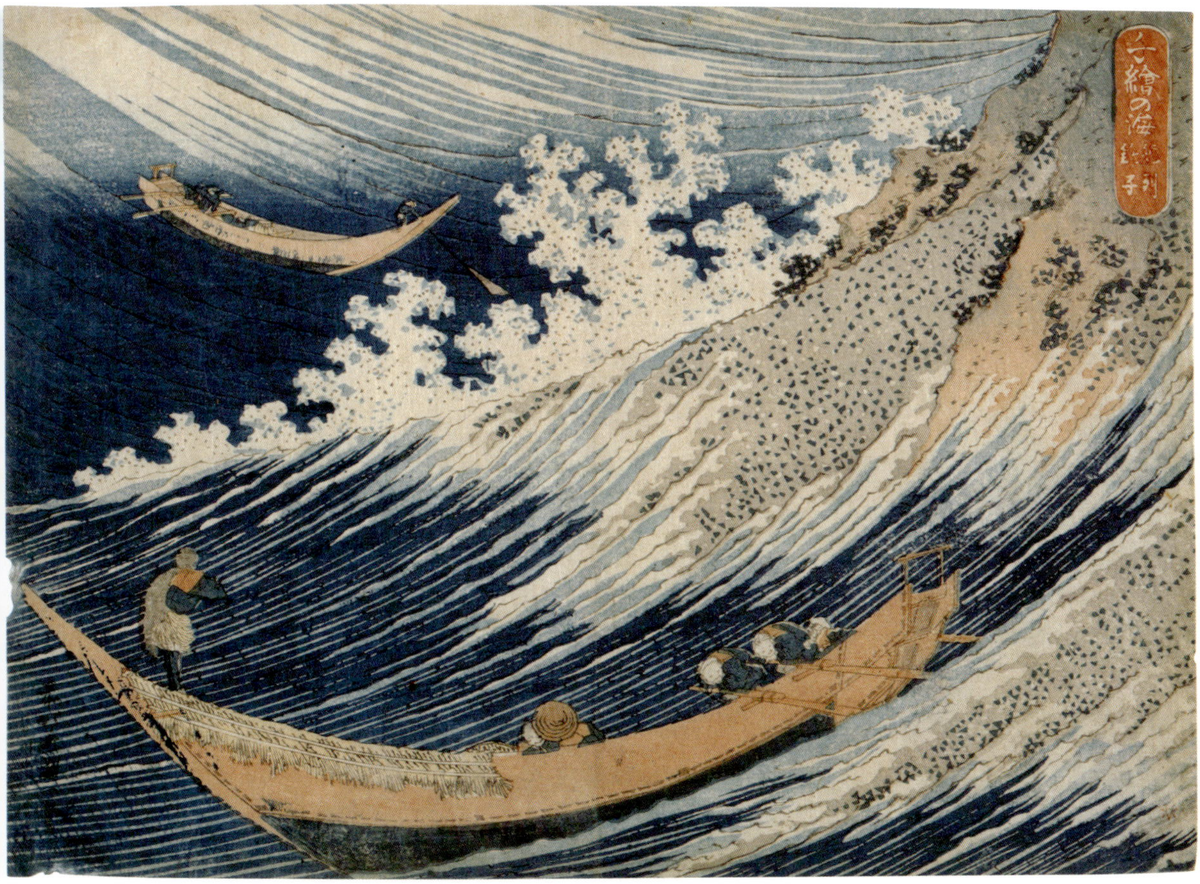

11-5　葛飾北斎　**千絵の海　相州 銚子**

中判錦絵　天保初期(1830～33)頃　千葉市美術館蔵

川や海で漁業を営む人々の暮らしを題材とした全10点からなるシリーズです。手前には引く波、遠くには打ち寄せる波を描き、さらに荒れ狂う波にあらがうように漁をする漁師たちの姿を捉えています。北斎の波への深い関心がうかがわれる一点です。

11-5　Katsushika Hokusai

One Thousand Pictures of the Sea: Chōshi in Sōshū

c. 1830–1833, *chūban nishiki-e*, Chiba City Museum of Art

A series of altogether ten prints depicting the life of fishermen working on the river or at sea. An ebbing wave is depicted in the foreground with another one rolling in in the distance. The fishermen are struggling against the raging waves to continue fishing. This is an example that demonstrates Hokusai's deep interest in waves.

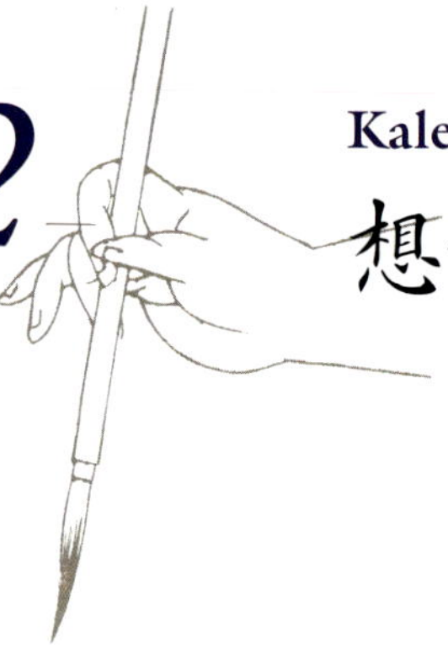

12 Kaleidoscopic Vistas Sparked by Imagination
想像力が生み出す多彩な富士

Thirty-six Views of Mount Fuji
冨嶽三十六景

北斎が富士図の連作に取り組んだ最初の作例は、文政6年(1823)、64歳の時に刊行した絵手本『今様櫛𨪙雛形(いまようせっきんひながた)』(図8-5)です。この中で、夏の富士、快晴の富士、橋下の富士など、富士山を用いた櫛のデザインを8図掲載しています。

天保元年(1830)、71歳頃から、富士山を題材とした風景画である「冨嶽三十六景」(図1-1~2, 2-1, 12-1~4, 40-2)の制作に取り組みます。このシリーズの大きな売りが、当時は「ベロ」と呼んでいたプルシアン・ブルーという舶来の絵具の使用です。この藍色の絵具によって、これまでの風景画にはなかった、鮮やかで透明感のある空や海が表現されるようになりました。売れ行きも好調だったようで、「三十六景」という題名にも関わらず、全部で46点が刊行されています。

「冨嶽三十六景」における北斎の狙いは、目に見える風景をそのまま写し取ることではありません。時には富士山を主役に、時には富士山をこっそりと隠れた脇役にしながら、北斎の頭の中に思い浮かんだ理想の富士山の風景を描きとどめようとしたのです。

その試みは、「冨嶽三十六景」完成直後の天保5年(1834)から刊行された『富嶽百景』(図2-6, 12-5~6)という絵本で一段上の高みに至ります。『富嶽百景』は、「冨嶽三十六景」のように具体的な場所から富士山を描く作例が多くありません。天候や四季、時刻と富士山をいかに組み合わせるか、あるいは人の思いもよらない視点でいかに富士山を眺めるかということが、さらに追及されているのです。北斎にとって富士山は単なる山ではなく、次から次へと新しいイメージが生まれてくる発想の源であったといえるでしょう。

The first example of Hokusai working on a series of pictures of Mount Fuji was *Modern Designs for Combs and Tobacco Pipes* (fig. 8-5), which was published in 1823, when Hokusai was aged 64. In it, there are eight pictures of comb designs depicting Mount Fuji in the summer, Mount Fuji on a fine day, Mount Fuji under a bridge, etc.

It was from 1830, when he was around 71, that he began working on *Thirty-six Views of Mount Fuji* (figs. 1-1~2, 2-1, 12-1~4, 40-2), i.e. landscapes with Mount Fuji as the subject. A major selling point of this series was the use of imported Prussian blue paint, which was called "*bero*" in those days. This deep-blue-colored paint made it possible to represent the sky and sea with vivid transparency unidentifiable in former landscape paintings. They sold well and despite the title "thirty-six views," altogether forty-six works were published.

Hokusai's aim in *Thirty-six Views of Mount Fuji* was not to depict the landscape exactly as it appeared in his eyes. At times, he would make Mount Fuji play the leading role and, on other occasions, he would have it recede to an unobtrusively hidden supporting role. By doing so, Hokusai was trying to portray the ideal views of Mount Fuji that came to mind.

His attempts achieved yet a higher level in a picture book entitled *One Hundred Views of Mount Fuji*, (figs. 2-6, 12-5~6) which was published from 1834, immediately after the completion of *Thirty-six Views of Mount Fuji*. In *One Hundred Views of Mount Fuji*, there are not so many examples of the mountain portrayed from specific locations as was the case in *Thirty-six Views of Mount Fuji*. How to combine the weather, season, and time of day with Mount Fuji or how to capture it from a totally unforeseen viewpoint was pursued further. To Hokusai, Mount Fuji was not simply a mountain but a source of inspiration from which one after another new image emerged.

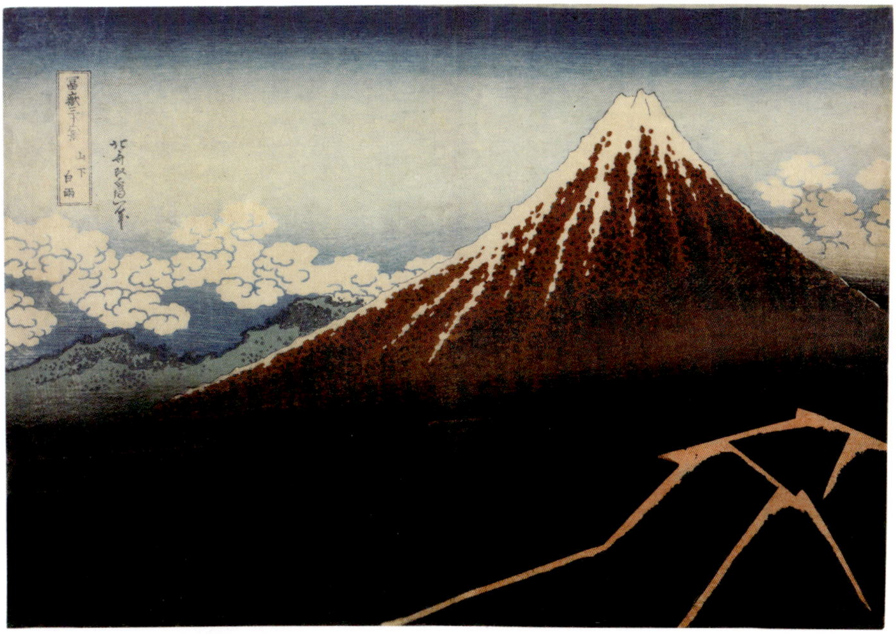

12-1 葛飾北斎 **冨嶽三十六景　山下白雨**
天保元〜4年(1830〜33)頃　大判錦絵　島根県立美術館(永田コレクション)蔵

山頂付近は雲ひとつない青空ですが、山麓は真っ黒に覆われており、白雨、すなわち突然のにわか雨に襲われている状況を表現しています。晴と雨、天空と地上という、相反するもの同士をひとつの画面の中に見事にまとめ上げた作品です。

12-1 Katsushika Hokusai
Thirty-six Views of Mount Fuji: Shower below the Summit
c. 1830–1833, *ōban nishiki-e*, Shimane Art Museum (Nagata Collection)

The sky is blue without a single cloud at the summit, but the foot of the mountain is covered in black, having been hit by a sudden shower. Contradictory elements, sunny and rainy, sky and earth, are brilliantly consolidated in a single image.

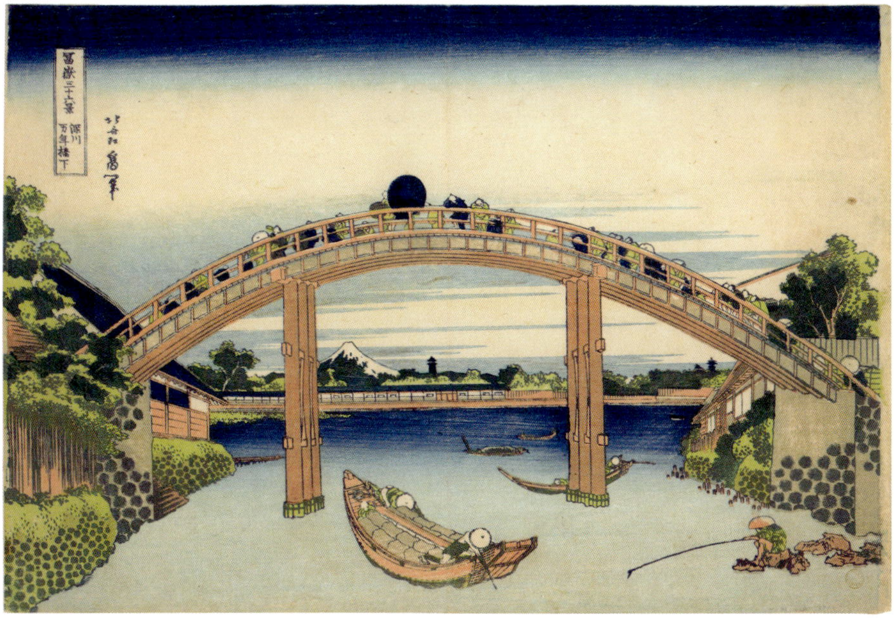

12-2 葛飾北斎 **冨嶽三十六景　深川万年橋下**
天保元〜4年(1830〜33)頃　大判錦絵　メトロポリタン美術館蔵

橋の下から富士山を眺めるという奇抜な構図になっています。橋は綺麗な弧を描いており、定規とコンパスを使って緻密に計算して描いたかのようです。幾何学的な画面構成を好んだ、北斎の個性が際立った作品です。

12-2 Katsushika Hokusai
Thirty-six Views of Mount Fuji: Under Mannen Bridge at Fukagawa
c. 1830–1833, *ōban nishiki-e*, The Metropolitan Museum of Art

An unusual composition in which Mount Fuji is seen from below a bridge. The bridge forms a handsome arc as if drawn with meticulous calculations using a ruler and a compass. Hokusai's originality in favor of geometric compositions stands out.

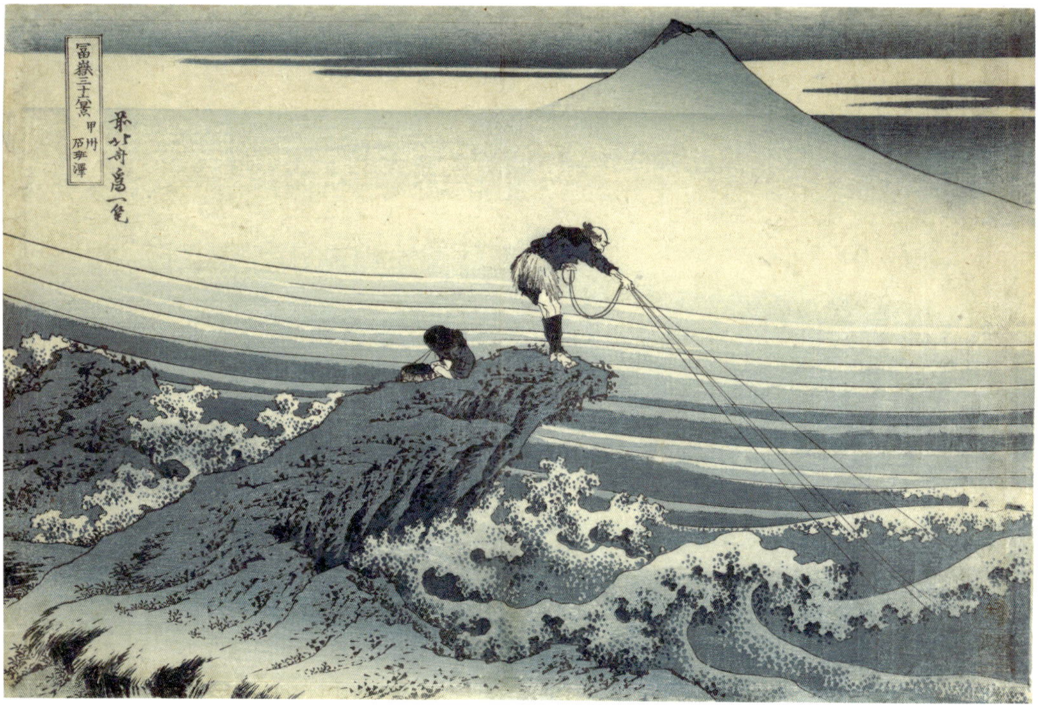

12-3 葛飾北斎 **冨嶽三十六景　甲州石班沢**
天保元～4年(1830～33)頃　大判錦絵　メトロポリタン美術館蔵

「冨嶽三十六景」には藍一色で画面全体を摺った藍摺の作品が含まれています。本図は、激しい川の流れに立ち向かう漁師とそれを見守る富士山が、透明感のある藍色のぼかしで表現されており、ベロの美しさが十分に伝わる一点となっています。

12-3 Katsushika Hokusai
Thirty-six Views of Mount Fuji: Kajikazawa in Kai Province
c. 1830–1833, *ōban nishiki-e*, The Metropolitan Museum of Art

There are *aizuri* works printed in Prussian blue only among the *Thirty-six Views of Mount Fuji*. Here, a fisherman confronts the fierce flow on the river with Mount Fuji watching over him. The Prussian blue gradation is applied with a feeling of limpidity, fulling conveying the splendor of *bero*.

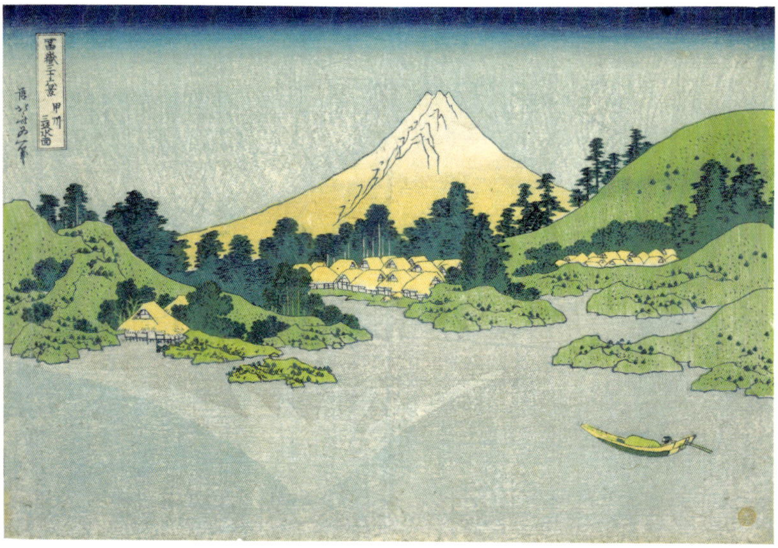

12-4 葛飾北斎 **冨嶽三十六景　甲州三坂水面**
天保元～4年(1830～33)頃　大判錦絵　メトロポリタン美術館蔵

目の前の富士山は雪のない夏の富士山ですが、河口湖の水面に映る富士山は、山頂に雪を頂いた冬の富士山になっています。夏と冬という、全く異なる二つの季節を一枚の画面で表現した、北斎らしい奇抜なアイデアが光る作品です。

12-4 Katsushika Hokusai
Thirty-six Views of Mount Fuji: Surface of the Water at Misaka in Kai Province
c. 1830–1833, *ōban nishiki-e*, The Metropolitan Museum of Art

The mountain in front of you is Mount Fuji in the summer with no snow, but the mountain reflected on Lake Kawaguchi is Mount Fuji in the winter capped with snow. Hokusai's unconventional idea of representing two entirely different seasons, summer and winter, in a single image is eye-catching.

12-5 葛飾北斎『富嶽百景』二編

天保6年(1835)　半紙本　国文学研究資料館蔵

竹林の間から見える富士山を描いた「竹林の不二」。竹の曲線と富士山の稜線がリズミカルに呼応しています。また、中景を省略して、竹林と富士山を対比することで、遠近感も演出されています。

12-5 Katsushika Hokusai

***One Hundred Views of Mount Fuji*, part 2**

1835, *hanshibon*,
National Institute of Japanese Literature

Fuji in a Bamboo Grove depicts Mount Fuji seen through a bamboo thicket. The curved lines of the bamboo and Mount Fuji's ridgeline rhythmically correspond. By omitting the mid-distance and setting the bamboo grove against Mount Fuji, Hokusai produces perspective, too.

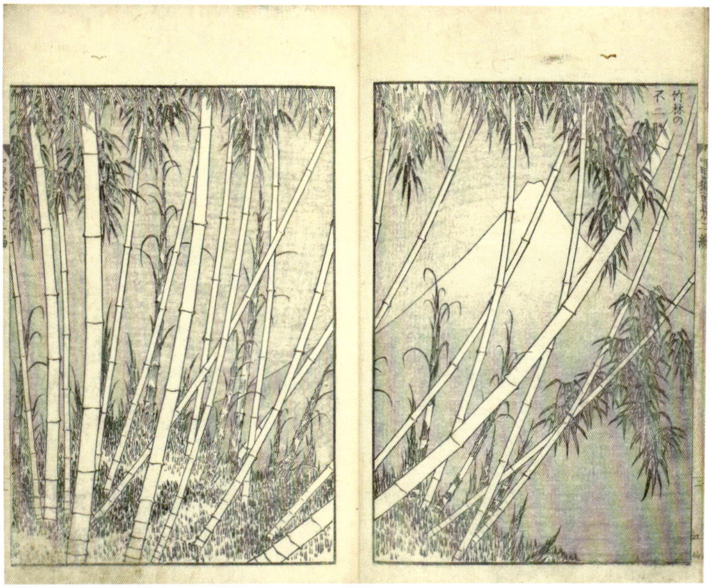

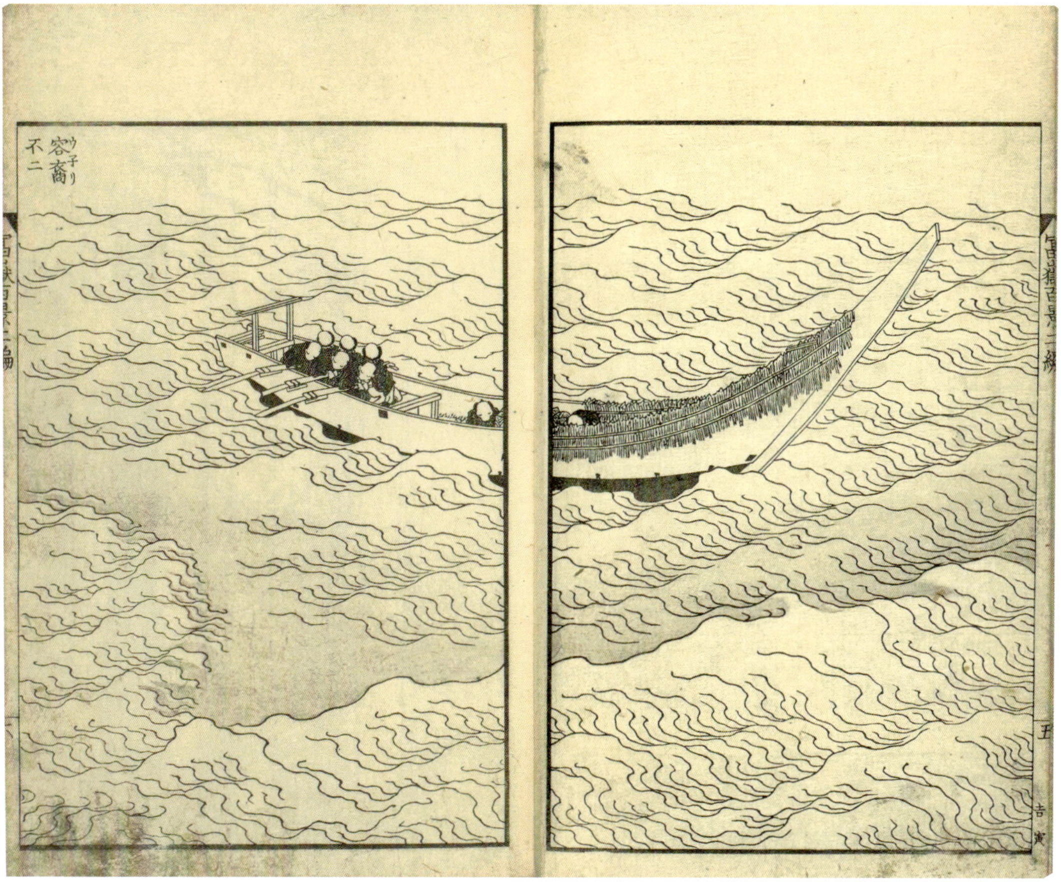

12-6 葛飾北斎『富嶽百景』二編

天保6年(1835)　半紙本　国文学研究資料館蔵

「容裔不二」。一見したところ、どこにも富士山の姿はありません。しかし、舟の浮かぶ水面に注目してみると、富士山の姿が映っており、波の動きによってその形がうねっていることが分かります。北斎らしい奇抜な視点の作品です。

12-6 Katsushika Hokusai

***One Hundred Views of Mount Fuji*, part 2**

1835, *hanshibon*, National Institute of Japanese Literature

Fuji on the Swell—at first sight, there is no sign of Mount Fuji. However, if you look at the water surface where the boat is afloat, Mount Fuji is reflected there with its shape changing according to the undulations. Another unconventional viewpoint typical of Hokusai.

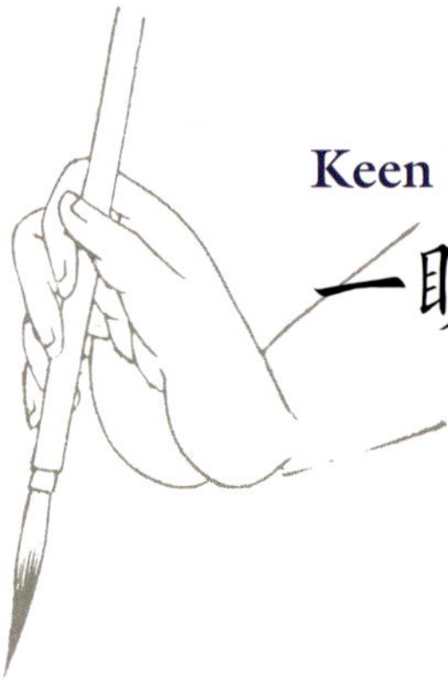

13 Keen Eye for the Right Moment
一瞬をとらえる観察眼

Pictures of Flowers and Birds
花鳥画

北斎は、『北斎漫画』を中心とした絵手本（→32頁参照）の中で、さまざまなジャンルを取り扱っていますが、その中で、花や鳥、さらには虫や魚なども含めた花鳥画と呼ばれる画題を数多く描いています。

一方、絵手本ではなく、独立した一枚摺の錦絵による花鳥画を集中的に制作するのが、70歳を過ぎた天保年間（1830~1844）前期頃です。ちょうど「富嶽三十六景」（→48頁参照）を始め、錦絵による風景画をいくつも刊行していた時期でした。北斎は高齢にも関わらず、風景画だけでなく、花鳥画というジャンルにも新たに取り組もうとしたのです。

北斎の錦絵による花鳥画にはいくつかの作例がありますが、天保初期に制作された横大判の10枚揃（図13-1）と、天保5年（1834）頃に制作された中判の10枚揃（図13-2）が特に注目されます。北斎の花鳥画には、中国絵画からの影響が感じられるとともに、花や鳥の細部まで見逃さない鋭い観察力と、緊迫感のある構図が大きな特徴となっています。

ちなみに、北斎と同時期、歌川広重（→100頁参照）も花鳥画を制作していました。広重の花鳥画は季節感に富んだ抒情性にあふれており、刊行された点数だけ比べると、当時の人気は広重の方に軍配が上がったようです。しかし北斎と広重、それぞれの花鳥画には両者の個性が発揮されており、優劣のつけがたいものになっています。

Hokusai dealt with a variety of genres in *Hokusai's Sketches* and other *edehon* (drawing manuals, see p. 32). Among them, he did many works on the subject known as flowers and birds, including insects, fish, etc.

Meanwhile, it was around the early part of the Tempō era (1830–1844), when Hokusai was over 70, that he intensively produced pictures of flowers and birds not as drawing manuals but as independent single-sheet *nishiki-e* (polychrome prints). This was the period during which he had just begun publishing *Thirty-six Views of Mount Fuji* (see p. 48) and numerous other landscapes in *nishiki-e*. Despite his advance in age, he had the vigor to work not only on landscapes but newly on the genre of flowers and birds.

There are a number of examples of pictures of flowers and birds represented in *nishiki-e* by Hokusai, among which a set of ten horizontal *ōban*-sized prints produced in the early Tempō era (fig. 13-1) and a set of ten *chūban*-sized prints produced circa 1834 (fig. 13-2) are particularly noteworthy. In addition to the influence of Chinese painting, marked characteristics of Hokusai's pictures of flowers and birds are his keen power of observation to spot even the minute details of a flower or a bird and his compositions with a tense atmosphere.

Incidentally, Utagawa Hiroshige (see p. 100) also produced pictures of flowers and birds around the same time as Hokusai. Hiroshige's pictures of flowers and birds are abundant in lyricism with a rich sense of the season, and compared solely by the number of works published, Hiroshige seems to have been more popular in those days. Even so, Hokusai and Hiroshige each display their individuality in their pictures of flowers and birds, making it hard to decide which is superior.

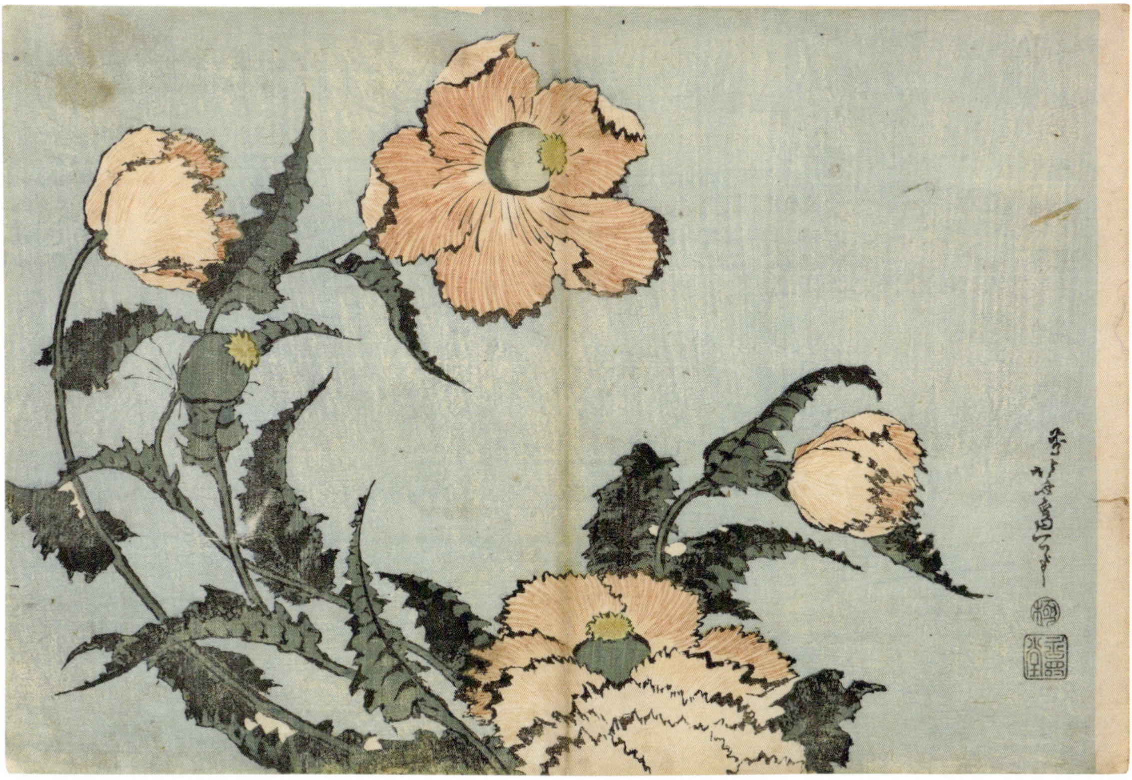

13-1 葛飾北斎 **芥子**

天保2〜3年(1831〜32)頃　大判錦絵

島根県立美術館(永田コレクション)蔵

芥子の花や葉の特徴をしっかりと観察しているだけでなく、強い風が吹き、茎がしなって花弁が揺らいだ瞬間の動きまでを捉えています。波や風といった形にならないものを描くことを得意とした、北斎らしい表現です。

13-1 Katsushika Hokusai ***Poppies***

c. 1831–1832, ōban nishiki-e,
Shimane Art Museum (Nagata Collection)

Not only does Hokusai carefully observe the characteristics of the flowers and leaves but he even captures the momentary movement of the stems bending and the petals fluttering as a strong wind blows. This is a representation distinctive of Hokusai, who was good at drawing formless subjects such as waves or the wind.

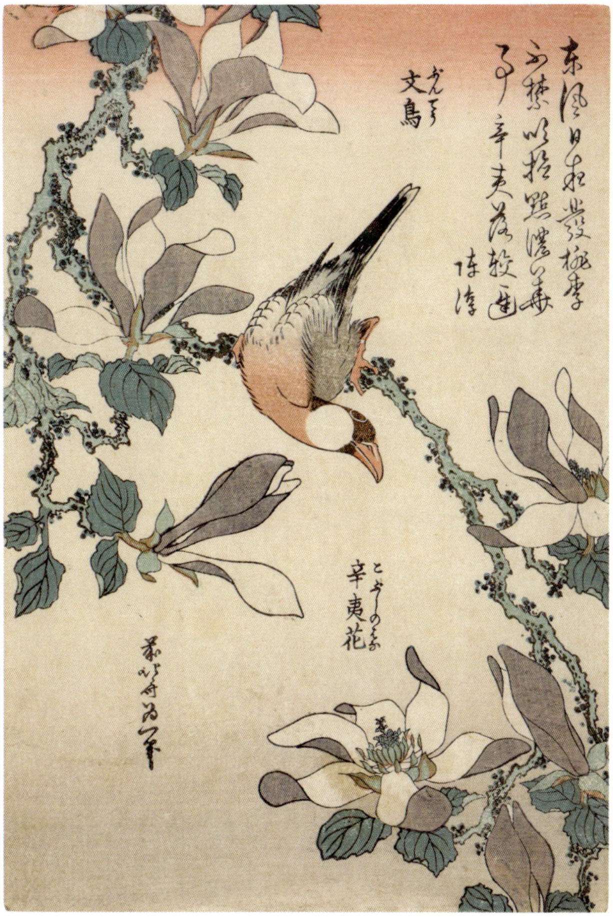

13-2 葛飾北斎 **文鳥　辛夷花**

天保5年(1834)頃　中判錦絵

島根県立美術館(永田コレクション)蔵

早春に白い花を咲かせる辛夷の枝に、愛玩用として飼育されていた文鳥が首をひねるようにして留まっています。中国・明代の文人画家である陳淳の五言絶句が添えられ、中国絵画の雰囲気も漂わせています。

13-2 Katsushika Hokusai

Java Sparrow and Magnolia

c. 1834, *chūban nishiki-e*, Shimane Art Museum (Nagata Collection)

A java sparrow kept as a pet is perching on a magnolia branch, which blooms with white flowers in early spring, and looking sideways. A poem by Chen Chun, a Chinese literati painter of the Ming dynasty, is added, providing the atmosphere of a Chinese painting.

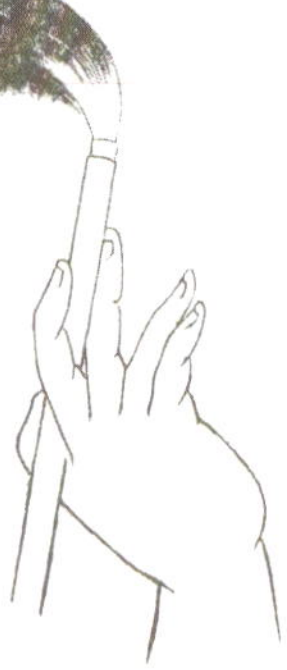

14 Ceaseless Aspiration in Proud Independence
挑み続けた孤高の晩年

Original Paintings
肉筆画

肉筆画とは、浮世絵師が自らの筆で直接紙や絹に描く絵画のことです。絵師と彫師と摺師が協力して制作する版画や版本と異なり、絵師の技量にすべてが委ねられます。また、数多くの枚数を摺る版画と違い、肉筆画は特別な注文を受けて制作する一点物のため、金銭的な価値も高い物でした。

北斎は生涯を通じて肉筆画を手がけていますが、集中して制作していた時期は大きく二つあります。ひとつは、北斎号を使い始めた享和から文化中期頃、すなわち40代の頃です。この時期は主に美人画を中心に制作しています（→20頁参照、図14-1）。

肉筆画に取り組んでいた二つ目の時期が、最晩年です。北斎は天保5年（1834）、75歳から画狂(がきょう)老人卍(ろうじんまんじ)という画号を用い始めました。この頃から版画や版本の制作数が減っていき、80歳を過ぎる頃には肉筆画に専念するようになります。和漢の故事や歴史、鍾馗や羅漢、あるいは龍虎や鷹、狐狸などの動物たちが主な画題として描かれました。一般的に浮世絵師による肉筆画といった場合、美人画や風俗画が最も大きな割合を占めています。晩年の北斎は、浮世絵のジャンルにこだわることなく、独自の世界を築き上げていったのです。

北斎は嘉永2年（1849）に90歳で亡くなるまで絵筆を手放すことなく、ひたすらに己の腕を研鑽し続けました（→84頁参照）。北斎の晩年の肉筆画には、画技を究めようとする熱い情熱が詰まっているといえるでしょう。

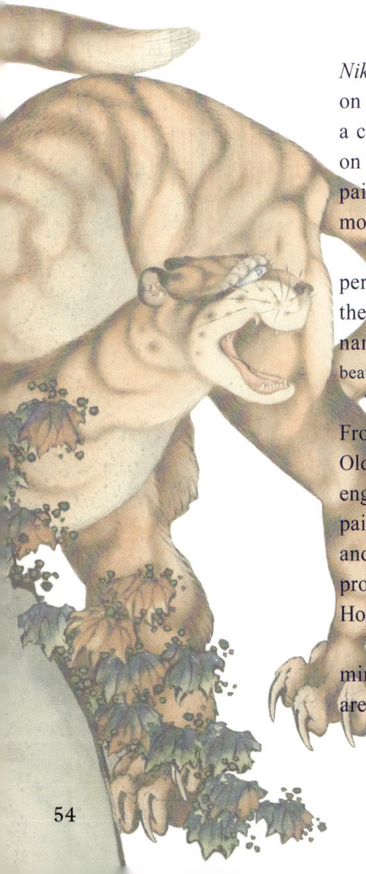

Nikuhitsuga (original paintings) refer to pictures painted by *ukiyo-e* artists with a paintbrush directly on paper or silk. Unlike prints or books printed from engraved woodblocks produced through a collaboration among the artist, the woodblock carver, and the printer, everything depended on the artist's skill. Moreover, unlike prints which were printed in large numbers, an original painting was a one-of-a-kind item produced according to a special order. Consequently, the monetary value of the work was high, too.

While Hokusai produced original paintings throughout his lifetime, there are largely two periods during which he worked concentratedly on original paintings. One was the period from the Kyōwa era (1801–1804) to the mid-Bunka era (1804–1818), when he began using the Hokusai name, i.e. when he was in his forties. In those days, he worked mainly on *bijinga* (pictures of beauties, see p. 20, fig. 14-1).

The second period during which he concentrated on original paintings was in his final years. From 1834, when Hokusai turned 75, he began using the artist name Gakyō Rōjin 卍 (卍. the Old Man Mad about Drawing). From then on, he produced less prints and books printed from engraved woodblocks, and by the time he was over 80, he devoted himself to producing original paintings. His main subjects were Japanese and Chinese tradition or history, Zhong Kui or Arhat, and animals such as dragons, tigers, hawks, foxes, or badgers. Generally speaking, the largest proportion of the original paintings by *ukiyo-e* artists are *bijinga* or genre scenes. Late in life, Hokusai built up a world of his own without adhering to the genre of *ukiyo-e*.

Until Hokusai died aged 90 in 1849, he never put his paintbrush down and continued single-mindedly to hone his artistic skills (see p. 84). The original paintings he produced in his later years are jammed with his fervent passion to master the art of painting.

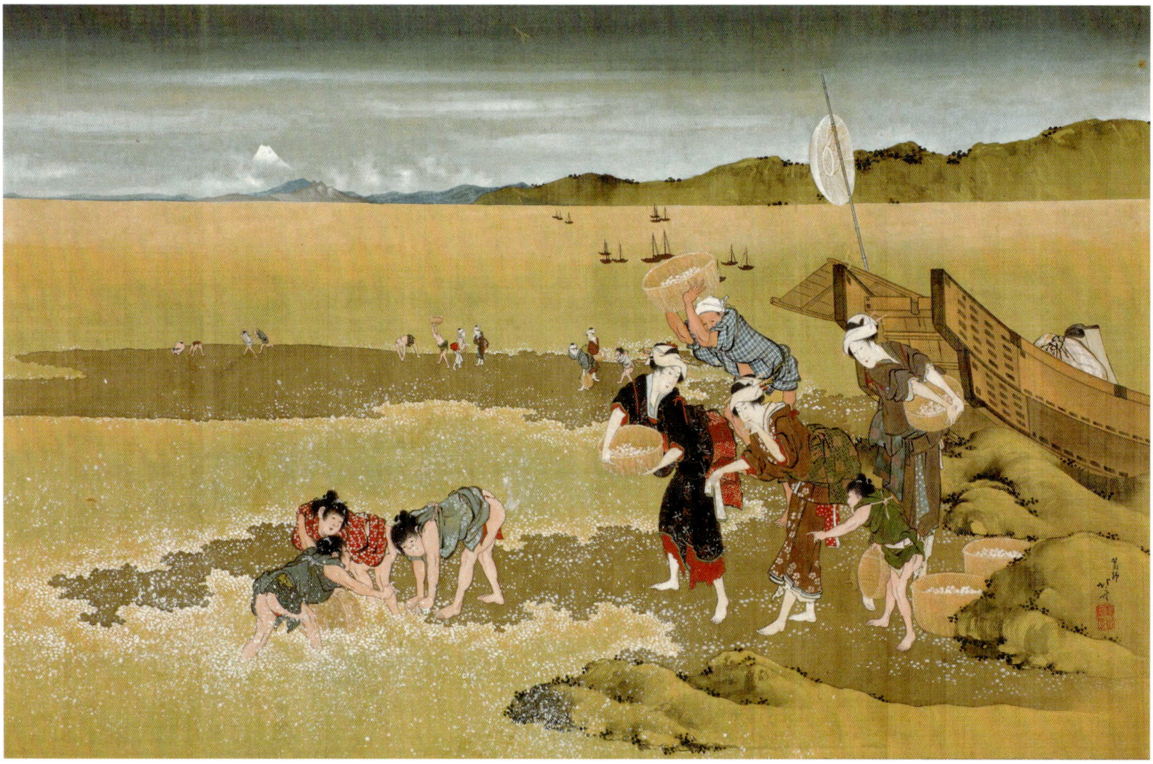

14-1 葛飾北斎 **潮干狩図**

文化4〜7年(1807〜10)頃　絹本着色　大阪市立美術館蔵　重要文化財

北斎40代後半頃の作品で、肉筆の美人画を数多く制作していた時期にあたります。潮干狩りに興じる人々は浮世絵風の表現ですが、背景の空や雲は油彩画を思わせる色彩になっており、北斎の画技の幅広さを感じさせます。

14-1 Katsushika Hokusai ***Shellfish Gathering at Low Tide***

c. 1807–1810, color on silk, Osaka City Museum of Fine Arts, Important Cultural Property

Hokusai painted this in his mid-forties, at a time when he was producing many *nikuhitsuga* (original paintings) of beauties. While the people merrily gathering shellfish are portrayed in an *ukiyo-e*-like manner, the coloring of the sky and clouds in the background calls oil painting to mind, revealing the breadth of Hokusai's artistic skills.

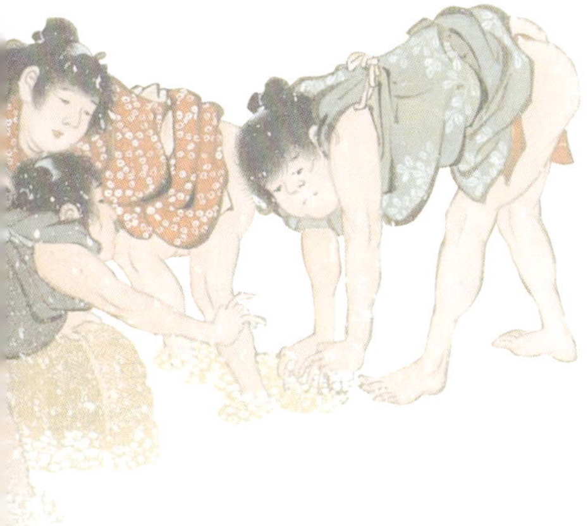

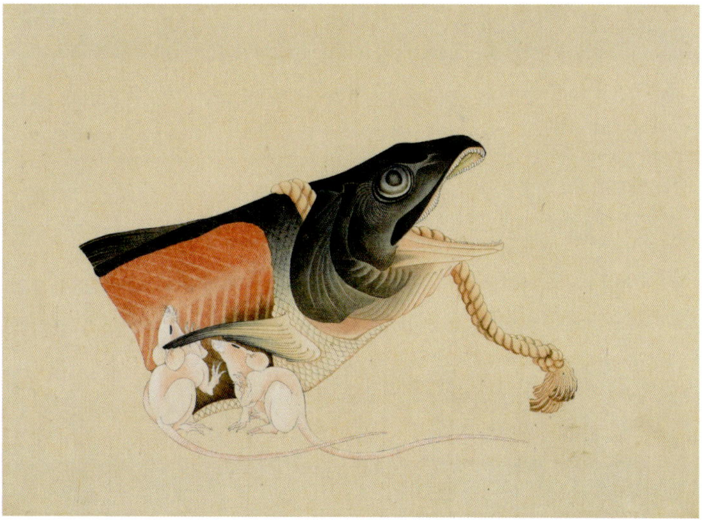

14-2 葛飾北斎 **『肉筆画帖』**

天保中〜後期(1835〜44)頃　紙本着色　島根県立美術館(永田コレクション)蔵

「塩鮭と鼠」を含む10図からなる肉筆の画帖です。天保の大飢饉の頃、北斎は肉筆の画帖を多く描き、絵草紙屋で販売していました(『北斎伝』)。この画帖がそれに該当するかは定かではありませんが、類似した画帖はいくつも確認されています。

14-2 Katsushika Hokusai ***Album of Brush Paintings***

c. 1835–1844, color on paper, Shimane Art Museum (Nagata Collection)

This is an album containing ten original paintings such as *Salted Salmon and Mice*. During the Tempo Famine (1833–1836), Hokusai produced a lot of albums of original paintings, which were sold at shops selling picture books and prints (*Hokusai-den*). Although we are not sure whether this is one such example, numerous similar examples have been confirmed.

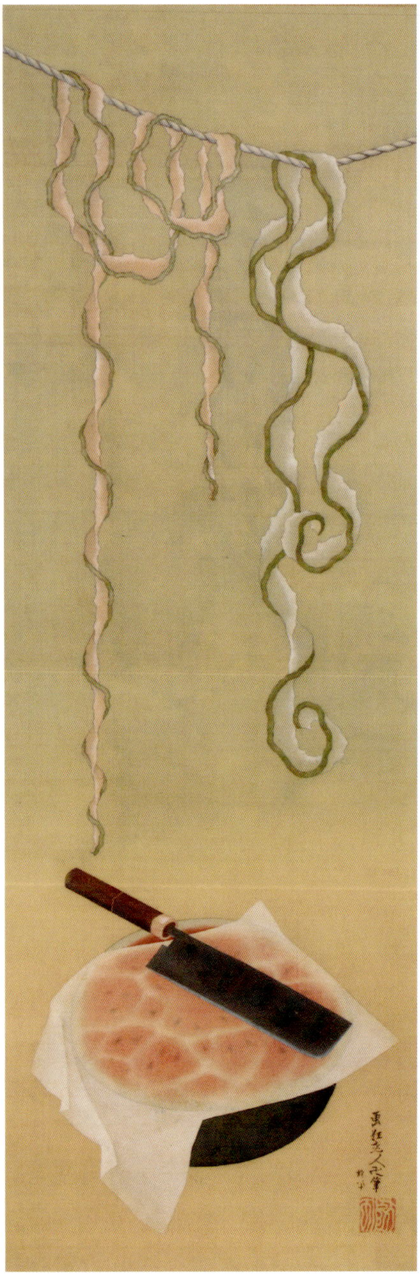

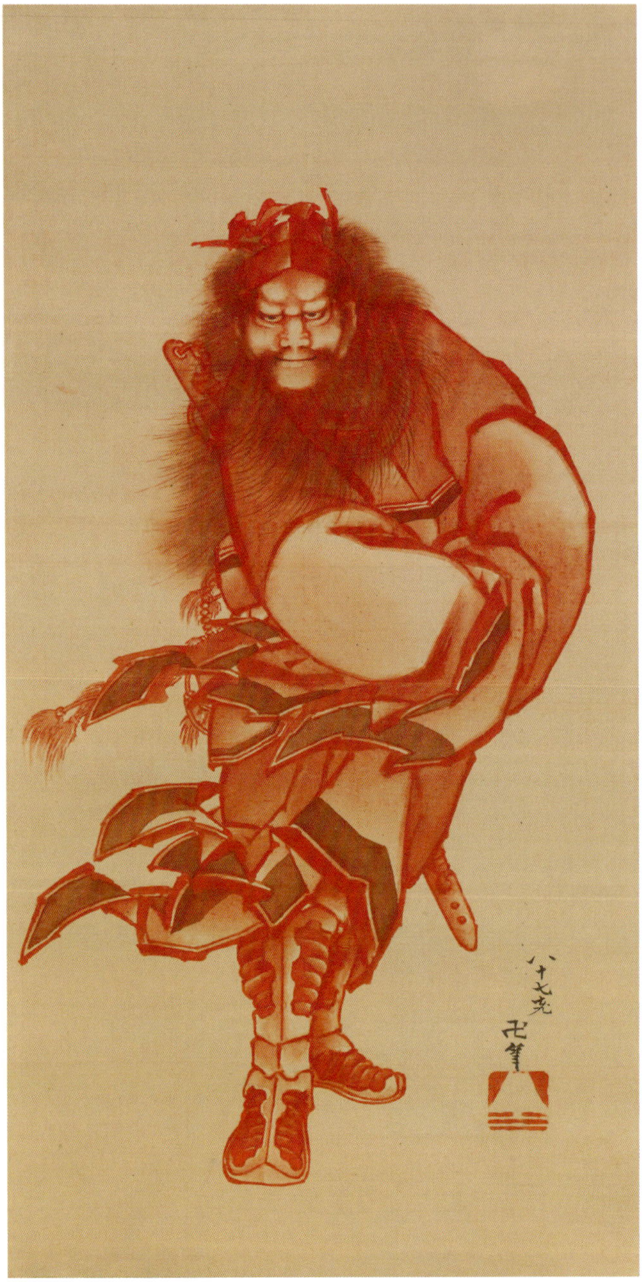

14-3 葛飾北斎 **西瓜図**

天保10年（1839） 絹本着色 宮内庁三の丸尚蔵館蔵

北斎晩年の80歳の制作。半分に切った西瓜の上に紙と庖丁が置かれ、上には西瓜の皮がぶら下げられています。一般的な浮世絵の画題から大きく逸脱したもので、宮中の乞巧奠（七夕）の儀式の見立てとの説もあります（今橋理子「伝説の記号―葛飾北斎筆「西瓜図」と七夕―」『東海大学紀要』18号、1995年）。

14-3 Katsushika Hokusai ***Watermelon and Knife***

1839, color on silk, Sannomaru Shozokan (The Museum of the Imperial Collections), The Imperial Household Agency

This was painted late in life, when Hokusai was aged 80. A piece of paper and a knife are placed on top of a watermelon, which has been cut in half. There is also rind hanging above. The subject matter deviates considerably from an ordinary *ukiyo-e* and some say that this painting is likened to the *kikkōden* (*tanabata*) ritual held in the Imperial Court.

14-4 葛飾北斎 **鍾馗図**

弘化3年（1846） 絹本着色 メトロポリタン美術館蔵

北斎が30代半ば頃に描いた朱描きの鍾馗図が現存していますが、87歳という最晩年においても鍾馗図を描いています。端午の節句の飾り物として好まれた鍾馗図の依頼はおそらく頻繁にあり、北斎はこの画題を生涯に渡って描き続けたのでしょう。

14-4 Katsushika Hokusai

Shōki (Zhong Kui) Painted in Red

1846, color on silk, The Metropolitan Museum of Art

A portrait of Shōki (Chinese: Zhong Kui) painted in red by Hokusai in his mid-thirties remains and he did the same subject again late in life, at age 87. As portraits of Shōki were popular as decorations for the Boys' Festival, they were frequently ordered and Hokusai probably continued to depict this subject matter throughout his lifetime.

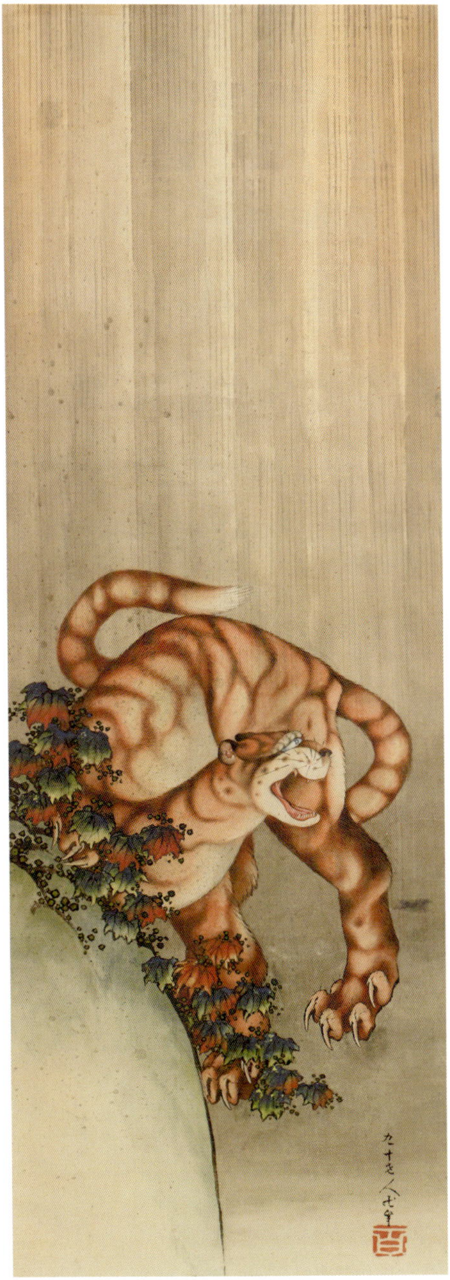

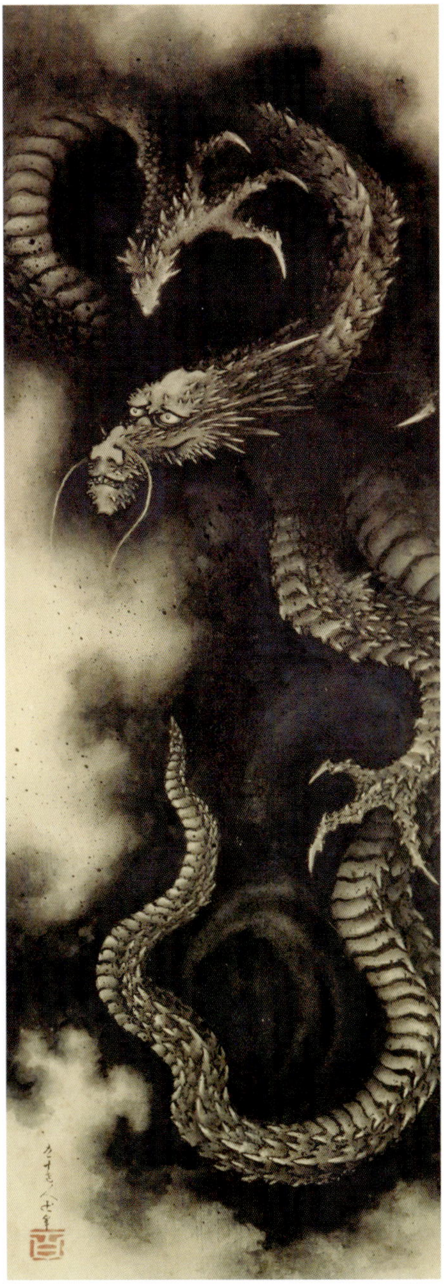

14-5 葛飾北斎 **雨中の虎図**

嘉永2年(1849)　紙本着色　太田記念美術館蔵

北斎が亡くなった90歳の時の制作です。激しい雨が降る中、虎が空中に向かって吼えています。長い間、一幅の作品と考えられていましたが、2005年、永田生慈により、右の「雲龍図」と対幅であることが発見され、虎の視線の先に龍がいることが判明しました。

14-6 葛飾北斎 **雲龍図**

嘉永2年(1849)　紙本着色　ギメ美術館蔵

黒雲の中に姿を現した龍です。「雨中の虎図」と並べることにより、天の龍と地の虎を対比させた北斎の作画意図が明確となります。亡くなる直前の絶筆に近い時期でありながら、大作というべき迫力に満ち溢れています。

14-5 Katsushika Hokusai ***Tiger in Rain***

1849, color on paper, Ōta Memorial Museum of Art

This was produced when Hokusai was 90, the year he passed away. The tiger is roaring towards the sky amidst heavy rain. This was long considered a single work. However, in 2005, Nagata Seiji discovered that it forms a pair with *Dragon in Rain Clouds* shown on the right. It turned out that the tiger was looking at the dragon.

14-6 Katsushika Hokusai ***Dragon in Rain Clouds***

1849, color on paper, Musée Guimet

The dragon appears within a black cloud. By placing this painting next to *Tiger in Rain*, the artist's intent to contrast the dragon in heaven and the tiger on earth becomes clear. Despite being painted just before Hokusai's death, close to his final work, it is brimming with impact fit to be described a monumental work.

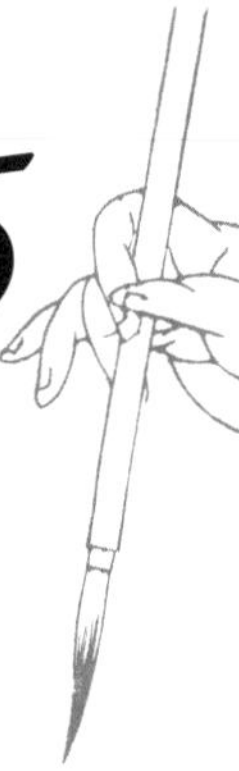

15 He Liked Writing Too
文章を書くのも大好き

Gesaku and *Senryū*
戯作と川柳

膨大な量の絵を描いていた北斎ですが、実は小説の文章を執筆していたこともあります。寛政12年(1800)、41歳の時、時太郎可候という名前で、『竈将軍勘略之巻』(図15-1)という黄表紙(→24頁参照)を執筆しました。挿絵も北斎自身によるものです。

北斎は、寛政13年(1801)に1冊、享和3年(1803)に2冊と、自画作の黄表紙を立て続けに発表しています。しかしながら、あまり評判は良くなかったのか、その後の刊行は確認されておりません。代わりに、曲亭馬琴とタッグを組んで読本挿絵を多数手がけていくことになります(→24頁参照)。自分の才能は物語の執筆よりも絵を描く方にあると、北斎は改めて認識しのたかもしれません。

なお、文化11年(1814)の『喜能会之故真通』(図9-1~2)や文政4年(1821)の『万福和合神』(図9-6)といった春画では、独特の擬音語が多用されていることから、文章も北斎自身によるものと考えられています。北斎は文章を書くことが好きだったと言えるでしょう。

晩年になると、川柳を作ることを趣味とするようになります。川柳とは、5・7・5の17音で人情や風俗を詠んだり、人や社会を風刺したりする短詩のことです。卍、万字、百姓などと号し、文政6年(1823)、64歳の頃から、『誹風柳多留』という川柳の句集への投句や句選を行っています。「其腰で夜も竿さす筏乗り」といった艶笑句や、「紅葉ふみわけぐんにやりと鹿の屎」といったスカトロジックな句が多いのが特徴で、弘化3年(1846)、87歳まで作った川柳として、225句が確認されています[1)]。

Besides creating a huge number of pictures, there was actually a time when Hokusai wrote novels. In 1800, at the age of 41, he wrote a *kibyōshi* (see p.24) entitled *The Book of Tactics of General Oven* (fig. 15-1) under the pen name Tokitarō Kakō. The illustrations are by Hokusai, too.

Hokusai continued to present *kibyōshi* written and illustrated by himself, one in 1801 and two in 1803. However, whether because they did not prove popular, there are no publications confirmed thereafter. Instead, he was to team up with Kyokutei Bakin on producing numerous *yomihon* illustrations (see p. 24). Perhaps he realized anew that his talent lay in drawing pictures more than in writing stories.

As regards *shunga* such as *Pine Seedlings on the First Rat Day* (1801, figs. 9-1~2) and *Myriad Gods of Conjugal Delights* (1821, fig. 9-6), the frequent use of characteristic onomatopoeia suggests that the text was written by Hokusai, too. It seems that Hokusai liked writing.

Late in life, Hokusai indulged in composing *senryū* (humorous verse). *Senryū* is a 17 syllable (5-7-5) short verse narrating human feelings and customs or satirizing people and the society. Under the pen names 卍, Manji, Hyakushō, etc., from 1823, when he was around 64, Hokusai submitted selected poems to *Haifū yanagidaru*, a collection of *senryū*. There are 225 *senryū*, many of which are comic poems with erotic content or scatological verse, confirmed as works composed by Hokusai until 1846, when he was 87.

1) 橋本秀信「北斎と葛飾派の川柳(一)」『北斎研究』25号、1998年

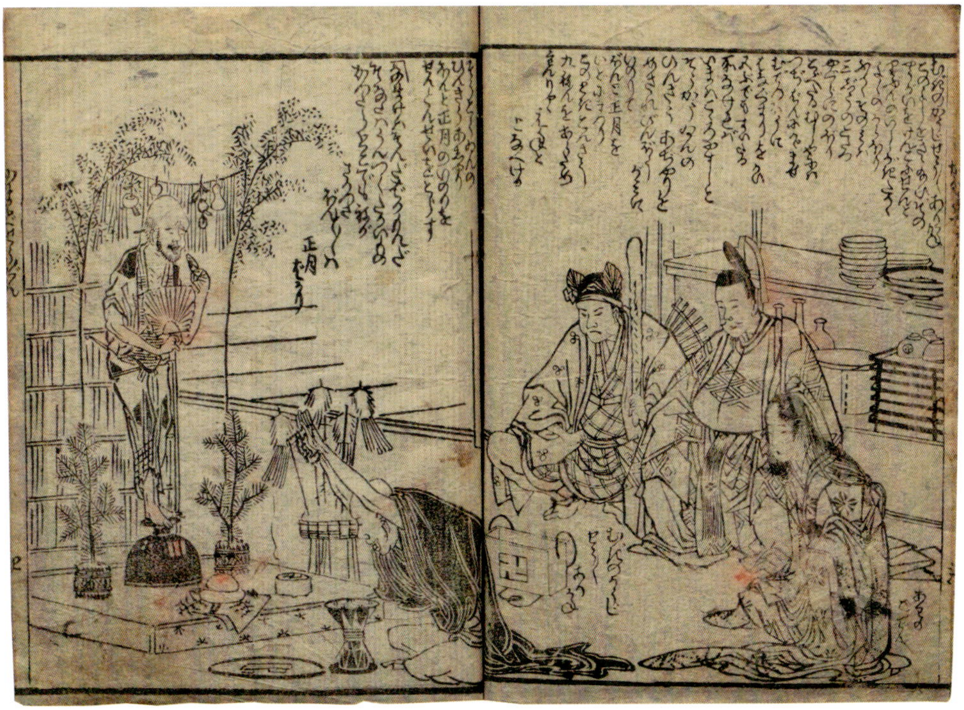

15-1　葛飾北斎『竈将軍勘略之巻』(かまどしょうぐんかんりゃくのまき)
寛政12年(1800)　中本　国立国会図書館蔵

北斎の黄表紙の処女作です。巻末に、悪い点があれば曲亭馬琴に添削してもらいたいと北斎自身が述べていることから、馬琴が制作に何らかの形で関与していたのではないかと考えられます。

15-1　Katsushika Hokusai
The Book of Tactics of General Oven
1800, *chūhon*, National Diet Library, Japan

This was Hokusai's maiden *kibyōshi*. At the end of the book, Hokusai mentions that he would like Kyokutei Bakin to correct him if there were any unsatisfactory points, suggesting that Bakin was involved one way or another in the production of this book.

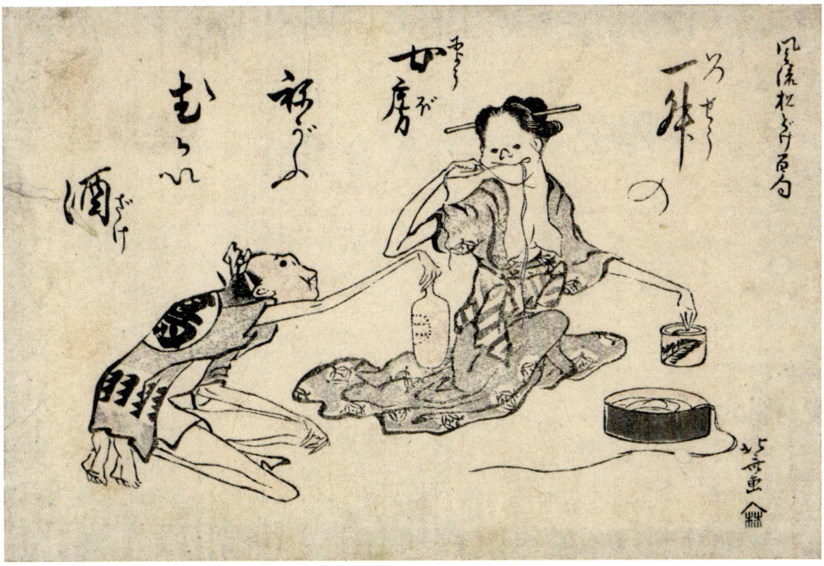

15-2　葛飾北斎　風流(ふうりゅう)おどけ百句(ひゃっく)　むかひ酒(ざけ)
文化8年(1811)頃　九つ切判錦絵　島根県立美術館(永田コレクション)蔵

北斎自身の川柳ではありませんが、北斎は川柳を賛とした戯画も手掛けています。この絵の川柳は「一升の女房ねがふむかい酒」。鳥羽絵(とばえ)と呼ばれる戯画に登場する、手足の長い人物たちが描かれています。

15-2　Katsushika Hokusai
One Hundred Comical Haiku: Hair of the Dog
c. 1811, *kokonotsugiriban nishiki-e*, Shimane Art Museum (Nagata Collection)

Although the *senryū* (humorous verse) are not by Hokusai himself, he also did caricatures with *senryū* added as inscriptions. The *senryū* inscribed here refers to "hair of the dog." People with long arms and legs who appear in caricatures known as *toba-e* are depicted.

16

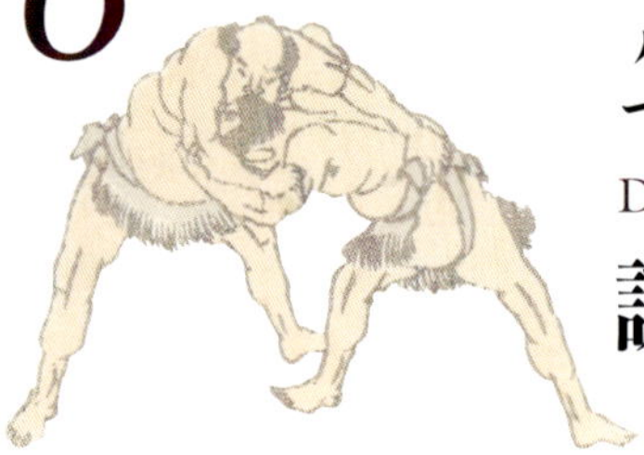

Born Near Ryōgoku
生まれは両国のほど近く

Date and Place of Birth
誕生日と生誕地

葛飾北斎は、宝暦10年（1760）9月23日に誕生しました。その根拠となるのが、天保15年（1844）11月1日に北斎が描いた「大黒天図」（図16-1）です。この絵の中に北斎自らが「宝暦十庚辰年九月甲子ノ出生」と署名しています。これによって、宝暦十庚辰年＝宝暦10年、九月甲子＝9月23日ということが分かり、北斎の誕生日が特定できるのです。なお残念なことに、この「大黒天図」は現在行方不明になっており、楢崎宗重（ならざきむねしげ）の『北斎論』（→124頁参照）に掲載されたモノクロの写真しか残っておりません。

また、飯島虚心の『葛飾北斎伝』（→124頁参照）によれば、北斎が産声をあげた場所は隅田川の東岸地域である本所割下水とされています。割下水とは排水路のことですので、その周辺になるのでしょう。本所割下水（南割下水）は、現在の東京都墨田区亀沢1～4丁目付近にあたります（図16-2）。北斎はこの東西約1km、南北約300 mの敷地のあたりで生まれたことになりますが、ピンポイントで生誕地を特定することは難しいようです。

現在、割下水は埋め立てられて道路になり、「北斎通り」という名前がつけられています。また、この場所には葛飾北斎生誕地の案内板（図16-3）やすみだ北斎美術館（→124頁参照）が建てられるなど、町をあげて北斎の顕彰が行われています。

Katsushika Hokusai was born on the twenty-third day of the ninth month of 1760. This date is based on *Daikokuten, The God of Wealth* (fig. 16-1) painted by Hokusai on the first day of the eleventh month of 1844. Hokusai signed this painting quoting this date of birth, enabling us to identify when he was born. Unfortunately, the whereabouts of the painting itself is currently unknown and a black-and-white photograph of it published in Narazaki Muneshige's *Hokusai-ron* (A study on Hokusai, see p. 124) is the only remaining evidence.

In *Katsushika Hokusai-den* (see p. 124), Iijima Kyoshin writes that the location where Hokusai uttered his first cry was Honjo Warigesui, a district on the east bank of the Sumida River. As *warigesui* means drainage, it must have been somewhere in the vicinity. Honjo Warigesui (Minamiwarigesui) is the area which now covers Kamezawa 1–4-chōme, Sumida-ku, Tokyo (fig. 16-2). Hokusai was born somewhere within this site of approximately 1 km from east to west and 300 m from north to south, but it is hard to pinpoint the exact location.

Nowadays, the entire neighborhood publicly honors Hokusai by naming the road running through this area from east to west "Hokusai-dōri," erecting a monument of "Katsushika Hokusai's birthplace" (fig. 16-3), building The Sumida Hokusai Museum (see p. 124), etc.

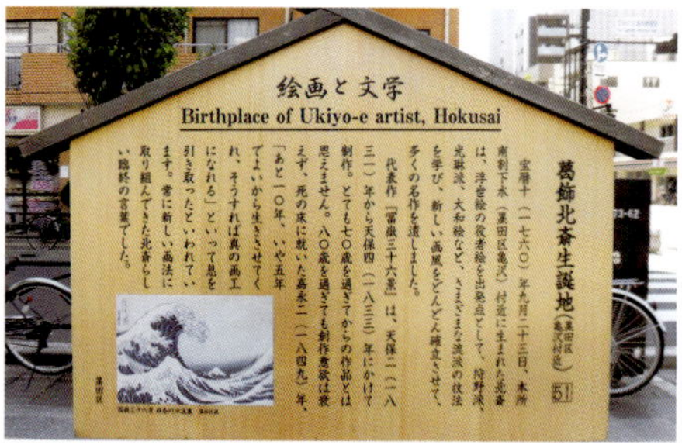

16-3
葛飾北斎生誕地の案内板
東京都墨田区亀沢2丁目7-7に設置された案内板。あくまでこの付近で誕生したものとして設置されています。

16-3
Information on Katsushika Hokusai's birthplace
An information board installed at 2-7-7 Kamezawa, Sumida-ku, Tokyo, though no more than a sign that he was born in this vicinity.

※本章のタイトル脇のカットは葛飾北斎『北斎漫画』三編（メトロポリタン美術館蔵）より作成。
The title illustrations for this chapter were taken from *Hokusai's Sketches*, part 3 (The Metropolitan Museum of Art)

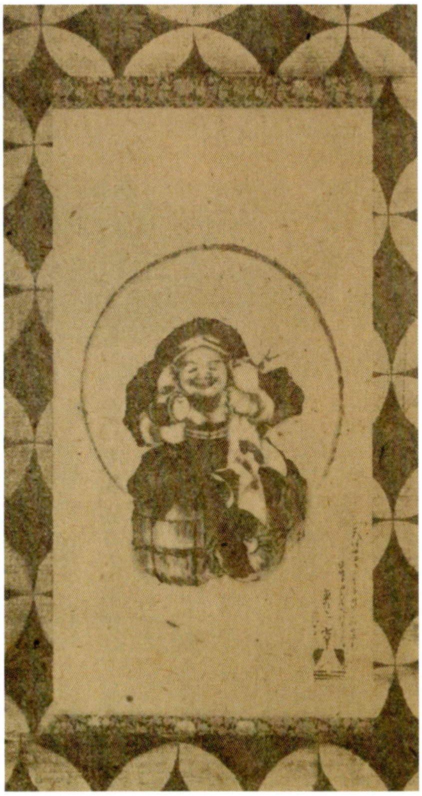

16-1 葛飾北斎 **大黒天図**（だいこくてんず）

楢崎宗重『北斎論』アトリヱ社・昭和19年（1944）より転載

北斎の誕生日を特定する根拠となる肉筆画。現在所在不明。「天保十五甲辰年子ノ月甲子ノ朔日子ノ刻　宝暦十庚辰年九月甲子ノ出生　画狂老人卍筆　齢八十五歳」の落款があり、天保15年（1844）11月1日、北斎85歳の時の制作であったことが分かります。

16-1 Katsushika Hokusai

Daikokuten, the God of Wealth

Reproduced from Narazaki Muneshige, *Hokusai-ron* [A study on Hokusai] (Atorie-sha, 1944)

This is the original painting which serves as the basis for determining Hokusai's date of birth. Current whereabouts unknown. The signature reveals that it was "painted on the first day of the eleventh month of 1844 by Manji, the Old Man Mad about Drawing born on the twenty-third day of the ninth month of 1760 and aged 85."

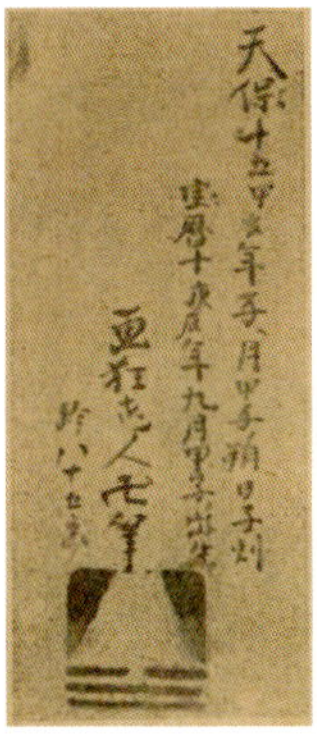

16-2 葛飾北斎の生誕地 Katsushika Hokusai's birthplace

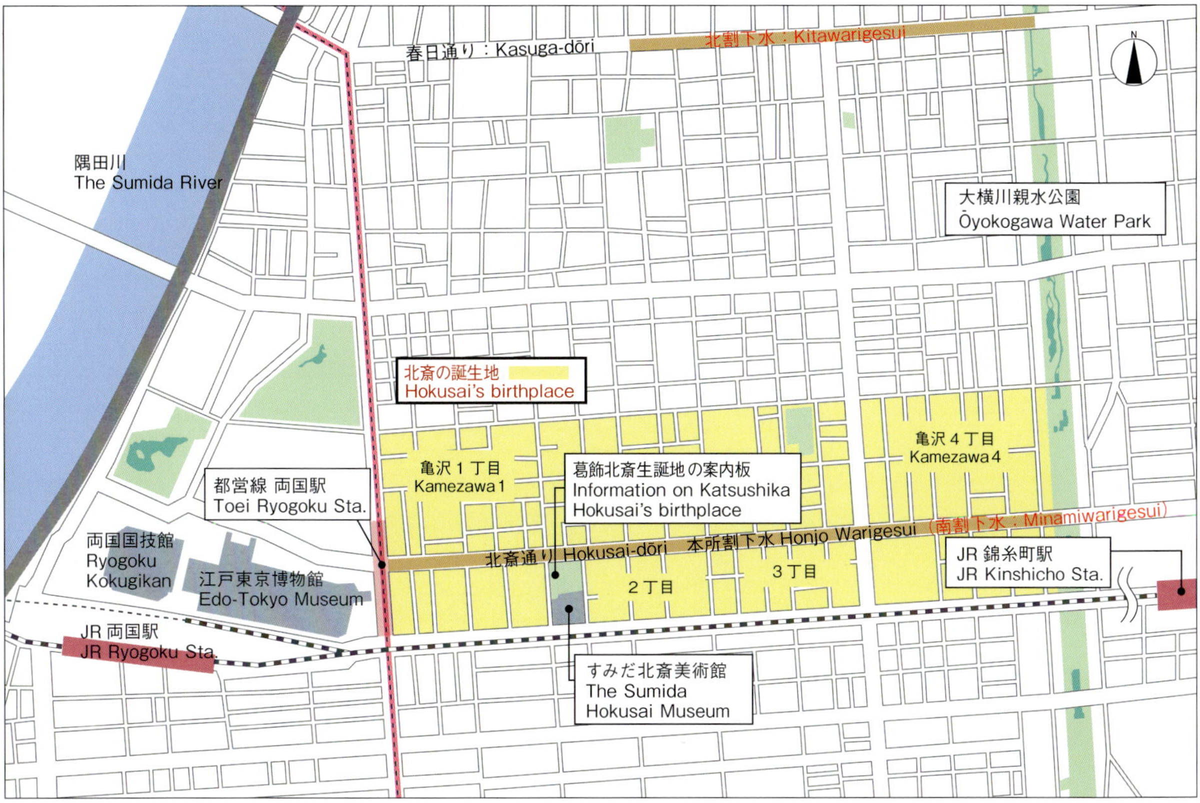

17

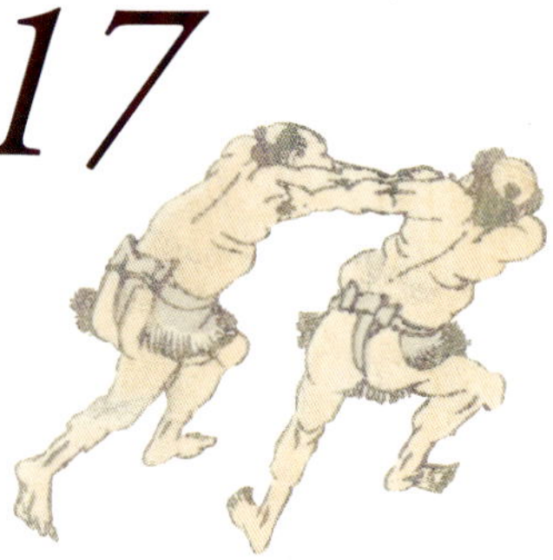

Fond of Drawing
幼い頃から絵を描くことが大好き

Childhood
幼少期

北斎の父親が誰であったについては、いくつかの説があり、はっきりと断定されていません。しかし近年、新史料と共に検証されたのが、幕府御用達の御鏡師（鏡職人）である二代中嶋伊勢の長男が、北斎の実の父親であるという説です[1]。

母親は、赤穂義士に討ち入られた吉良上野介の家臣である小林平八郎の孫娘だったと伝えられています（『北斎伝』）。また、北斎に兄弟や姉妹がいたかは定かではありません。

北斎は、10代か20代の頃、父親の弟、すなわち叔父にあたる三代中嶋伊勢の養子になったとの説があります[2]。しかし、北斎は御鏡師の跡職を継ぐことなく、息子である富之助（→64頁参照）に四代目を継がせ、自分は浮世絵師としての仕事に専念し続けました。

北斎の幼名は時太郎、後に鉄蔵と改めています（『北斎伝』）。『富嶽百景』初・二編の跋文で「己(おのれ)六才より物の形状(かたち)を写(うつす)の癖(へき)ありて」と北斎自身が記しているように、6歳という小さな頃から絵を描くことが大好きだったようです。しかし、初めから浮世絵師を目指しておらず、14, 15歳から19歳頃までは、版木の文字を彫る仕事をしていました（『北斎伝』）。なぜ彫師の仕事をやめ、浮世絵師に転向したのかは分かりませんが、おそらく絵を描くことが北斎にとって一番やりたいことだったのでしょう。

1）岸文和「北斎伝記の再検討ー新出史料『御鏡師中嶋伊勢御目見願』を手がかりに」『美術フォーラム21』34号、2016年
2）岸文和　前掲書〔註1〕

There are various views about who Hokusai's father was and it has not been clearly affirmed. Recently checked against new historical materials is the theory that Hokusai's real father was the eldest son of Nakajima Ise II, an official shogunal mirror caster.

His mother is said to have been the granddaughter of Kobayashi Heihachirō, a retainer of Kira Kōzukenosuke, the official of the Tokugawa shogunate who was killed by retainers of the Akō clan (*Hokusai-den*). Whether Hokusai had brothers or sisters remains unknown.

When Hokusai was in his teens or twenties, he was adopted by his father's younger brother, that is to say, his uncle Nakajima Ise III. However, Hokusai did not succeed his adoptive father to the position of mirror caster. He had his son Tominosuke (see p. 64) take over as Nakajima Ise IV and Hokusai himself continued concentrating on his work as an *ukiyo-e* artist.

Hokusai's childhood name was Tokitarō and he was later renamed Tetsuzō (*Hokusai-den*). As Hokusai himself wrote in the postscript to *One Hundred Views of Mount Fuji* (parts 1, 2), "I was in the habit of copying the shapes of things from when I was 6 years old," it seems that he loved drawing pictures from the young age of 6. At first, he did not have an eye on becoming an *ukiyo-e* artist. From the age of 14 or 15 to around 19, he was engaged in carving letters on printing blocks (*Hokusai-den*). Why he gave up his job as a carver and switched to an *ukiyo-e* artist is unclear, but drawing pictures was probably what he wanted to do most of all.

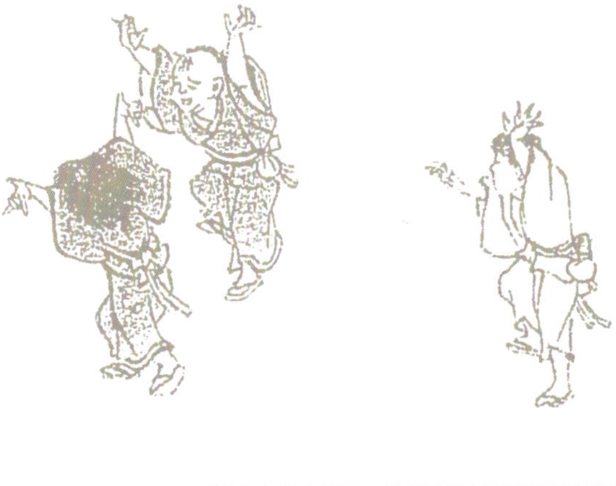

※葛飾北斎『北斎漫画』一編（国立国会図書館蔵）より作成。
From *Hokusai's Sketches*, part 1 (National Diet Library, Japan)

17-1 葛飾北斎の家系図　Katsushika Hokusai's family tree

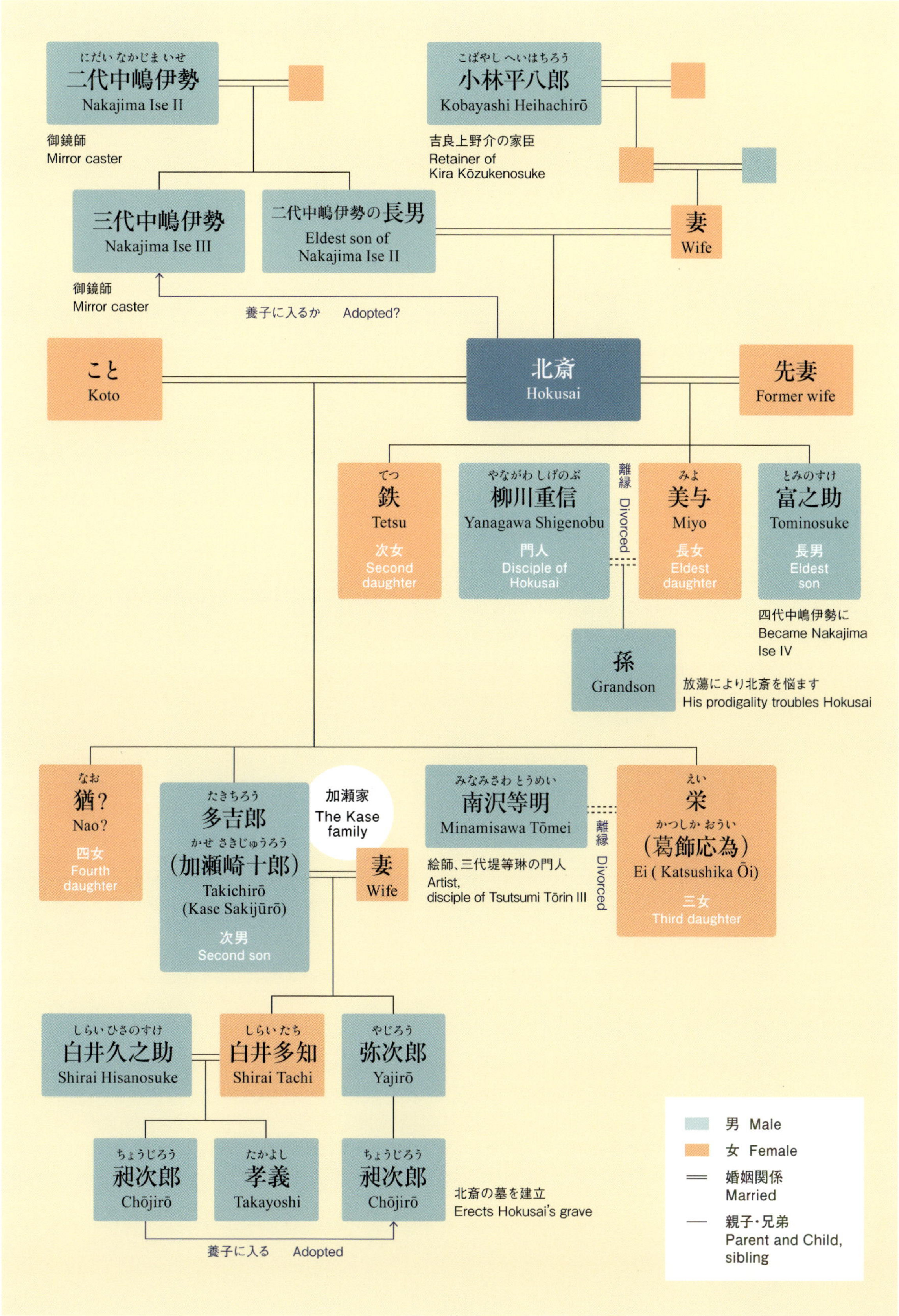

18

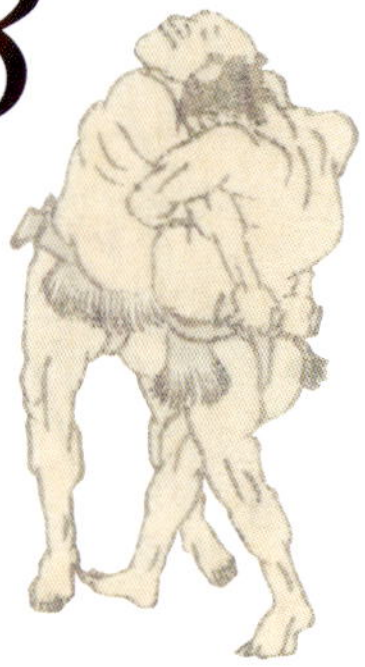

His Daughter Was a Gifted Artist Too
娘も才気あふれる女絵師

Wives and Children
妻と子供たち

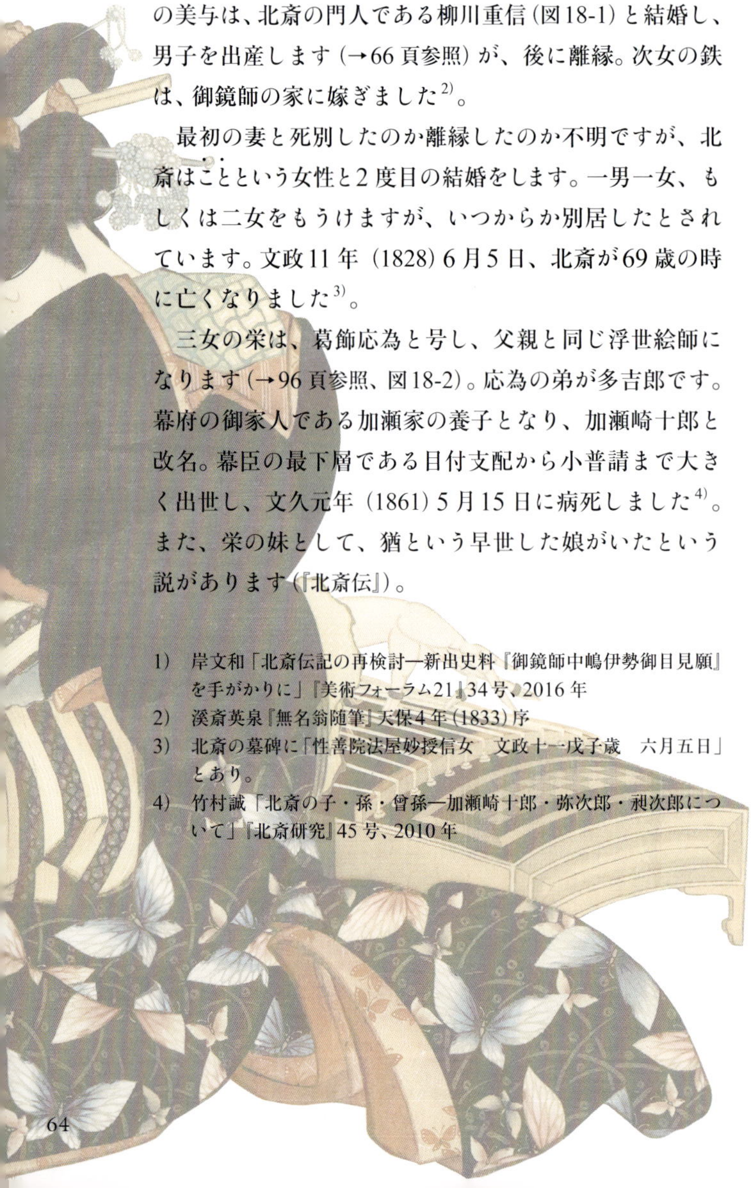

北斎は2回結婚し、5人、もしくは6人の子どもがいたと伝えられています(→63頁、葛飾北斎の家系図参照)。

最初に結婚した女性の素性は分からず、名前も不明です。おそらく北斎が20代の時に結婚し、一男二女をもうけました。長男は富之助。北斎が養子となった御鏡師である中嶋家の跡職を、北斎に代わって享和3年(1803)に相続しますが、文化13年(1816)頃に早世します[1]。長女の美与は、北斎の門人である柳川重信(図18-1)と結婚し、男子を出産します(→66頁参照)が、後に離縁。次女の鉄は、御鏡師の家に嫁ぎました[2]。

最初の妻と死別したのか離縁したのか不明ですが、北斎はことという女性と2度目の結婚をします。一男一女、もしくは二女をもうけますが、いつからか別居したとされています。文政11年(1828)6月5日、北斎が69歳の時に亡くなりました[3]。

三女の栄は、葛飾応為と号し、父親と同じ浮世絵師になります(→96頁参照、図18-2)。応為の弟が多吉郎です。幕府の御家人である加瀬家の養子となり、加瀬崎十郎と改名。幕臣の最下層である目付支配から小普請まで大きく出世し、文久元年(1861)5月15日に病死しました[4]。また、栄の妹として、猶という早世した娘がいたという説があります(『北斎伝』)。

1) 岸文和「北斎伝記の再検討―新出史料『御鏡師中嶋伊勢御目見願』を手がかりに」『美術フォーラム21』34号、2016年
2) 溪斎英泉『無名翁随筆』天保4年(1833)序
3) 北斎の墓碑に「性善院法屋妙授信女　文政十一戊子歳　六月五日」とあり。
4) 竹村誠「北斎の子・孫・曾孫―加瀬崎十郎・弥次郎・昶次郎について」『北斎研究』45号、2010年

Hokusai is said to have married twice and had five or six children (see p. 63, Katsushika Hokusai's family tree).

Both the identity and name of the first woman Hokusai married remain unknown. He probably married in his twenties and had a son and two daughters. The son was called Tominosuke. In 1803, Tominosuke succeeded to the professional name of the Nakajima family, an official shogunal mirror caster who adopted Hokusai, on behalf of Hokusai. However, he died young circa 1816. The eldest daughter, Miyo, married Yanagawa Shigenobu (fig. 18-1), a disciple of Hokusai, and gave birth to a boy (see p. 66), but later divorced. The second daughter, Tetsu, married into an official shogunal mirror caster's family.

It is not clear whether Hokusai was bereaved of or divorced his first wife, but he got married for the second time to a woman named Koto. They had a son and one or two daughters, but, from a certain stage, appear to have lived apart. Koto died on the fifth day of the sixth month of 1828, when Hokusai was 69.

Hokusai's third daughter, Ei, took the name of Katsushika Ōi, and, like her father, became an *ukiyo-e* artist (see p. 96, fig. 18-2). Ōi's younger brother was Takichirō. He was adopted by the Kase family, a retainer of the Tokugawa shogun, and became Kase Sakijūrō. Sakijūrō got promoted significantly from *metsuke* (inspector), the lowest rank among the shogun's retainers, to *kobushin* (minor construction worker) until he died from a disease on the fifteenth day of the fifth month of 1861. There is also an opinion that Ei had a younger sister, Nao, who suffered a premature death *(Hokusai-den)*.

18-1 曲亭馬琴作・柳川重信画

『南総里見八犬伝(なんそうさとみはっけんでん)』巻之一

文化11年(1814)　半紙本　国立国会図書館蔵

曲亭馬琴の代表作である読本『南総里見八犬伝』。その挿絵を最初に担当していたのが柳川重信でした。北斎の画風に縛られず、独自の作風による美人画や役者絵を描いています。

18-1 Kyokutei Bakin

Nansō Satomi hakkenden, vol. 1

illust. Yanagawa Shigenobu, 1814, *hanshibon*, National Diet Library, Japan

Nansō Satomi hakkenden (Satomi and the eight "dogs") is the most important *yomihon* among the novels by Kyokutei Bakin. The illustrations for the first volume were provided by Yanagawa Shigenobu. He depicted beauties and actors in a style of his own without being restricted by that of Hokusai.

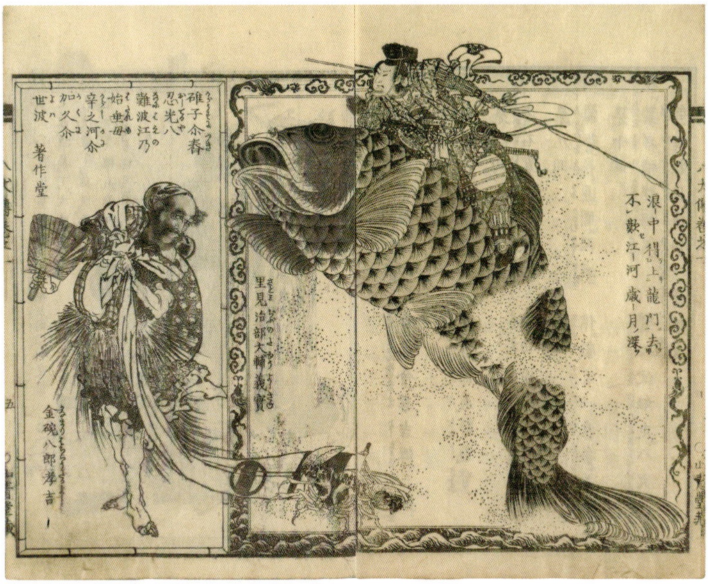

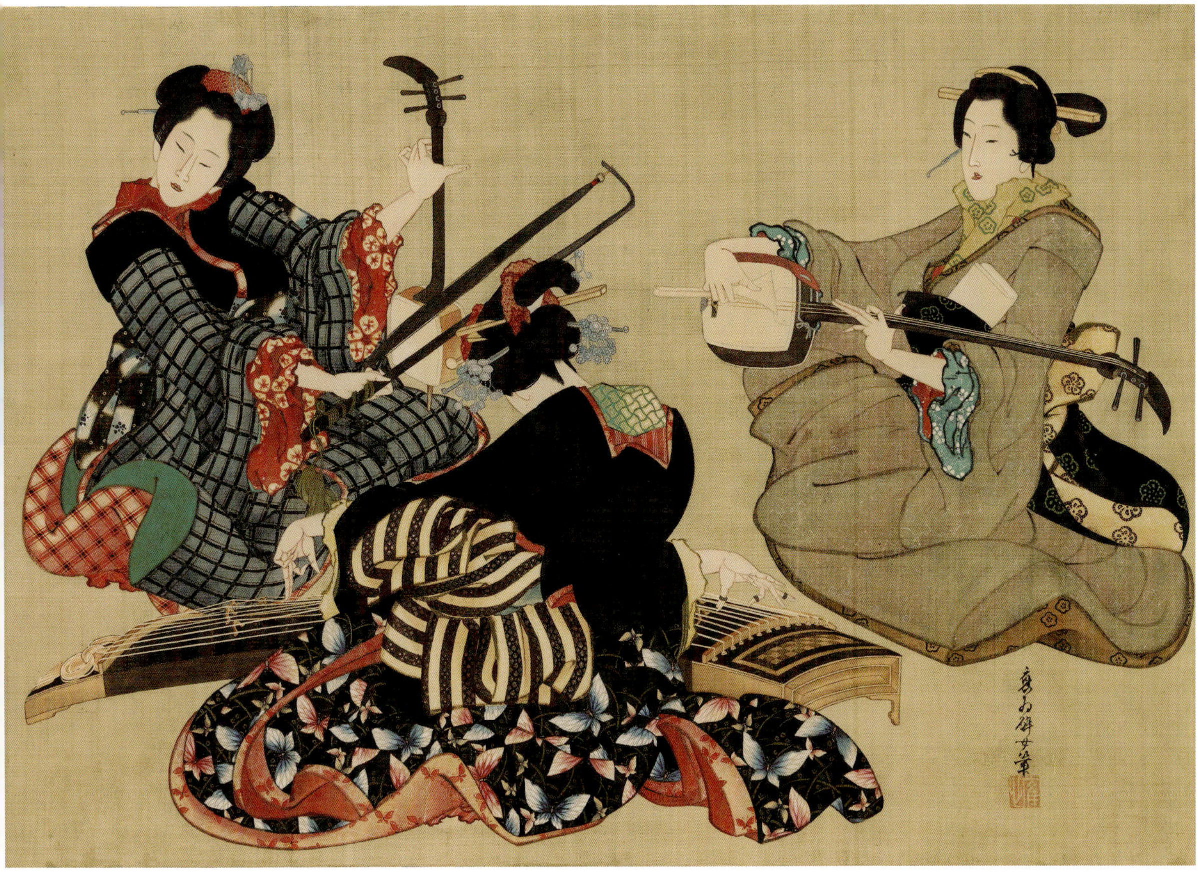

2020 Museum of Fine Arts, Boston.

18-2 葛飾応為　**三曲合奏図(さんきょくがっそうず)**

弘化(1844〜48)頃　絹本着色　ボストン美術館蔵

美人画の腕は北斎を上回るともいわれた応為。3人の女性たちが胡弓、箏、三味線を合奏している場面を描いています。応為の肉筆美人画の代表作で、「応ゐ酔女筆」という、自らを「酔女」と号した洒落た落款も特徴です。

18-2 Katsushika Ōi

Three Women Playing Musical Instruments

c.1844–1848, color on silk, Museum of Fine Arts, Boston

Some say that Ōi was better at pictures of beauties than Hokusai. This painting shows three women playing a *kokyū*, a *koto*, and a *shamisen*. It is a representative example of the original paintings by Ōi and is characterized by the witty signature, "Painted by the drunkard Ōi."

19

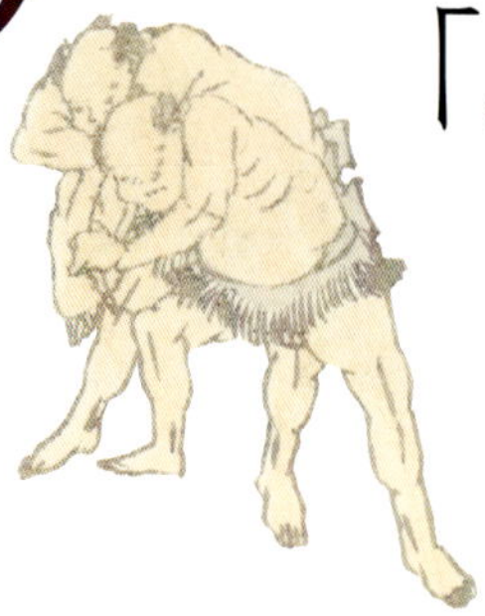

Dogged by a "Devil" Late in Life
「悪魔」に晩年を悩まされ

Grandchildren and Descendants
孫と子孫

北斎の長女・美与と柳川重信との間に生まれた男子（名前は不明）は、晩年の北斎を大きく悩ませました。『北斎伝』に紹介された北斎の自筆の手紙によれば、文政12年（1829）、孫の放蕩による不始末によって、北斎はいろいろと尻拭いをさせられたとのことです。また、天保5～6年（1834～35）頃、北斎は浦賀に潜居したとされますが、その理由のひとつとして、孫の放蕩によって発生したトラブルから逃げるためであったことが挙げられています（『北斎伝』）。

さらに、天保13～14年（1842～43）、北斎は毎朝小さな紙に唐獅子や獅子舞の図を描き（図19-1）、丸めて家の外に捨てていましたが、その理由は「これ我が孫なる悪魔を払ふ禁呪なり」であったといいます（『北斎伝』）。これが確かだとするならば、北斎は10年以上も「悪魔」のような孫に悩まされていたことになります。

また、北斎の次男である多吉郎、後の加瀬崎十郎には、弥次郎と多知という一男一女がいます。弥次郎は、天保12年（1841）に生まれ、家督を継いで御家人となり、慶応2年（1866）、26歳の若さで亡くなりました。多知は白井家に嫁ぎ、孝義と祖次郎（ちょうじろう）（→84頁参照）の二男をもうけます。祖次郎は加瀬家の養子となり、弥次郎の跡を継ぎました[1]。

その後の北斎の子孫についてはこれまで詳しく触れられていませんでしたが、近年、白井孝義の子孫が現在でも続いていることが報告されました[2]。

1) 竹村誠「北斎の子・孫・曾孫―加瀬崎十郎・弥次郎・祖次郎について」『北斎研究』45号、2010年
2) 内藤正人「北斎の裔―幕臣白井家の系譜と、その遺品」『浮世絵芸術』177号、2019年

In his later years, Hokusai was afflicted considerably by the boy (name unknown) born to Hokusai's eldest daughter, Miyo, and Yanagawa Shigenobu. According to a letter handwritten by Hokusai and cited in *Hokusai-den*, in 1829, Hokusai had to bear various consequences of his grandson's dissipated misconducts. Furthermore, Hokusai is said to have gone into hiding in Uraga circa 1834–1835. One of the reasons is considered to have been that he needed to run away from the trouble his prodigal grandson had caused (*Hokusai-den*).

Every morning between 1842 and 1843, Hokusai drew pictures of Chinese lions and the lion dance (fig. 19-1) on tiny pieces of paper, which he crumpled up and threw out of the house. This is said to have been "a spell to drive the evil spirit of my grandson away" (*Hokusai-den*). If this was true, it would mean that Hokusai was afflicted by his "devil"-like grandson for ten or more years.

Hokusai's second son, Takichirō, who was later renamed Kase Sakijūrō, had a son named Yajirō and a daughter named Tachi. Born in 1841, Yajirō succeeded his father as head of the family and became a retainer of the Tokugawa shogun, but died in 1866 at the young age of 26. Tachi married into the Shirai family and bore two sons, Takayoshi and Chōjirō (see p. 84). Chōjirō was adopted by the Kase family and succeeded Yajirō.

Details of Hokusai's descendants thereafter have not been mentioned hitherto in detail, but, in recent years, it has been reported that Shirai Takayoshi's descendants live on to this day.

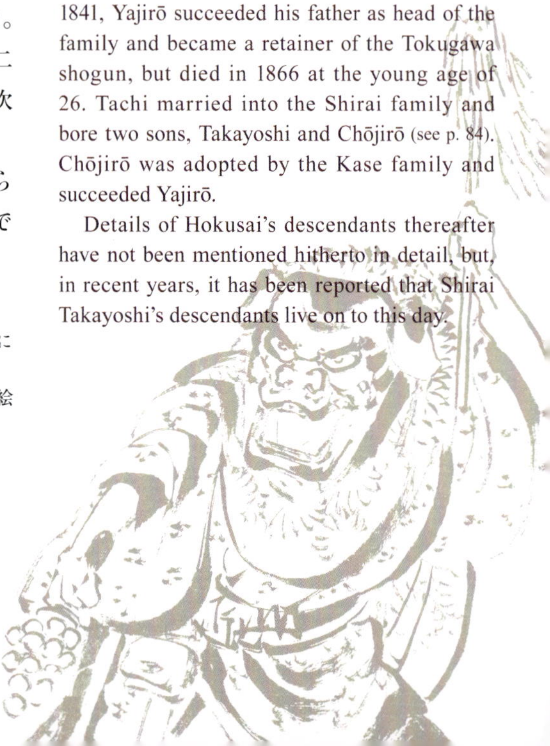

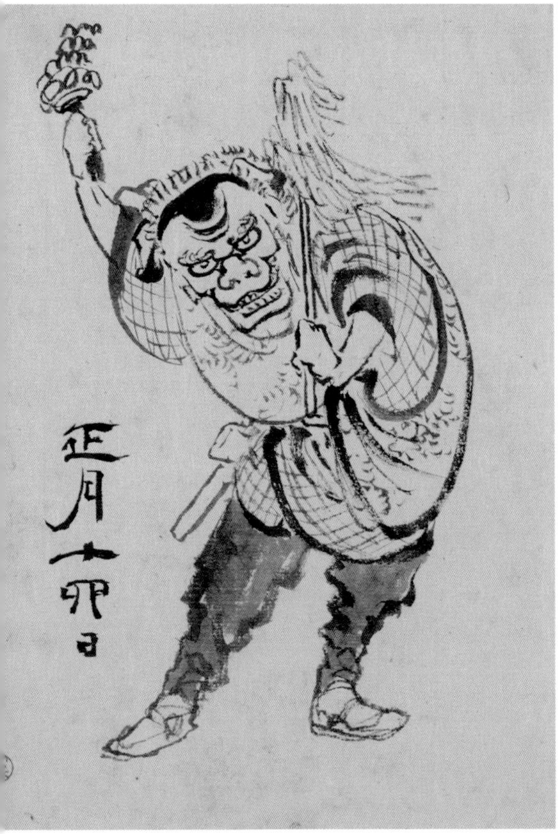

1月14日

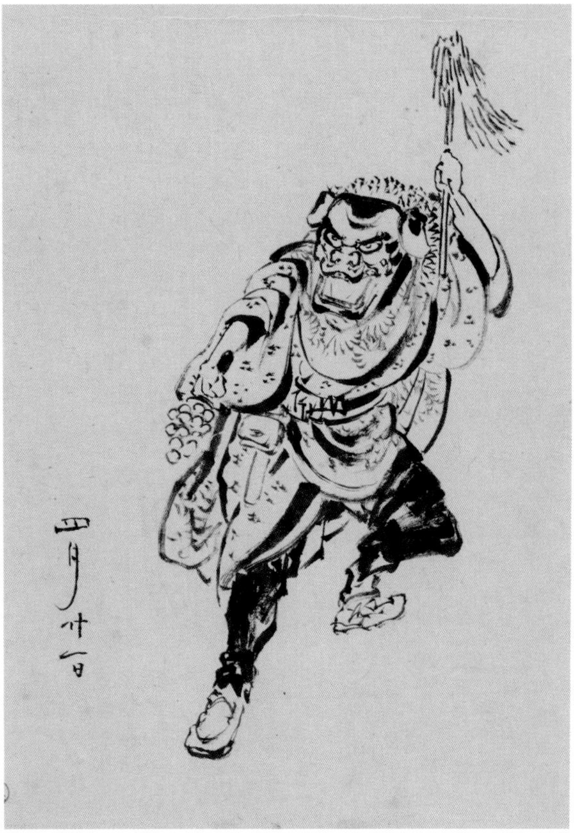

4月21日

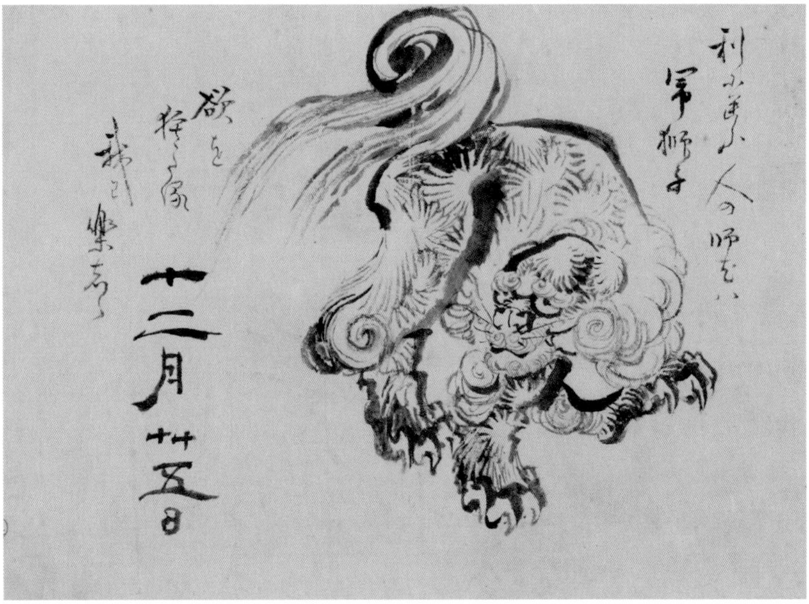

撮影：落合晴彦
Photo by Ochiai Haruhiko

12月25日

19-1 葛飾北斎　**日新除魔図**（にっしんじょまず）

天保13〜14年（1842〜43）　紙本墨画　九州国立博物館蔵　重要文化財

九州国立博物館が所蔵する「日新除魔図」219点は、松代藩士である宮本慎助の旧蔵。宮本慎助は北斎に絵の注文をしていましたが、受け取りに行った際に完成していなかったため、北斎の娘である応為から代わりに「日新除魔図」の束を受け取りました。

19-1 Katsushika Hokusai ***Daily Exorcisms***

1842–1843, ink on paper, Kyushu National Museum, Important Cultural Property

The 219 “Daily Exorcisms” included in the collection of Kyushu National Museum formerly belonged to Miyamoto Shinsuke, a retainer of the Matsushiro domain. Miyamoto Shinsuke had commissioned Hokusai to do a painting. However, when he went to collect it, it had not yet been completed. Instead, he received a bundle of “Daily Exorcisms” from Hokusai’s daughter Ōi.

20

Heedless of Appearance and Tidiness
身なりかまわず散らかし放題

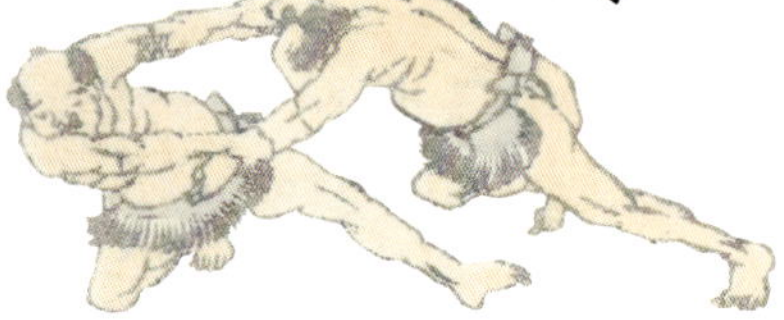

Clothing and Living
衣装と住居

北斎が普段どのような衣服を着て、どのような家に住んでいたのかについて、『北斎伝』にはさまざまな記録があります。

まず、北斎は普段の身だしなみにまったく気をつかっていませんでした。絹の服や流行の服を着たりせず、粗い手織りの紺縞の木綿を着て、柿色の袖なし半纏を羽織っていたそうです。また、6尺余り（約1.8 m）の天秤棒を杖とし、雨の日は草鞋を、晴れの日は麻裏草履を履いていたといいます。さらに、『北斎伝』の中では「常に弊衣（ぼろぼろの衣服）を着し」「衣服破れたりと雖厭はす」といった言葉でも表現されるほどでした。

また、北斎の住居は、「懶惰にして居室を掃除せす」と『北斎伝』にあるように、普段から掃除をしないためにゴミが散らかり、蜘蛛が巣を張るほど汚れていました。部屋の汚さが限界に達すると引っ越したともいわれています（→72頁参照）。北斎が本所亀沢町榿馬場に住んでいた時の家を実際に訪れたことのある門人の露木孔彰が、北斎の家の様子を絵にしています（図20-1）。

歌舞伎役者の三代目尾上菊五郎が、幽霊の絵を依頼するため、北斎の家を訪れたことがありました。北斎の家があまりに汚いのに驚き、乗って来た駕籠の中にあった毛氈を運び入れ、それを部屋に敷いてから座ったほどであったといいます。北斎にとって絵を描くことが一番大事で、身の回りのことは度を過ぎるほど無頓着だったようです。

In *Hokusai-den*, there are a variety of records on what sort of clothes Hokusai usually wore and what sort of a house he lived in.

To begin with, Hokusai did not care at all about his everyday personal appearance. Instead of wearing silk or clothes in fashion, he was dressed in coarsely handwoven navy-blue striped cotton, over which he would slip on a persimmon colored sleeveless short coat. It is said that he used an approximately 1.8-meter-long shouldering pole as a walking stick and wore straw sandals on rainy days and hemp-soled sandals on sunny days. In *Hokusai-den*, there are even expressions such as "always wore rags" and "did not mind at all even if his clothes were torn."

As for his residence, according to *Hokusai-den*, Hokusai was "slothful and did not clean his room." As he was not in the habit of cleaning, there was litter all over the place and the room was dirtily covered in cobwebs. Some say that he moved when his room became too dirty (see p. 72). Tsuyuki Kōshō, who actually visited the house where Hokusai lived in Honjo Kamezawa-chō Hannoki Baba, did a picture of Hokusai's abode (fig. 20-1).

The *kabuki* actor Onoe Kikugorō III once visited Hokusai to order a picture of a ghost. Shocked by the untidiness, he is said to have brought the rug in the *kago* (palanquin) he had come on into Hokusai's room and laid it before sitting down. To Hokusai, drawing pictures was his prime concern and he did not care in the slightest about keeping neat and tidy.

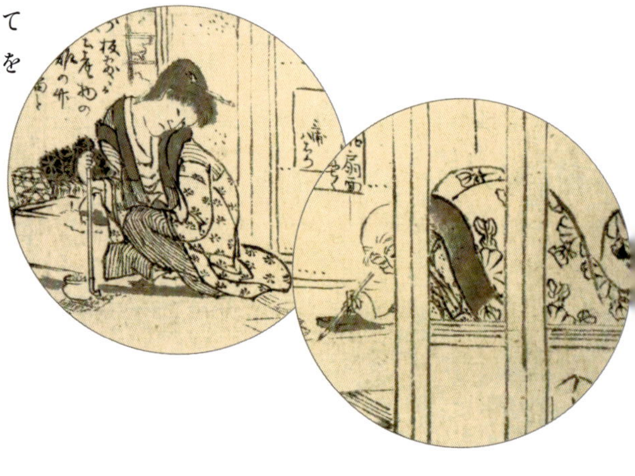

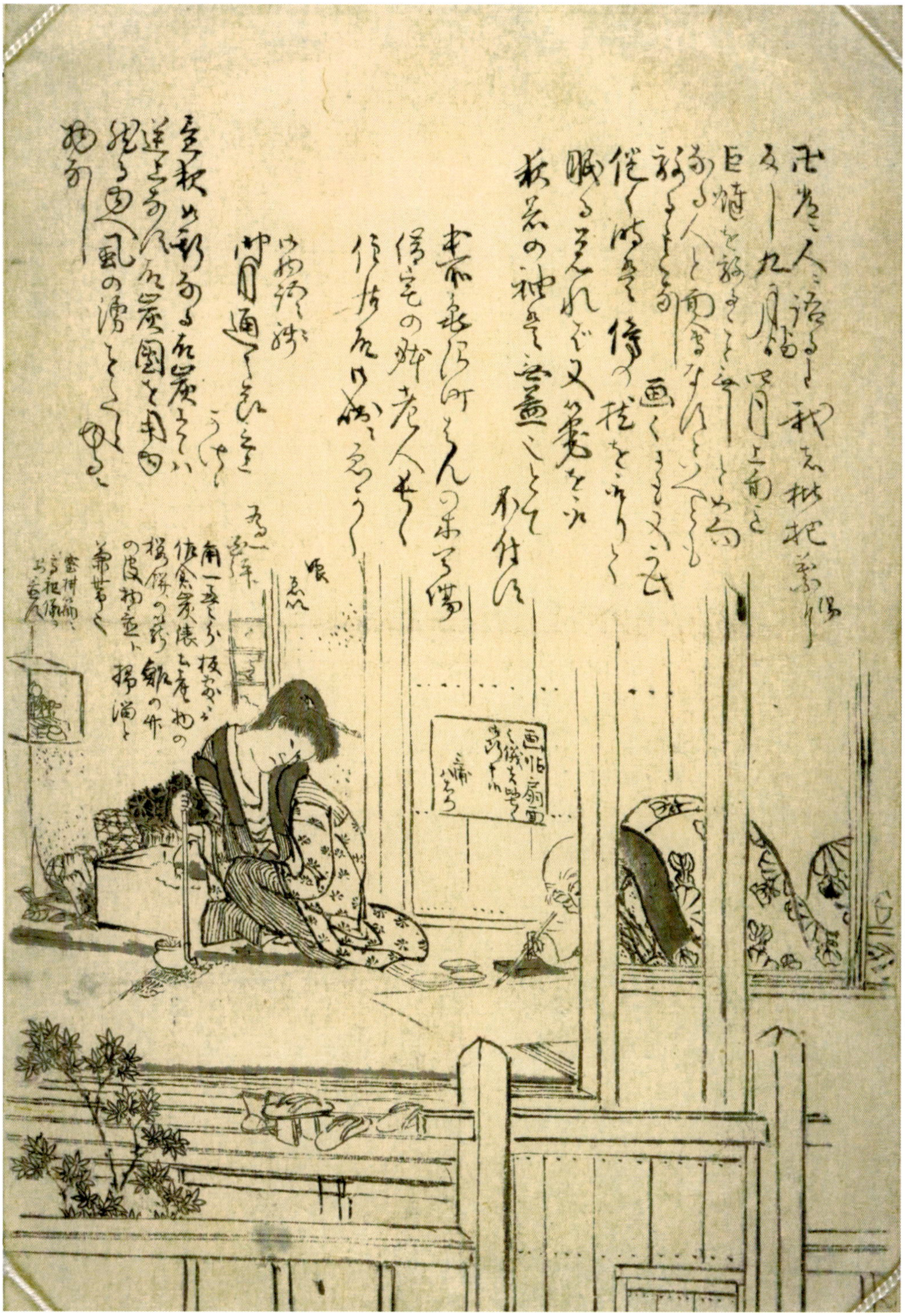

20-1 露木孔彰　**北斎仮宅之図**

明治26年(1893)以前　紙本墨画　国立国会図書館蔵

布団にくるまって絵を描いている北斎を、娘の応為が煙管を片手に眺めています。部屋は汚れていて、炭の俵や桜餅の籠、寿司を包む竹の皮などが散らかっていました。左端、柱に打ち付けられている蜜柑箱の中には、北斎が信仰していた日蓮の像が安置されています (→ 78 頁参照)。

20-1 Tsuyuki Kōshō

Hokusai and Ōi in Their Lodgings

before 1893, ink on paper, National Diet Library, Japan

Rolled up in a *futon*, Hokusai is drawing and his daughter Ōi watches him with a pipe in hand. The room is in a mess with charcoal sacks, baskets containing sweets, bamboo sheaths wrapped around *sushi*, etc. scattered all over the place. Enshrined inside the tangerine box nailed to the pillar on the far left is a statue of Nichiren, whom Hokusai believed in (see p. 78).

21

Nondrinker and Sweet Tooth

酒は飲まず、甘いもの好き

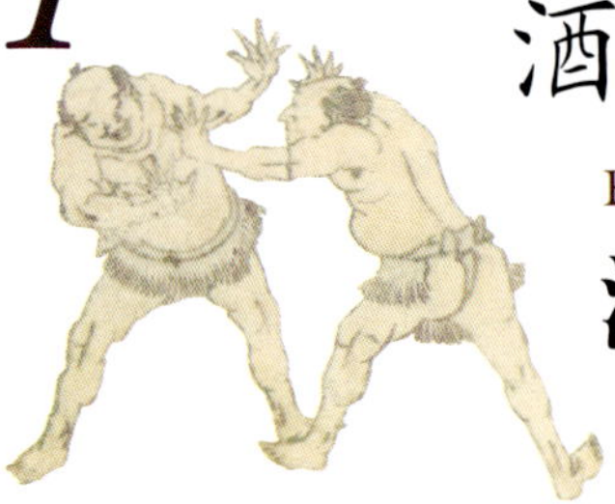

Eating and Drinking

酒と食事

北斎がどのような食事や飲み物を好んでいたかについては、『北斎伝』にさまざまな記録があります。

まず、北斎はお酒を全く飲まない下戸であることが、多くの人たちに証言されています。北斎が描いた読本挿絵や絵本の中に、「酔中筆」と北斎自身が記している例がいくつかあります（図21-2）。しかし、これらは本当に酒に酔いながら描いたのではなく、拙い表現となってしまったことの言い逃れであったと考えられます。

その一方で、北斎は甘いお菓子には目がありませんでした。本所石原の菓子商であった戸崎某は、北斎の家を訪問するごとに必ず大福餅を七つ八つお土産に持っていきました。その時北斎はとても喜び、舌を鳴らして食べたそうです。

そもそも北斎は、食事そのものに関心がなかったようです。煮売酒店（惣菜や酒を売る店）の隣に住んでいた時は、三食とも隣の店から食事を運んでいたため、家には食器がひとつもなく、土瓶と茶碗が２、３個あっただけでした。また、買ってきた料理を食べる時も、わざわざ他の器に移すことなく、箸を使わずにそのまま手づかみで食べていたそうです。ただ、蕎麦は好きだったようで、若い修業時代には朝から晩まで絵を描いた後に蕎麦を２杯食べて寝たり、亡くなるまで寝る前には必ず蕎麦を食べたりしていたという逸話も残っています。

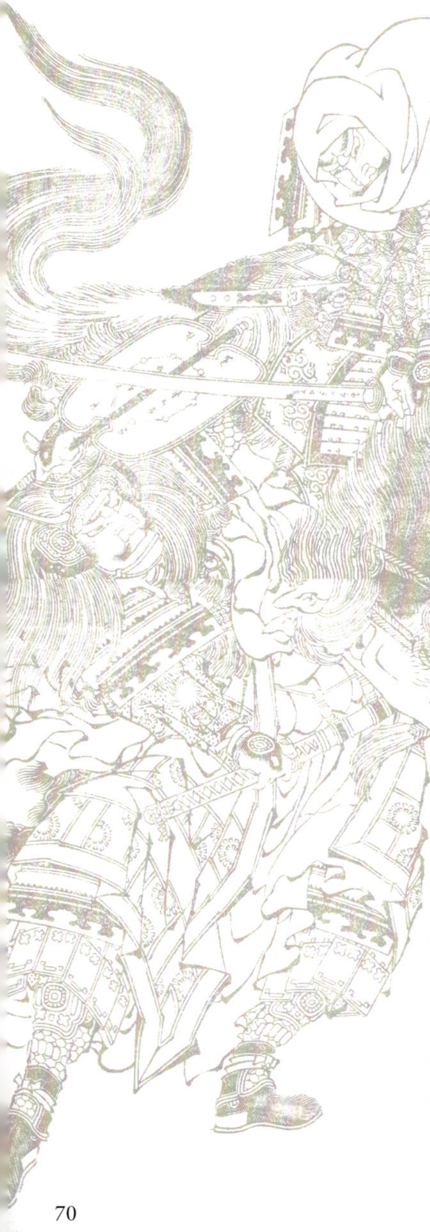

There are various records of what sort of meals and drinks Hokusai liked in *Hokusai-den*.

First of all, many people have testified that Hokusai did not drink alcohol at all. There are several examples of illustrations in reading books or picture books by Hokusai personally inscribed "painted while drunk" (figs. 21-2). However, they were not really painted when he was drunk. It may have been an excuse for the clumsy representation.

Meanwhile, Hokusai had a weakness for sweets. A Mr. Tozaki, a confectioner in Honjo Ishihara, always took seven or eight *daifuku* (sweet bean paste wrapped in steamed glutinous rice) as a present whenever he visited Hokusai's house. Hokusai would be very happy and smack his lips over them.

It seems that Hokusai was not interested in meals. When he was living next door to a cooked-food and liquor shop, he had three meals a day delivered from the neighboring shop and therefore owned no tableware except for a teapot and two or three teabowls. When eating the food he had purchased, he did not bother to put it on a different plate. He simply ate it with his fingers without using chopsticks. One exception was *soba* noodles. Anecdotes remain that, as a young trainee, after drawing pictures from morning to night, he would have two bowls of *soba* and fall asleep or that he always had *soba* before going to bed until his death.

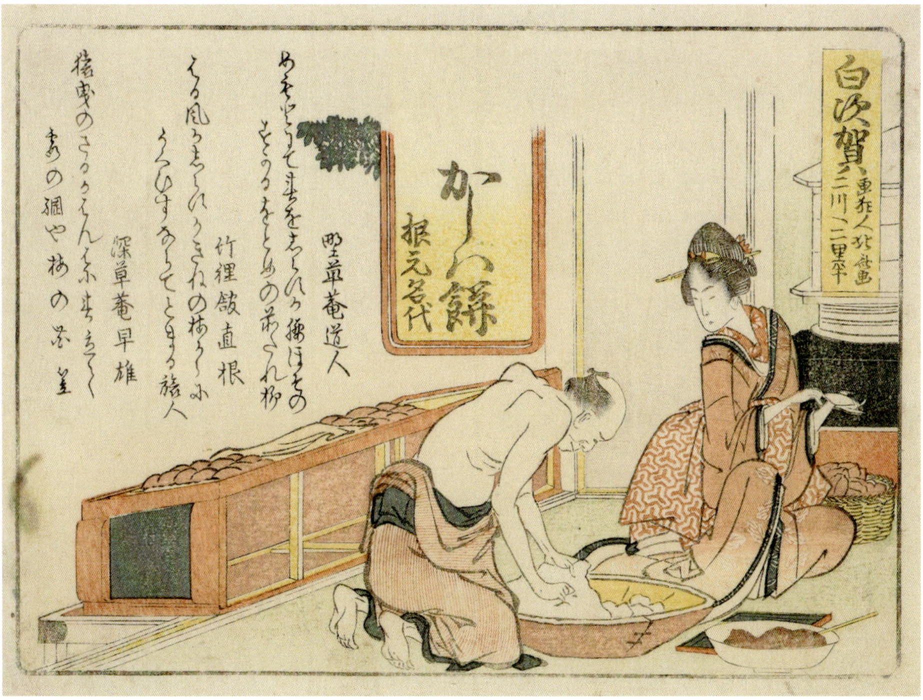

21-1　葛飾北斎
春興五十三駄之内　白須賀
享和4年（1804）　九つ切判摺物　島根県立美術館（永田コレクション）蔵

東海道の宿場町を題材とした狂歌摺物です。白須賀宿（静岡県湖西市）と二川宿（愛知県豊橋市）の間にある猿が馬場は、餡の入った餅を柏の葉で包んだ柏餅が名物として知られています。柏餅を作る店の様子が描かれていますが、おそらくこのような甘い柏餅は北斎の大好物だったことでしょう。

21-1　Katsushika Hokusai
New Year Kyōka Gathering, Fifty-three Stations of the Tōkaido: Shirasuka
1804, *kokonotsugiriban surimono*, Shimane Art Museum(Nagata Collection)

A *kyōka surimono* (single-sheet woodblock print) of the post towns along Tōkaidō. Sarugababa, located between Shirasuka (Kosai-shi, Shizuoka) and Futagawa (Toyohashi-shi, Aichi), is famous for *kashiwamochi*, a cake of pounded rice containing sweet bean paste and wrapped in an oak leaf. This depicts a shop where this local specialty is being made. Hokusai would have loved sweet rice cakes like this.

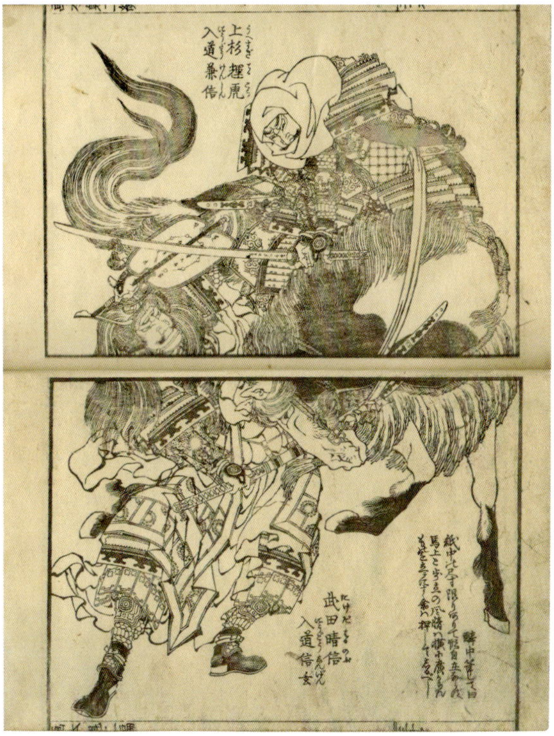

21-2　葛飾北斎　**『絵本武蔵鐙』**
天保7年（1836）　半紙本　太田記念美術館蔵

上杉謙信と武田信玄が対峙する場面。北斎は画面の右下に「酔中筆して曰　紙中の尺寸限りありて形自在ならず　馬上と歩立の風情は横に広からんものを立ニ記す　余は押してしるべし」と書き込んでいます。縦長の構図であまり上手く描けなかったことを、「酔中筆」という言葉で言い訳しているようです。

21-2　Katsushika Hokusai
Picture Book, The Stirrups of Musashi
1836, *hanshibon*, Ōta Memorial Museum of Art

The scene in which Uesugi Kenshin and Takeda Shingen confront each other. The inscription by Hokusai in the lower right reads, "Painted while drunk. With limited space, I couldn't depict the forms at will. The mounted warrior and the one on foot should be spread sideways, but I had to capture them vertically. The rest is left to your imagination." Hokusai seems to be trying to justify his being unable to capture the scene perfectly in a vertical composition with the words "painted while drunk."

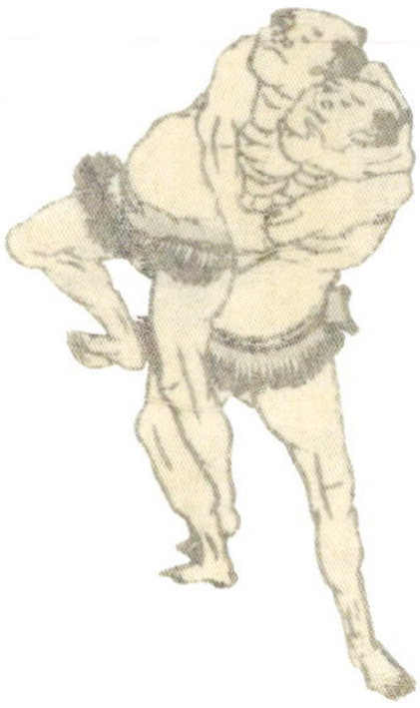

22 Wanderer with No Fixed Abode
居所不定の引っ越し魔

Moving House
引っ越し

『北斎伝』の序文の冒頭には、「画工北斎畸人也。年九十而移居九十三所。」と、北斎が畸人、すなわち、風変わりな人物で、90年の生涯で93回も引っ越しをしたことが述べられています。さらに『北斎伝』には、75歳までに56回ほど引っ越したとありますので、晩年には毎年1年に2、3回は引っ越さなければならない計算です。実際に住んだとされる住居は20数か所程度ですが、この信じ難い引っ越しの多さこそ、北斎の風変わりな性格を象徴する重要なエピソードであったといえます。

多い時には1日で3回も引っ越したとも言いますので、北斎がどこに住んでいるのか、当時の人たちも分からなくなってしまったのは当然でしょう。天保7年（1836）と天保13年（1842）に刊行された『広益諸家人名録』という著名人の住所を記した人名録に北斎の名前があるのですが、いずれも「居所不定」と書かれています。

北斎がそれほどたくさん引っ越した理由のひとつに、部屋の掃除をするのが面倒だったことがあります。しかし、引っ越しをするにもお金がかかりますので、それならば人を雇って代わりに掃除をしてもらった方がはるかにお得です。四方梅彦という戯作者がその疑問を北斎に尋ねたところ、転居を100回した寺町百庵という俳人がおり、その百庵にならって自分も100回引っ越しをしたいと語ったそうです（『北斎伝』）。残念ながら、100回にはあと7回足らず、百庵の記録に届くことは叶いませんでした。

The Introduction of *Hokusai-den* begins as follows. "The painter Hokusai was an eccentric man. He moved ninety-three times in his ninety-year-long lifetime." The same book continues that he moved fifty-six times until the age of 75, which means that he would have moved two or three times a year late in life. There are twenty or so abodes that he is considered to actually have lived in. The unbelievable frequency of Hokusai's moves is indeed an important episode that symbolizes how out-of-the-way a character he had.

There is even an opinion that Hokusai moved as many as three times a day. Therefore, it is no wonder that even the people of the time became unable to tell where he was living. Hokusai's name is included in *Kōeki shoka jinmeiroku*, directories of distinguished people's addresses published in 1836 and 1842. In both versions, Hokusai is listed, "whereabouts unknown."

One of the reasons Hokusai moved so often was that he found cleaning the room a bother. However, moving house costs money. If he could afford to move, it would have been far more reasonable to hire someone to do the cleaning for him. A popular novelist named Yomono Umehiko put this question to Hokusai, who replied that there was a *haiku* poet named Teramachi Hyakuan who moved 100 times. Hokusai said he wanted to follow Hyakuan's example and move 100 times, too (*Hokusai-den*). Unfortunately, Hokusai ended seven times short of Hyakuan's record of 100 times.

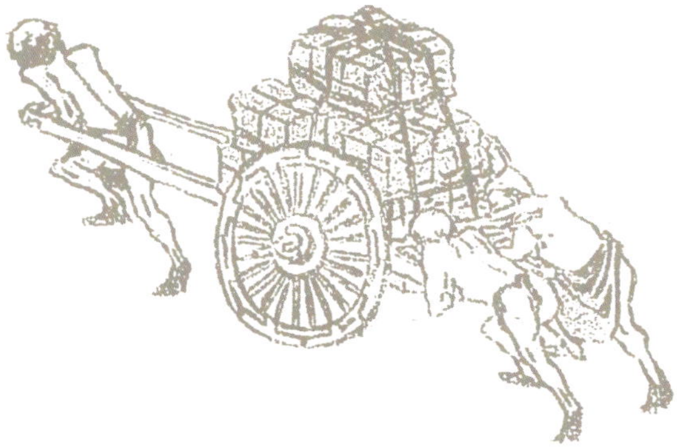

※葛飾北斎『北斎漫画』二編（国立国会図書館蔵）より作成。
From *Hokusai's Sketches*, part 2 (National Diet Library, Japan)

22-1 北斎引越しMAP〈北斎が住んだとされる主な場所〉 Map of Hokusai's residences

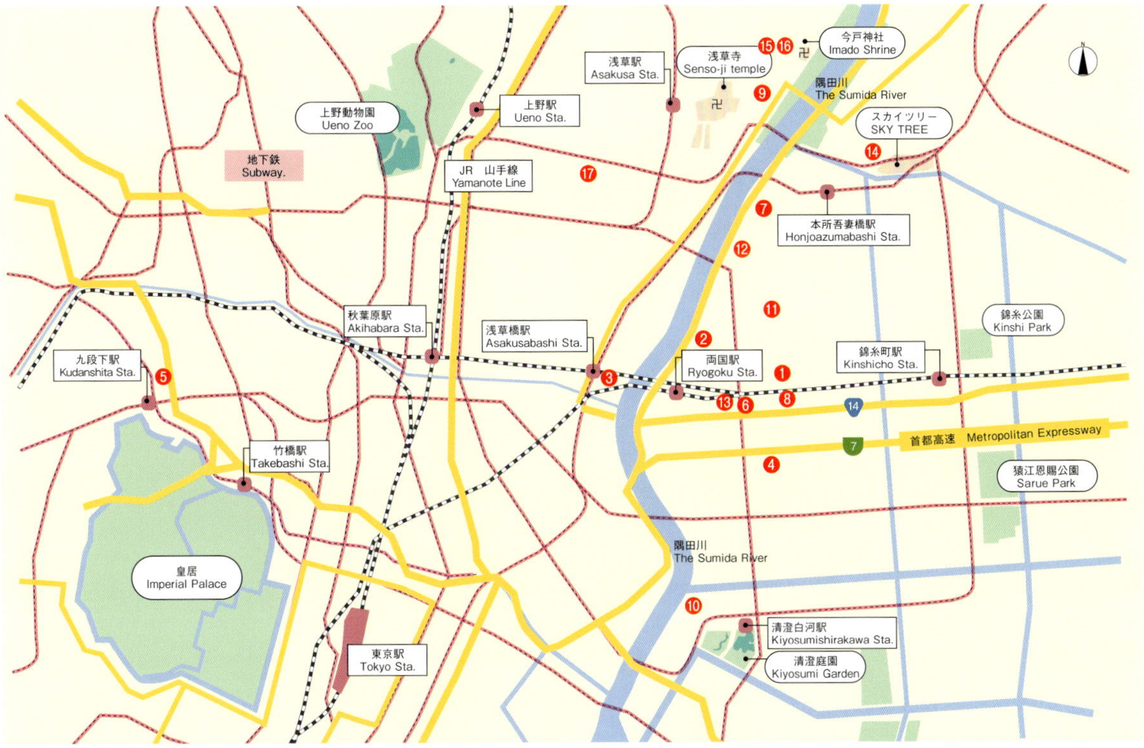

	地名 Location	現在のおおよその場所 Current address (approximate)	年代(西暦) Year	年齢 Age
1	本所割下水 Honjo Warigesui	墨田区亀沢1～4丁目 Kamezawa 1–4 chōme, Sumida-ku	宝暦10年 (1760)	1歳　生誕地(『北斎伝』) Birthplace
2	横網町 Yokoamichō	墨田区横網1・2丁目 Yokoami 1, 2 chōme, Sumida-ku		幼少期に居住(『北斎伝』) Childhood home
3	浅草大六天神脇町 Asakusa Dairoku Tenjin Wakimachi	台東区柳橋1丁目 Yanagibashi 1 chōme, Taitō-ku	寛政7~8年 (1795~96)頃	36~37歳(『浮世絵師之考』)
4	本所林町三丁目 Honjo Hayashichō	墨田区立川・菊川 Tatekawa and Kikukawa, Sumida-ku	寛政10年 (1798)頃	39歳(『古画備考』)
5	元飯田町中坂下 Motoiida-machi Nakazaka-shita	千代田区九段北1丁目 Kudankita 1 chōme, Chiyoda-ku	文化3年 (1806)	47歳　曲亭馬琴宅に寄宿(『苅萱後伝玉櫛笥』) Lodges at Kyokutei Bakin's house.
6	本所亀沢町 Honjo Kamezawachō	墨田区両国4丁目付近 Around Ryōgoku 4 chōme, Sumida-ku	文化5年 (1808)	49歳　新宅を構える(「北斎新築報条」) Builds a new house.
7	蛇山(中之郷原庭町) Hebiyama (Nakanogō Haraniwachō)	墨田区東駒形 Higashikomagata, Sumida-ku	文化12年 (1815)	56歳(『踊独稽古』)
8	本所緑町 Honjo Midorichō	墨田区緑1～3丁目 Midori 1–3 chōme, Sumida-ku	文政3年 (1820)	61歳(『北斎論』)
9	浅草藪の内明王院地内 The precincts of Myōō-in Asakusa Yabunouchi	台東区花川戸1丁目 Hanakawado 1 chōme, Taitō-ku	天保元年 (1830)	71歳(『北斎伝』)
10	万年橋周辺 Around Mannenbashi	江東区清澄 Kiyosumi, Kōtō-ku	天保7年 (1836)	77歳(『和漢絵本魁』)
11	本所石原片町 Honjo Ishiwara Katamachi	墨田区石原1・2丁目 Ishiwara 1, 2 chōme, Sumida-ku	天保10年 (1839)	80歳(『北斎伝』)
12	本所達磨横町 Honjo Daruma Yokochō	墨田区東駒形1丁目 Higashikomagata 1 chōme, Sumida-ku	天保10年 (1839)	80歳　火災に遭う(『北斎伝』) Suffers a fire.
13	本所亀沢町榿馬場 Honjo Kamezawachō Hannokibaba	墨田区両国4丁目 Ryōgoku 4 chōme, Sumida-ku	天保13年 (1842)頃	83歳(『北斎伝』)
14	向島小梅村 Mukōjima Koumemura	墨田区向島・押上付近 Around Mukōjima and Oshiage, Sumida-ku	弘化元年 (1844)	85歳(嵩山房宛稿料受取証)
15	浅草田町一丁目 Asakusa Tamachi 1 chome	台東区浅草6丁目 Asakusa 6 chōme, Taitō-ku	弘化4年 (1847)	88歳(神山熊三郎宛北斎書簡)
16	浅草聖天町遍照院境内 The precincts of Henshō-in, Asakusa Shōdenchō	台東区浅草6丁目 Asakusa 6 chōme, Taitō-ku	嘉永元年 (1849)	90歳　最後の引っ越し(『北斎伝』) Final move
17	誓教寺 Seikyō-ji	台東区元浅草4丁目 Motoasakusa 4 chōme, Taitō-ku		北斎の墓所 Hokusai's grave

参考文献：永田生慈「葛飾北斎年譜」『北斎研究』22号、1997年

23

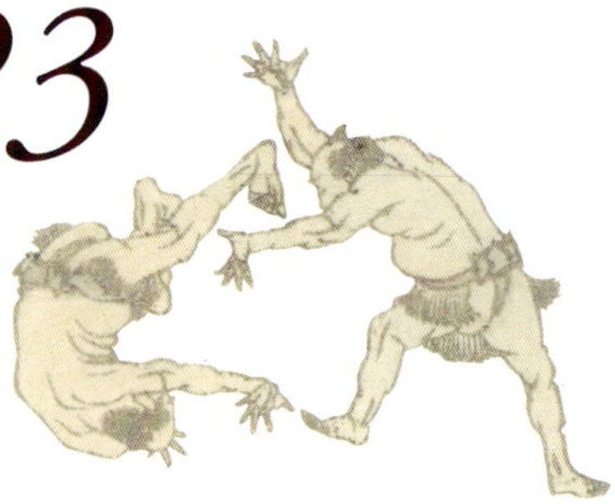

Big Ears, Long Face?

耳が大きく顔が長い?

Hokusai's Features

北斎の顔

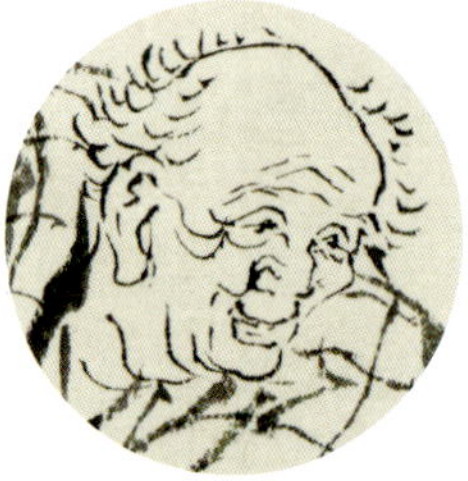

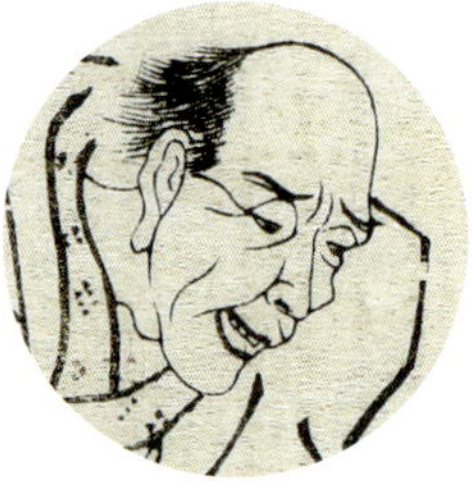

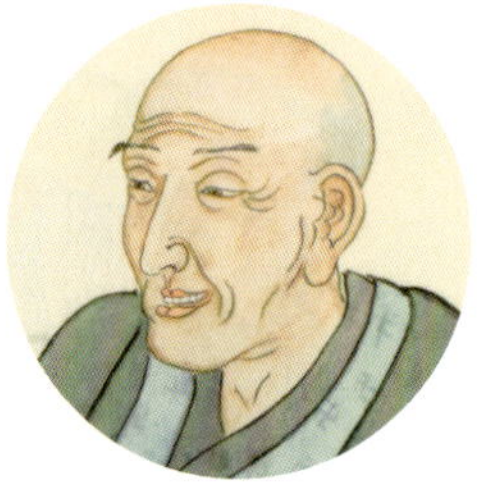

北斎はどのような顔をしていたのでしょうか。直接北斎に会っている考証家の関根只誠の証言によれば、「痩せて鼻目常人に異ならされども、たゝ耳は、頗巨大なり」と、耳が非常に大きかったことが印象に残っているとのことです(『北斎伝』)。

北斎の肖像画として、北斎自身によるもの、あるいは、北斎以外の絵師によるものなど、いくつかの作品が指摘されています[1)]。北斎の自画像として信憑性が高いもののひとつに、北斎が八十三歳の時に描いたとされる作品(図23-1)があります。顔はやや丸型で、髪の毛はぼさぼさ。顔の皺も多く見られます。

一方、北斎と実際に接点のあった絵師が描いた北斎像として、花笠文京作・歌川国芳画『日本奇人伝』の挿絵(図23-2)や、渓斎英泉が描いた肖像画に基づく挿絵(図23-3)などがあります。国芳や英泉が描いた北斎像は顔つきが面長で、北斎自身の自画像と比べると、同一人物と断定できるほど同じような顔にはなっていません。

北斎は必ずしも自分の顔を本物そっくりに描こうとしていなかったかもしれません。状況に応じて、自分の姿を自在に変えていた可能性も考えられるのです。だとすると、国芳や英泉といった他人が描いた姿の方が、より実際の姿に近いといえるでしょう。

1) 山本陽子「葛飾北斎の肖像画における自己演出」(『明星大学研究紀要 人文学部』第52号、2016年)に過去の北斎肖像画に関する研究が簡潔にまとめられています。

What did Hokusai look like? According to Sekine Shisei, who met Hokusai in person, "Although he was thin with normal eyes and nose, his ears were very big." (*Hokusai-den*).

Several portraits of Hokusai are known, some by Hokusai himself and those by other artists, etc. One of the self-portraits considered authentic is a work assumed to have been painted when Hokusai was 83 (fig. 23-1). He has a roundish face, untidy hair, and many wrinkles.

To give some examples of portraits of Hokusai painted by artists who actually had contact with Hokusai, there is an illustration in *Nihon kijinden* (Biographies of eccentric people of Japan) written by Hanagasa Bunkyō and illustrated by Utagawa Kuniyoshi (fig. 23-2) and an illustration based on a portrait painted by Keisai Eisen (fig. 23-3). Kuniyoshi and Eisen depict Hokusai with an oval face. Compared with Hokusai's self-portrait, each model's face is not similar enough to be identified as the same person.

Perhaps Hokusai did not necessarily intend to depict the exact likeness of his face. It is quite possible that he altered his looks as desired according to the circumstances. In that case, the portraits by other people such as Kuniyoshi and Eisen may have been closer to Hokusai's actual appearance.

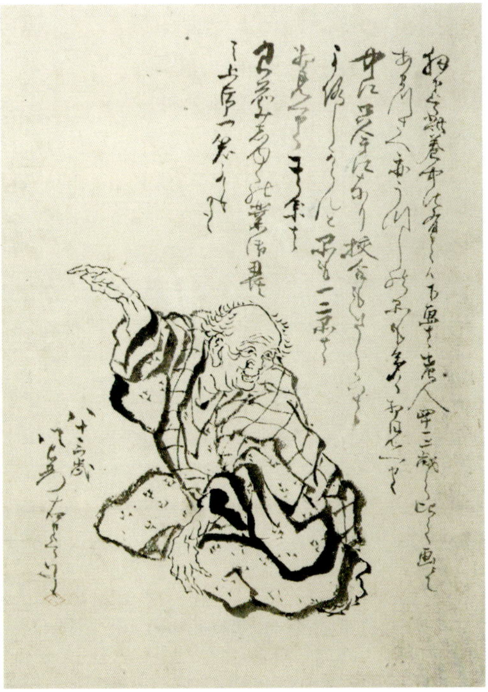

Nationaal Museum van Wereldculturen.Coll.no.:RV-3513-1496

23-1 葛飾北斎 **北斎自画像**

天保13年(1842)　紙本墨画　ライデン国立民族学博物館蔵

北斎が版元に宛てた文章に添えた自画像。「八十三歳　八右衛門右申上候」とあるように、83歳の姿です。この頃の北斎は三浦屋八右衛門としばしば自らを名乗っていました。

23-1 Katsushika Hokusai

Self-Portrait

1842, ink on paper, Museum Volkenkunde, Leiden

This is a self-portrait which Hokusai attached to a letter he sent to a publisher. It is inscribed, "My name is Hachiemon and I am aged 83." It shows the artist at 83. In those days, Hokusai often went under the name Miuraya Hachiemon.

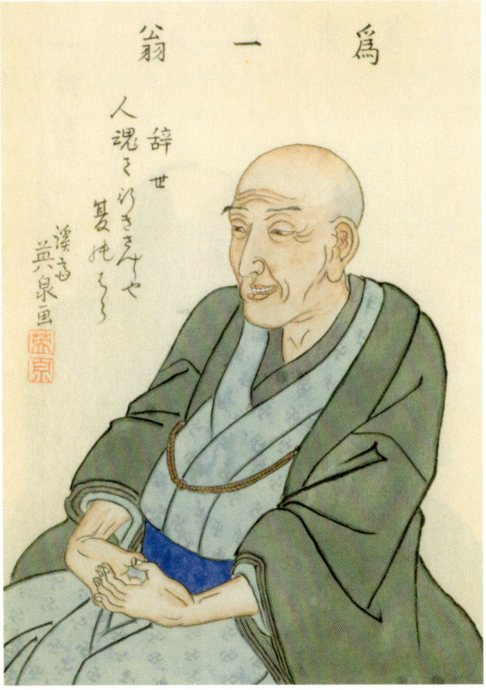

23-3 木村默老作 **『戯作者考補遺』**

写本　慶應義塾図書館蔵

渓斎英泉が描いた北斎の肖像画ですが、原本は焼失しており、本図は明治期に写されたものです。北斎80歳頃の姿を捉えています。

23-3 Kimura Mokurō

Gesakusha-kōhoi

(A supplement to a study of *gesaku* writers)

handwritten copy, Keio University Library

This is a portrait of Hokusai by Keisai Eisen. The original book was destroyed in a fire and this is a copy made in the Meiji era. It shows Hokusai at around 80 years old.

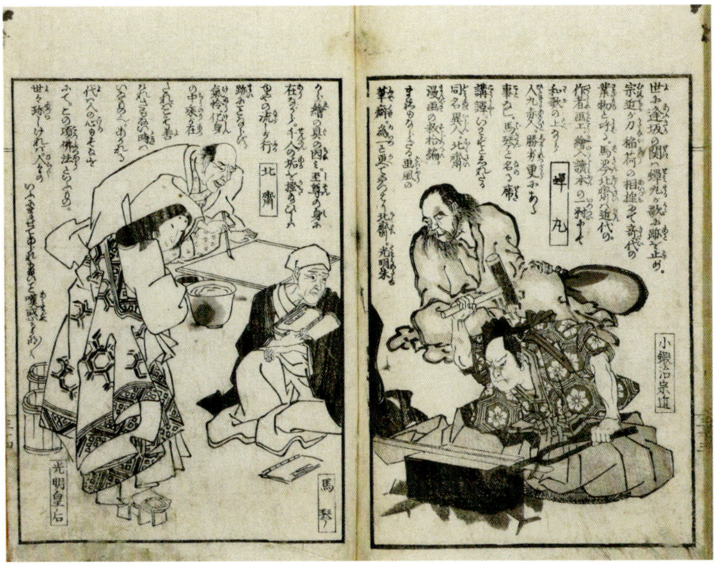

23-2 花笠文京作・歌川国芳画

『日本奇人伝』下巻

嘉永2年(1849)　半紙本

島根県立美術館(永田コレクション)蔵

左上で絵筆を走らせているのが北斎です。国芳は北斎とも面識がありましたので、実際の姿に近いものと思われます。

23-2 Hanagasa Bunkyō

***Nihon kijinden* (Biographies of eccentric people of Japan), vol. 2**

illust. Utagawa Kuniyoshi, 1849, *hanshibon,*
Shimane Art Museum (Nagata Collection).

Hokusai is the man with a paintbrush in hand in the upper left. As Kuniyoshi knew Hokusai in person, it should be fairly close to his actual look.

24

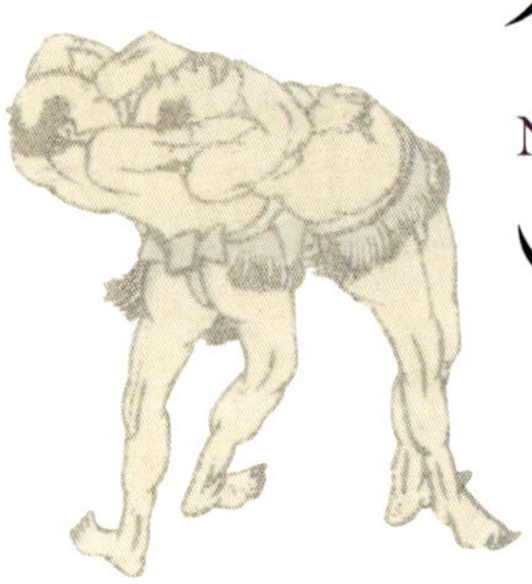

Unbending Challenger
不屈のチャレンジ精神の証

Numerous Artist Names
いくつもの画号

一般的に、浮世絵師が名前を頻繁に変えることは多くありません。例えば歌川広重の場合、一幽斎や一立斎といった斎号は改めていますが、広重という画号は生涯使い続けました。また、歌川国貞は歌川豊国と名前を改めますが、これは師匠の名前を襲名するという特殊なケースです。不特定多数の人々に商品を販売しなくてはならない浮世絵師にとって、改名を頻繁に行なうことは客たちの混乱を招くだけで、メリットはほとんどありません。

しかしながら、北斎に限っては、右頁の一覧から分かるように、その画号を頻繁に変えているのです。

その理由として、北斎はお金に困った時、画号を門人に譲って幾ばくかのお金をもらっていたという説があります(『北斎伝』)。実際、宗理という画号は門人の琳斎宗二へ、戴斗という画号は門人の斗円楼北泉に譲られています。

しかし、それ以上の理由として、あるジャンルを極めたと思ったら、名前を変えることで心機一転し、新たな課題に取り組もうという、北斎のひとつのところにとどまらない開拓精神の強さがあるのでしょう。ただし、北斎という画号は、最も広く知られていたこともあり、晩年になっても「葛飾前北斎戴斗筆」「前北斎為一筆」などのように、新しい画号と併記するほど思い入れは強かったようです。

Generally speaking, it is not very often that an *ukiyo-e* artist frequently changes names. For example, in the case of Utagawa Hiroshige, he did change his "sai" pseudonyms such as Ichiyūsai and Ichiryūsai, but he continued to use the artist name Hiroshige throughout his lifetime. In the case of Utagawa Kunisada, he changed his name to Utagawa Toyokuni, but this was an exceptional case in which he succeeded to his master's professional name. To an *ukiyo-e* artist who had to sell merchandise to an unspecified large number of people, there was hardly any advantage of frequently changing names as it would only confuse the customers.

However, in Hokusai's case, as indicated in the list shown on the right, he frequently changed his artist name.

Some say that this was because when Hokusai was short of money, he would transmit his artist name to a disciple in exchange for a certain amount of money (*Hokusai-den*). In fact, his artist name Sōri was transmitted to his pupil Rinsai Sōji and his artist name Taito to his pupil Toenrō Hokusen.

Nevertheless, an even stronger reason may have lain in Hokusai's great pioneering spirit of not remaining in one place. Once he felt he had mastered a certain genre, he would make a fresh start by changing names and begin working on a new theme. Partly as the artist name Hokusai was widely recognized, he seems to have been deeply attached to this name to the extent that, late in life, he would sign with both his former and new names such as "Katsushika sakino [*former*] Hokusai Taito hitsu [*painted by*]" or "Sakino [*former*] Hokusai Iitsu hitsu [*painted by*]."

北斎の主な画号の変遷　Major changes in Hokusai's artist names

※画号の使用時期は、絵画の署名として用いていた大よその時期によります。

*The period of usage roughly outlines when Hokusai employed that name as his signature.

20代～30代半ば　In His Twenties to Mid-Thirties

①
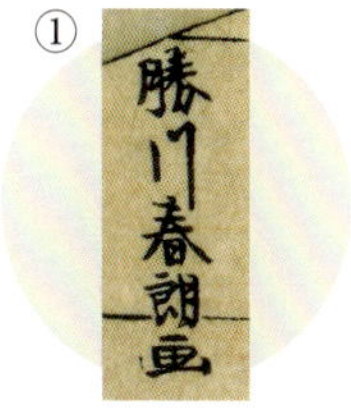

勝川春朗画
Katsukawa Shunrō *ga*
3-1

かつかわしゅんろう
勝川春朗（①）Katsukawa Shunrō（①）
安永8～寛政6年（1779～94）20～35歳
1779–1794, aged 20-35

ぐんばてい
群馬亭　Gunbatei
天明5～6年（1785～86）26～27歳
1785–1786, aged 26-27

くさむら しゅんろう
叢 春 朗　Kusamura Shunrō
寛政5～6年（1793～94）34～35歳
1793–1794, aged 34-35

30代後半　In His Late Thirties

②
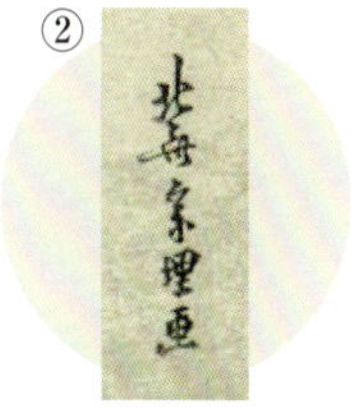

北斎宗理画
Hokusai Sōri *ga*
4-2

そうり
宗理　Sōri
寛政6～10年（1794～98）35～39歳
1794–1798, aged 35-39

ほくさいそうり
北斎宗理（②）Hokusai Sōri（②）
寛政8～10年（1796～98）37～39歳
1796–1798, aged 37-39

40代　In His Forties

③
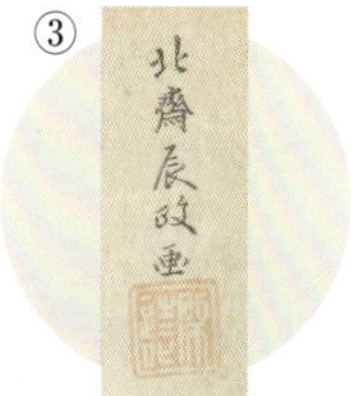

北斎辰政画「師造化」
Hokusai Tokimasa *ga*
"Shizōka"
25-1

④
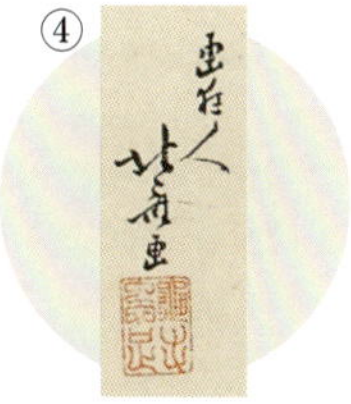

画狂人北斎画
「亀毛蛇足」
Gakyōjin Hokusai *ga*
"Kimōdasoku"
5-3

⑤
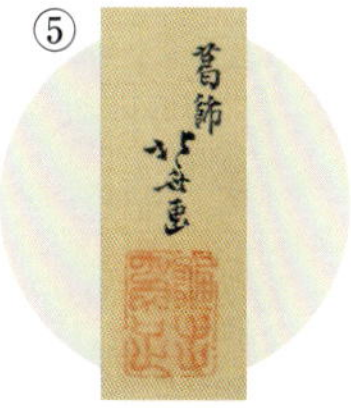

葛飾北斎画「亀毛蛇足」
Katsushika Hokusai *ga*
"Kimōdasoku"
5-5

かこう
可候　Kakō
寛政10～享和3年（1798～1803）39～44歳
1798–1803, aged 39-44

ほくさいときまさ
北斎辰政（③）Hokusai Tokimasa（③）
寛政10～文化元年（1798～1804）39～45歳
1798–1804, aged 39-45

ふせんきょほくさい
不染居北斎　Fusenkyo Hokusai
寛政11年（1799）40歳
1799, aged 40

ときたろうかこう
時太郎可候　Tokitarō Kakō
寛政12～文化元年（1800～1804）41～45歳
1800–1804, aged 41-45

がきょうじんほくさい
画狂人北斎（④）Gakyōjin Hokusai（④）
享和元～文化3年（1801～1806）42～47歳
1801–1806, aged 42-47

がきょうろうじんほくさい
画狂老人北斎　Gakyō Rōjin Hokusai
文化元～2年（1804～05）45～46歳
1804–1805, aged 45-46

きゅうきゅうしんほくさい
九々蜃北斎　KyūKyūshin Hokusai
文化2年（1805）46歳
1805, aged 46

かつしかほくさい
葛飾北斎（⑤）Katsushika Hokusai（⑤）
文化2～12年（1805～15）46～56歳
1805–1815, aged 46-56

50代　In His Fifties

⑥
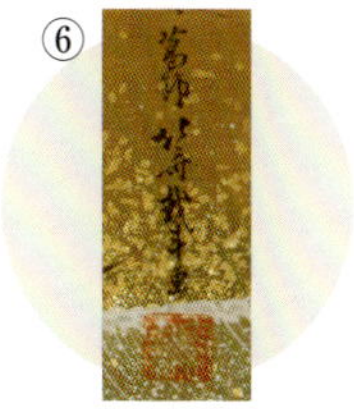

葛飾北斎戴斗画「雷震」
Katsushika Hokusai
Taito *ga* "Raishin"
31-2

たいと
戴斗（⑥）Taito（⑥）
文化7～文政2年（1810～1819）51～60歳
1810–1819, aged 51-60

60代～70代半ば　In His Sixties to Mid-Seventies

⑦
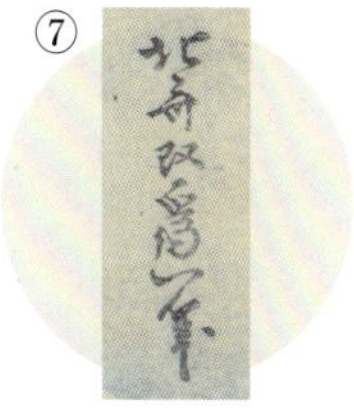

北斎改為一筆
Hokusai *aratame*
Iitsu *hitsu*
12-1

いいつ
為一（⑦, ⑧）Iitsu（⑦, ⑧）
文政3～天保5年（1820～34）61～75歳
1820–1834, aged 61-75

⑧
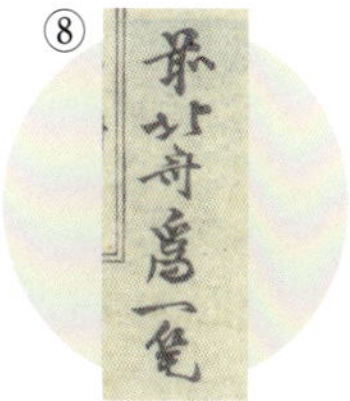

前北斎為一筆
Sakino Hokusai Iitsu *hitsu*
12-3

70代半ば～90歳　In His Mid-Seventies to Ninety

⑨
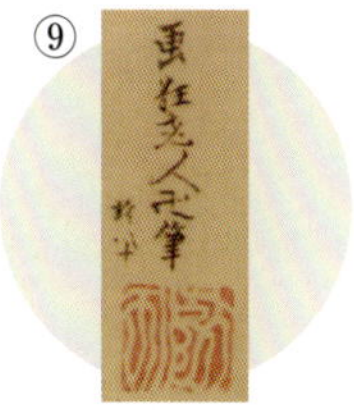

画狂老人卍筆
齢八十
Gakyō Rōjin 卍 *hitsu*
yowai hachiju
14-3

がきょうろうじんまんじ
画狂老人卍（⑨, ⑩）
Gakyō Rōjin 卍（⑨, ⑩）
天保5～嘉永2年（1834～49）75～90歳
1834–1849, aged 75-90

⑩
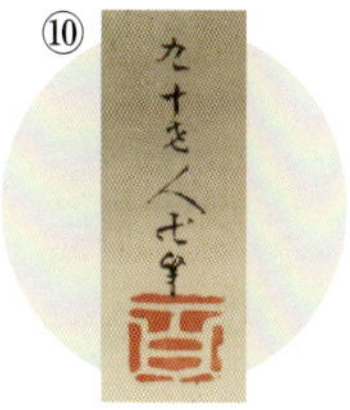

九十老人卍筆「百」
Kyūjū Rōjin 卍 *hitsu*
"Hyaku"
14-5

25

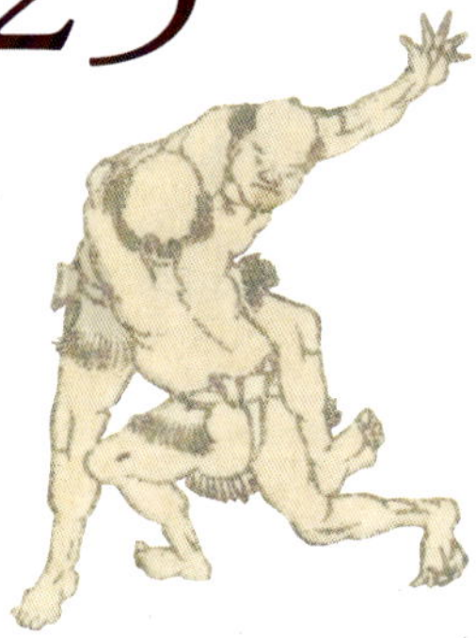

Name Chosen from Faith in Myōken
「北斎」の由来は妙見信仰

Religious Belief
信仰心

北斎の主要な画号のひとつである「北斎辰政」は、北斎が妙見菩薩を信仰していたことに由来しています(『北斎伝』)。妙見菩薩とは北極星あるいは北斗七星を神格化した天部の仏のことで、北極星を北辰ということにちなんで、北斎は「北斎辰政」と名乗りました(図25-1)。「戴斗」という画号も、斗＝北斗七星を戴くということに由来していると考えられます。

現在の東京都墨田区業平5丁目にある、日蓮宗の法性寺という寺の境内に、妙見菩薩を祀る柳島妙見堂がありました。北斎はこの柳島妙見堂にお礼参りをする途中、雷が落ちるのに遭遇して田んぼに落ち、その頃から名声を得るようになったという逸話が伝えられています(『北斎伝』)。

また、北斎は日蓮宗に帰依しており、池上本門寺や堀之内妙法寺には、時々参詣していたといいます(『北斎伝』)。常に法華経の普賢品の呪文を唱えており、そうしながら道を歩く時は、知り合いにあっても気が付かないほど集中していました(『北斎伝』)。自宅には、蜜柑箱を柱に打ち付け、その中に日蓮の像を祀っており(図20-1)、日蓮を描いた作品もいくつか制作しています。

ただし、北斎の墓がある誓教寺(→84頁参照)は、日蓮宗ではなく浄土宗の寺です。

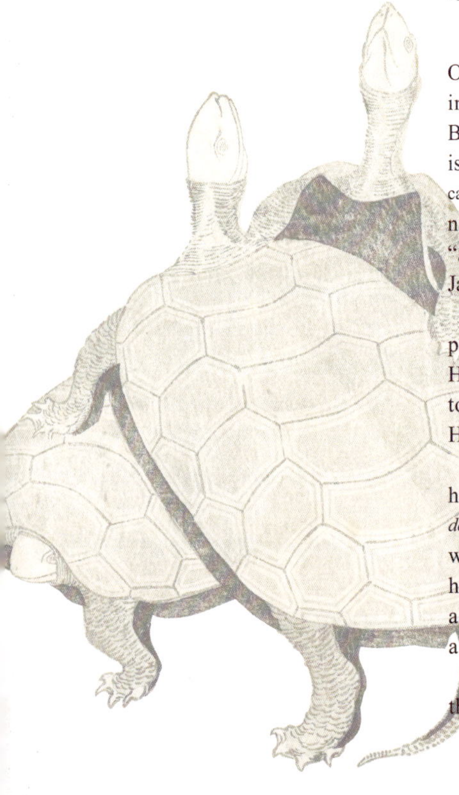

One of Hokusai's main artist names, "Hokusai Tokimasa," derives from his faith in the Buddhist deity Myōken Bosatsu (*Hokusai-den*). Myōken Bosatsu is a celestial Buddha regarded a deification of the North Star or the Big Dipper. As the North Star is also known as Hokushin, Hokusai used the two characters "*hoku*" and "*shin* (which can also be read *toki*)" and signed himself as "Hokusai Tokimasa" (fig. 25-1). The artist name "Taito" would also appear to derive from the Big Dipper as the character for "*tai*" means to receive and "*to*" is the second character in "Hokutoshichisei," the Japanese name for the Big Dipper.

In the precincts of Hosshou Temple of the Nichiren sect, which is located in the present Narihira 5-chōme, Sumida-ku, Tokyo, there was Yanagishima Myouken Hall, where Myōken Bosatsu was enshrined. There is an anecdote that on his way to visiting this Yanagishima Myouken Hall to offer thanks, lightning struck and Hokusai fell into a rice paddy, after which he gained fame (*Hokusai-den*).

Hokusai was a devout believer in the Nichiren sect of Buddhism and is said to have paid occasional visits to Ikegami Honmon-ji and Horinouchi Myōhō-ji (*Hokusai-den*). He constantly recited an incantation in the *Fugenhon* of the Lotus Sutra, even while walking on the street. On such occasions, he was so focused on chanting that he would walk by without noticing an acquaintance (*Hokusai-den*). At home, he nailed a tangerine box to the pillar, in which he enshrined a statue of Nichiren (fig. 20-1). He also did paintings of Nichiren.

Seikyō-ji, the temple where Hokusai's grave is located (see p. 84), is not a temple of the Nichiren sect but of the Jōdo sect.

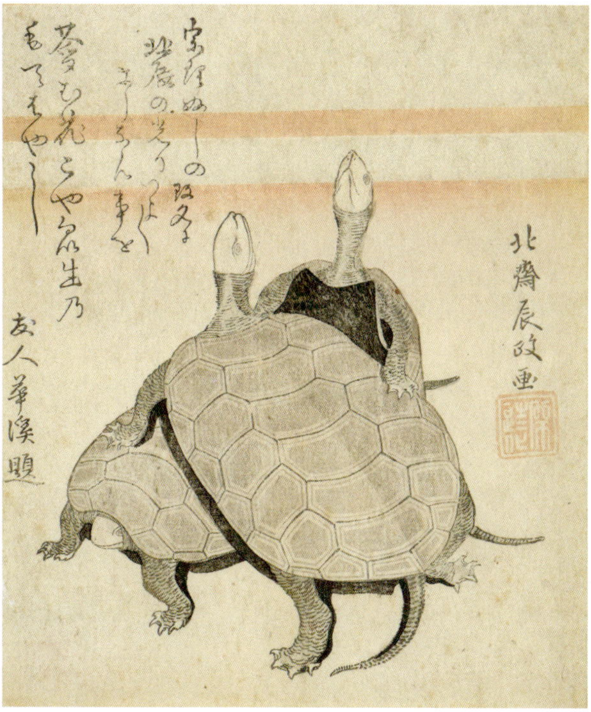

25-1 葛飾北斎 **亀図**（かめず）

寛政10年（1798）　色紙判摺物

島根県立美術館（永田コレクション）蔵

北斎が宗理から北斎辰政に改名した際、それを友人たちに知らせるために配った摺物です。書家の稲葉華溪（いなばかけい）が、「宗理ぬしの改名に北辰の光いよいよましなん事を」と、北辰（北極星）の光が増して北斎がこれからも活躍するようにという賛を記しています。

25-1 Katsushika Hokusai

Three Terrapins

1798, *shikishiban surimono*, Shimane Art Museum (Nagata Collection)

This is a *surimono* (single-sheet woodblock print) Hokusai distributed to his friends in order to announce his change of name from Sōri to Hokusai Tokimasa. The calligrapher Inaba Kakei inscribed a panegyric reading, “May the light of Hokushin glow all the more on the occasion of Sōri’s change of name.” Hokushin is another name for the North Star and consists of the characters Hokusai chose for his new name. Thus, it is a wish for Hokusai’s continued success.

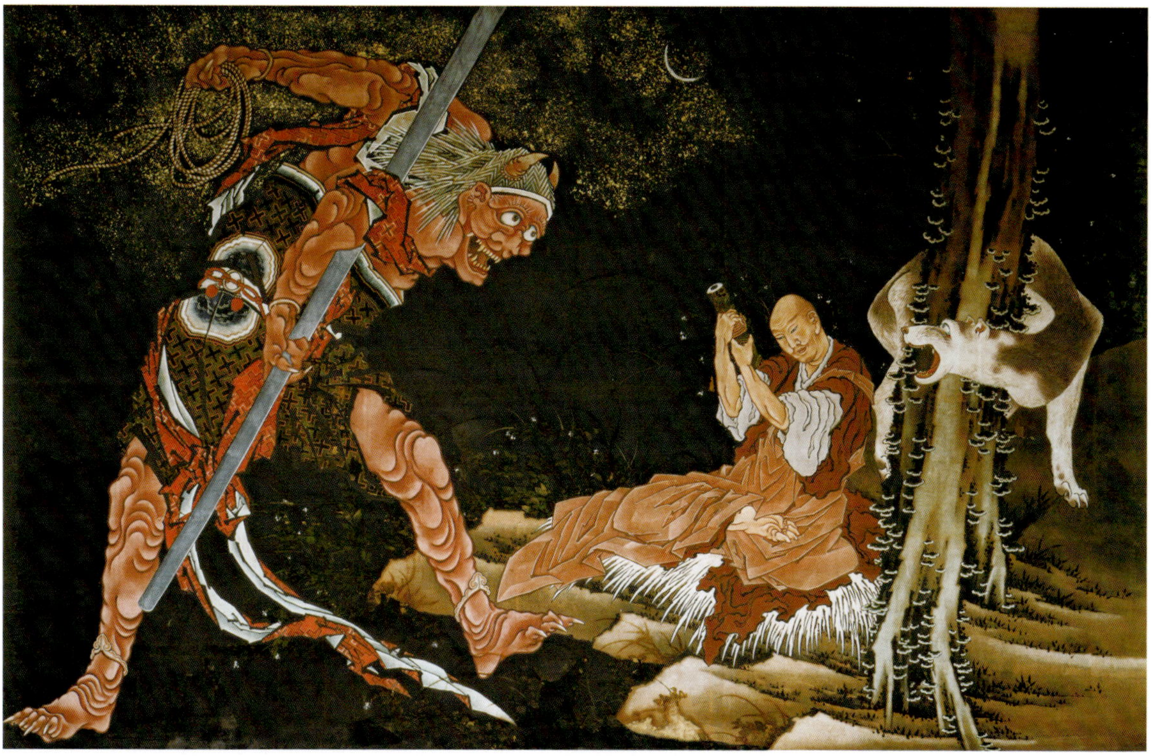

25-2 葛飾北斎 **弘法大師修法図**（こうぼうだいししゅうほうず）

弘化年間（1844～48）　紙本着色　西新井大師總持寺蔵

北斎は日蓮宗以外の仏教絵画も描きました。本図は、弘法大師（空海）が西新井の地を訪れた際、鬼の姿で描かれた病魔を法力でもって調伏し、疫病の流行を鎮めたという、西新井大師の縁起を題材にしています。

25-2 Katsushika Hokusai

The Priest Kōbō Daishi Exorcising a Demon

1844–1848, color on paper, Nishiarai Daishi Soji-ji

Hokusai did Buddhist paintings related to sects other than the Nichiren sect, too. In this painting, the subject matter is the foundation of the temple Nishiarai Daishi.When Kōbō Daishi (Kūkai) visited Nishiarai, he exorcised the demon of ill health with the power of Buddhist dharma and got the epidemic under control.

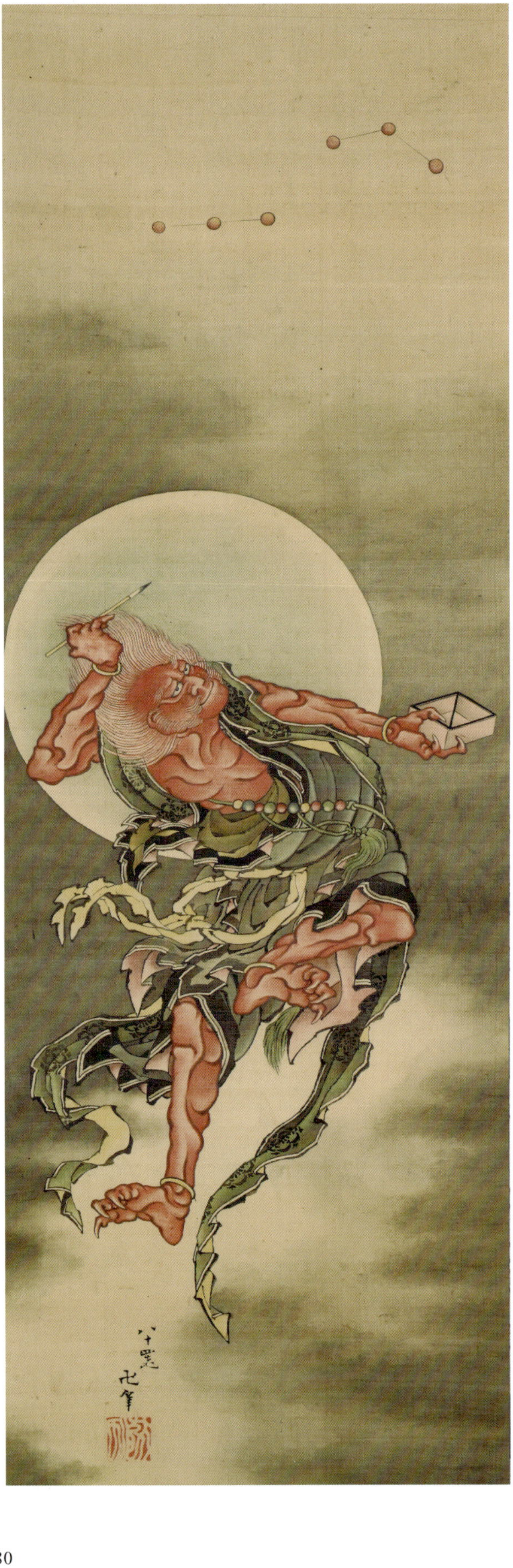

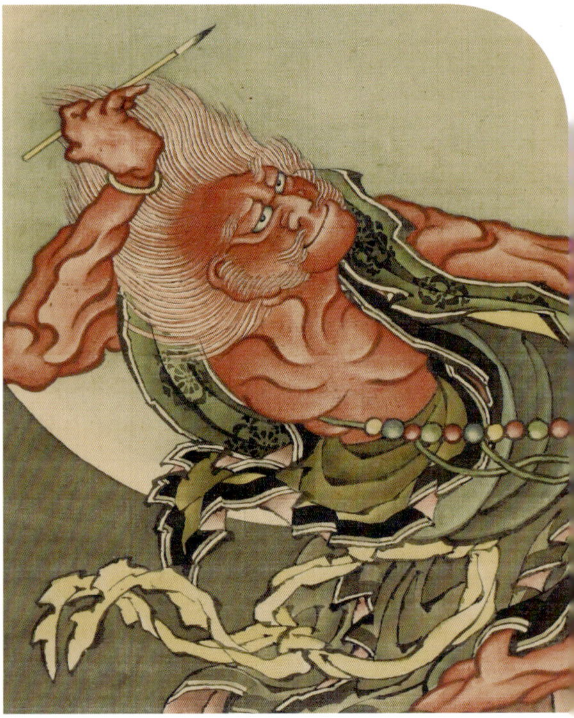

25-3 葛飾北斎

文昌星図

天保14年（1843）　絹本着色　島根県立美術館（永田コレクション）蔵

文昌星は北斗七星第一の星のこと。文学を司る神とされ、右手に筆、左手に升を持っています。また、天空上部には六星が配されています。北斗信者である北斎だけに、力強い、神秘的な画面となっています。

25-3 Katsushika Hokusai

Bunshōsei

1843, color on silk, Shimane Art Museum (Nagata Collection)

Bunshōsei refers to the first star of the Big Dipper. It is regarded the god of literature holding a writing brush in the right hand and a measuring cup in the left hand. Six stars are depicted higher up in the sky. Reflecting Hokusai's belief in the Big Dipper, it is a powerful and mystical painting.

Column

金銭にこだわりなし 経済感覚

Nonchalant about Money: Sense of Economy

北斎の制作量の多さを考えれば、さぞかしたくさんの収入があったと思うかも知れません。実際、北斎の画料は高かったようです。絵本を１丁描くにあたり、通常の絵師であれば金２朱のところ、北斎はその倍となる金1分をもらっていました（『北斎伝』）。

では、北斎が裕福な暮らしをしていたかといえば、そのようなことはありません。着る物に困るほど、貧乏な暮らしをしていました。手元にお金がないため、版元に画料の前借をお願いする手紙を送ったりすることもありました。

北斎が貧乏だった理由には、経済感覚の欠如があるようです。『北斎伝』によれば、貰った画料を袋から出さずに机の上に放って置き、商人たちが集金に来ると、額を確認せずに袋ごと渡していたそうです。貯金をしたり裕福な暮らしをしたりということに全く興味がなく、絵を描くことが第一であったのでしょう。

このような逸話もあります[1]。オランダの商館長（カピタン）から男女の生涯を描いた絵巻物を依頼された際、カピタン付きの医者からも同様の注文を受けました。完成した絵巻物を持っていくと、カピタンからは約束通りの金を貰いますが、医者からは半額に値切られます。北斎は医者の無理に従うのは日本の恥になると考え、絵巻物を渡さずに持ち帰ってしまいました。たとえ一文にならなくても、絵師としてのプライドが北斎にとっては大事だったのです。

1) 朝岡興禎編『古画備考』嘉永３年（1850）起筆

Judging from the magnitude of the works Hokusai produced, he would certainly appear to have earned a lot of money. Indeed, it seems that his works were costly. Whereas a standard artist charged two gold *shu* for a picture book, Hokusai asked for double that price, one gold *bu* (*Hokusai-den*).

Thus, Hokusai would appear to have been well-off, but that was not the case. He was so badly off that he was in need of clothing. He even sent a letter to his publisher requesting an advance on a commission for a painting as he did not have any cash on hand.

It seems that Hokusai owed his poverty to his sense of economy. According to *Hokusai-den*, he left the commission he received for a painting in its envelope without checking the amount enclosed, and when a merchant came to collect his bills, he would hand over the envelope without checking the contents. He had no interest whatsoever in saving money or leading an affluent life. Drawing pictures was his prime concern.

There is also an anecdote about when Hokusai was asked to do a picture scroll of men's and women's lives by a Dutch *kapitan*. Hokusai also received a similar commission from the *kapitan's* doctor. When he delivered the finished works, the *kapitan* gave him the money he had promised, but the doctor tried to bargain the price down to half the initial amount. Believing that giving in to the doctor would disgrace Japan, Hokusai took the picture scroll home without handing it over to the doctor. Even if he could not earn a single penny, to Hokusai, his pride as an artist was more important.

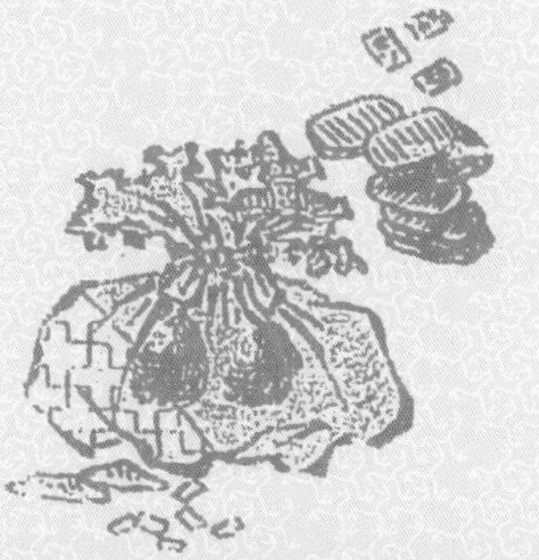

※葛飾北斎『北斎漫画』三編（国立国会図書館蔵）より作成。
From *Hokusai's Sketches*, part 3 (National Diet Library, Japan)

26

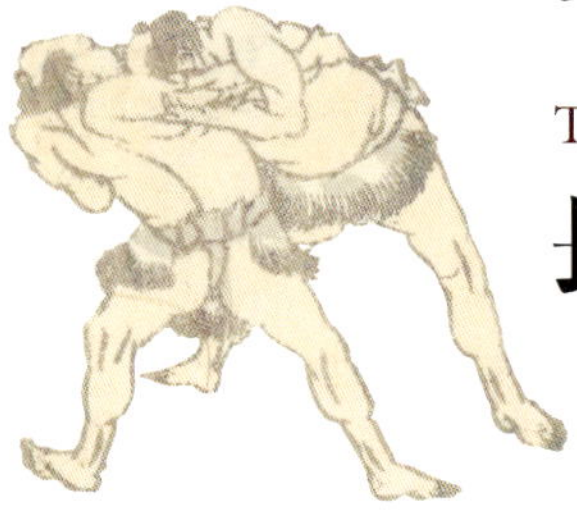

Home Remedies?
手作りの薬の力？
The Secret of Longevity
長寿の秘訣

北斎は90歳まで長生きしましたが、同時期に活躍した浮世絵師たち、例えば、渓斎英泉が58歳、歌川広重が62歳、歌川国芳が65歳と還暦前後でその多くが亡くなっています。長生きとされた歌川国貞にしても没年は79歳です。

北斎は、名立たる浮世絵師たちの中で最も長寿であっただけでなく、亡くなる直前まで絵筆を握るほどの健康を維持していました（図26-1）。北斎が87歳頃、眼鏡もかけず、背も屈んでおらず、雨の中を西両国から日本橋まで行き来しても平気だったことを、笠亭仙果が手紙に記しています[1)]。

その秘訣として、北斎が宮本慎助に贈った「日新除魔図」（図19-1）の中に、焼酎に龍眼と砂糖を入れたものを60日置いて、朝晩猪口で2杯ずつ飲めば長寿の薬になると、北斎自身が記したものが貼り込まれています（図26-2）。しかし、絵を描きたいという情熱こそが北斎の健康を支えていたのではないでしょうか。北斎は80歳を過ぎた年齢にも関わらず、自分は猫一匹も満足に描くことができないと溜息をついたといいます（『北斎伝』）。その年齢になっても画技を研鑽しようという真摯な姿勢が、生きる活力となったのでしょう。

ちなみに北斎は、68～69歳の頃、中風、すなわち脳卒中を患いました。柚子を使った薬を自ら作り、元のように回復したといいますが（『北斎伝』）、もしこの時に運悪く亡くなっていたとしたら、「冨嶽三十六景」（→48頁参照）は誕生していませんでした。だとするならば、北斎の現在における評価は大きく変わっていたことでしょう。

1) 土山節子「笠亭仙果の書簡にみえる北斎晩年のおもかげ」『日本歴史』150号、1960年

Compared to Hokusai, who lived to the great age of 90, many of the other *ukiyo-e* artists who were active during the same period passed away at around 60 years old. For example, Keisai Eisen died at the age of 58, Utagawa Hiroshige at 62, and Utagawa Kuniyoshi at 65. Even Utagawa Kunisada, who is considered to have lived a long life, died aged 79.

Not only was Hokusai the most long-lived among noted *ukiyo-e* artists but he remained healthy enough to continue painting until immediately before his death (fig. 26-1). A letter written by Ryūtei Senka describes how Hokusai, at around age 87, thought nothing of going back and forth between Nishiryōgoku and Nihombashi in the rain without spectacles and without stooping.

The secret of such longevity is described by Hokusai himself in *Daily Exorcisms* (fig. 19-1), which he gave to Miyamoto Shinsuke. In it, Hokusai writes, if you put longan and sugar in *shōchū*, leave it for sixty days, and drink two *sake* cupsful of it every morning and night, it works for longevity (fig. 26-2). However, in Hokusai's case, it was probably his enthusiasm to draw pictures that supported his health. Despite being over 80 years old, Hokusai is said to have sighed that he could not draw even a single cat properly (*Hokusai-den*). His sincere attitude to devote himself, at that age, to studying drawing techniques must have been what gave him the vitality to live on.

When Hokusai was around 68 or 69, he suffered paralysis, that is to say, a stroke. He is said to have made his own medicine with *yuzu*, a citron, and recovered (*Hokusai-den*). If he had unluckily died on that occasion, *Thirty-six Views of Mount Fuji* (see p. 48) would not have been created. In that case, no doubt Hokusai's present fame would have changed considerably.

ふじごしりゅうず
26-1 葛飾北斎 **富士越龍図**

嘉永2年（1849） 絹本淡彩 北斎館蔵

「嘉永二己酉年 正月辰ノ日 宝暦十庚辰ノ年出生 九十老人卍筆」との落款があることから、制作日が嘉永２年１月11日か23日であることが明らかとなる貴重な作例です。亡くなる約３カ月前でも、さらなる高みを目指そうという北斎の気概が感じられます。

26-1 Katsushika Hokusai

Dragon Rising above Mount Fuji

1849, wash on silk, Hokusai Museum

This is a rare example in which the signature reveals that it was painted on the eleventh or twenty-third day of the first month of 1849 by the old man Manji, 90 years of age, born in 1760. Even three or so months before his death, Hokusai was still full of mettle in pursuit of further eminence.

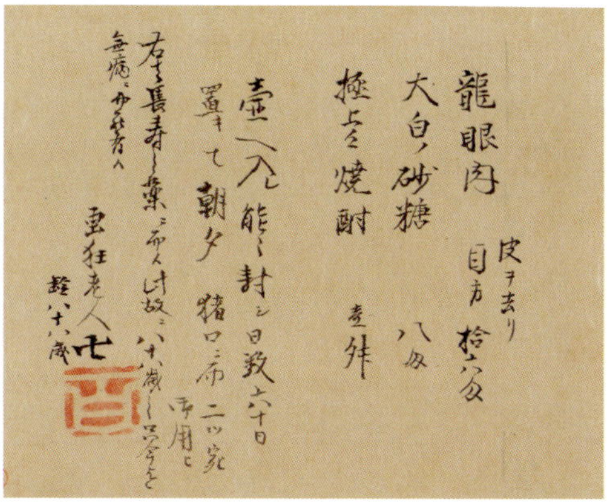

撮影：落合晴彦 Photo by Ochiai Haruhiko

26-2 葛飾北斎

ちょうじゅのくすりちょうごうほう
長寿之薬調合法

弘化4年（1847） 紙本墨書 九州国立博物館蔵 重要文化財

北斎はこの長寿の薬によって、88歳の今まで病気をせずに過ごせたと記しています。「日新除魔図」（図19-1）の画帖に収録。

26-2 Katsushika Hokusai

How to Compound an Elixir of Life

1847, ink on paper, Kyushu National Museum, Important Cultural Property

Hokusai writes that this elixir of life enabled him to live to the present age of 88 without any health problems. It is included in his sketchbook of "Daily Exorcisms"(fig.19-1).

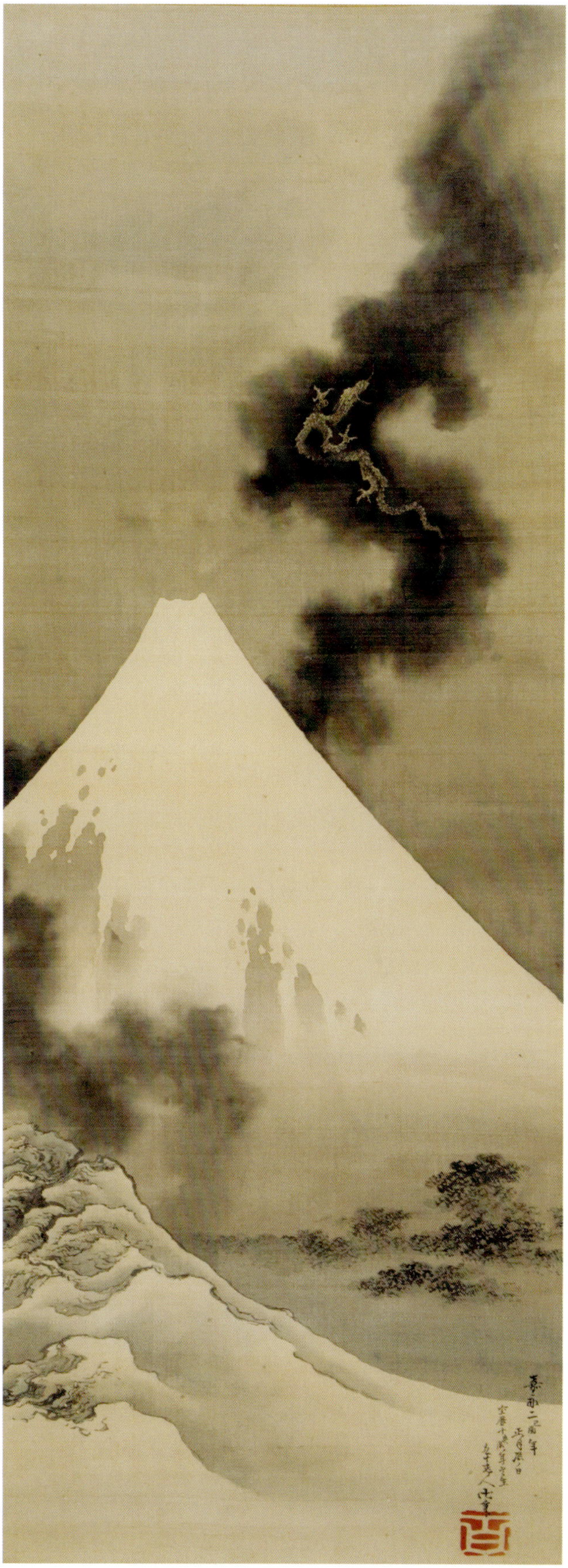

27 The Old Man Mad about Drawing Rests in Asakusa

画狂老人の魂、浅草に眠る

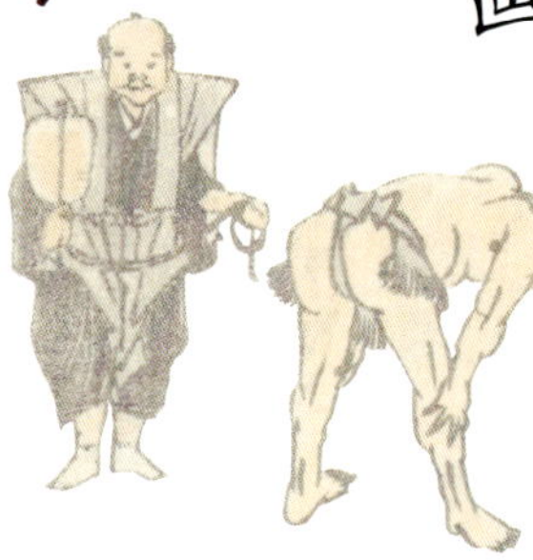

Deathbed and Grave

死に際と墓

北斎は、嘉永2年(1849)、90歳という年齢でありながら精力的に活動しており、12点もの肉筆画の現存が確認されています[1)]。しかし、ついに病にかかり、4月18日午前4時頃、浅草聖天町にある遍照院(東京都台東区浅草6丁目)の境内にあった長屋で、その生涯を閉じます。北斎は亡くなる直前、大きく息をして「天我をして十年の命を長ふせしめは(あと10年生きられれば)」と言い、しばらくして「天我をして五年の命を保たしめは、真正の画工となるを得へし(5年生きられれば本当の絵師になれるのに)」という言葉を残し、帰らぬ人となったといいます(『北斎伝』)。

翌4月19日に葬式が行なわれ、誓教寺(東京都台東区元浅草4丁目)という浄土宗の寺に葬られました。誓教寺の過去帳によれば、北斎の戒名は「南牕院奇誉北斎居士」といいます。現在、誓教寺には、「画狂老人卍墓」と刻まれた北斎の墓がありますが、この墓は北斎が亡くなった際のものではなく、北斎の曾孫である加瀬祟次郎(ちょうじろう)(→63頁参照)により、明治に入ってから建造されたものです。

ちなみに、現在でも、北斎の命日である4月18日になると、誓教寺において「北斎忌」という追悼法要が行われています。

1) ティモシー・クラーク「逆順で語る晩年の北斎」『北斎—富士を越えて—』(展覧会図録)、あべのハルカス美術館、2017年

In 1849, despite being aged 90, Hokusai continued working vigorously and the existence of as many as twelve original paintings can be confirmed. However, in the end, he fell ill and at around four in the morning on the eighteenth day of the fourth month, his life came to a close in a tenement house within the precincts of Henjō-in, a temple in Asakusa 6-chōme (Sumida-ku, Tokyo). Just before passing away, he is said to have commented, "If only I could have lived for ten more years," and, after a while, continued, "If only I could have lived for five more years, I would have become a true artist." With that, he was never to return (*Hokusai-den*).

Hokusai's funeral was held the following day, on the nineteenth day of the fourth month, and he was buried in Seikyō-ji, a temple of the Jōdo sect in Motoasakusa 4-chōme (Sumida-ku, Tokyo). According to the death register at Seikyō-ji, Hokusai's posthumous Buddhist name is "Nansōin Kiyo Hokusai Koji." Nowadays, Hokusai's grave in Seikyō-ji is inscribed "Grave of an Old Man Mad about Drawing" but it does not date from Hokusai's time. It was erected by Hokusai's great-grandson, Kase Chojirō, (see p. 63) in the Meiji era (1868-1912).

Even today, on April 18, the anniversary of Hokusai's death, "Hokusai-ki," a memorial service, is held at Seikyō-ji.

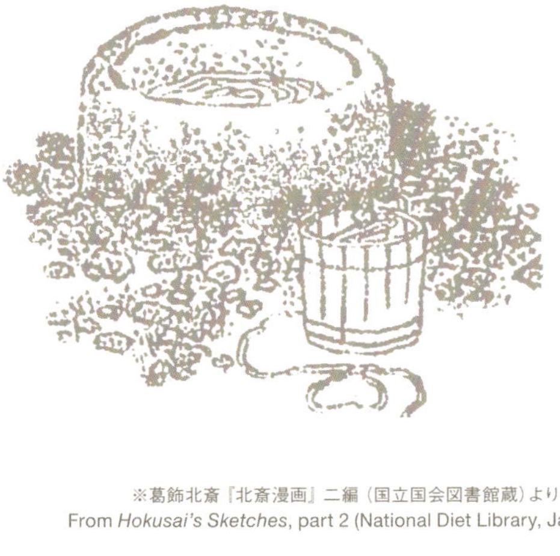

※葛飾北斎『北斎漫画』二編(国立国会図書館蔵)より作成。
From *Hokusai's Sketches*, part 2 (National Diet Library, Japan)

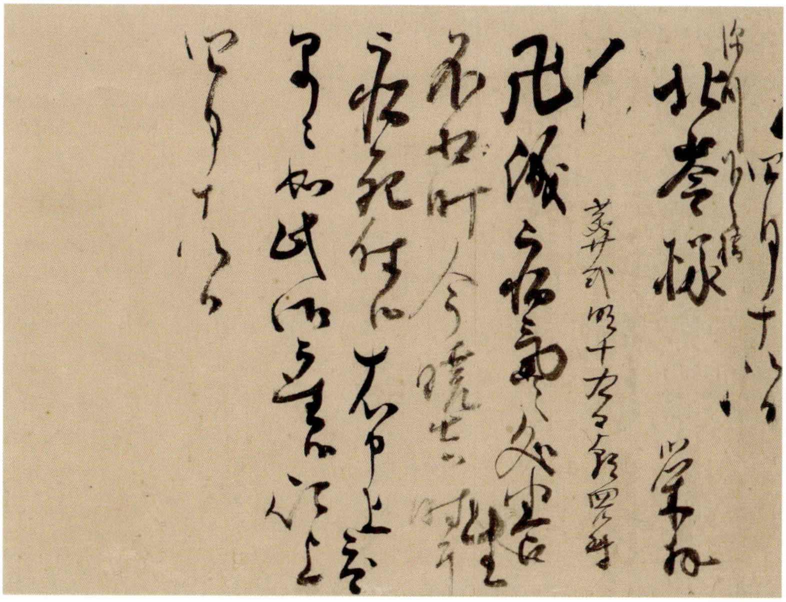

27-1 葛飾応為 **北斎死亡通知書**

嘉永2年(1849)　紙本墨書　島根県立美術館
(永田コレクション・府川家資料)蔵

娘の応為が、北斎の門人である府川北岑に宛てた北斎の死亡通知書。卍（北斎）は病気で養生していましたがかなわず、今朝4時ごろに病死しました。葬式は明日19日の午前10時ごろに執り行いますと記されています。

27-1 Katsushika Ōi
Announcement of Hokusai's Death
1849, ink on paper, Shimane Art Museum (Nagata Collection, Fukawa Family Materials)

This is an announcement of Hokusai's death written by his daughter Ōi and addressed to Hokusai's disciple Fukawa Hokushin. It reads, "Although 卍 (Hokusai) was recuperating from an illness, he died around four o'clock this morning. The funeral will take place at around ten a.m. tomorrow, on the nineteenth."

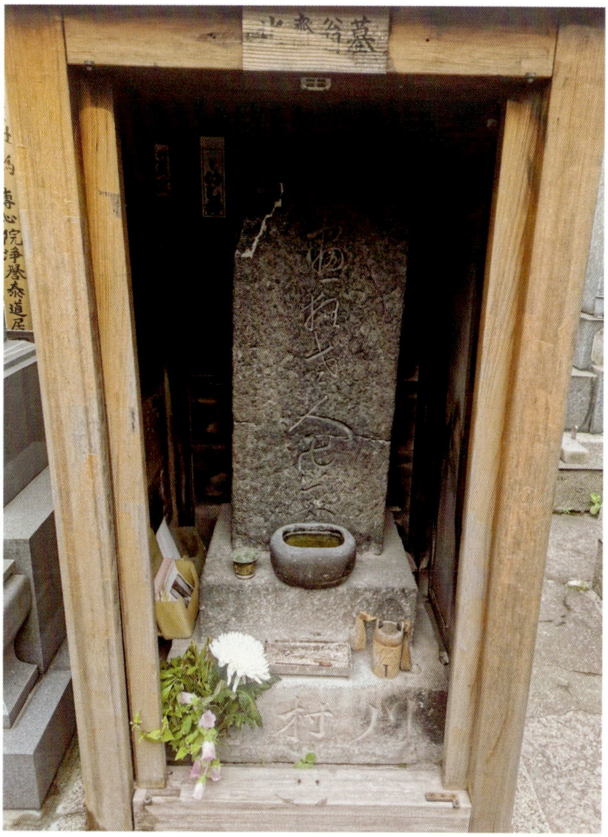

27-2 **葛飾北斎の墓**
誓教寺

墓の右側面には
「飛と魂でゆくきさんじや夏の原　行年九十」
という北斎の辞世の句が刻まれています。

27-2 **Katsushika Hokusai's grave**
Seikyō-ji, Tokyo

Hokusai's farewell poem, "Disembodied as a spirit, I shall lightly roam the summer fields. Died at the age of 90." is inscribed on the right-hand side of the grave.

28

Master Portraitist of Actors and Beauties

役者絵と肉筆美人画の名手

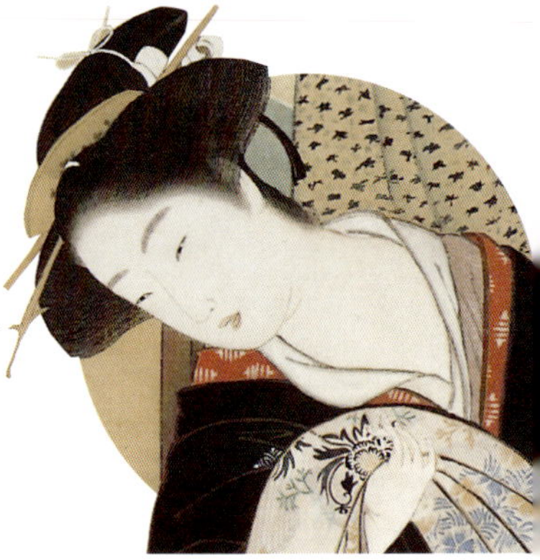

Hokusai's Teacher Katsukawa Shunshō

師匠・勝川春章

北斎が浮世絵師を目指してその門を叩いたのが勝川春章です（→14頁参照）。近年、勝川春章の生年について、通説よりも17歳若返り、寛保3年（1743）であることが指摘されました[1]。すなわち、北斎が19歳で入門した時、春章は36歳。北斎にとって、父親よりもやや若いくらいの年齢差でした。

春章は、明和5年（1768）頃から、歌舞伎役者の顔をそっくりに描くという新機軸を試みます（図28-1）。それによって、伝統的な鳥居派の役者絵をしのぐ人気を獲得し、役者絵界の第一人者となりました。次世代の東洲斎写楽（→90頁参照）や歌川豊国の登場を準備したという面でも、春章は浮世絵の歴史に重要な功績を残した絵師といえるでしょう。

さらに春章は、天明3年（1783）頃から肉筆による美人画の制作に精力を注ぎ始めます。版画とは趣きの異なる優雅な美人画は、細部に至るまで丁寧な彩色をしている点が特徴です（図28-2）。春朗時代、北斎は肉筆美人画をほとんど制作していませんが、後に肉筆美人画を手がける中で（→20頁参照）、春章から学んだことは大きな糧になっていたことでしょう。

ちなみに、春章には春好、春英、春潮といった多くの門人がいますが、北斎は、兄弟子の勝川春好とは大変に仲が悪く、北斎が勝川派を離脱した理由のひとつに数えられています。北斎の門人である露木孔彰によれば（『北斎伝』）、北斎が描いた絵草紙問屋の看板を見た春好が、出来の悪さを笑い、北斎の面前で引き裂いて打ち捨てました。北斎はその場は耐え忍びますが、いつか世界一の絵師になって見返してやると心の中で誓います。北斎は晩年、自分の腕が上達したのは、春好が自分を辱めたからだと語っていたそうです。

1） 神谷勝広「勝川春章伝記小考」『浮世絵芸術』173号、2017年

Aiming to become an *ukiyo-e* artist, Hokusai became a pupil of Katsukawa Shunshō (see p. 14). Recent studies have revealed that Katsukawa Shunshō was born in 1743, seventeen years earlier than the hitherto commonly accepted birthdate. That is to say, when Hokusai became Shunshō's pupil, Hokusai was aged 19 and Shunshō 36. In terms of age difference, to Hokusai, Shunshō would have been slightly younger than his father.

From around 1768, Shunshō struck out in a new direction of portraying exact images of *kabuki* actors' faces (fig. 28-1). They proved more popular than the traditional prints of *kabuki* actors produced by the Torii school and Shunshō became the foremost authority in that genre. He also rendered distinguished achievements in the history of *ukiyo-e* by preparing the emergence of the next generation, namely Tōshūsai Sharaku (see p. 90) and Utagawa Toyokuni.

From around 1783, Shunshō began putting his energy into the production of original paintings of beauties. These elegant *bijinga* (pictures of beauties) had a charm different from prints and featured elaborate coloring attentive to the details (fig. 28-2). There are hardly any original paintings of beauties by Hokusai dating from the period during which he used the artist name Shunrō. However, when working on original paintings of beauties later on (see p. 20), what he learned from Shunshō definitely would have proved useful.

Shunshō had many pupils such as Shunkō, Shun'ei, and Shunchō. Hokusai did not get on with Katsukawa Shunkō, a senior pupil, and their discord is counted as one of the reasons that Hokusai seceded from the Katsukawa school. According to Tsuyuki Kōshō, who was Hokusai's pupil (*Hokusai-den*), when Shunkō came across a print wholesaler's signboard produced by Hokusai. he laughed at the poor craftsmanship and pulled it to pieces before Hokusai. Although Hokusai endured that incident, he vowed to himself that one day he would become the greatest artist in the world and put Shunkō to shame. Late in life, Hokusai is said to have mentioned that it was because Shunkō humiliated him that he became so competent.

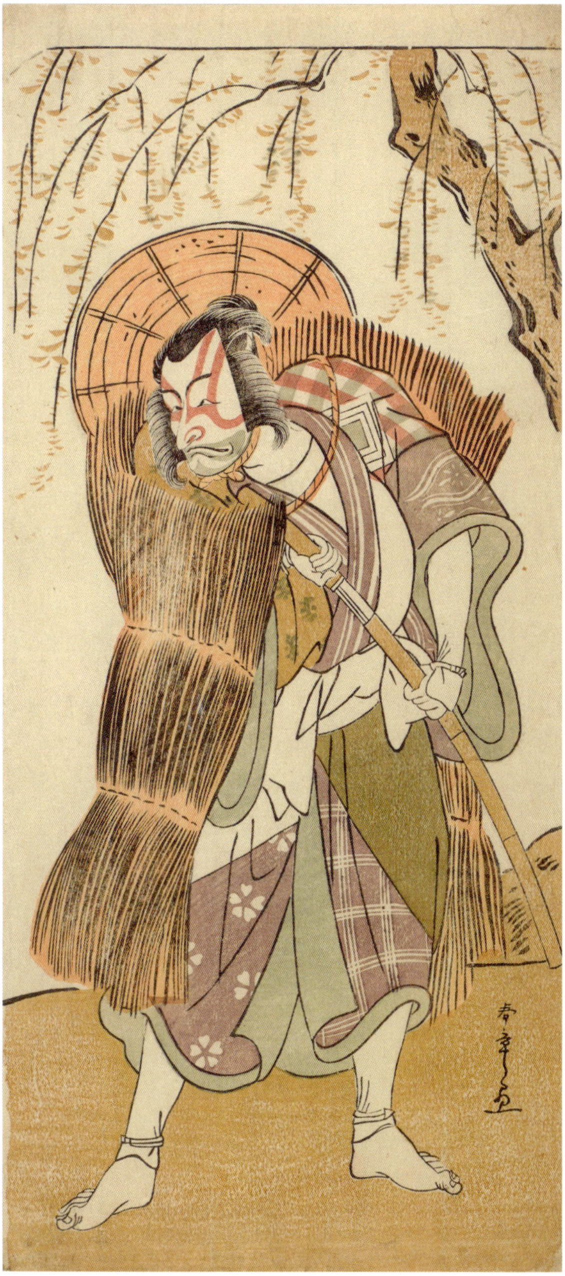

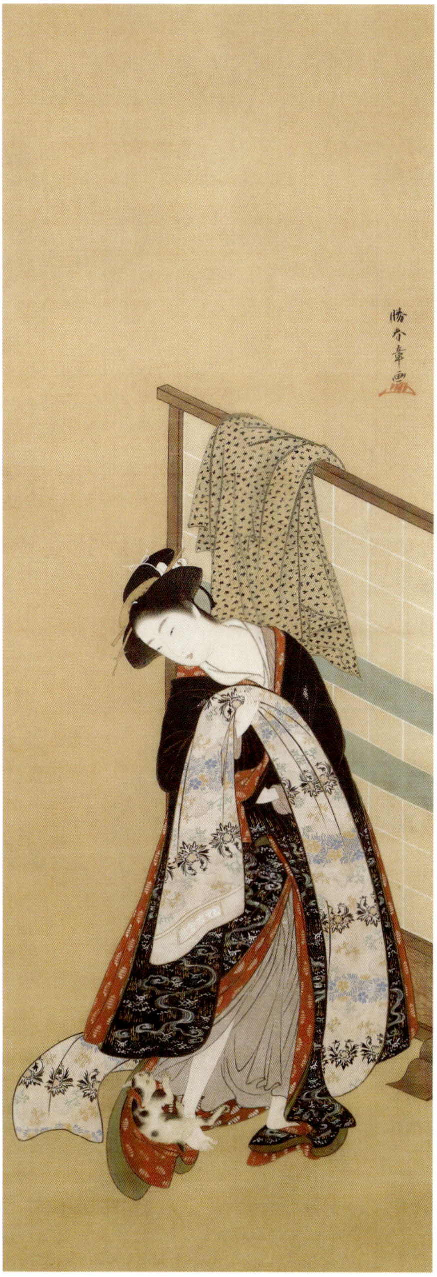

28-1 勝川春章

ごだいめいちかわだんじゅうろう　あくしちびょうえかげきよ

五代目市川団十郎の悪七兵衛景清

安永5年(1776)　細判錦絵　太田記念美術館蔵

春章以前の鳥居派の役者絵では、役者名や配役名を記載するのがほとんどでしたが、春章の役者絵ではそれらが記載されず、似顔絵だけで判断されるようになりました。また、役者たちの体の動きを写実的に捉えようとする意識も高まっています。

28-1 Katsukawa Shunshō

The Actor Ichikawa Danjūrō V as Akushichibyōe Kagekiyo

1776, *hosoban nishiki-e*, Ōta Memorial Museum of Art

The actor's name and the part he was playing were recorded in most of the actor prints by the Torii school prior to Shunshō. In Shunshō's works, there was no mention and they were to be judged from the likeness. There was also more attention paid to capturing the movements of the actor's body realistically.

28-2 勝川春章

こねこ　びじんず

子猫に美人図

安永9～天明2年(1780～82)頃　絹本着色　太田記念美術館蔵

春章の肉筆美人画は、錦絵と異なり、上等な絵具を使って、着物の模様の細部まで丁寧に描写されています。このような緻密な彩色の手法は、北斎の肉筆美人画に明らかに受け継がれています。

28-2 Katsukawa Shunshō

A Kitten and a Woman

c. 1780–1782, color on silk, Ōta Memorial Museum of Art

Unlike his *nishiki-e* (poluychrome prints), Shunshō used high-quality pigments for his original paintings of beauties and painted the *kimono* pattern carefully in detail. This method of elaborate coloring was definitely inherited by Hokusai in his original paintings of beauties.

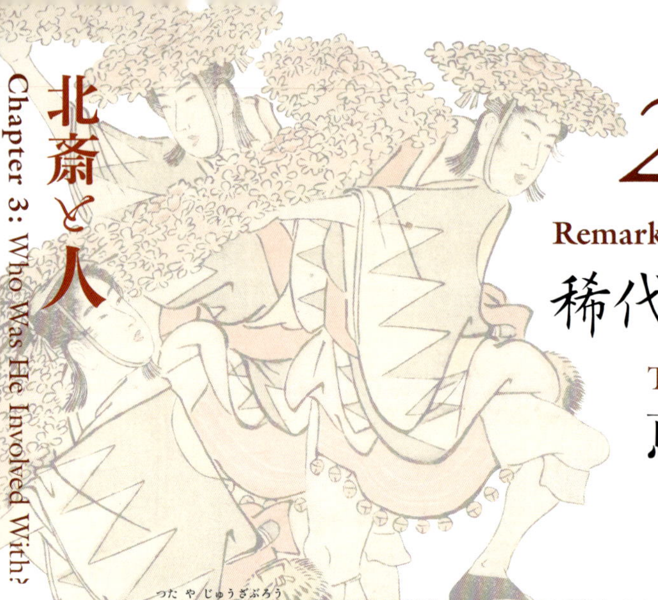

29

Remarkable Publisher and Producer

稀代の出版プロデューサー

Tsutaya Jūzaburō
蔦屋重三郎

蔦屋重三郎は出版物を制作・販売する版元ですが、喜多川歌麿や東洲斎写楽といった浮世絵師、あるいは、さまざまな戯作者たちの才能を発掘した名プロデューサーとしても知られています。

北斎が蔦屋重三郎の元から錦絵を刊行するのは、寛政元年（1789）、30歳頃以降のことです。子ども絵や役者絵、風俗画（図29-1）、黄表紙の挿絵などが確認でき、実力のある若手絵師としてそれなりの評価をされていたことでしょう。しかしこの頃、蔦屋重三郎が刊行した喜多川歌麿（→90頁参照）の美人大首絵が巷間で大評判になっていたことを考えると、蔦屋重三郎にとって北斎の存在はそれほど大きくなかったように思われます。

蔦屋重三郎が北斎を一目置く存在とみなすようになったのは、北斎が宗理号（→76頁参照）を襲名し、新たな画風を切り開いてからのことでしょう。その頃北斎は、『四方の巴流』や『柳の絲』（図4-1）といった蔦屋重三郎の元から刊行された狂歌絵本（→16頁参照）において、北尾重政や北尾政演（山東京伝）、鳥文斎栄之などの著名な絵師たちと共に挿絵を担当しています。

北斎がいよいよその個性を花開かせようとしていた寛政9年（1797）、蔦屋重三郎は48歳の若さで亡くなります。蔦屋重三郎は、その後の北斎の華々しい活躍を見ることが叶わなかったのです。ただし、版元としての蔦屋重三郎は番頭が二代目を継ぎ、北斎もさまざまな狂歌絵本（図4-2～5、29-2）や錦絵（図5-4）を蔦屋重三郎の元から刊行します。

Tsutaya Jūzaburō was a publisher who made and sold publications, but he is also known to have been active as a noted producer who discovered the talents of *ukiyo-e* artists such as Kitagawa Utamaro and Tōshūsai Sharaku and a variety of *gesaku* (popular fiction) writers.

It was in 1789, from when Hokusai turned 30 onwards, that his *nishiki-e* (polychrome prints) were published by Tsutaya Jūzaburō. Pictures of children and *kabuki* actors, genre scenes (fig. 29-1), *kibyōshi* (illustrated novels of comical content for adults bound in "yellow covers") illustrations, etc. by Hokusai are known to have been published by Tsutaya Jūzaburō, confirming that Hokusai was appreciated to a certain extent as a competent young artist. However, bearing in mind that the half-length portraits of beauties by Kitagawa Utamaro (see p. 90), which Tsutaya Jūzaburō published, created such a sensation, from Tsutaya Jūzaburō's point of view, Hokusai's existence probably was not so significant.

It was after Hokusai assumed the name Sōri (see p. 76) and cut open a new artistic style that Tsutaya Jūzaburō came to acknowledge Hokusai's superiority. In those days, together with prominent artists such as Kitao Shigemasa, Kitao Masanobu (Santō Kyōden), Chōbunsai Eishi, etc., Hokusai did illustrations for *kyōka* picture books (see p. 16) such as *Yomo no haru* and *Willow Tresses* (fig. 4-1), which were published by Tsutaya Jūzaburō.

In 1797, when Hokusai's originality was finally about to effloresce, Tsutaya Jūzaburō passed away at the young age of 48. Unfortunately, Tsutaya Jūzaburō did not live long enough to witness the brilliant work by Hokusai that followed. Nevertheless, Tsutaya Jūzaburō's head clerk took over as Tsutaya Jūzaburō II, from whom a variety of Hokusai's *kyōka* picture books (figs. 4-2~5, and 29-2) and *nishiki-e* (fig. 5-4) were published.

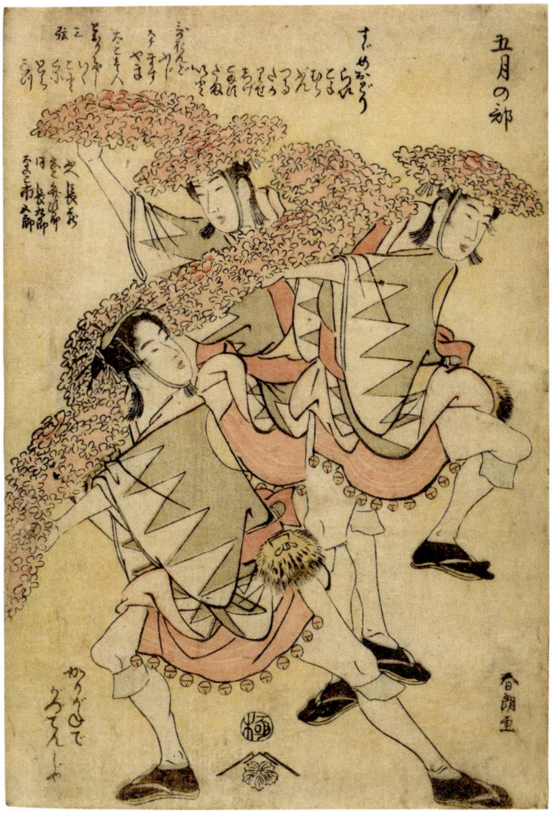

29-1 葛飾北斎　**五月の部　すずめおどり**

寛政3〜5年(1791〜93)頃　中判　島根県立美術館(永田コレクション)蔵

北斎がまもなく勝川派を離脱しようとする30代前半に描かれた作品です。吉原遊廓の俄狂言という年中行事を題材にした揃物で、参加している芸者たちの名前が列記されています。

29-1 Katsushika Hokusai

The Fifth Month: Sparrow Dance

c. 1791–1793, *chūban*, Shimane Art Museum (Nagata Collection)

Hokusai produced this in his early thirties, shortly before seceding from the Katsukawa school. It is part of a set of prints depicting *niwaka kyogen*, a farce held at the pleasure quarters of Yoshiwara as an annual event. The names of the *geisha* taking part are listed.

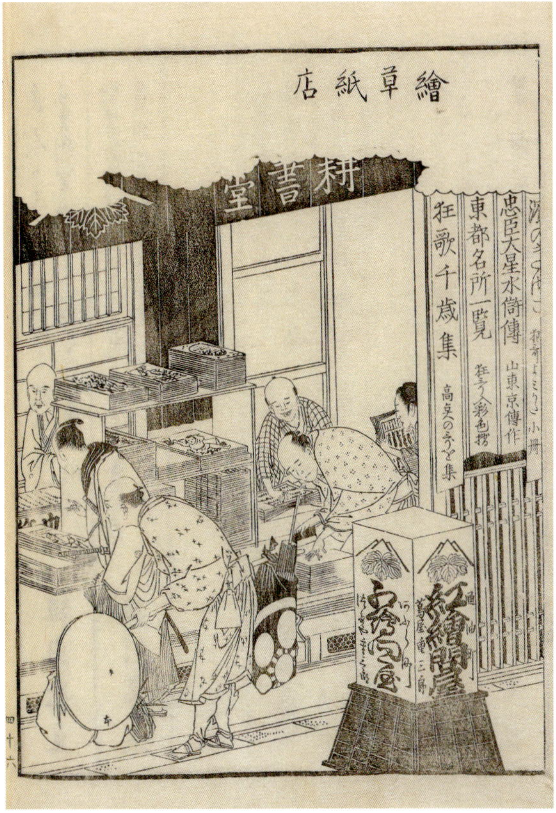

29-2 葛飾北斎『**東遊**』

寛政11年(1799)　大本　島根県立美術館(永田コレクション)蔵

本書の版元である耕書堂こと蔦屋重三郎の店先の様子を伝えています。場所は通油町、現在の東京都中央区日本橋大伝馬町にあたります。錦絵が山積みの状態で販売されており、客はそれを眺めて購入しました。店先には北斎が手掛けた『東都名所一覧』(図4-3)の宣伝も掲げられています。

29-2 Katsushika Hokusai ***Pleasures in the Eastern Capital***

1799, *ōhon*, Shimane Art Museum (Nagata Collection)

Portrayed here is the storefront of Kōshodō, Tsutaya Jūzaburō's shop, from which this book was published. It was located in Tōriaburachō, the present Nihombashi Ōdenmachō, Chuō-ku, Tokyo. *Nishiki-e* (polychrome prints) were stacked up for sale and customers could look at them before purchasing them. Hokusai's *Famous Places in Edo at a Glance* (fig. 4-3) is advertised at the storefront.

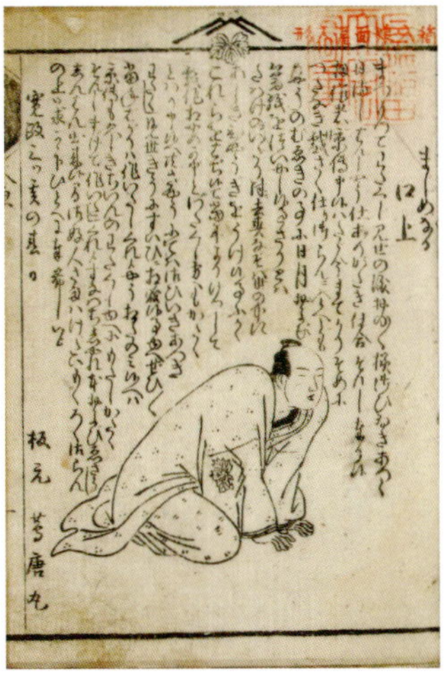

29-3 山東京伝作『**箱入娘面屋人魚**』

寛政3年(1791)　中本　早稲田大学図書館蔵

物語の冒頭、蔦屋重三郎の姿が描かれています。出版規制が強まる中、戯作の執筆に乗り気でなかった作者の山東京伝に、無理矢理頼み込んで書いてもらったという刊行の経緯を述べたものです。蔦屋重三郎の姿はこのような草双紙の中に時折登場しています。

29-3 Santō Kyōden ***Hakoiri musume men'ya ningyo***

1791, *chūhon*, Waseda University Library

Tsutaya Jūzaburō appears at the beginning of this story. There is an explanation on how the publisher forced Santō Kyōden, who was reluctant to write *gesaku* (popular fiction) at a time when publishing regulations were being tightened, to contribute a story. Tsutaya Jūzaburō is occasionally depicted in illustrated storybooks like this one.

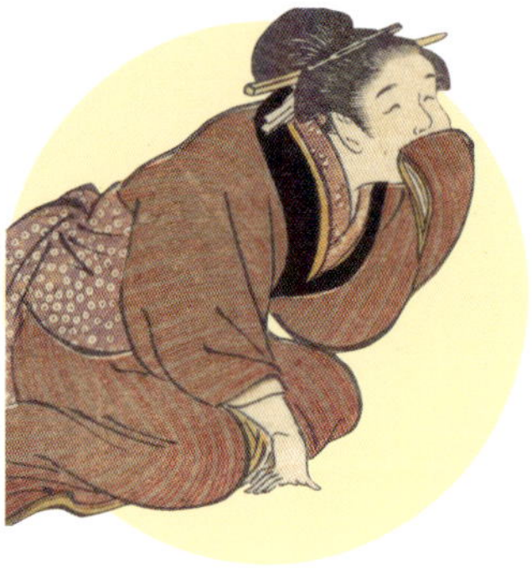

30

Celebrated Artists of the Same Generation
同世代の人気絵師たち

Kitagawa Utamaro and Tōshūsai Sharaku
喜多川歌麿と東洲斎写楽

浮世絵の歴史を眺めた時、喜多川歌麿と東洲斎写楽は、北斎よりも一世代前に位置づけられている印象があります。しかし、歌麿と写楽が巷間で話題となっていたのは北斎が30代の頃で、実は絵師としての活動時期は重なっているのです。

喜多川歌麿の生年は不詳ですが、北斎より10歳以上年上ということはないでしょう。歌麿は、寛政4年（1792）頃から蔦屋重三郎の元で刊行した、女性たちの上半身を大きく捉えた美人大首絵によって台頭しました。すでに北斎も蔦屋重三郎の元から錦絵を出しているので（→88頁参照）、歌麿の存在を知らないはずがありません。寛政期の北斎の美人画には歌麿からの影響を少なからず感じさせます（図29-1）。北斎と歌麿が個人的にどの程度の交流をしていたかは分かりませんが、狂歌絵本である『狂歌歳旦江戸紫』や『男踏歌』（図4-2、30-1）では挿絵を分担していました。

東洲斎写楽は、寛政6年（1794）5月、蔦屋重三郎の元から歌舞伎役者の大首絵を発表して話題を集めますが、翌年には突如姿を消した謎の絵師です。写楽が登場した年、北斎は勝川派から離れ、役者絵はもちろん錦絵の制作からも遠ざかっていました。写楽の正体は北斎であるという説を唱える研究者もいますが、現在、阿波の能役者である斎藤十郎兵衛であるという説が有力視されています。だとするならば、斎藤十郎兵衛の生年は宝暦13年（1763）。写楽は北斎よりも3歳年下となります。自分も手がけていた役者絵のジャンルで突然活躍した写楽の存在を、北斎はどのような気持ちで眺めていたのでしょうか。

Looking at the history of *ukiyo-e*, we get the impression that Kitagawa Utamaro and Tōshūsai Sharaku belong to one generation before Hokusai. Yet, Utamaro and Sharaku were much talked about when Hokusai was in his thirties. Hence, the period during which they were active as artists overlaps with Hokusai.

Although the exact year of Kitagawa Utamaro's birth remains unknown, he could not have been more than ten years older than Hokusai. He came to the fore from around 1792 thanks to the *ōkubi-e* (half-length portraits) of beautiful women published by Tsutaya Jūzaburō. As Hokusai had already had his *nishiki-e* (polychrome prints) published by Tsutaya Jūzaburō (see p. 88), he certainly would have been aware of Utamaro's existence. Hokusai's *bijinga* (pictures of beauties) dating from the Kansei era (1789–1801) demonstrate not a little influence of Utamaro (fig. 29-1). Although we do not know how well Hokusai and Utamaro knew each other on a personal level, they were allotted illustrations for the same *kyōka* picture books, *The Purple of Edo* and *The Stamping Song of Men* (figs. 4-2, 30-1).

Tōshūsai Sharaku is an enigmatic artist who, having presented half-length portraits of *kabuki* actors through Tsutaya Jūzaburō in the fifth month of 1794 and been much talked about, suddenly disappeared the following year. The year Sharaku appeared was the period during which Hokusai seceded from the Katsukawa school and withdrew not only from prints of actors but also from the production of *nishiki-e*. There are scholars who claim that the true identity of Sharaku was Hokusai, but the opinion that he was a *noh* actor of Awa named Saitō Jūrobē is currently regarded more likely. In that case, as Saitō Jūrobē was born in 1763, Sharaku would have been three years younger than Hokusai. How would Hokusai have felt about the sudden emergence and success of Sharaku in the genre of prints of *kabuki* actors, which he, too, had been working on?

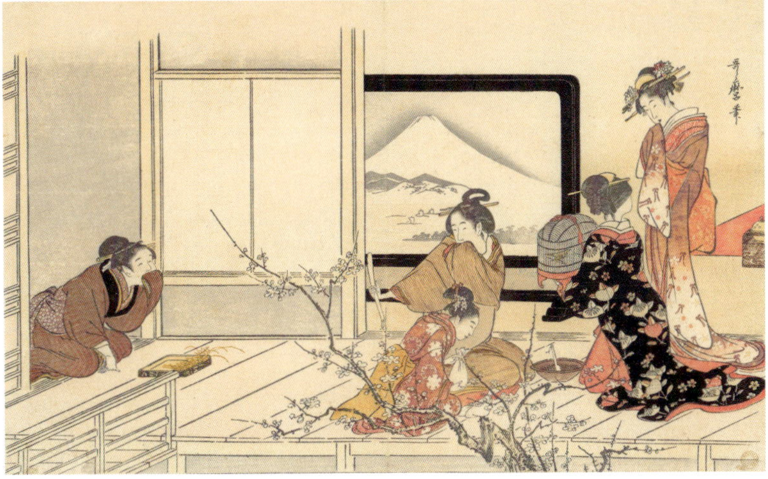

30-1 喜多川歌麿ほか画

男踏歌

寛政10年(1798) 大本
メトロポリタン美術館蔵

歌麿による狂歌絵本の挿絵です。全6図の挿絵の内、歌麿と北斎(図4-2)、そして三代堤 等琳、北尾重政、易祇、鳥文斎栄之がそれぞれ1図ずつ担当しています。北斎は、狂歌絵本というジャンルで、着実に人気絵師たちの仲間入りをしていることが分かります。

30-1 ***The Stamping Song of Men***

illust. Kitagawa Utamaro et al.
1798, *ōhon*, The Metropolitan Museum of Art

This is an illustration by Utamaro in a *kyōka* picture book. There are altogether six illustrations in this book. Besides Utamaro and Hokusai (fig. 4-2), there are one each by Tsutsumi Tōrin III, Kitao Shigemasa, Ekishi, and Chōbunsai Eishi. This shows that Hokusai had steadily got included among the popular artists who illustrated *kyōka* picture books.

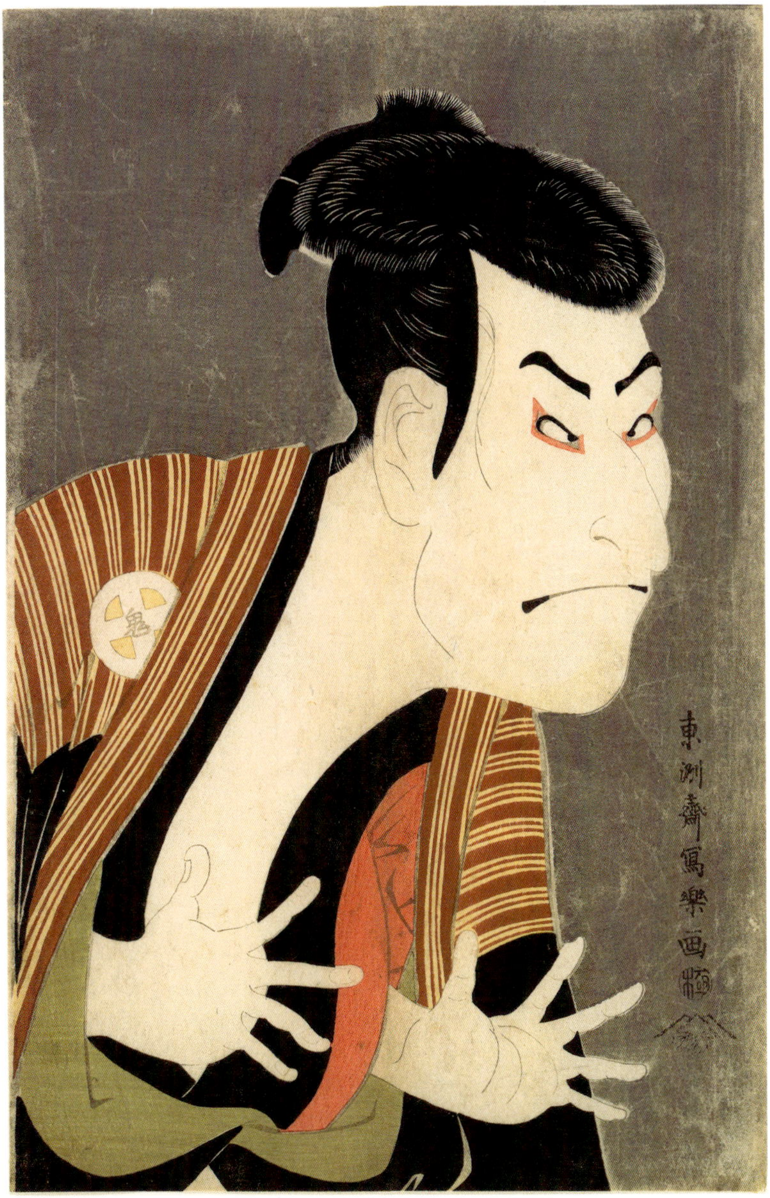

30-2 東洲斎写楽

三代目大谷鬼次の江戸兵衛

寛政6年(1794) 大判錦絵
メトロポリタン美術館蔵

写楽が最初に発表した役者大首絵28点のうちの1点です。雲母摺の背景に役者の顔が大きく浮かび上がっていますが、役者を美化せず、顔の特徴を誇張して描く点が特徴です。師匠の勝川春章とは異なる、新しい役者絵の登場を、北斎は目の当たりにしたことになります。

30-2 Tōshūsai Sharaku

The Actor Ōtani Oniji III as Edobē

1794, *ōban nishiki-e*,
The Metropolitan Museum of Art

This is one of the first twenty-eight *ōkubi-e* (half-length portraits) that Sharaku presented. The actor's head emerges largely against a *kirazuri* background with mica mixed into the printing ink. It is distinguished in the way Sharaku exaggerates the facial features without beautifying the actor. Hokusai would have witnessed the emergence of this new type of actor prints different from his master Katsukawa Shunshō with his own eyes.

31

Despite Quarrels, They Made a Great Pair

喧嘩もするが名コンビ

Kyokutei Bakin

曲亭馬琴

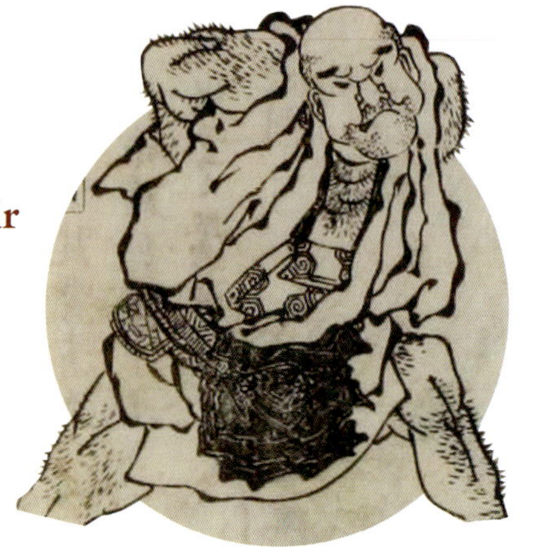

北斎はさまざまな戯作者が執筆した読本に挿絵を描いていますが（→24頁参照）、最も作画量が多いのが曲亭馬琴の執筆によるものです。馬琴の代表作といえば『南総里見八犬伝』ですが、それを手がける前、北斎と二人三脚で読本を制作していました。

北斎と馬琴がタッグを組み始めたのは、享和4年（1804）の『小説比翼文』です。それ以来、『新編水滸画伝』や『椿説弓張月』など、文化12年（1815）までの間に13点もの読本を制作します（後編や続編などは合わせて1点としています）。特に文化4～5年（1807～08）は制作数が最も多い時期でした。

『苅萱後伝玉櫛笥』において、馬琴自らが序文で「丙寅年画工北斎子、著作堂に遊ぶこと、春より夏のはじめに至て三四箇月」と語っているように、文化3年（1806）の春から夏にかけての3ヵ月、北斎は馬琴の家（著作堂）に居候し、共に制作に励んでいたようです。

読本挿絵では、作者（馬琴）が指示を出して絵師（北斎）がそれに従って描くのですが、その制作をめぐって、馬琴と北斎が喧嘩をしたという逸話がいくつか伝わっています。例えば、『占夢南柯後記』の口絵（図31-1）で、馬琴が登場人物の口に草履をくわえさせようと指示したところ、北斎は誰がこんな汚い物を口にするかと反論し、絶交に至ったというのです[1]。ただし、この後も両者は合作を続けており、不仲説に根拠がないことも実証されています[2]。馬琴は、北斎が挿絵を描いた高井蘭山作『新編水滸画伝』二編について、「画はさすがに北斎に候へば、不相替よろしく候」と、殿村篠斎に宛てた手紙の中で褒めていますので、少なくとも北斎の技量は高く評価していたことでしょう。

Hokusai did illustrations for many *yomihon* written by various *gesaku* (popular fiction) writers (see p. 24), among which he did the most illustrations for those written by Kyokutei Bakin. Bakin is best known for *Nansō Satomi hakkenden* (Satomi snd the eight "dogs"), but before writing that epic novel, he worked closely together with Hokusai in producing *yomihon*.

Hokusai and Bakin teamed up for the first time in 1804 to produce *Shōsetsu hiyokumon*. From then on, until 1815, they produced as many as thirteen *yomihon* such as *New Illustrated Edition of the Water Margin* and *Strange Tales of the Bow Moon* (counting sequels as part of one work). The years 1807 to 1808 were when they produced the most works.

In the Introduction to *Karukaya kōden tamakushige*, Bakin writes that for three or four months from the spring to early summer of 1806, Hokusai stayed at Bakin's house (Chosadō) and they worked together.

Yomihon illustrations were produced by the author (Bakin) giving instructions and the artist (Hokusai) drawing accordingly. There are several anecdotes about Bakin and Hokusai quarrelling about such productions. For example, when working on the frontispiece for *Yumeawase nanka kōki* (fig. 31-1), Bakin instructed Hokusai to do a picture of the character in the story holding a pair of sandals in his mouth, to which Hokusai refuted, "Who would put such dirty things in their mouth?" and broke off their friendship. However, even after that, they continued to collaborate and their discord has been proved unfounded. In a letter Bakin wrote to Tonomura Jōsai, he comments on the second part of *New Illustrated Edition of the Water Margin* written by Takai Ranzan and illustrated by Hokusai as follows. "The illustrations, as might be expected of Hokusai, are unexchangeable." Judging from such praise, Bakin was at least highly appreciative of Hokusai's talent.

1）『絵画叢誌』第20巻、1888年
2）鈴木重三『人間北斎』緑園書房、1963年

31-1 曲亭馬琴作・葛飾北斎画
『占夢南柯後記』巻之一
文化9年（1812） 半紙本 早稲田大学図書館蔵

中央にいる坊主頭の男性が問題の人物。馬琴が北斎に手渡した下書きでは、この男性は口に草履をくわえていますが、北斎の挿絵では草履をくわえていません。絶交説は疑わしいですが、馬琴の最初の構想が変更されたことは確かです。

31-1 Kyokutei Bakin
Yumeawase nanka kōki, vol. 1
illust. Katsushika Hokusai
1812, *hanshibon*, Waseda University Library

The man with a shaven head at the center is the character in question. In the draft that Bakin handed to Hokusai, this man was holding a pair of sandals in his mouth, but the sandals are not to be seen in Hokusai's illustration. It is hard to believe that Hokusai and Bakin broke off their friendship, but it is true that Bakin's initial idea was altered.

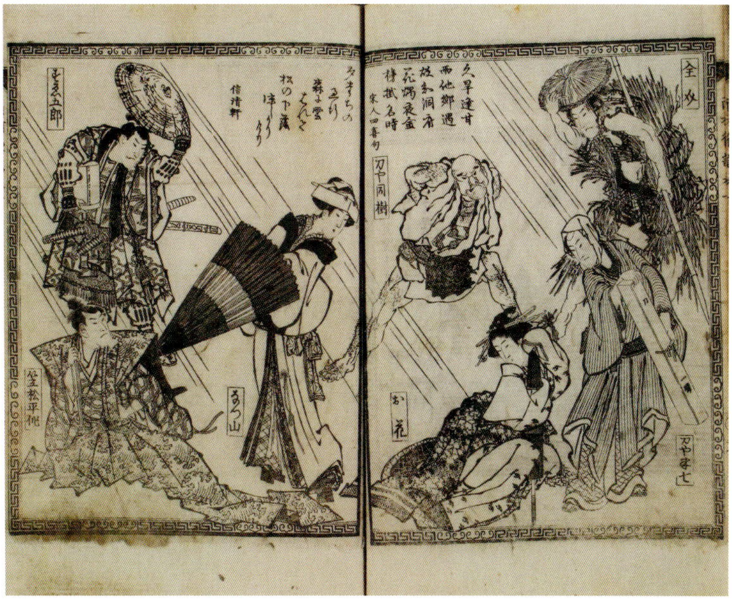

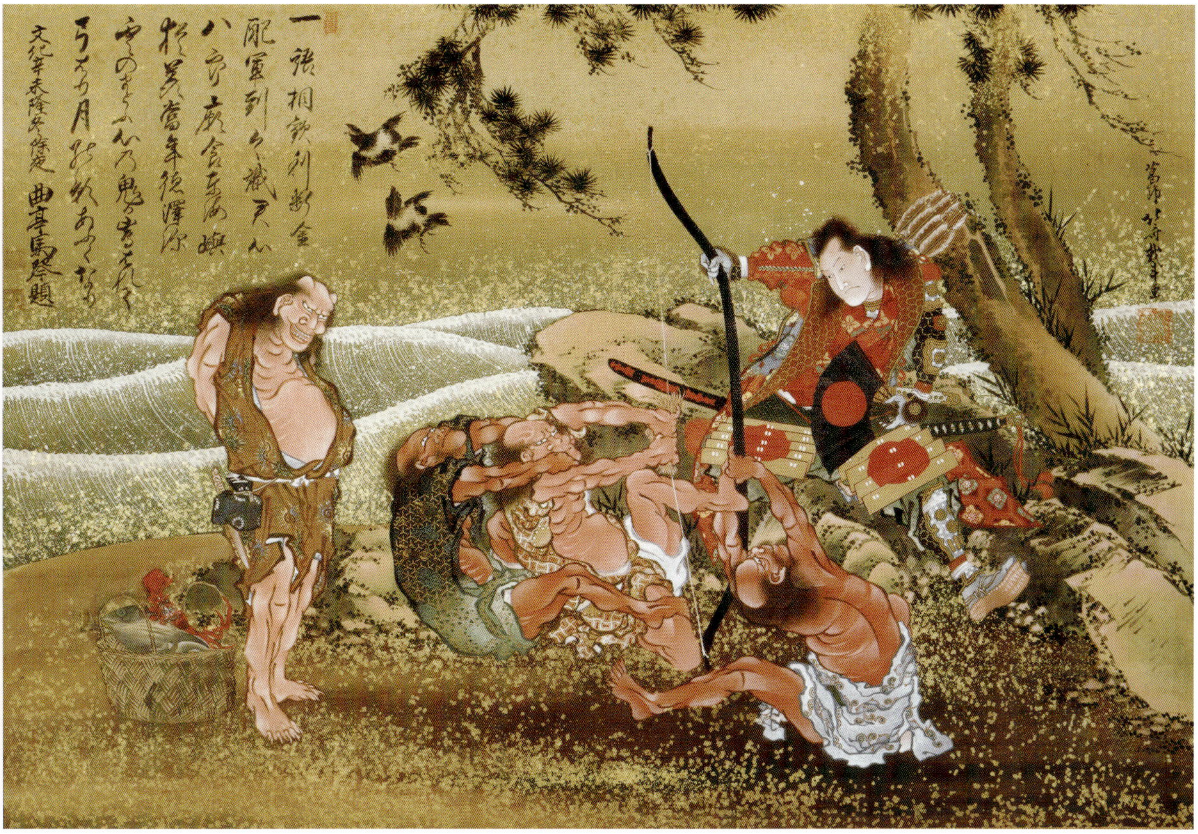

AKG/PPS通信社

31-2 葛飾北斎 **鎮西八郎為朝図**
文化8年（1811） 絹本着色 大英博物館蔵

『椿説弓張月』の完結を祝して、版元の平林庄五郎から依頼を受けた作品です。『椿説弓張月』の冒頭の挿絵（図6-2）を肉筆画として描き直したもので、左上には馬琴直筆による漢詩と和歌の賛が添えられており、貴重な合作となっています。

31-2 Katsushika Hokusai
Warrior Hero Tametomo and the Inhabitants of Onoshima Island
1811, color on silk, The British Museum

This is a painting commissioned by the publisher Hirabayashi Shōgorō to celebrate the completion of *Strange Tales of the Bow Moon*. Hokusai reproduced the first illustration (fig. 6-2) in *Strange Tales of the Bow Moon* as an original painting. Bakin wrote in a Chinese poem and a Japanese poem in the upper left of the painting, making it a rare collaboration.

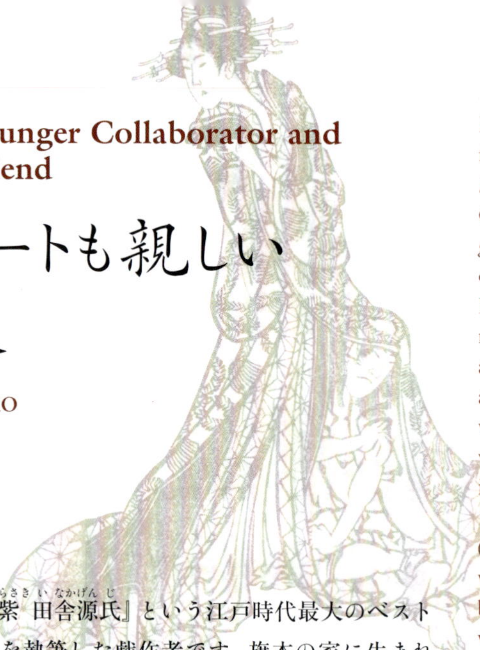

32 Younger Collaborator and Friend

プライベートも親しい年下の友

Ryūtei Tanehiko
柳亭種彦

柳亭種彦は、『偐紫田舎源氏』という江戸時代最大のベストセラーとなった合巻を執筆した戯作者です。旗本の家に生まれた武士でしたが、文化4年(1807)、25歳の頃に読本作家としてデビューします。まだ駆け出しである文化5～8年(1808～11)、種彦は6点の読本を執筆していますが、そのうち『霜夜星』(図10-2)や『総角物語』後編(図32-1)など、4点の挿絵を担当したのが23歳年上の北斎でした。北斎はその数年前から馬琴とタッグを組んで読本を制作し(→92頁参照)、大きな話題となっていました。種彦にとってデビュー時点で北斎に挿絵を描いてもらったことは、幸先の良いスタートだったといえるでしょう。

また、文化9年(1812)、橘崑崙が越後の怪談や奇談をまとめた『北越奇談』(図32-2)が刊行されますが、種彦がこの書を校訂し、北斎が挿絵を描くという協同作業も行っています。

しかも、断片的に残されている種彦の日記によれば[1)]、文化5～7年(1808～10)頃、2人は仕事上だけでなく、プライベートでも親しい交流をしていたことが確認できます。互いの家を行き来するだけでなく、一日中一緒に遊んだり、種彦が北斎に読本の構想を語ったりということもありました。

文化9年(1812)頃から種彦は合巻の執筆が中心となり、種彦の戯作に北斎が挿絵を描いた作例は確認できません[2)]。しかし、その後も長きに渡って2人の交流は続いていたようで、文政6年(1823)の『今様櫛きん雛形』(図2-5、8-5)や天保5年(1834)の『富嶽百景』初編など、北斎のいくつかの絵手本に種彦が序文を執筆しています。また、文政9年(1826)に種彦が執筆した考証随筆『還魂紙料』では、北斎が古画を模写した挿絵をいくつも描いています。

1) 朝倉治彦校訂『柳亭種彦日記』秋山書店、1979年
2) ただし、天保3年(1832)の『花雪吹縁柵』や天保4年(1833)の『出世奴小万之伝』といった合巻において、北斎は種彦の求めに応じて表紙の一部分を描いています。

Ryūtei Tanehiko was a *gesaku* (popular fiction) writer who wrote *Nise Murasaki inaka Genji* (Bogus Murasaki, Bumpkin Genji), which became the best-selling *gōkan* (literally, "bound-together volumes" of illustrated fiction) of the Edo period. He was a warrior born to a direct retainer of the shogun, but debuted as a *yomihon* writer in 1807, when he was around 25. Between 1808 and 1811, while still a novice writer, Tanehiko wrote six *yomihon*, of which four including *Stars on a Frosty Night* (fig. 10-2) and *Agemaki monogatari*, part 2 (fig. 32-1) were illustrated by Hokusai, who was 23 years older. Hokusai had been working on *yomihon* together with Kyokutei Bakin from a few years before that (see p. 92) and they were much talked about. To Tanehiko, having Hokusai illustrate his books just after his debut was certainly a promising beginning.

In 1812, *Strange Stories of the Northern Province of Echigo* (fig. 32-2), a collection of ghost tales and strange stories written by Tachibana Konron, was published. Tanehiko revised this book and Hokusai collaborated by providing the illustrations.

Moreover, according to fragments of Tanehiko's diaries that remain, the two not only worked together but were also personal friends between 1808 and 1810. Besides visiting each other at home, they spent the whole day enjoying themselves together and Tanehiko once told Hokusai about his ideas for *yomihon*.

From circa 1812, as Tanehiko began to concentrate on writing *gōkan*, no examples of Tanehiko's *gesaku* illustrated by Hokusai can be confirmed. However, they seem to have kept in touch with each other for many years and Tanehiko wrote the introduction for a number of *edehon* (drawing manuals) such as *Modern Designs for Combs and Tobacco Pipes* (figs. 2-5, 8-5) in 1823 and *One Hundred Views of Mount Fuji*, part 1 in 1834. When Tanehiko wrote *Sukikaeshi* (Recycled Paper), essays on bibliographic studies of Edo literature, in 1826, Hokusai provided copies of old paintings as illustrations.

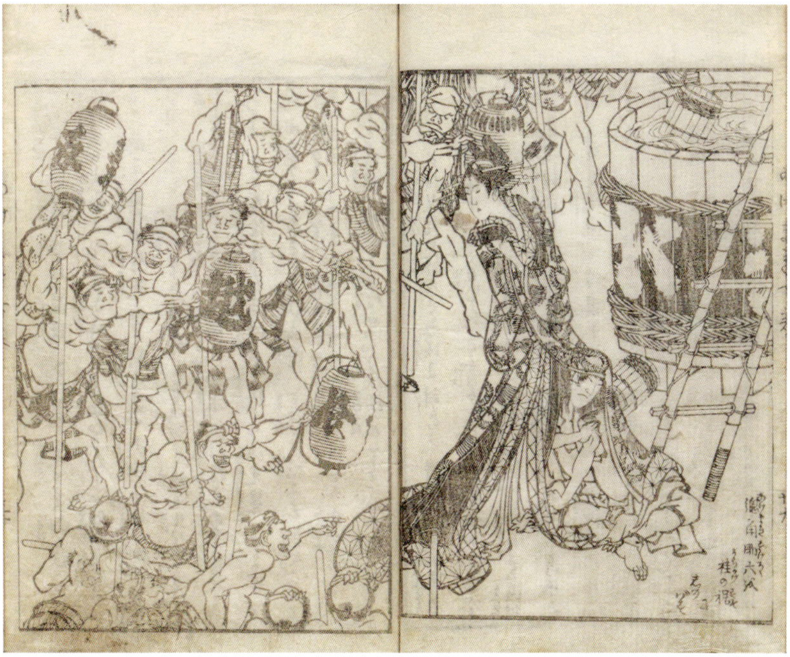

32-1　柳亭種彦作・葛飾北斎画

『総角物語（あげまきものがたり）』後編　下巻

文化6年（1809）　半紙本
国立国会図書館蔵

文化５年に刊行された前編は優遊斎桃川（ゆうゆうさいとうせん）が挿絵を描いていましたが、後編は北斎が担当しています。

32-1 Ryūtei Tanehiko

Agemaki monogatari, part 2, vol. 2

illust. Katsushika Hokusai
1809, *hanshibon*, National Diet Library, Japan

Part 1, published in 1808, was illustrated by Yūyūsai Tōsen, but Part 2 was illustrated by Hokusai.

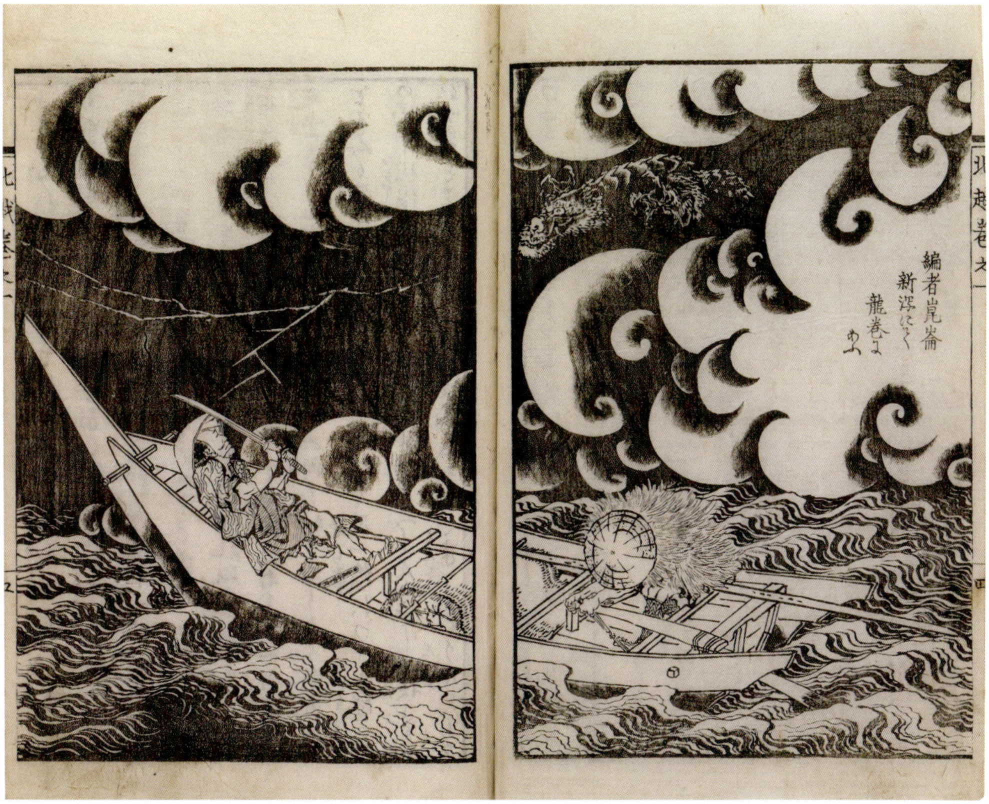

32-2　橘崑崙作・柳亭種彦校訂・葛飾北斎画

『北越奇談（ほくえつきだん）』巻之一

文化9年（1812）　半紙本　島根県立美術館（永田コレクション）蔵

新潟に向かう舟に乗っていた作者の橘崑崙（たちばなこんろん）が、竜巻に遭遇した時の逸話を挿絵として描いています。黒雲の中にうごめく龍の姿が見えます。

32-2 Tachibana Konron

Strange Stories of the Northern Province of Echigo, vol.1

rev. Ryūtei Tanehiko, illust, Katsushika Hokusai
1812, *hanshibon*, Shimane Art Museum (Nagata Collection)

This is an illustration of an anecdote about the author Tachibana Konron, who was confronted with a tornado on board a boat heading to Niigata. You can see a dragon wriggling in the black clouds.

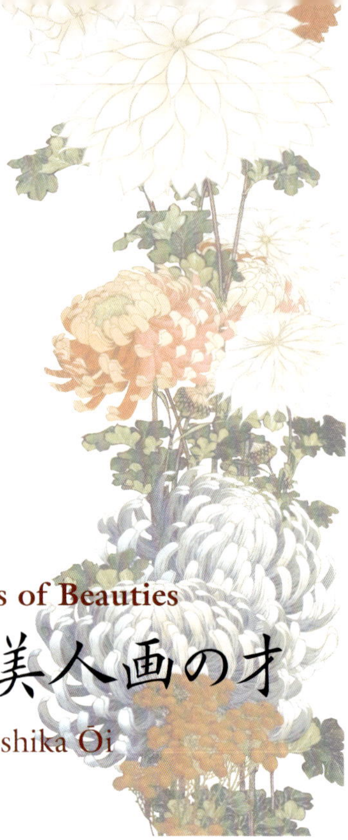

33

Hats off to Her Portraits of Beauties

北斎も認めた美人画の才

Hokusai's Daughter Katsushika Ōi

娘・葛飾応為

北斎の三女である栄(→64 頁)は、葛飾応為と号し、父親と同じ浮世絵師の職につきました。応為の作とされる肉筆画は10 数点しかなく、絵師としての実力は断片しか知ることができません。北斎の手伝いが仕事の中心で、応為への依頼が少なかったためでしょう。しかし、北斎が「余の美人画は、阿栄におよはさるなり、彼は妙に画きて、よく画法にかなへり」(『北斎伝』)と語ったとされるように、応為の美人画(図18-2、33-1)には北斎も認める個性を感じさせます。また、「夜桜美人図」(図33-2)や「吉原格子先之図」(図33-3)に特徴的な光と闇の描写は、北斎とも異なる応為独自の表現として注目されるでしょう。

応為の生涯について分かっていることは少なく、生没年もはっきりと確定できていません。ただし、応為の性格については『北斎伝』にいろいろな逸話が記されており、父親に似た変わり者であったことがうかがえます。例えば、服装にはこだわらず、料理はしないで煮売店(今でいう惣菜屋)で毎日買ってきていたといいます。掃除もあまり好きではなかったようで、ゴミも部屋に散らかったまま。しかも、北斎とは違い、酒も煙草も好むという豪気な性格でした。顔はそれほど美人ではなく、アゴが出ていたので、北斎からは「アゴアゴ」と呼ばれていたそうです(図33-4)。

細かいところにこだわらない性格だったからこそ、北斎とも良好な関係が続いたのでしょう。応為は北斎が亡くなるまで共に暮らし、北斎の手助けをし続けました。晩年の北斎の肉筆画には、80 歳を過ぎたとは思えない緻密な彩色の作例がいくつかありますが、応為がサポートしていたであろうことが推測されます(図33-5)。

Hokusai's third daughter, Ei (see p. 64), assumed the name Katsushika Ōi and took up the same occupation as her father, an *ukiyo-e* artist. There are no more than ten-odd original paintings attributed to Ōi and only fragments of her proficiency as an artist are known. This may be due to the fact that she worked mainly as assistant to Hokusai and did not receive many commissions herself. However, Hokusai is said to have commented, "My *bijinga* [pictures of beauties] are no match for those by Aei [another name for Ei]. She is skillful at painting and knows the techniques" (*Hokusai-den*). Indeed, the *bijinga* by Ōi (figs. 18-2, 33-1) display an originality that even Hokusai acknowledged. Her characteristic representations of light and dark in *Girl Composing a Poem under the Cherry Blossom in the Night* (fig. 33-2) and *Display Room in Yoshiwara at Night* (fig. 33-3) are noteworthy as expressions of Ōi's own and different from Hokusai.

Little is known about Ōi's lifetime and even the dates of her birth and death are yet to be confirmed. Nevertheless, various anecdotes regarding her character recorded in *Hokusai-den* reveal that, like her father, she was quite eccentric. For example, she did not care about her attire, did not cook, and bought food at a delicatessen-like shop every day. It seems that she was not fond of cleaning either and litter remained scattered across the room. Moreover, unlike Hokusai, she was dynamic in character and enjoyed drinking and smoking. She was not so attractive and as she had a projecting chin (*ago* in Japanese), Hokusai is said to have called her "Ago Ago" (fig. 33-4).

Perhaps it was thanks to the way Ōi did not worry about the details that she was able to get on with Hokusai. She lived with Hokusai until his death and continued to give him a hand. Among the original paintings dating from Hokusai's later years, there are some examples in which the coloring is so intricate that it is hard to believe the artist was over 80, suggesting that Ōi may have been supporting him (fig. 33-5).

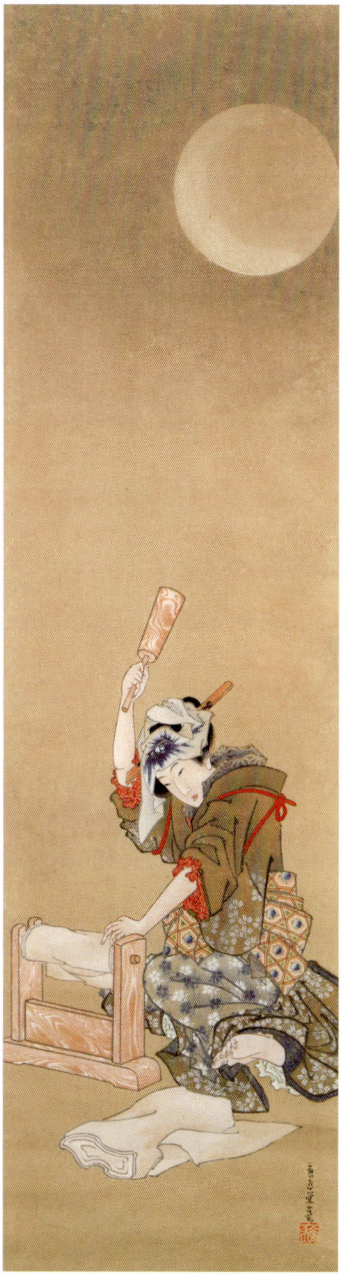

Image: TNM Image Archives

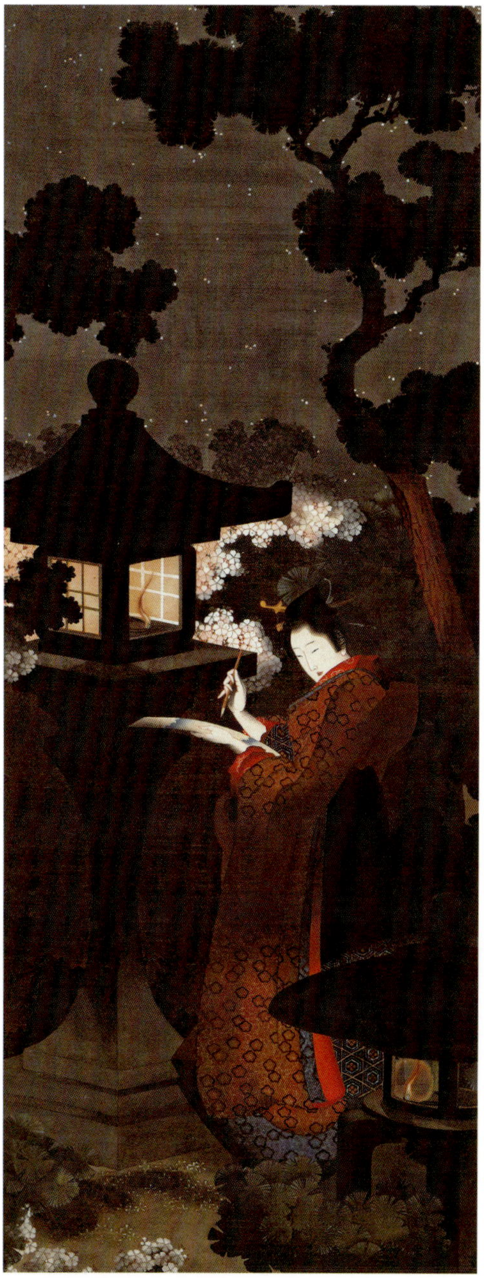

33-1 葛飾応為　**月下砧打ち美人図**

弘化～嘉永（1844～54）頃　紙本着色　東京国立博物館蔵

満月が輝く屋外で、女性が織り上がった布を柔らかくするために砧で叩いています。女性の顔や着物の衣紋線の描き方は北斎と似通っています。また、着物の裾や帯の模様、あるいは砧の木目など、細部を丁寧に描き込む特徴が見られます。

33-1 Katsushika Ōi

Woman Fulling Cloth by Moonlight

c. 1844–1854, color on paper, Tokyo National Museum

Outdoors under a glowing full moon, a woman beats newly woven cloth with a fulling block to soften it. The woman's face and the *kimono* lines are depicted in a style similar to Hokusai. The way Ōi scrupulously paints in the details such as the patterns on the lower part of the *kimono* and *obi* (sash) or the woodgrain on the fulling block is distinctive, too.

33-2 葛飾応為　**夜桜美人図**

19世紀中頃　絹本着色　メナード美術館蔵

石燈籠の明かりを頼りに、女性が短冊に何かを書きつけようとしています。周囲は真っ暗ですが、燈籠の光で女性や桜が部分的に明るく照らし出されています。夜空に星がまたたいているのも、光に対する応為の繊細な感覚によるものでしょう。

33-2 Katsushika Ōi

Girl Composing a Poem under the Cherry Blossoms in the Night

mid-19th century, color on silk, Menard Art Museum

A young woman is trying to write something on a strip of paper under the light from a stone lantern. The surroundings are pitch-dark, but the light from the stone lantern shines brightly on certain parts of the girl and the cherry blossoms. The stars twinkling in the sky are also signs of Ōi's subtle sensibility towards light.

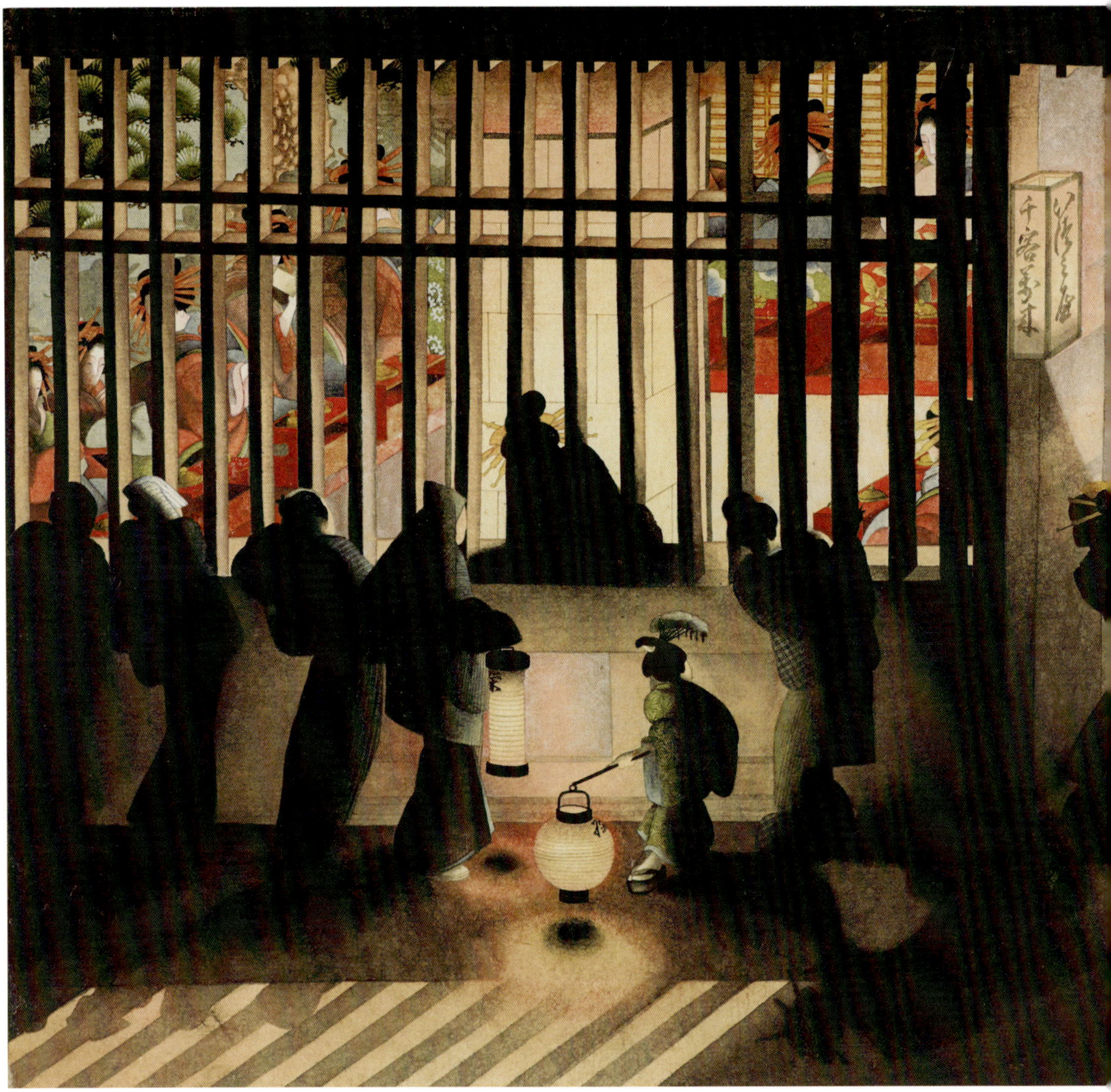

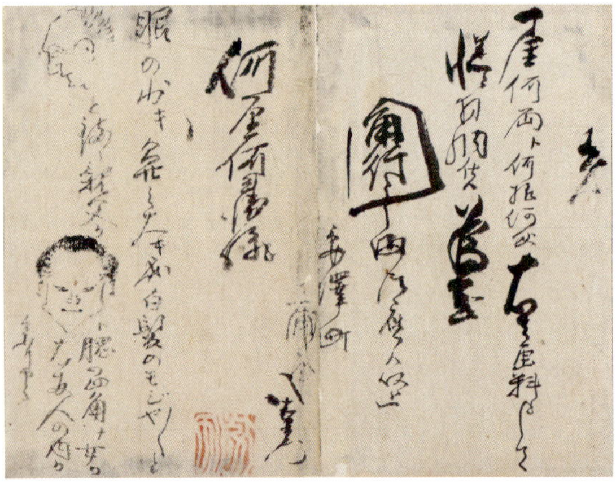

◀ 33-4　葛飾北斎　画料請求書

弘化年間(1844～48)頃　紙本墨書　島根県立美術館(永田コレクション)蔵

誰に宛てたものか分かりませんが、北斎の自筆による画料請求書です。後半に自分か応為が受け取りに行くとして、北斎と応為、2人の似顔絵が描かれています。応為は「腮の四角ナ女」としてその面貌が記されています。

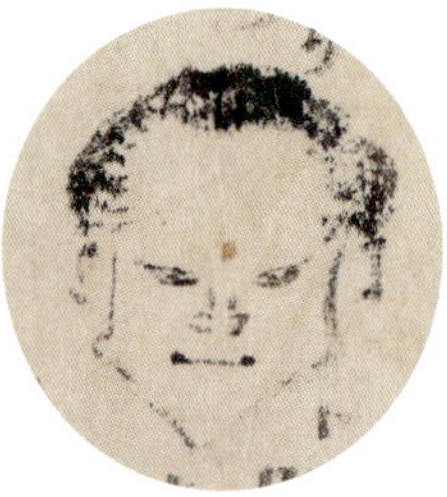

◀ 33-4 Katsushika Hokusai

Artist's Bill

c. 1844–1848, ink on paper,
Shimane Art Museum (Nagata Collection)

This request of payment for artistic work provided was handwritten by Hokusai, but we do not know whom it is addressed to. The latter half states that either he or Ōi will go to collect the money, adding sketches of both Hokusai and Ōi. The daughter's features are described with the inscription, "a woman with a square chin."

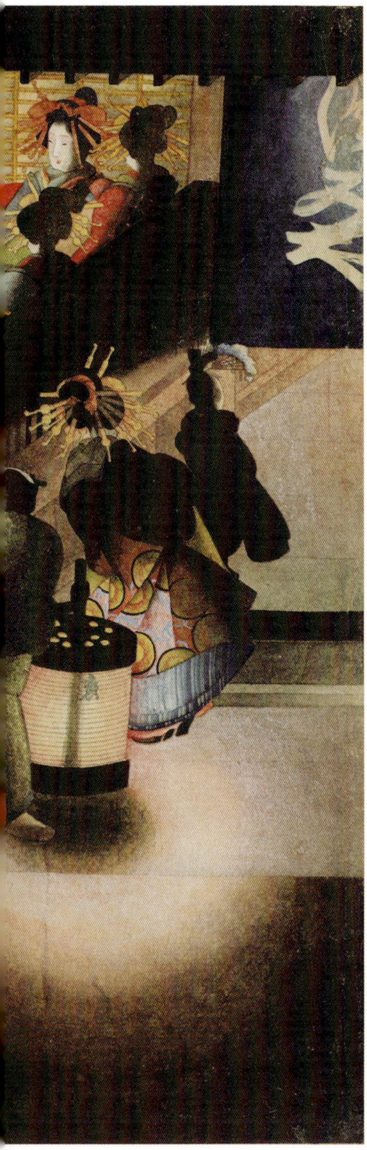

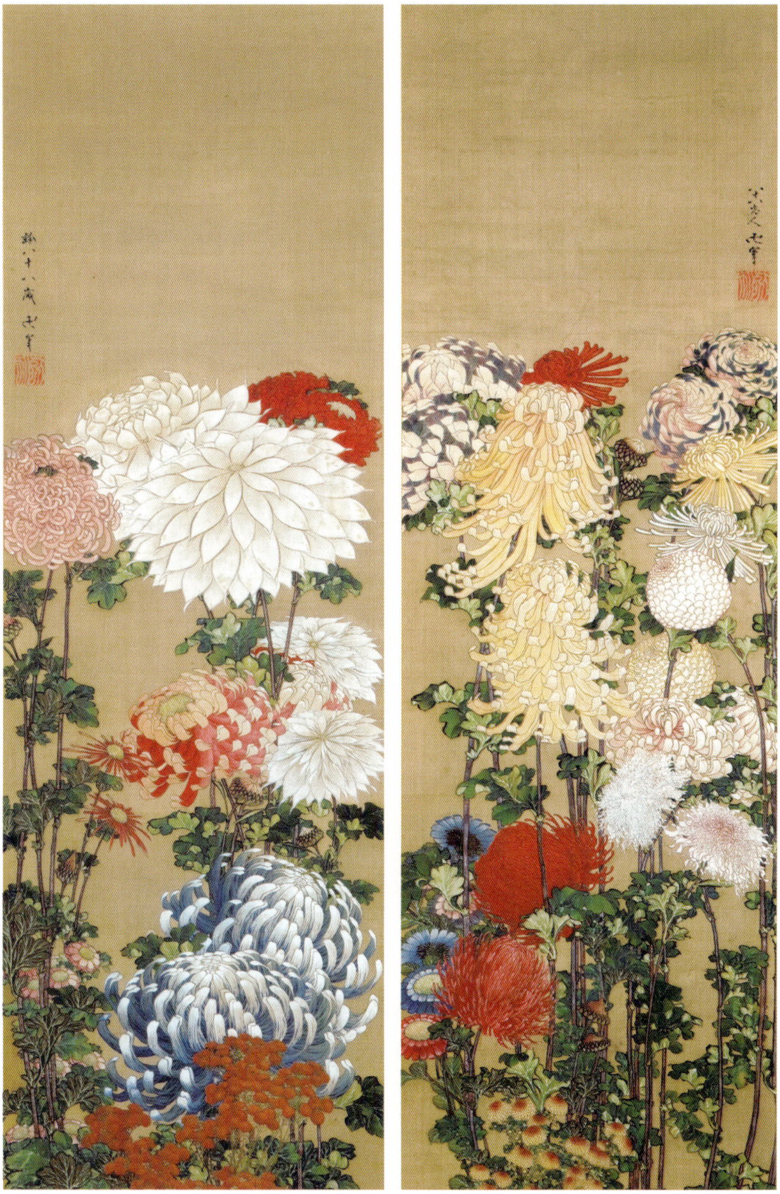

▲**33-3**　葛飾応為
吉原格子先之図
文政7〜嘉永(1824〜54)頃　紙本着色
太田記念美術館蔵

きらびやかな衣装に身を包んだ花魁たちが並ぶ、吉原遊廓の張見世の夜の景です。室内から発せられたまばゆい明かりと、人々の表情が見えないほどの闇という強烈な明暗の対比によって、幻想的な空間が生み出されています。

▲**33-3**　Katsushika Ōi
Display Room in Yoshiwara at Night
c. 1824–1854, color on paper, Ōta Memorial Museum of Art

Courtesans dressed in gorgeous costumes are seated in a row. This is how they awaited their customers at night in the pleasure quarters of Yoshiwara. The stark contrast between the dazzling light shed from indoors and the darkness outside, so dim that there is no telling of the onlookers' expressions, produces a visionary space.

33-5　葛飾北斎　**菊図**
弘化4年(1847)　絹本着色　北斎館蔵

北斎88歳の落款がありますが、その緻密な彩色から、制作の経緯についてさまざまな議論のある作品です。応為の作ではないかとの指摘もあるように（久保田一洋『北斎娘応為栄女集』藝華書院、2015年）、応為が積極的に関与していた可能性も考えられています。

33-5　Katsushika Hokusai　***Chrysanthemums***
1847, color on silk, Hokusai Museum

The sign and seal suggest that this was painted when Hokusai was aged 88, but the elaborate coloring has given rise to debates regarding the circumstances under which this was produced. Some argue that it is by Ōi and there is also a possibility that she was actively involved in the production.

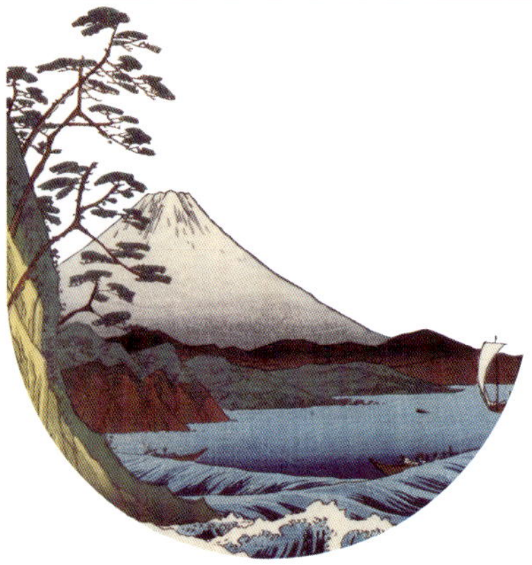

34

Archrival Landscapist
風景画の好敵手

Utagawa Hiroshige
歌川広重

歌川広重は北斎よりも37歳年下で、親と子以上に年齢が離れていますが、北斎が「冨嶽三十六景」(→48頁参照)を刊行した数年後に「東海道五拾三次之内」を発表していることから、しばしばライバルとして比較されています。

実は、2人が風景画を刊行していた時期は、わずかしか重なりません。北斎が風景画の錦絵を集中的に手掛けていたのは、70歳を過ぎた晩年の天保元~5年(1830~34)頃の5年程度。一方、広重は天保2年(1831)頃、35歳頃の「東都名所」によって世間からの注目を浴びるようになり、天保4年(1833)頃の「東海道五拾三次之内」(図34-1)でようやく一人前の絵師としてのスタートを切ったばかりでした。

その後の広重は、風景画の第一人者として、62歳で亡くなるまで活躍し続けます。風景画に限れば、制作数でも活動期間でも、広重のほうが北斎をはるかに上回っているのです。芸術的な評価はともかく、あくまで商業的な判断だけでいえば、花鳥画同様(→52頁参照)、風景画も広重の方に軍配が上がったといえるでしょう。

北斎が広重をどのように考えていたかの記録はありませんが、広重は北斎のことを強く意識していたようです。『冨士見百図』という絵本の序文で、広重は北斎の『富嶽百景』(図2-6, 12-5~6)について、「絵組のおもしろきを専らとし不二は其あしらひにいたるも多し」と、北斎は構図の面白さがメインで、富士山はおまけのようだと評しています。一方、自分の作品は、「予がまのあたりに眺望せしを其侭にうつし置たる」と、自分が眺めた風景を写実的に描いていることを主張しています。広重は、自分と北斎の表現の個性の違いについて、しっかりと認識していたようです。

Utagawa Hiroshige was thirty-seven years younger than Hokusai. Their age difference was larger than that of a father and son. Yet, as Hiroshige presented *Fifty-three Stations of the Tōkaidō* a few years after Hokusai had published *Thirty-six Views of Mount Fuji* (see p. 48), they are often compared as rivals.

In fact, the periods during which these two artists published landscapes overlap for only a very short time. It was for only five years or so between 1830 and 1834, late in Hokusai's life when he was over 70, that Hokusai worked concentratedly on *nishiki-e* (polychrome prints) of landscapes. Meanwhile, Hiroshige began to attract attention circa 1831, when he was about 35, with *Famous Places in the Eastern Capital. Fifty-three Stations of the Tōkaidō* (fig.34-1) presented circa 1833, finally marked his start as a full-fledged artist.

From then on, Hiroshige continued working as the foremost authority on landscapes until he died aged 62. As far as landscapes were concerned, Hiroshige produced far more works than Hokusai and was active for a longer period. Leaving the artistic worth aside, from a commercial point of view only, Hiroshige can be considered the winner regarding landscapes, as was the case with pictures of flowers and birds (see p. 52).

There are no records on how Hokusai regarded Hiroshige, but Hiroshige seems to have been highly conscious of Hokusai. In the Introduction to a picture book entitled *One Hundred Sights of Mount Fuji*, Hiroshige comments on Hokusai's *One Hundred Views of Mount Fuji* (figs. 2-6, 12-5~6) as follows. "He concentrates entirely on intriguing compositions and, in many cases, Mount Fuji ends up as an adornment." In other words, according to Hiroshige, the appeal of the composition was Hokusai's focal point and Mount Fuji was no more than an extra addition. In contrast, Hiroshige claims his own works "are true-to-life representations of the view before my eyes." Hiroshige was fully aware of the difference of individuality compared to Hokusai's expressions.

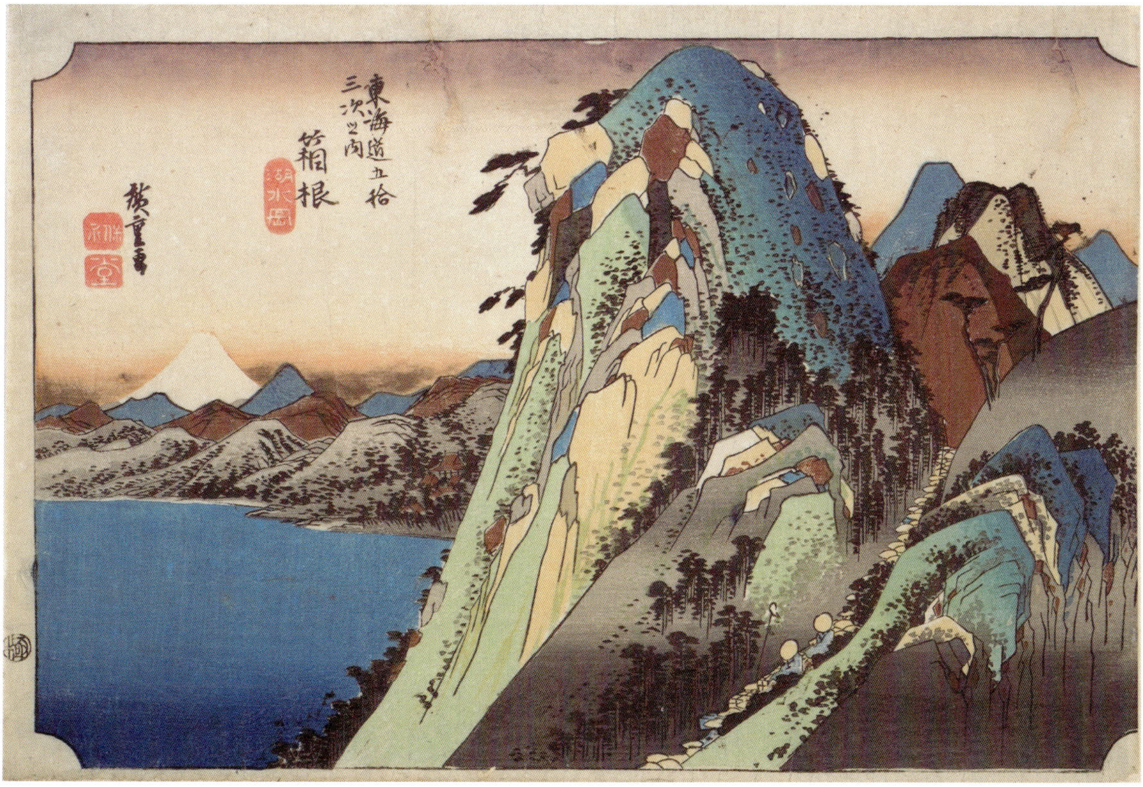

34-1 歌川広重

東海道五拾三次之内　箱根　湖水図

天保4年(1833)頃　大判錦絵　メトロポリタン美術館蔵

「東海道五拾三次之内」は東海道の宿場町を描いた全55点からなる揃物。その数年前に刊行された北斎の「冨嶽三十六景」とともに、浮世絵の風景画の歴史を切り開いた作品として位置付けられています。

34-1 Utagawa Hiroshige

Fifty-three Stations of the Tōkaidō: The Lake at Hakone

c. 1833, *ōban nishiki-e*, The Metropolitan Museum of Art

Fifty-three Stations of the Tōkaidō is a set of altogether fifty-five prints depicting the stations along Tōkaidō. Together with Hokusai's *Thirty-six Views of Mount Fuji*, which was published a few years earlier, it is regarded a milestone that opened up the history of *ukiyo-e* landscapes.

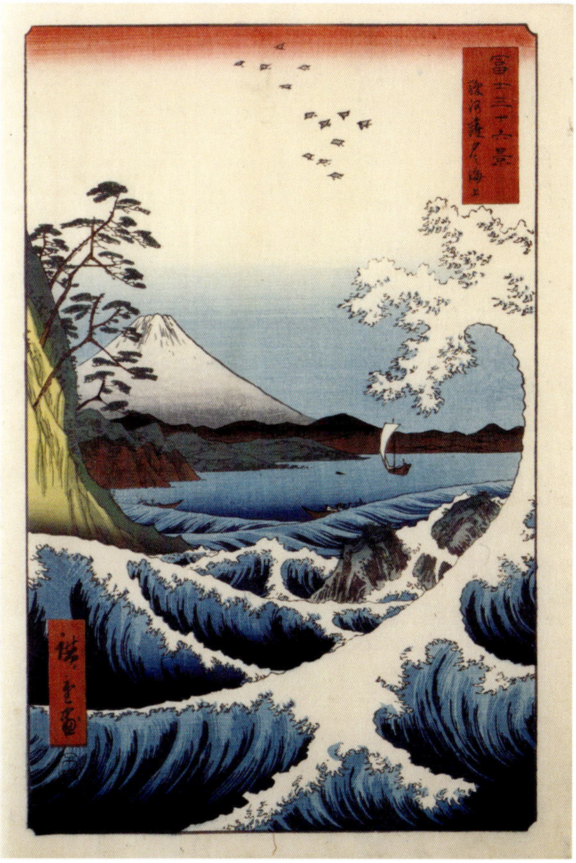

34-2 歌川広重

冨士三十六景　駿河薩タ之海上

安政6年(1859)　大判錦絵　山梨県立博物館蔵

北斎の「冨嶽三十六景　神奈川沖浪裏」(図2-1)を強く意識した作品です。見たままの景色を描くことにこだわった広重らしく、北斎とは違い、手前の波と遠くの富士山と間の景色をしっかりと描くことで、現実味を出しています。

34-2 Utagawa Hiroshige

Thirty-six Views of Mount Fuji: Sea at Satta Pass in Suruga Province

1859, *ōban nishiki-e*, Yamanashi Prefectural Museum

Hiroshige was strongly conscious of Hokusai's *Thirty-six Views of Mount Fuji: Great Wave off the Coast of Kanagawa* (fig. 2-1). Characteristic of Hiroshige, who adhered to depicting a landscape as it appeared, unlike Hokusai, he presents a sense of reality by firmly portraying the scenery between the waves in the foreground and Mount Fuji in the distance.

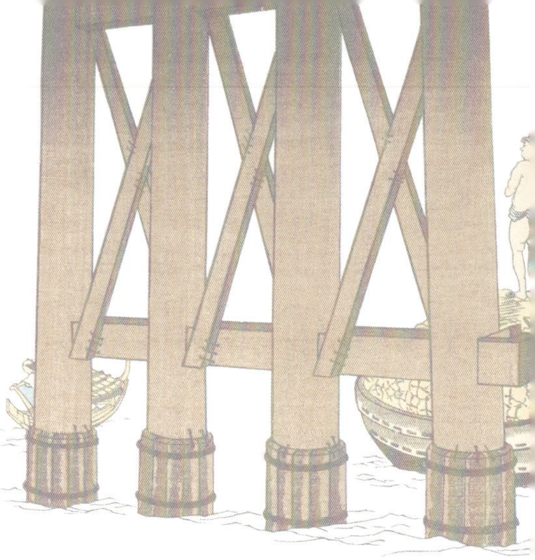

35

Friendship Transcending Schools

流派を超えた交流

Utagawa Kuniyoshi

歌川国芳

歌川国芳は武者絵や戯画で人気の浮世絵師ですが、その出世作となったのが、文政10年(1827)頃、31歳頃から刊行された「通俗水滸伝豪傑百八人之一個(人)」(図35-1)です。中国の小説『水滸伝』に登場する豪傑たちを描いた、迫力ある武者絵の揃物となっています。

国芳が『水滸伝』を題材として選んだ背景には、当時すでに『水滸伝』がブームであったことがあります。『水滸伝』の翻訳本が刊行されるだけでなく、挿絵を加えた翻案もいくつか刊行されていました。その中のひとつに曲亭馬琴・高井蘭山作・葛飾北斎画の読本『新編水滸画伝』(図6-1)があります。おそらく国芳は、北斎の挿絵による読本に目を通し、いかに自分のオリジナリティを発揮するかを模索したことでしょう。

国芳は他にも北斎の作品からアイデアの着想を得ています。例えば、巨大なワニザメで有名な代表作「讃岐院眷属をして為朝をすくふ図」では、北斎の読本挿絵『椿説弓張月』を参照しています。また、「東都冨士見三十六景」(図35-2)という風景画が、北斎の「冨嶽三十六景」(→48頁参照)を念頭に置いていることは明らかでしょう。

『北斎伝』によれば、国芳は北斎のことを慕っていました。国芳はある時、北斎の門人である大塚道庵を通じて北斎と面会しようとします。北斎は、一度会うことは構わないが、その後たびたび訪れるようになるのは国芳のためによくないと返事をしました。なぜなら、国芳が歌川派から流派を変えて葛飾派になったと世間から疑われてしまうのを心配したからです。その後、国芳は北斎と会い、絵について大いに語り合いました。北斎は流派の違いを意識し、国芳と適切な距離で付き合おうとしていたようです。

Utagawa Kuniyoshi is an *ukiyo-e* artist who was popular for his pictures of warriors and his caricatures. The work which brought him into prominence was *108 Heroes of the Water Margin for Everyman* (fig. 35-1), which was published from circa 1827, when he was around 31 years old. They are a series of impressive portraits of the heroes in a Chinese novel entitled *Water Margin*.

Kuniyoshi's choice of *Water Margin* as his subject matter was backed by the fact that the novel was already enjoying a boom in those days. Not only was a Japanese translation published but there were also a number of adaptations with additional illustrations published. One such example was the *yomihon, New Illustrated Edition of the Water Margin* (fig. 6-1), written by Kyokutei Bakin and Takai Ranzan and illustrated by Katsushika Hokusai. Kuniyoshi probably looked through this storybook illustrated by Hokusai and pondered how to display his own originality.

Kuniyoshi also got ideas from other works by Hokusai. For example, in his masterpiece *Retired Emperor Sutoku Sends His Retainers to Rescue Tametomo*, which is famous for its giant ferocious shark, Kuniyoshi referred to Hokusai's illustration in the *yomihon* entitled *Strange Tales of the Bow Moon*. As regards the landscapes entitled *Thirty-six Views of Mount Fuji Seen from Edo* (fig. 35-2), it is obvious that Kuniyoshi had Hokusai's *Thirty-six Views of Mount Fuji* (see p. 48) in mind.

According to the biography *Hokusai-den*, Kuniyoshi revered Hokusai. One day, Kuniyoshi tried to arrange a meeting with Hokusai through one of Hokusai's disciples, Ōtsuka Dōan. Hokusai replied that he would not mind meeting Kuniyoshi once, but it would not be good for Kuniyoshi if he were to keep coming again. Hokusai was worried that people might suspect that Kuniyoshi had switched from the Utagawa school to the Katsushika school. In due course, Kuniyoshi visited Hokusai and they held lengthy discussions on painting. Hokusai seems to have taken care to maintain a certain distance from Kuniyoshi bearing in mind that he belonged to a different school.

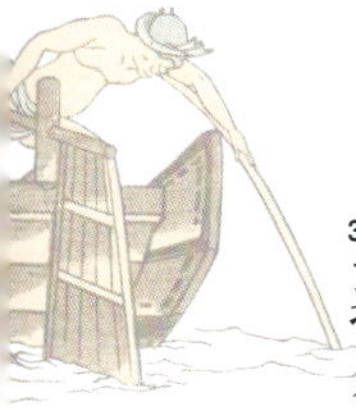

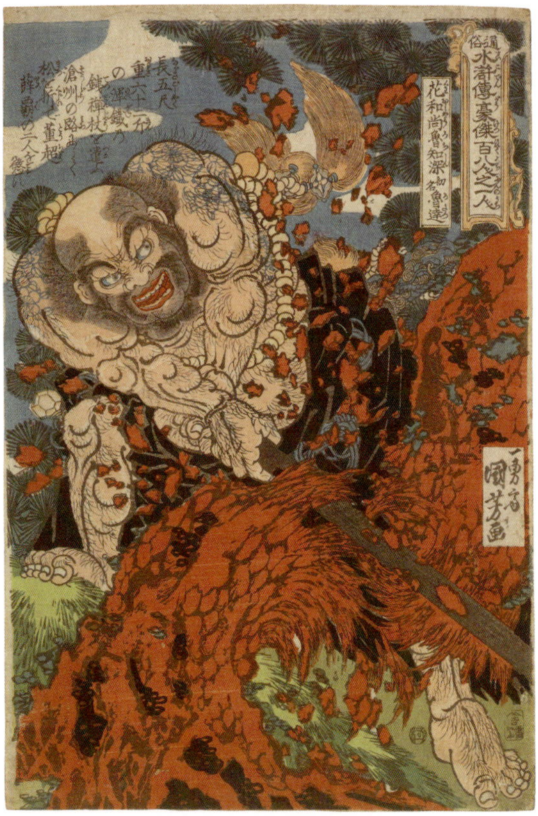

35-1 歌川国芳

通俗水滸伝豪傑百八人之一人 花和尚魯知深 初名魯達

文政10年(1827)　大判錦絵　山口県立美術館・浦上記念館蔵

『水滸伝』のヒーローたちを描いた全74点の揃物。北斎も読本挿絵や絵本を中心に武者絵を数多く描いていますが、一枚摺の錦絵において武者絵の人気が高まったのは、やはり国芳の功績が大きいでしょう。

35-1 Utagawa Kuniyoshi

108 Heroes of the Water Margin for Everyman: Kaoshō Rochishin

1827, *ōban nishiki-e*, Hagi Uragami Museum

A set of altogether seventy-four portraits of the heroes in the Chinese novel *The Water Margin*. Hokusai also did numerous portraits of warriors mainly as *yomihon* illustrations and picture books, but the surge in the popularity of single-sheet *nishiki-e* can definitely be attributed largely to Kuniyoshi's achievements.

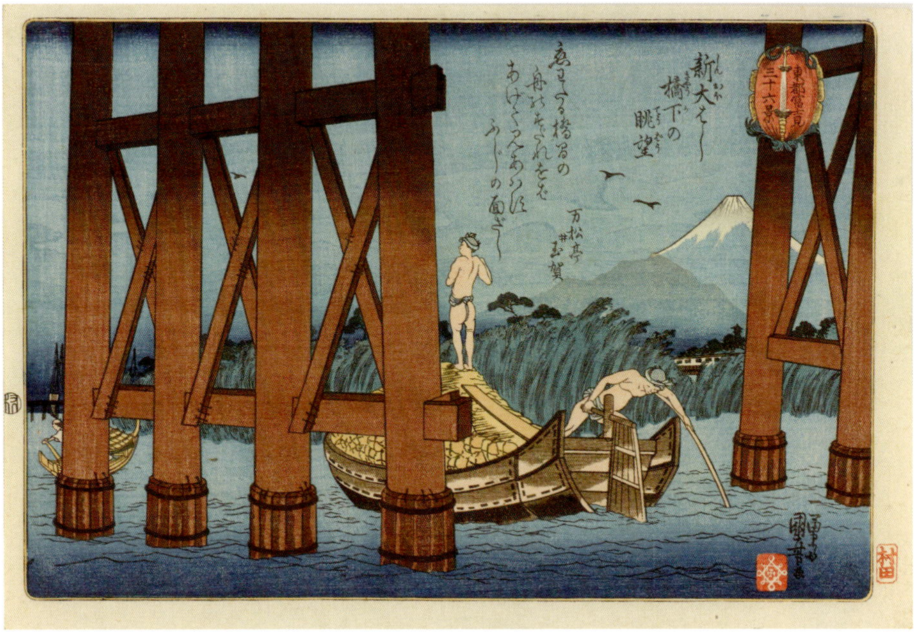

35-2 歌川国芳

東都冨士見三十六景　新大はし橋下の眺望

天保14年(1843)頃　大判錦絵　太田記念美術館蔵

橋の下から富士山を眺めるという奇抜な視点は、北斎の「冨嶽三十六景　深川万年橋下」(図12-2)と共通しますが、国芳の作品は人間の視点に近い高さから風景を眺めており、北斎の作品よりも臨場感を強く感じさせます。

35-2 Utagawa Kuniyoshi

Thirty-six Views of Mount Fuji Seen from Edo: View from beneath Shin'ōhashi Bridge

c. 1843, *ōban nishiki-e*, Ōta Memorial Museum of Art

The unconventional viewpoint of looking at Mount Fuji from beneath a bridge is shared by Hokusai's *Thirty-six Views of Mount Fuji: Under Mannen Bridge at Fukagawa* (fig. 12-2). In Kuniyoshi's case, the mountain is viewed from a height closer to a person's viewpoint, providing it with a more true-to-life ambience compared to Hokusai's work.

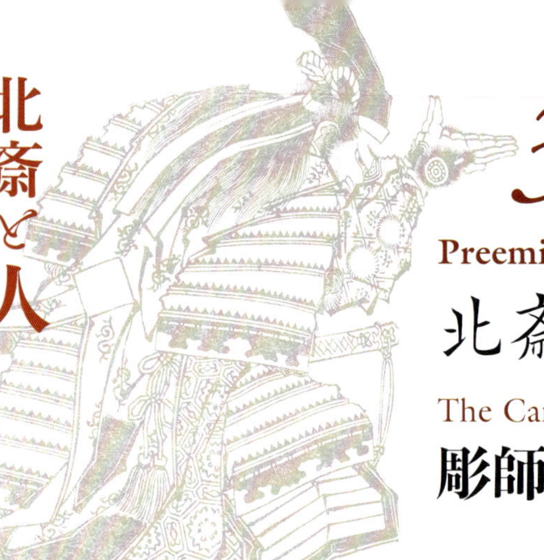

36

Preeminent Skills Appreciated by Hokusai

北斎が認める卓抜した技術

The Carver Egawa Tomekichi

彫師・江川留吉

木版画である錦絵や絵本を制作するには、絵師だけでなく、彫師や摺師の力が必要です。当然のことながら、彫師や摺師もそれぞれ技量が異なりますから、それによって作品の良し悪しが変わってきます。

北斎は彫りの作業について強いこだわりがありました。特に江川留吉（えがわとめきち）という彫師の腕前を高く評価しています。江川留吉は、文化9年（1812）刊の読本『北越奇談』（図32-2）や、文政6年（1823）刊の絵手本『今様櫛𥿻雛形（いまようせっきんひながた）』（図2-5, 8-5）、天保5、6年（1834、35）刊の絵本『富嶽百景』（図2-6, 12-5~6）初編・二編など、北斎の版本をいくつも手掛けた彫師です。生没年は分かっていませんが、当代有数の彫りの名手で、絵本を専らとし、一枚摺である錦絵は彫らなかったそうです[1]。

『北斎伝』には、天保6年（1835）、北斎が版元である小林新兵衛らに宛てた手紙が紹介されていますが、その中で、武者絵本〔おそらく『和漢絵本魁』と『絵本武蔵鐙』（図21-2, 36-1）〕や読本『釈迦御一代記図会（しゃかごいちだいきずえ）』（図6-6）の彫りは江川留吉に頼んで欲しいと、しつこいまでに訴えています。江川留吉が指揮した『富嶽百景』の彫りが素晴らしかったためで、北斎は満足いく作品を仕上げるために、腕の立つ彫師の技術が不可欠だったのです。

また、天保7年（1836）、同様に版元の小林新兵衛らに宛てた手紙で、北斎は、人の顔を彫る時の注意事項を、わざわざ挿絵を描いて説明しています（図36-2）。目に下瞼を付けずに彫るように、あるいは、歌川派の鼻の形にならないようになど、ごくわずかな違いにしか過ぎないようにも見えますが、北斎にとって、歌川派の画風と似てしまわないようにするためには、彫りについて細かく目配りをする必要があったのです。

1）大野静方「江戸時代の彫刻師」『浮世絵と版画』大東出版社、昭和17年（1942）

Nishik-e (polychrome prints) and picture books were woodblock prints, which required not only an artist but also a carver and a printer. Of course the ability of each carver and printer differed and, accordingly, the quality of the work would vary.

Hokusai was extremely fastidious about the carving process. He held the carver Egawa Tomekichi's skills in particularly high esteem. Egawa Tomekichi was a carver who worked on many of Hokusai's books composed of woodblock prints including the *yomihon Strange Stories of the Northern Province of Echigo* (fig. 32-2) published in 1812, the *edehon* (drawing manual) *Modern Designs for Combs and Tobacco Pipes* (figs. 2-5, 8-5) published in 1823, and the picture books *One Hundred Views of Mount Fuji*, parts 1 and 2 (figs. 2-6, 12-5~6) published in 1834 and 1835. Although the years of his birth and death remain unknown, he was one of the best carvers of his time. He is said to have worked exclusively on picture books and did not carve single-sheet *nishiki-e*.

A letter Hokusai wrote to his publisher Kobayashi Shinbē in 1835 is introduced in the biography *Hokusai-den*. In it, Hokusai insists that the carving of his warrior picture books〔probably *Picture Book of Japanese and Chinese Warriors* and *Picture Book, The Stirrups of Musashi* (figs. 21-2, 36-1)〕and his *yomihon Illustrated Life of Shakamuni* (fig. 6-6) should be done by Egawa Tomekichi. This was because the carving of *One Hundred Views of Mount Fuji* supervised by Egawa Tomekichi was superb and the skills of a proficient carver were indispensable for Hokusai to accomplish a satisfying work.

In another letter to Kobayashi Shinbē in 1836, Hokusai even went as far as giving detailed precautions on carving a human face by providing illustrations (fig. 36-2). Carve the eye without defining the lower eyelid, do not carve the nose in the shape of an Utagawa school nose, etc. Such details may seem trivial, but to Hokusai, in order to make sure that his style did not resemble the style of the Utagawa school, it was necessary to pay close attention to the carving.

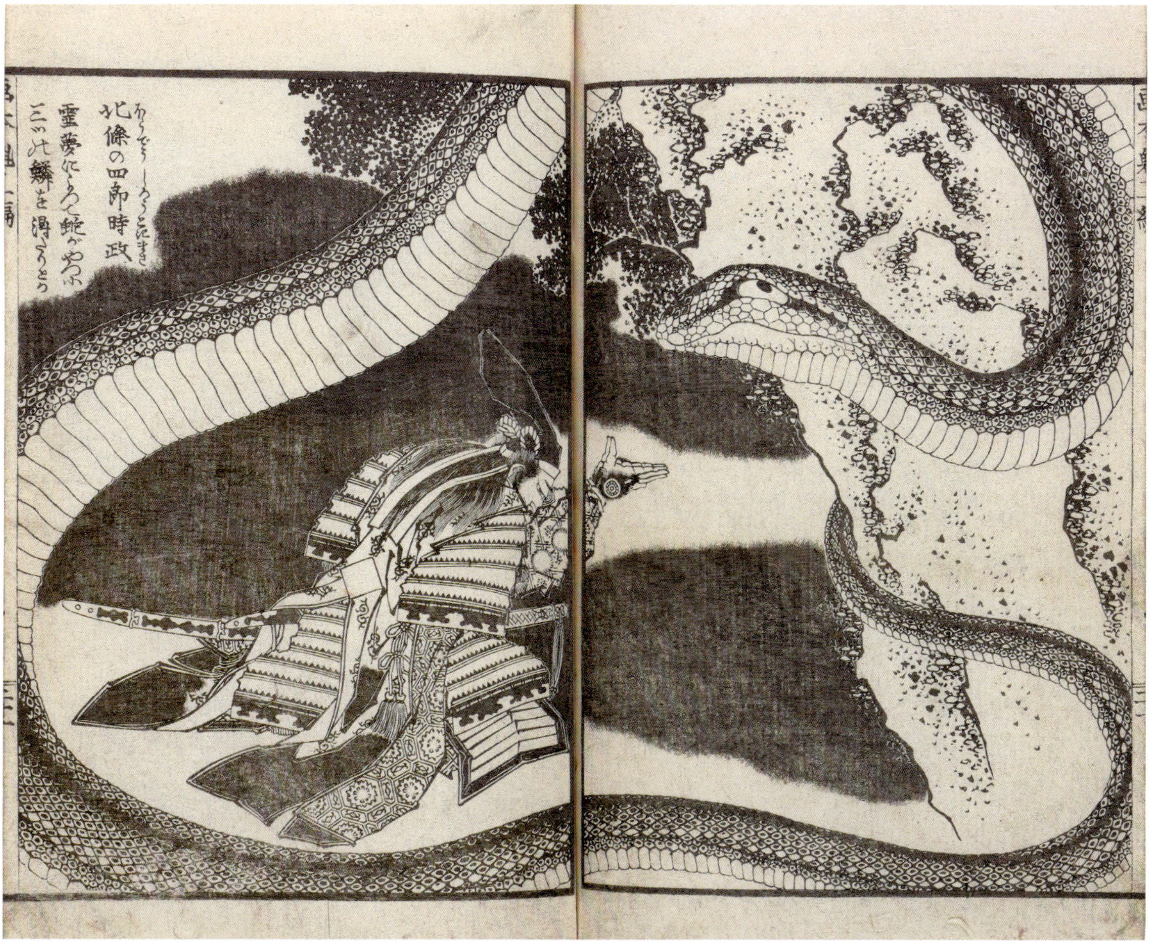

36-1 葛飾北斎 『絵本武蔵鐙(えほんむさしあぶみ)』

天保7年(1836)　半紙本　島根県立美術館(永田コレクション)蔵

日本の武者を集めた絵本。奥付では、北斎が「七十七齢　前北斎改画狂老人卍筆」と署名したすぐ左隣に「彫工　江川留吉」と名前が並んで記されています。蛇の鱗や武者の鎧など、高度な彫りの技術がうかがえます。

36-1 Katsushika Hokusai

Picture Book, The Stirrups of Musashi

1836, *hanshibon*, Shimane Art Museum (Nagata Collection)

This is a picture book of Japanese warriors. Next to Hokusai's signature, "Aged 77, Drawn by the former Hokusai renamed Manji, the Old Man Mad about Drawing," on the left-hand side, it says, "Carver, Egawa Tomekichi." His high degree of carving techniques is demonstrated in the snake's scales and the warriors' armor.

36-2 飯島虚心

『葛飾北斎伝(かつしかほくさいでん)』

明治26(1893)年　半紙本　国立国会図書館蔵

北斎が版元に宛てた手紙の中で、彫師の杉田金助に向けて説明しています。杉田金助は以前に北斎の描いた『唐詩選画本(とうしせんえほん)』の彫りを担当していますが、人物の顔の彫り方が北斎にとっては気に入らなかったようです。

36-2 Iijima Kyoshin

Katsushika Hokusai-den
(A biography of Katsushika Hokusai)

1893, *hanshibon*, National Diet Library, Japan

In a letter to the publisher, Hokusai gives instructions for the carver Sugita Kinsuke. Sugita Kinsuke had formerly been in charge of the carving of Hokusai's *Illustrated Anthology of Tang-Dynasty Poems*, but it seems that Hokusai was unhappy about the way he carved the figures' faces.

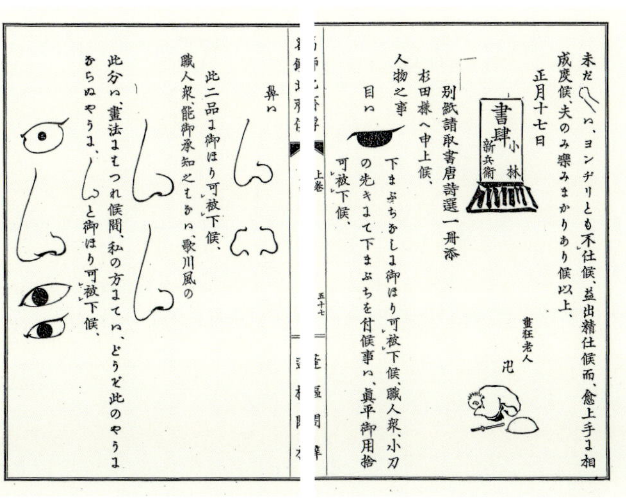

未だ〈ハ、ヨンデリとも不仕候、益出精仕候而、愈上手ニ相成度候、夫のみ楽みまかりあり候以上、
正月十七日
画狂老人　卍
書肆　小林新兵衛
別紙請取書唐詩選一冊添
杉田様へ申上候、
人物之事
目ハ
下まぶちかしニ御ほり可被下候、職人衆、小刀の先キニて下まぶちを付候事ハ、眞平御用捨可被下候、
鼻ハ
此二品ニ御ほり可被下候、
職人衆、能御承知之もあれ、歌川風の
此分ハ、書法ニもつれ候間、私の方ニてハ、どうぞ此のやうニあらぬやうニ、と御ほり可被下候、

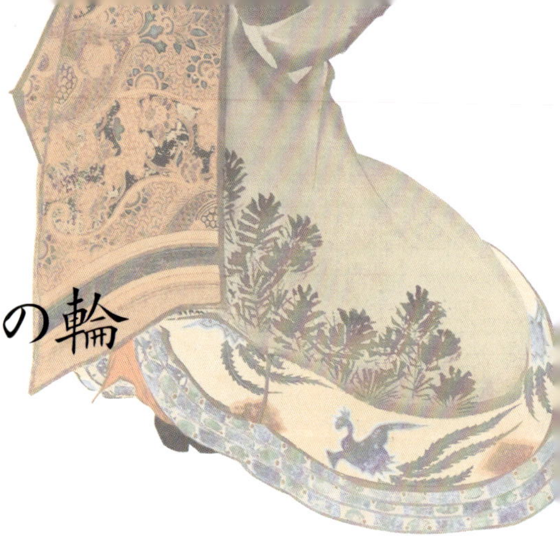

37

Followers all over Japan
日本中に広がる弟子の輪

Disciples
門人たち

北斎には数多くの門人がおり、直弟子と孫弟子を数えれば230名以上にのぼるとの指摘があります[1)]。『北斎伝』には、北斎は「自教授することを好ます、其の門人たらんを請ふものあれは、自画きし刻板の画手本を出たし、先つ画かしめ、そここゝと、短所を指して、教へたるのみ」だったとあります。すなわち、手取り足取り教えるのではなく、『北斎漫画』のような絵手本（→32頁参照）を手本とさせ、簡単に悪い点を指摘する程度の教え方でした。それでも北斎の教えを乞いたいという絵師はたくさんいたのでしょう。

北斎の門人たちは、北斎が開拓したさまざまな分野を継承しています。菱川宗理（図37-1）や蹄斎北馬（図37-2）は肉筆美人画を得意とし、柳々居辰斎（図37-3）や昇亭北寿（図37-4）は洋風の風景画に個性を発揮しました。狂歌摺物や狂歌本の挿絵のジャンルでは、魚屋北渓（図37-5）や柳々居辰斎（図37-6）、読本挿絵では柳川重信（→64頁参照, 図18-1）が活躍しています。そして、北斎の娘である葛飾応為（→96頁参照）は、絵師として北斎の仕事をサポートしました。

さらに、名古屋（→114頁参照）には牧墨僊や東南西北雲、沼田月斎、大坂（→116頁参照）には千鶴斎北洋や雪花亭北洲、春陽斎北敬、小布施（→120頁参照）には高井鴻山といったように、江戸の町以外にも高名な弟子たちが多くいたのも大きな特徴です。

北斎の門人たちは、北斎の画風を忠実に守ろうとする絵師もいれば、独自の画風を築こうとする絵師もいました。同じ一門として一括りにするには、それぞれがあまりに個性的であったといえるでしょう。

1） 永田生慈『葛飾北斎』吉川弘文館、2000年

Hokusai had many disciples. It has been pointed out that his immediate pupils and second-generation pupils amounted to 230 or more. According to the biography *Hokusai-den*, Hokusai "did not like giving lessons. If someone wanted to become a disciple, all Hokusai would do was hand the pupil a sample print he had made, have the pupil copy it, and instruct the pupil by pointing out each one of the defects." That is to say, rather than spoon-feeding the pupil, Hokusai would have the pupil follow drawing manuals (see p. 32) like *Hokusai's Sketches* and point out the pupil's weak points in brief. Even so, there must have been quite a few artists who wanted to be taught by Hokusai.

Hokusai's disciples inherited a variety of fields pioneered by their master. Hishikawa Sōri (fig. 37-1) and Teisai Hokuba (fig. 37-2) were good at original paintings of beauties and Ryūryūkyo Shinsai (fig. 37-3) and Shōtei Hokuju (fig. 37-4) exerted their individuality in Western-style landscapes. Totoya Hokkei (fig. 37-5) and Ryūryūkyo Shinsai (fig. 37-6) were actively involved in *kyōka* prints and illustrations for *kyōka* books and Yanagawa Shigenobu (see p. 64, fig. 18-1) in *yomihon* illustrations. Hokusai's daughter, Katsushika Ōi (see p. 96) supported Hokusai's work as an artist.

Also noteworthy is the fact that Hokusai had many distinguished disciples in cities other than Edo, too. In Nagoya (see p. 114), there were Maki Bokusen, Tōnansei Hokuun, and Numata Gessai; in Osaka (see p. 116), Senkakusai Hokuyō, Sekkatei Hokushū, and Shun'yōsai Hokkei; and in Obuse (see p. 120), Takai Kōzan.

Among Hokusai's disciples, there were artists who faithfully observed Hokusai's artistic style and others who tried to establish a style of their own. Each one of them was so distinctive that it is hard to summarize them altogether as a single school.

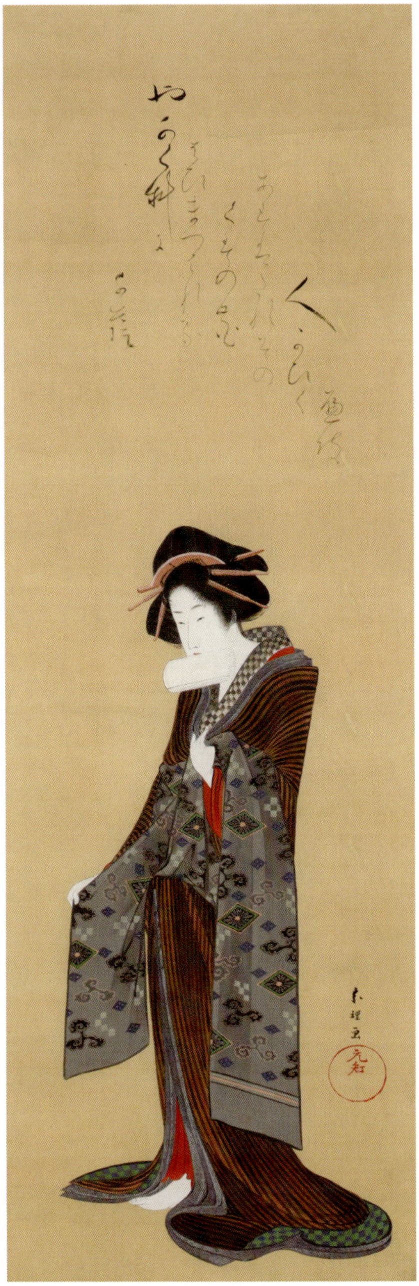

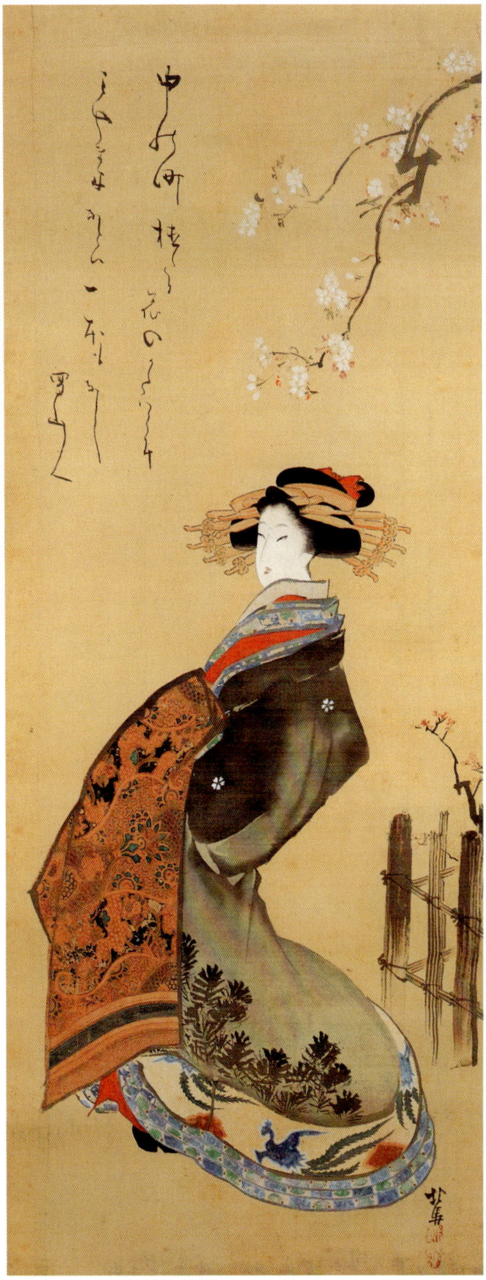

37-1 菱川宗理 **帯をなおす美人図**

寛政10〜文化(1798〜1818)頃　絹本着色

島根県立美術館(永田コレクション)蔵

菱川宗理は北斎が宗理と号していた30代後半頃の門人です。はじめ宗二と号していましたが、寛政10年（1798）に宗理号を襲名しました。宗理時代の北斎の作風に類似した肉筆美人画を主に制作しています。

37-1 Hishikawa Sōri

Beauty Adjusting Her Sash

c. 1798–1818, color on silk, Shimane Art Museum (Nagata Collection)

Hishikawa Sōri was a disciple of Hokusai when the master was in his late thirties and was working under the name Sōri. Hishikawa began under the name Sōji and succeeded to the Sōri name in 1798. He produced mainly original paintings of beauties similar in style to Hokusai during his Sōri period.

37-2 蹄斎北馬 **桜下花魁の図**

文化〜文政6年(1804〜23)頃　絹本着色　太田記念美術館蔵

北馬は北斎の門人の筆頭に挙げられる絵師で、読本挿絵や狂歌絵本、摺物の他、本図のような肉筆美人画を多数制作しています。初めは北斎からの影響が色濃く見られましたが、徐々に独自の画風を確立していきました。

37-2 Teisai Hokuba

Courtesan under the Cherry Blossoms

c. 1804–1823, color on silk, Ōta Memorial Museum of Art

Regarded the top artist among Hokusai's disciples, Teisai Hokuba produced many *yomihon* illustrations, *kyōka* picture books, single-sheet woodblock prints, and original paintings of beauties like the present example. His early works were heavily influenced by Hokusai, but he gradually established an artistic style of his own.

37-3 柳々居辰斎
近江八景　石山秋月
文化(1804～18)頃　大判錦絵　太田記念美術館蔵

辰斎は、狂歌摺物や読本挿絵、肉筆画を制作しました。錦絵としては、西洋の透視図法や陰影法を取り入れた洋風風景画を手掛けています。洋風風景画は北斎が40代半ば頃に集中して手掛けていたジャンルで、辰斎の作品には北斎からの大きな影響がうかがえます。

37-3 Ryūryūkyo Shinsai
Eight Views of Ōmi Province: The Autumn Moon at Ishiyama
c. 1804–1818, *ōban nishiki-e*, Ōta Memorial Museum of Art

Shinsai produced *kyōka surimono* (single-sheet woodblock prints), *yomihon* illustrations, and original paintings. Regarding *nishiki-e* (polychrome prints), he did Western-style landscapes employing Western perspective and shading. Western-style landscapes was a genre that Hokusai worked on concentratedly around his mid-forties and Hokusai's influence is strongly noticeable in Shinsai's works.

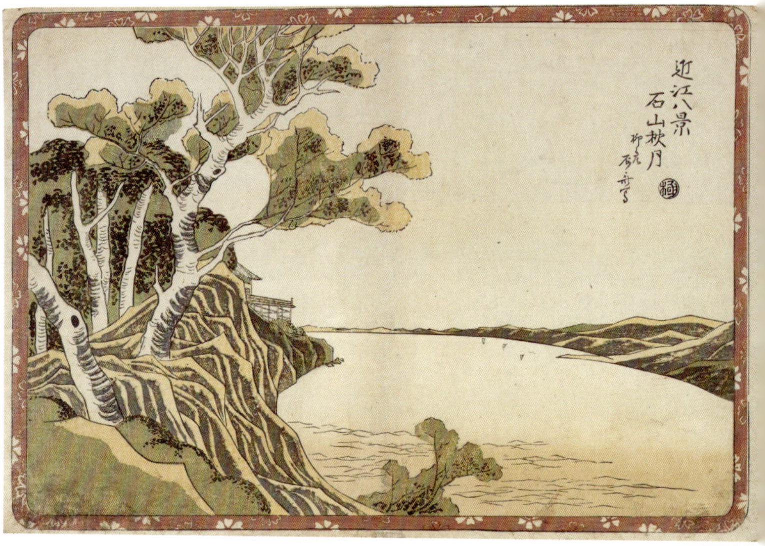

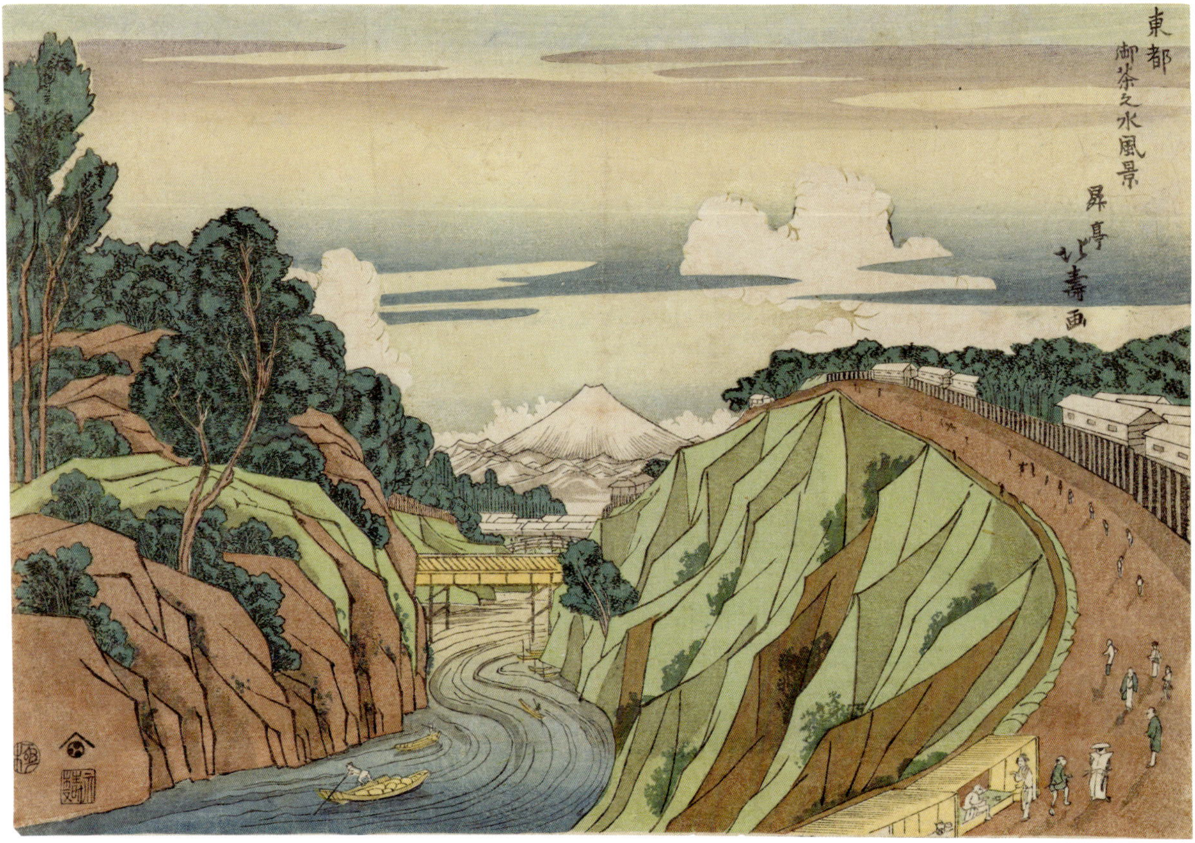

37-4 昇亭北寿　**東都御茶之水風景**
文化元～6年(1804～09)頃　大判錦絵　太田記念美術館蔵

北寿は北斎が得意とした洋風風景版画を継承し、多くの風景画を手掛けました。本図において、崖を三角形で連ねたり、明るい色面と暗い色面で陰影を示したりしていますが、北斎の影響から抜け出し、北寿独自の描法を追求しようとしていることが認められます。

37-4 Shōtei Hokuju ***View of Ochanomizu in Edo***
c. 1804–1809, *ōban nishiki-e*, Ōta Memorial Museum of Art

Inheriting the techniques of Western-style landscape prints that Hokusai was good at, Hokuju produced many landscapes. Here, as evident in the way the bluffs are represented as overlapping triangles or the shading with bright color planes and dark ones, Hokuju has broken away from Hokusai's influence and seems to be pursuing drawing techniques of his own.

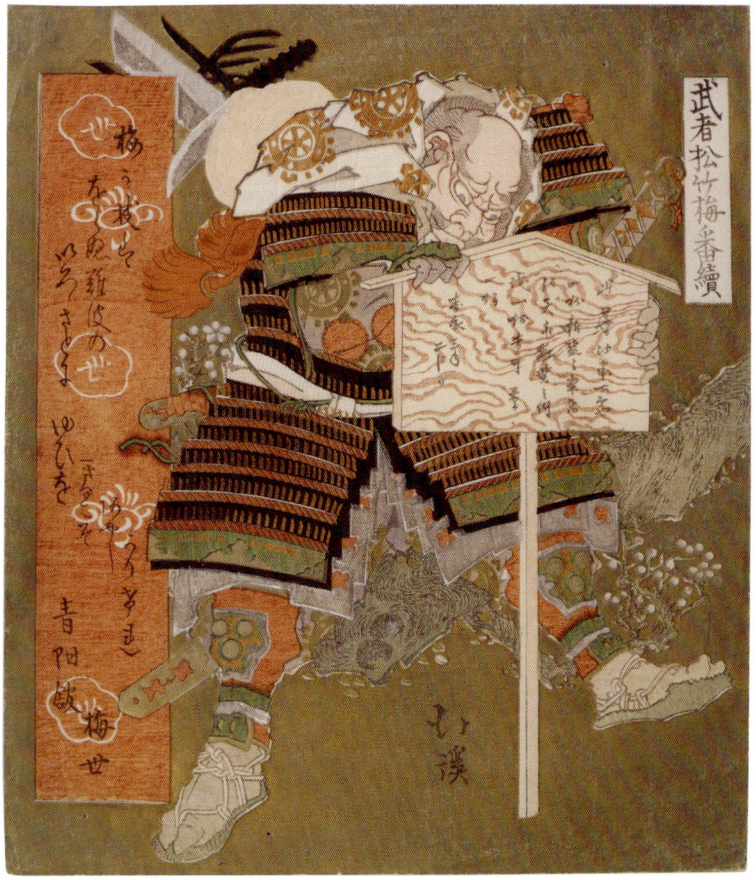

37-5 魚屋北溪

武者松竹梅番続　梅　武蔵坊弁慶

文政後期(1822〜30)頃　色紙判摺物　千葉市美術館蔵

北溪は、北斎の門人として、蹄斎北馬に並ぶ双璧とされています。魚屋を営んでいたことから、魚屋という画号を用いました。狂歌絵本や狂歌摺物のジャンルにおいて、北斎の画風を忠実に継承し、数多くの作品を制作しました。

37-5 Totoya Hokkei

Designs of Warriors Likened to Pine, Bamboo, and Plum: Plum, Musashi-bō Benkei

c. 1822–1830, *shikishiban surimono*, Chiba City Museum of Art

Totoya Hokkei was regarded one of the two greatest disciples of Hokusai alongside Teisai Hokuba. As he ran a fish shop, he used the artist name Totoya, which means fishmonger in Japanese. He faithfully inherited Hokusai's artistic style in the genres of *kyōka* picture books and *kyōka surimono* (single-sheet woodblock prints) and produced a considerable number of works.

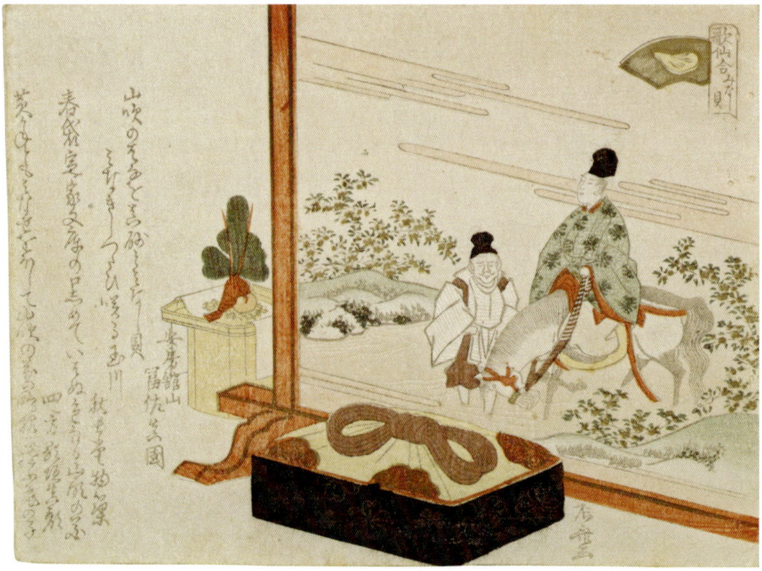

37-6 柳々居辰斎

歌仙合　みなし貝

文化6年(1809)　九つ切判摺物　千葉市美術館蔵

辰斎は洋風風景画（図 37-3）だけでなく、狂歌摺物も制作しています。狂歌摺物では、一般的な錦絵ではあまり描かれることのない、さまざまな道具類も画題となりました。

37-6 Ryūryūkyo Shinsai

Contest of Poet Immortals: Waterless Shell

1809, *kokonotsugiriban surimono*, Chiba City Museum of Art

It was not only Western-style landscapes (fig. 37-3) that Shinsai produced. He also did *kyōka surimono* (single-sheet woodblock prints), in which implements that would not be treated as subject matters in normal *nishiki-e* (polychrome prints) were portrayed.

38 Art Appreciated by Foreigners Too

異邦人にも喜ばれた画技

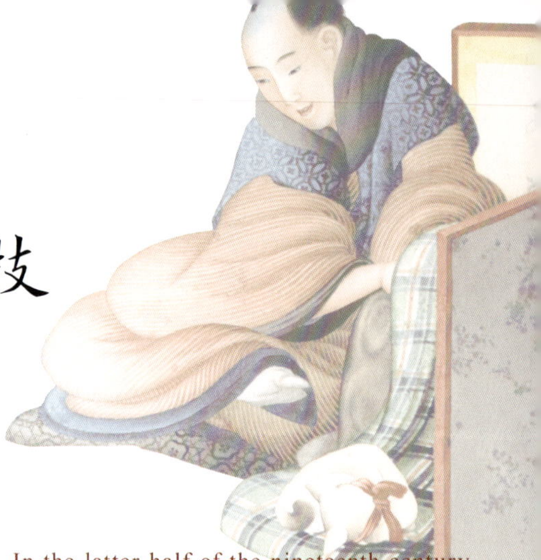

The Dutch

オランダ人

19世紀後半、北斎の作品はフランスを中心としたヨーロッパ各地で愛好され、ジャポニスムと呼ばれる日本美術ブームを起こすひとつの要因となります。しかし、北斎が存命中の頃から、その名前はヨーロッパ人たちに知られるところでした。

江戸時代の日本は、ヨーロッパとの窓口が長崎の出島に限定されていました。そこで商館長（カピタン）を務めるオランダ人たちは、日本に関する情報収集のためにさまざまな工芸品や日用品を手に入れているのですが、その中に北斎の絵画がありました。

まず、文政5年（1822）、江戸の町を訪問したカピタンのブロムホフは、『北斎漫画』初編から10編を購入しています。ブロムホフがこの時北斎と直接会ったという資料はありませんが、ブロムホフは北斎に絵画制作の発注をしたとの推測があります[1)]。

次に文政9年（1826）、カピタンであるデ・ステューレルと商館医のシーボルトが江戸を訪れた際、北斎が描いた肉筆画を受け取り、母国へと持ち帰っています。以前にブロムホフが発注したものに加え、デ・ステューレルやシーボルトが追加で依頼をしたのでしょう。庶民たちの日常の生活や職人たちの仕事、江戸の町の名所など、日本を知るための内容となっています。一般的な錦絵や肉筆画とは異なる色遣いとなっているのが特徴で、北斎が単独で制作したのではなく、娘の葛飾応為（→96頁参照）や魚屋北渓（→106頁参照）、二代葛飾戴斗など、門人たちの手が加わった工房制作であったと考えられています[2)]。これらの作品は、現在、オランダのライデン国立民族学博物館とフランス国立図書館に所蔵されています。

1) マティ・フォラー「葛飾北斎とシーボルトの出会い」『北斎 Siebold & Hokusai and his Tradition』（展覧会図録）、東京新聞、2007年
2) マティ・フォラー、前掲書［註1］

In the latter half of the nineteenth century, Hokusai's works were appreciated in France and other parts of Europe and became one of the causes of the boom for Japanese art known as Japonisme. Hokusai's name was already known to the Europeans during his lifetime.

In Japan during the Edo period (1603-1868), contact with European countries was restricted to Dejima in Nagasaki. In order to gather information on Japan, the chief factors (*kapitans*) of the Dutch trading post there obtained a variety of craftwork and commodities, among which Hokusai's pictures were included.

To begin with, the *kapitan* Jan Cock Blomhoff who visited Edo in 1822 purchased parts 1 to 10 of *Hokusai's Sketches*. Although there is no evidence that Blomhoff met Hokusai in person on that occasion, there is speculation that he placed an order for Hokusai to produce a considerable number of paintings.

After that, in 1826, the *kapitan* Johan Willem de Sturler and the resident physician at Dejima Philipp Franz von Siebold visited Edo, collected some original paintings by Hokusai, and took them back to the Netherlands. In addition to what Blomhoff had ordered, de Sturler and Siebold had probably ordered some more works. They were pictures of the commoners' daily life, artisans' work, sights in Edo, etc., i.e. content to find out about Japan. They are characterized by their use of color, differing from ordinary *nishiki-e* (polychrome prints) and original paintings. Presumably Hokusai did not produce them alone. They are considered to have been produced in the studio with the assistance of his daughter Katsushika Ōi (see p. 96) and disciples such as Totoya Hokkei (see p. 106) and Katsushika Taito II. These works are currently kept in the National Museum of Ethnology, Leiden and the Bibliothèque nationale de France.

38-1 葛飾北斎 **端午の節句**

文政7〜9年(1824〜26)頃 紙本着色 ライデン国立民族学博物館蔵

屋根の上にある物干台の上にいる家族たち。背後には、鯉幟や鍾馗の幟が飾られ、5月5日の端午の節句であることが分かります。マティ・フォラー氏は北斎と応為の制作であると推定しています。

38-1 Katsushika Hokusai ***Boys' Festival***

c. 1824–1826, color on paper, National Museum of Ethnology, Leiden

A family are gathered on a clothes-drying platform on the roof. Carp streamers and a banner of Shōki (Chinese: Zhong Kui) decorate the background, indicating that it is the Boys' Festival. Matthi Forrer presumes that this is by Hokusai and Ōi.

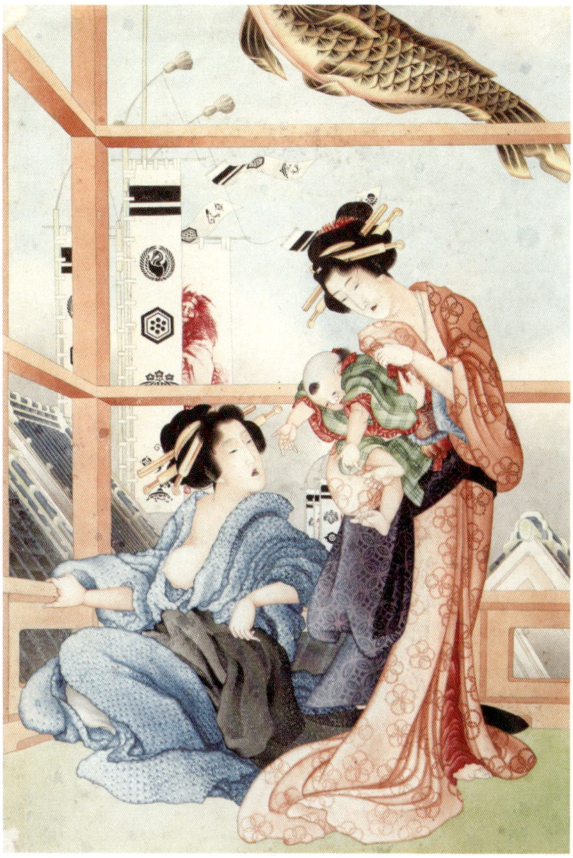

Nationaal Museum van Wereldculturen.Coll.no.:RV-1-4482-h

▼38-2 葛飾北斎 **節季の商家**

文政7〜9年(1824〜26)頃 紙本着色 ライデン国立民族学博物館蔵

師走の決算期（節季）を迎えた商家の様子。算盤をはじく番頭の脇にある大福帳に文政7年を示す記述があり、本図の制作年を推定する貴重な情報となっています。マティ・フォラー氏は、この作品も北斎と応為の制作であると推定しています。

▼38-2 Katsushika Hokusai ***Year-end Accounts***

c. 1824–1826, color on paper, National Museum of Ethnology, Leiden

This shows a merchant family at the end of the year, when they have to settle accounts. There is an entry marked 1824 in the account book placed by the chief clerk counting on the abacus, which serves as valuable information for dating this work. Matthi Forrer presumes that this is by Hokusai and Ōi.

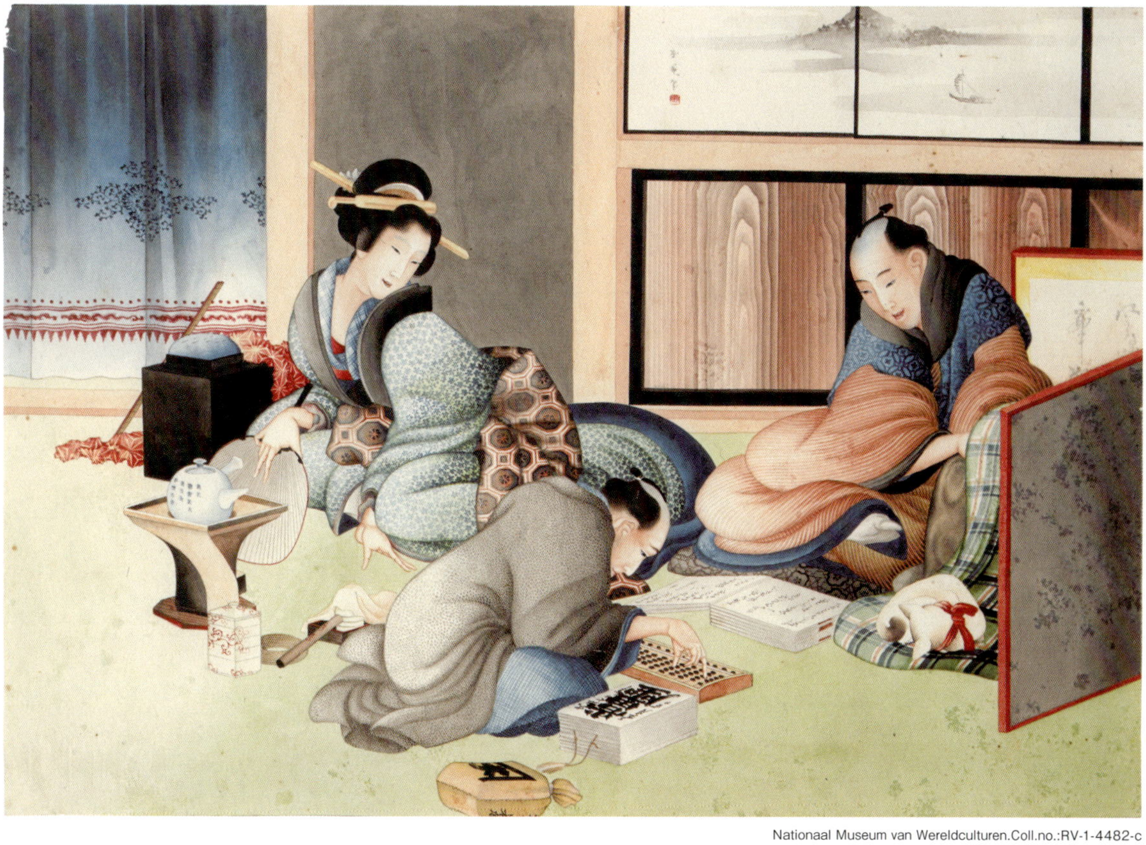

Nationaal Museum van Wereldculturen.Coll.no.:RV-1-4482-c

39 Gaze on the Sea
海を眺めた地

Chiba
千葉

北斎は日本各地を旅していますが、文化3年（1806）、47歳の時に、現在の千葉県木更津市まで出かけました。畳ヶ池付近にあった水野清右衛門の家に逗留し、「唐仙人の楽遊」（現在所在不明）という襖絵や、木更津市長須賀にある日枝神社に奉納するための大絵馬「富士の巻狩り図」（図39-1）を制作しました[1]。

北斎は木更津から江戸に戻る際、陸路ではなく、船に乗った可能性が指摘されています[2]。江戸湾を俯瞰した鳥瞰図「総房海陸勝景奇覧」（図39-2）や、木更津沖から弁才船越しに富士山を眺めた「冨嶽三十六景　上総ノ海路」を制作するにあたり、この時の旅行の記憶が生かされているのかも知れません。

さらに、北斎は晩年になってからも2回、千葉県に出かけています。その証拠となるのが、「総房旅客」という北斎自身の落款です。ひとつは、天保5～6年（1834～35）頃の団扇絵「鷹」に「総房旅客前北斎改画狂老人卍」という落款が、もうひとつは、天保11年（1840）の鳥瞰図「唐土名所之絵」に「総房旅客　画狂老人卍齢八十一」という落款があります。すなわち、75～76歳頃と81歳の時に千葉県を旅行していたと推測されるのです。ただし、具体的にどの場所を訪れたかまでは定かではありません。

なお、千葉県いすみ市にある行元寺には、「波の伊八」こと武志伊八郎信由という彫工が制作した「波に宝珠」という欄間があり、北斎はこれから「冨嶽三十六景　神奈川沖浪裏」（図2-1）の着想を得たという説があります[3]。しかしながら、現時点では、北斎が行元寺まで訪れたという確実な資料はまだ見つかっておりません。

1）　永田生慈「房総の旅客葛飾北斎─長須賀滞在と、その作品─」『浮世絵芸術』35号、1972年

2）　永田生慈「北斎旅行考」『財団法人北斎館　北斎研究所　研究紀要』第2集、2009年

3）　片岡栄『名工波の伊八、そして北斎』文芸社、2015年

Hokusai traveled all over Japan. In 1806, at the age of 47, he went to Chiba, the present Kisarazu-shi. He stayed at Mizuno Seiemon's house in the environs of Tatamigaike and produced a *fusuma* (sliding door) painting entitled *Tōsennin no gakuyū* (whereabouts unknown) and *Boar Hunt at the Foot of Mount Fuji* (fig. 39-1), a large votive wooden tablet presented to Hie Shrine in Nagasuka, Kisarazu.

On the way back from Kisarazu to Edo, it is possible that Hokusai returned not by land but on a boat. His memories of this cruise may have borne fruit as *Bird's-eye View over Land and Sea on Chiba Peninsula* (fig. 39-2) and *Thirty-six Views of Mount Fuji: At Sea off Kazusa*.

Hokusai went to Chiba twice more in his later years. This is proved by his signatures "Sōbō ryokaku [literally, traveler in Chiba]." One is the signature on *Hawk*, a round fan dating from circa 1834–1835 and signed "Traveler in Chiba, the former Hokusai renamed Manji, the Old Man Mad about Drawing." The other is his signature in *Famous Places in China, a* bird's-eye view dating from 1840 and signed "Traveler in Chiba, Manji, the Old Man Mad about Drawing aged 81." These signatures suggest that Hokusai traveled to Chiba when he was 75 or 76 and 81 years old. However, it is not clear which part of Chiba it was that he visited.

At Gyōgan-ji, a temple in Isumi-shi, Chiba, there is a *ranma* (carved wooden panel used as a decorative transom above sliding doors) entitled *Curving Waves and Peaked Treasure Orbs* and made by the carver Takeshi Ihachirō Nobuyoshi a.k.a. "Nami no Ihachi [Ihachi the wave carver]." Some say that Hokusai got the idea for *Thirty-six Views of Mount Fuji: Great Wave off the Coast of Kanagawa* (fig. 2-1) from this work. However, at present, there is no clear evidence that Hokusai went as far as Gyōgan-ji.

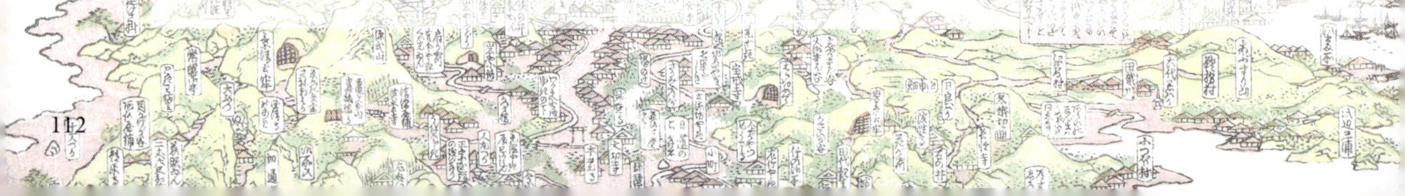

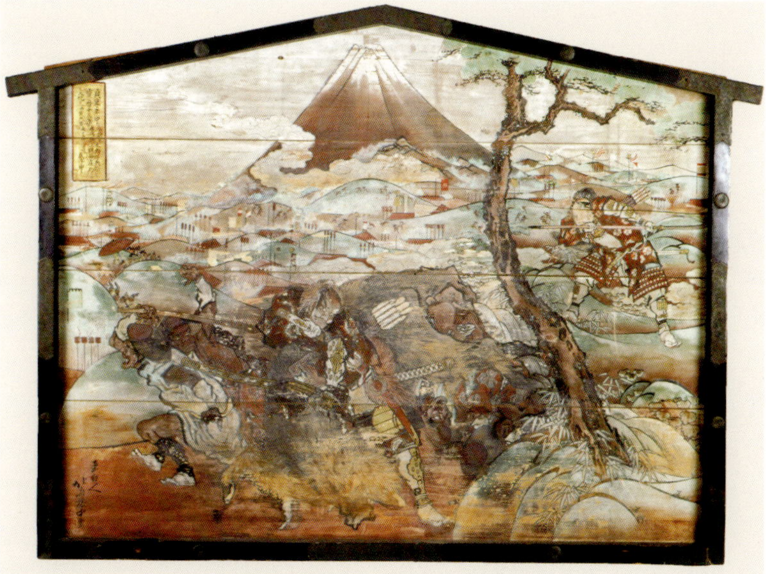

39-1 葛飾北斎

富士の巻狩り図

文化3年(1806)　板絵着色
木更津市長須賀・日枝神社蔵

建久４年（1193）、源頼朝が富士の裾野で巻狩りを行った際に、仁田四郎忠常が猪を退治したという、武者絵の伝統的な画題を描いた絵馬です。中央縦 139.5cm、横 180.5cm という、北斎の作品の中でも巨大な画面を誇っています。

39-1 Katsushika Hokusai

Boar Hunt at the Foot of Mount Fuji

1806, color on board, Hie Jinja, Nagasuka, Kisarazu-shi, Chiba

When Minamoto no Yoritomo went hunting at the foot of Mount Fuji in 1193, Nitta Shirō Tadatsune killed a boar. This traditional subject matter for a warrior painting is painted on a votive wooden tablet. 139.5 cm tall at the center and 180.5 cm wide, this is a substantial piece among Hokusai's works.

『図説 木更津のあゆみ』(平成24年 木更津市発行)より転載
Reproduced from *Zusetsu Kisarazu no ayumi* (An illustrated history of Kisarazu, Kisarazu City, 2012)

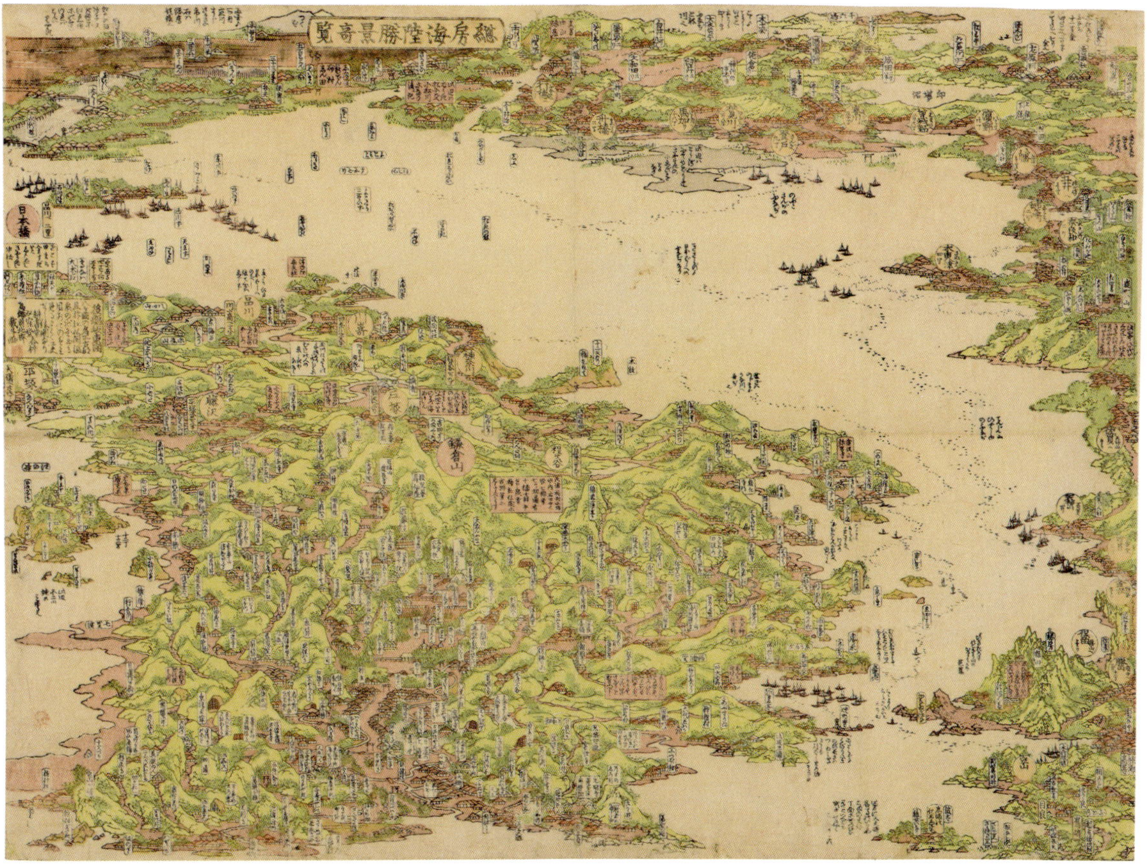

39-2 葛飾北斎　**総房海陸勝景奇覧**

文政元年(1818)頃　大々判錦絵　島根県立美術館(永田コレクション)蔵

三浦半島を手前に大きく描き、江戸湾を挟んで画面右手に房総半島を描いています。北斎が訪れた木更津は画面の右端に小さく描かれる程度ですが、北斎が宿泊した場所に近い畳ヶ池も描き込まれており、実体験が生かされていると考えられます。

39-2 Katsushika Hokusai

Bird's-eye View over Land and Sea on Chiba Peninsula

c. 1818, *ōōban nishiki-e*, Shimane Art Museum (Nagata Collection)

Miura Peninsula is depicted largely in the foreground and, with Edo Bay lying in between, Bōsō Peninsula lies towards the right. Kisarazu, where Hokusai went to, appears small at the right edge. However, as Tatamigaike, close to where he stayed, is written in, it appears to be based on his real experience.

40 Where *Hokusai's Sketches* Was Created
『北斎漫画』が生まれた地

Nagoya
名古屋

北斎は2度、名古屋に滞在したことが知られています。1回目は文化9年（1812）秋、53歳の時でした。この頃の北斎は、読本挿絵の第一人者として、全国的にその名前が知れ渡っていました。また、すでに尾張・三河地方の狂歌師たちとつながりがあり、狂歌摺物の制作に携わっていました（図40-1）。名古屋では北斎が来ることを待ち望んでいた人が多くいた、という状況だったのです。

文化9年、関西旅行の途中に名古屋に立ち寄った北斎は、尾張藩士で北斎の門人となる牧墨僊の家に数ヵ月滞在します。墨僊の家で300図余りの下絵を描き、これを元にして誕生したのが『北斎漫画』初編（→32頁参照）でした。文化11年（1814）、名古屋の版元である永楽屋東四郎が江戸の角丸屋甚助の協力を得て刊行します。

再び名古屋を訪れたのは、それから5年後の文化14年（1817）、58歳の時でした。花屋町に滞在し、版元からの依頼による絵本の版下絵を制作します[1]。この年の10月5日、西掛所（現在の本願寺名古屋別院）で巨大達磨の半身像を描くライブパフォーマンスを行なっています（→28頁参照）。その後、大坂まで足を伸ばしました（→116頁参照）。

北斎が名古屋の風景を描いた作品として、「冨嶽三十六景　尾州不二見原」（図40-2）があります。有名な名所ではないにも関わらず、あえてこの場所を選んでいるのは、北斎が滞在していた場所から1.5キロほどの近さにあったからでしょう。北斎は名古屋での滞在を思い出しながら、この作品を描いたと思われます。

1）　武田酔霞「葛飾北斎尾張名古屋の生活」『浮世絵』10号、1916年

Hokusai is known to have stayed in Nagoya twice. The first time was in the autumn of 1812, when he was 53 years old. In those days, he was known all over Japan as the leading authority on *yomihon* illustrations. He already had connections with *kyōka* poets in Owari and Mikawa and was involved in the production of *kyōka surimono* (single-sheet woodblock prints, fig. 40-1). There were many people looking forward to Hokusai's arrival in Nagoya.

When Hokusai stopped by at Nagoya while traveling around the Kansai region in 1812, he stayed at Maki Bokusen's house for a few months. Bokusen was a retainer of the Owari domain and became a disciple of Hokusai. While staying at Bokusen's, Hokusai produced over 300 sketches, which led to the emergence of the first part of *Hokusai's Sketches* (see p. 32). It was published in 1814 by Eirakuya Tōshirō, a publisher in Nagoya, with the cooperation of Kadomaruya Jinsuke, a publisher in Edo.

Hokusai's second visit to Nagoya took place five years later, in 1817, when he was 58. He stayed in Hanayachō and worked on the master drawings for a picture book commissioned by a publisher. On the fifth day of the tenth month that year, he gave a live performance in which he painted a huge half-length portrait of Bodhidharma at Nishikakesho (the present Hongan-ji Nagoya Betsu-in, see p. 28). After that, Hokusai went on to Osaka (see p. 116).

As a landscape of Nagoya depicted by Hokusai, there is *Thirty-six Views of Mount Fuji: Fujimi-bara in Owari Province* (fig. 40-2). The reason he chose this location although it was not a famous sight was probably that it was close to where he was staying, just 1.5 kilometers away. Hokusai probably produced this work reminiscing of his stay in Nagoya.

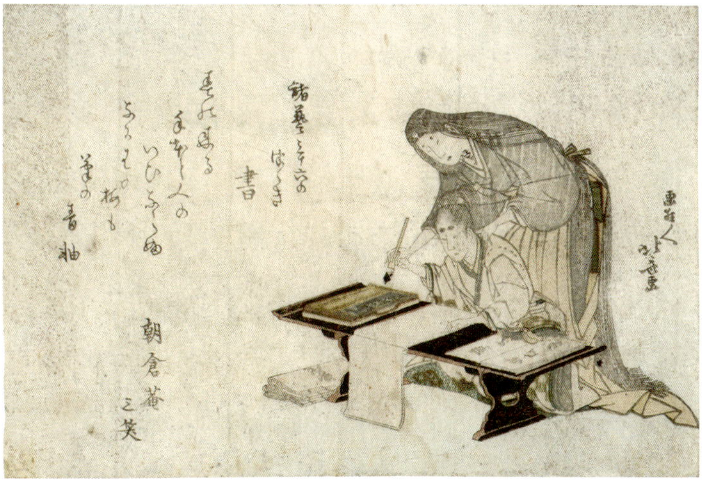

40-1 葛飾北斎

諸芸三十六のつつき　書

享和元～3年（1801～03）頃　四つ切判摺物
名古屋市博物館蔵

尾張・三河地方の狂歌サークルである三河擣衣連。本図はそのリーダーである浅倉庵三笑からの注文を受けて制作された摺物で、三笑の狂歌が賛として添えられています。実際に北斎が名古屋を訪れる10年ほど前の制作であり、北斎の名前は以前から名古屋の人々に知られていたと推測されます。

40-1 Katsushika Hokusai

Thirty-six Accomplishments, Calligraphy

c. 1801–1803, *yotsugiriban surimono*,
Nagoya City Museum

There was a *kyōka* circle in the Owari and Mikawa district called Mikawa Tōiren. Its leader Asakuraan Sanshō commissioned this *surimono* (single-sheet woodblock print) and a *kyōka* composed by Sanshō is inscribed as a caption. It was produced ten or so years before Hokusai actually visited Nagoya, implying that the artist's name was already known among the citizens of Nagoya.

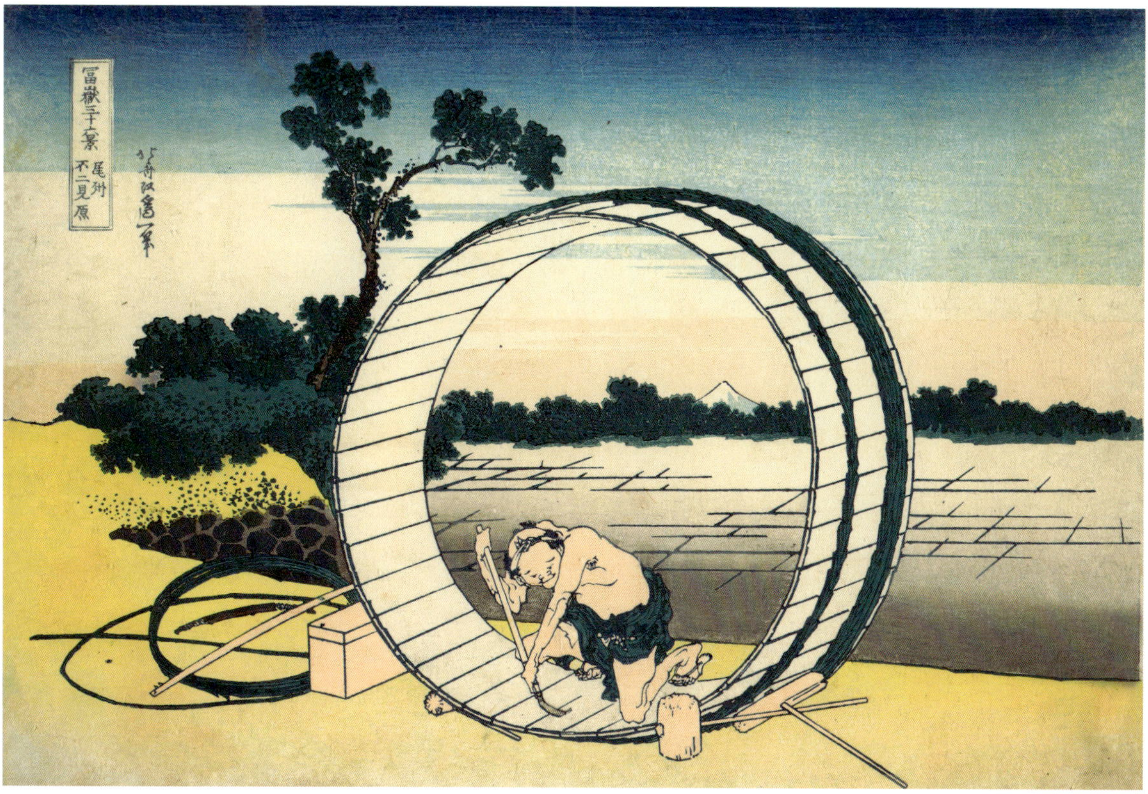

40-2 葛飾北斎

冨嶽三十六景　尾州不二見原

天保元～4年（1830～33）　大判錦絵　メトロポリタン美術館蔵

現在の愛知県名古屋市中区富士見町周辺にあった富士見原。ここから富士山は見えず、聖岳が富士山と見誤られていました。また、聖岳は独立峰ではないため、北斎は想像でこの風景を描いたと考えられます（種田祐司「富士見原から富士山がみえた?!」『北斎だるせん！』〈展覧会図録〉、名古屋市博物館、2017年）。

40-2 Katsushika Hokusai

Thirty-six Views of Mount Fuji: Fujimi-bara in Owari Province

1830–1833, *ōban nishiki-e*, The Metropolitan Museum of Art

Fujimi-bara was located near the present Fujimi-cho, Nagoya-shi, Aichi. Mount Fuji cannot be seen from this point. Mount Hijiri was mistaken for Mount Fuji. Moreover, as Mount Hijiri is part of a mountain range and does not stand on its own, it is possible that Hokusai created this landscape exercising his imagination.

41 Renowned among the Locals
響き渡る北斎の名

Osaka
大坂

北斎と馬琴による読本は大坂でも流行し、『三七全伝南柯夢』や『椿説弓張月』（図2-3, 6-2～4）は、文化5～6年（1808～09）、歌舞伎となって上演されるほどでした。北斎は読本挿絵の絵師として広く人気を博し、大坂の絵師たちにも影響を与えていたのです。

北斎が実際に大坂を訪れたのは、文化14年（1817）に名古屋に滞在した後（→114頁参照）、翌文化15年（文政元年、1818）のことであったと考えられています。その証拠のひとつに、『北斎伝』に「一説に、北斎尾州名古屋より伊勢に行き、紀州に入り、夫より大坂京都を歴遊し、江戸に帰りしといふ」という記述があります。ただし、伊勢、紀州、京都に滞在した資料はまだ確認されておらず、大坂にだけ活動の可能性が認められています。

北斎が大坂を訪れた目的として指摘されているのが、文政2年（1819）4月に刊行された『北斎画式』（図41-1）の版下絵を制作することです[1]。『北斎漫画』と同様、絵を学ぶ人のための絵手本で、北斎は大坂の版元である秋田屋太右衛門から依頼を受け、文政元年（1818）9月9日までには完成させたことが、その序文からうかがえます。

興味深いのは、『北斎画式』の奥付に「摂陽浪花校合門人」として、千鶴亭北洋、雪花亭北洲、春陽斎北敬という3名の絵師の名前が挙げられていることです。文化15年1月まで、雪花亭北洲は春好、春陽斎北敬は謹多楼春陽と名乗り、役者絵の絵師として十分な活躍をしていましたが、同年5月までに、北洲、北敬と画号を改めました（図41-2）[2]。このことから、文化15年の早い時期に北斎が来坂し、北洲と北敬、そしてそれまで活動が認められてない北洋が北斎に弟子入りしたと考えられるのです。

1）永田生慈「北斎旅行考」『財団法人北斎館　北斎研究所　研究紀要』第2集、2009年
2）北川博子「北斎の大坂の弟子たち」『北斎―風景・美人・奇想―』（展覧会図録）、大阪市立美術館、2012年

The *yomihon* produced by Hokusai and Bakin proved popular in Osaka, too. So much so that *Sanshichi zenden nanka no yume* and *Strange Tales of the Bow Moon* (figs. 2-3, 6-2～4) were staged as *kabuki* performances in 1808–1809. Hokusai gained wide reputation as a *yomihon* illustrator and influenced the artists in Osaka, too.

It was in 1818, after his stay in Nagoya in 1817 (see p. 114), that Hokusai is considered to have visited Osaka in person. This is backed partly by the following account in the biography *Hokusai-den*. "One theory holds that Hokusai went from Bishū Nagoya to Ise, then to Kishū, and from there, made a tour of Osaka and Kyoto before returning to Edo." Nevertheless, no evidence of Hokusai having stayed in Ise, Kishū, and Kyoto has been confirmed so far. Only the possibility of his activities in Osaka has been verified.

What has been pointed out as the purpose of Hokusai's visit to Osaka is the production of the master drawings for *The Form of Paintings of Hokusai* (fig. 41-1), which was published in 1819. Like *Hokusai's Sketches*, this was a drawing manual for people learning to draw and paint. The introduction to this textbook explains that Hokusai was commissioned by Akitaya Taemon, a publisher in Osaka, and completed it by the ninth day of the ninth month of 1818.

It is interesting that the names of three artists, namely Senkakutei Hokuyō, Sekkatei Hokushū, and Shun'yōsai Hokkei, are listed as "disciples of Setsuyō Naniwa Kyōgō" in the colophon at the end of *The Form of Paintings of Hokusai*. Until the first month of 1818, Sekkatei Hokushū used the name Shunkō and Shun'yōsai Hokkei took the name Kintarō Shun'yō and both artists were busily engaged in producing pictures of actors. Yet, from the fifth month of 1818, these two artists renamed themselves Hokushū and Hokkei (fig. 41-2). Consequently, it is possible that Hokusai arrived in Osaka early in 1818 and Hokushū, Hokkei, and, in addition, Hokuyō, whose work has not been confirmed prior to that, became disciples of Hokusai.

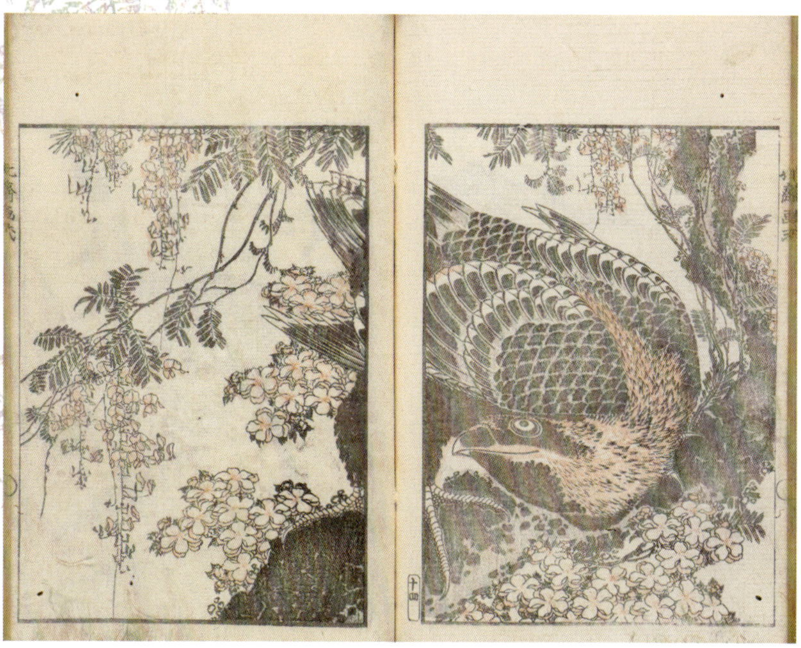

41-1 葛飾北斎 『北斎画式』
文政2年(1819)　大本　島根県立美術館(永田コレクション)蔵

見開きの画面に、伝説上の人物や庶民の暮らし、風景、花鳥など、さまざまなジャンルを描いた絵本です。『北斎漫画』よりも、絵画として観賞する目的の度合いが高くなっています。

41-1 Katsushika Hokusai ***The Form of Paintings of Hokusai***
1819, *ōhon*, Shimane Art Museum (Nagata Collection)

This is a picture book with a variety of genres such as the lives of legendary characters and commoners, landscapes, flowers, and birds presented as double-page spreads. Compared to *Hokusai's Sketches*, the purpose of this book was more to have the pictures appreciated.

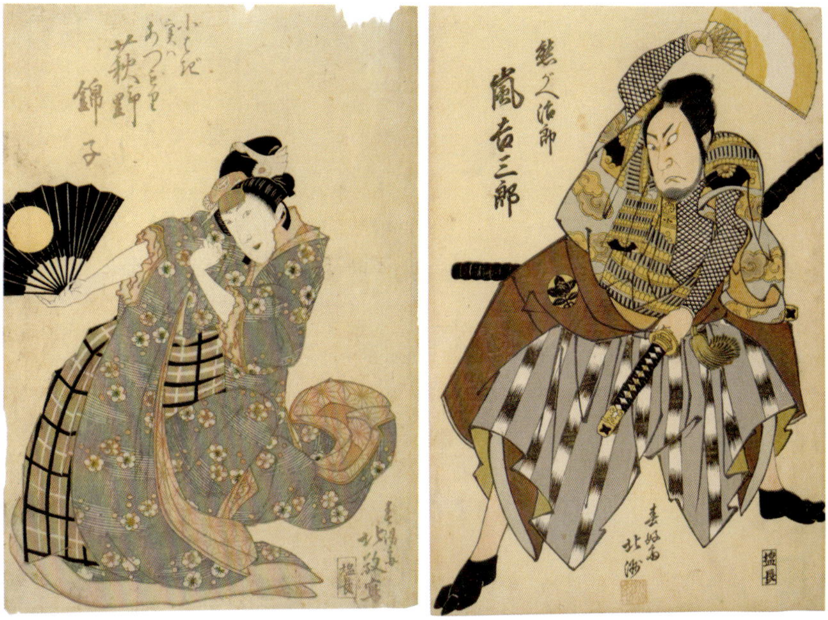

41-2 春陽斎北敬・雪花亭北洲
小はぎ実はあつもり 荻野錦子　熊がへ治郎 嵐吉三郎
文政元年(1818)　大判錦絵2枚続　阪急文化財団 池田文庫蔵

文政元年（1818）5月に上演された芝居を題材にした役者絵です（荻野錦子の「荻」を画中文では「萩」と表記）。北洲、北敬がこの時までに画号を改め、北斎門下となったことを示す貴重な作例となっています。また北洲の署名の下にある印章「よしのやま」は、かつて北斎が使用していた印章です。

41-2 Shun'yōsai Hokkei and Sekkatei Hokushū
Ogino Kinshi as Atsumori (Disguised as Kohagi) and Arashi Kichisaburō as Kumagae Jirō
1818, diptych *ōban nishiki-e*, Ikeda Bunko, Hankyu Culture Foundation

These are actor prints depicting a play performed in the fifth month of 1818. They are valuable examples indicating that Hokushū and Hokkei had changed their artist names and become disciples of Hokusai by then.The "Yoshino-yama" seal under Hokushū's signature is one that Hokusai used to employ.

42 Living in Hiding?
正体を隠して潜んだ地？

Uraga
浦賀

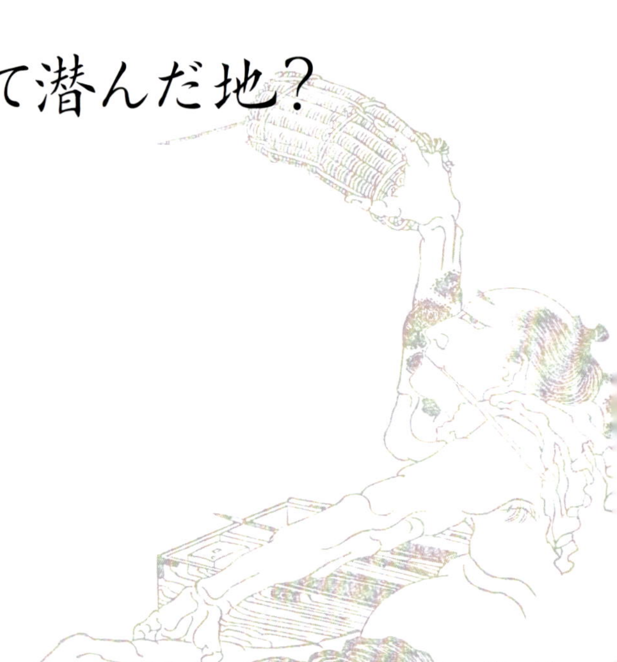

北斎は、天保5～6年（1834～35）、75～76歳頃、現在の神奈川県横須賀市東部の浦賀に潜居していたと『北斎伝』にあります。しかも、正体を隠し、三浦屋八右衛門という偽名を名乗っていました。その理由として、借金から逃げるためであったとか、孫（→66頁参照）の放蕩によって問題が発生したためであったなど、いくつかの説が考えられています。

『北斎伝』に掲載されている北斎の手紙から類推するに、この頃に北斎が江戸の町を離れていたことは確かなようです。しかし、飯島虚心も『北斎伝』で浦賀を実地調査していますが、浦賀に滞在していたという確かな証拠はまだ見つかっておりません。

貴重な資料となるのが、北斎没後の嘉永3年（1850）に刊行された武者絵本『絵本和漢誉（えほんわかんのほまれ）』です。この絵本の中に、「豆相ノ旅客前北斎改　画狂老人卍筆　時七十六歳」とあります（図42-1）。すなわち、天保6年に、北斎は豆州（ずしゅう）（現静岡県東部）と相州（そうしゅう）（現神奈川県）を旅していたようです。そうすると、北斎は浦賀にずっと潜居していたわけではないことになります。また、同じ天保5～6年頃、北斎は千葉にも出かけていたと推測されています。この時期、はたして北斎はどこに出かけていたのか、今後さらなる検討が必要でしょう。

なお、北斎が浦賀を描いた作品として「千絵の海　相州浦賀」（図42-2）があります。ただし、この作品は天保初期の制作と推定されますので、北斎が浦賀に潜居する前に手掛けたことになります。もちろん、北斎がこの作品を描くより以前に、浦賀を訪れていた可能性は十分に考えられます。

According to the biography *Hokusai-den*, Hokusai lived in hiding in Uraga, in the east part of the present Yokosuka-shi, Kanagawa, between 1834 and 1835, when he was 75 or 76. Concealing his identity, he went under the alias Miuraya Hachiemon. Several reasons have been suggested for this. Some say that he wanted to escape his debts and others advocate that there were problems caused by his grandson's prodigality (see p. 66).

Judging from Hokusai's letters published in *Hokusai-den*, he definitely was not in Edo in those days. Yet, although Iijima Kyoshin, the author of *Hokusai-den*, too, conducted an on-the-spot survey of Uraga in order to write the biography, conclusive evidence that Hokusai stayed in Uraga still has not been found.

A significant source is *Picture Book, The Glory of Japan and China*, which was published in 1850, after Hokusai's death. This picture book includes the inscription "Painted by a traveler in Zushū (the east part of the present Shizuoka Prefecture) and Sōshū (the present Kanagawa Prefecture), the former Hokusai, renamed Manji, the Old Man Mad about Drawing, aged 76" (fig. 42-1). This suggests that Hokusai was touring the provinces of Izu and Sagami in 1835. In that case, he would not have been living in hiding all the time in Uraga. There is also a possibility that he went to Chiba around the same time, between 1834 and 1835. Where Hokusai actually went to during this period needs to be investigated further in the future.

Uraga is depicted by Hokusai in *One Thousand Pictures of the Sea: Uraga in Sagami Province* (fig. 42-2). However, this work is considered to have been produced in the early Tempō era (1830-1844), which would mean before he went into hiding in Uraga. Of course, it is perfectly possible that Hokusai had visited Uraga before working on this view.

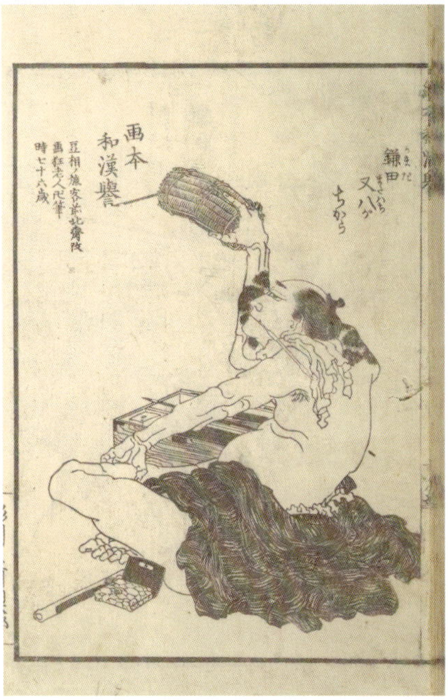

42-1 葛飾北斎 『絵本和漢誉（えほんわかんのほまれ）』

嘉永3年(1850) 半紙本 メトロポリタン美術館蔵

北斎が天保6年（1835）、76歳の時に描いたことが、最終図となる「鎌田又八がちから」の書き入れ（「豆相ノ旅客前北斎改 画狂老人卍筆 時七十六歳」）から判明します。北斎はこの時期、『和漢絵本魁（わかんえほんさきがけ）』『絵本武蔵鐙（えほんむさしあぶみ）』（図36-1）といった他の武者絵本も制作していました。本書は何らかの理由で刊行作業が遅れ、15年後にようやく出版されました。

42-1 Katsushika Hokusai

Picture Book, The Glory of Japan and China

1850, *hanshibon*, The Metropolitan Museum of Art

Judging from the entry in the final picture *Kamata Matahachi's Strength*, we know that this was drawn in 1835, when Hokusai was aged 76. At that time, he was also producing other warrior picture books such as *Picture Book of Chinese and Japanese Warriors* and *Picture Book, The Stirrups of Musashi* (fig. 36-1). For some reason or other, the publication process of this book was delayed and it finally came out fifteen years later.

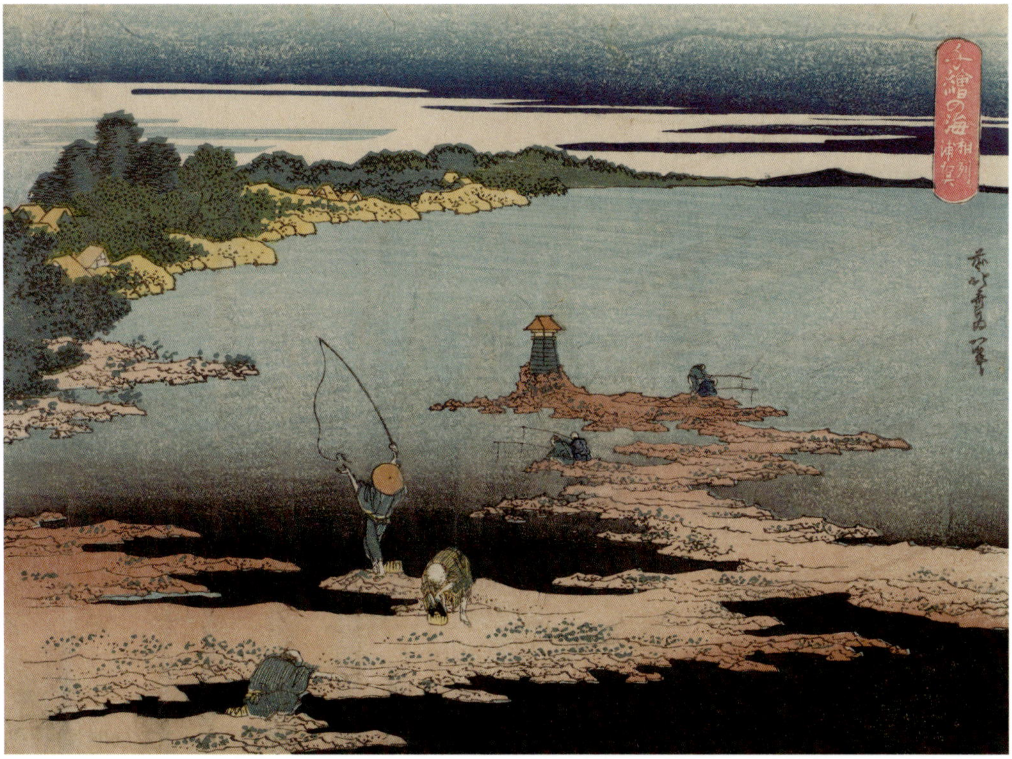

42-2 葛飾北斎 千絵（ちえ）の海（うみ） 相州浦賀（そうしゅううらが）

天保初期(1830〜33)頃 中判錦絵 ボストン美術館蔵

現在の神奈川県横須賀市、浦賀港の入口に位置する岩場の突端に設けられた灯明堂と、その周辺で釣りをする人たちです。北斎はさらに15年ほど前となる文化14年（1817）、『北斎漫画』七編の中で「相模浦賀」と題して灯明堂を描いているので、50代後半にはこの場所を知っていた可能性があります。

42-2 Katsushika Hokusai

One Thousand Pictures of the Sea: Uraga in Sagami Province

c. 1830–1833, *chūban nishiki-e*, Museum of Fine Arts, Boston

This shows a votive light shrine built on the tip of a rocky stretch located at the entrance to the present Uraga Port in Yokosuka-shi, Kanagawa and people fishing around it. Fifteen or so years earlier, in 1817, Hokusai depicted this votive light shrine in *Hokusai's Sketches*, vol. 7 under the title *Sagami Uraga*. Consequently, it is possible that he was already familiar with this place in his late fifties.

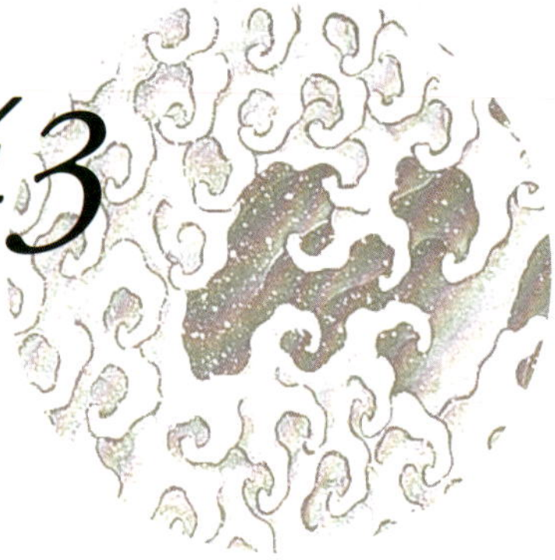

43 Trips in the Final Years

最晩年に訪れた地

Obuse

小布施

北斎は80歳を過ぎた最晩年に、現在の長野県上高井郡にある小布施町を2度訪れています。北斎を小布施へと呼び寄せ、滞在中の世話をしたのが、門人である高井鴻山（たかいこうざん）です。鴻山は、若い頃に京都や江戸に遊学し、天保7年（1836）、小布施に戻って家業の造り酒屋を営んでいました。北斎とは江戸にいた時分に交流が生まれています。

北斎が初めて小布施に滞在したのは天保15年（1844）、85歳の時です。この時は北斎一人だけでしたが、翌弘化2年（1845）、2度目の来訪では、娘の葛飾応為を同行させました。

北斎は小布施に滞在中、鴻山の尽力により、注目すべき作品の制作に関わっています。ひとつは祭屋台の天井絵です。天保15年には東町祭屋台の「龍図」と「鳳凰図」を、弘化2年には上町祭屋台の「男浪図」（図43-3）と「女浪図」（図43-4）を手掛けました。なお、「男浪図」と「女浪図」の縁には、花や鳥、動物などが描かれていますが、これらは北斎が下絵を描き、鴻山が彩色しています。

もうひとつは、岩松院本堂の天井に描かれた巨大な「鳳凰図」（図43-2）です。江戸にいた北斎が彩色した下絵（図43-1）を鴻山に送り届け、鴻山がそれを元に完成させたと考えられます。

北斎が嘉永2年（1849）に亡くなった後も、娘の応為は小布施との交流が続いていました。鴻山が応為に菊図の注文をし、嘉永6年（1853）3月に買い取っています。また、応為が小布施の某宛てに送った手紙として、栗の礼状と、赤絵具の製法を指導したものが残されています。

参考：久保田一洋『北斎娘・応為栄女集』藝華書院, 2015年

Very late in life, at past 80 years of age, Hokusai visited Obuse-machi in the present Kamitakai-gun, Nagano twice. It was Takai Kōzan, a disciple, who invited Hokusai to Obuse and looked after him while he was there. As a young man, Kōzan had studied away from home in Kyoto and Edo. Upon his return to Obuse in 1836, he ran the family business, a *sake* brewery. Kōzan had met Hokusai when he was in Edo.

Hokusai stayed in Obuse for the first time in 1844, when he was 85 years old. On that occasion, he visited Obuse alone. On his second visit the following year, in 1845, he was accompanied by his daughter, Katsushika Ōi.

Thanks to the good offices of Kōzan, Hokusai got involved in notable works during his stay in Obuse. One was the ceiling paintings for some festival floats. In 1844, he did *Dragon* and *Phoenix* for the Higashimachi festival float. In 1845, he produced *Masculine Waves* (fig. 43-3) and *Feminine Waves* (fig. 43-4) for the Kanmachi festival float. There are flowers, birds, animals, etc. on the borders of *Masculine Waves* and *Feminine Waves*. The underdrawings for these border decorations were provided by Hokusai and Kōzan did the coloring.

Another project was a huge *Phoenix* (fig. 43-2) painted on the ceiling of the main hall of the temple Ganshō-in. An underdrawing colored by Hokusai in Edo (fig. 43-1) was delivered to Kōzan, and Kōzan is considered to have completed the painting based on that underdrawing.

Even after Hokusai died in 1849, his daughter Ōi kept in touch with Obuse. Kōzan commissioned Ōi to paint a picture of chrysanthemums and purchased it in the third month of 1853. Letters written by Ōi to someone in Obuse also remain. One is a letter of thanks for chestnuts and another gives instructions on how to make red paint.

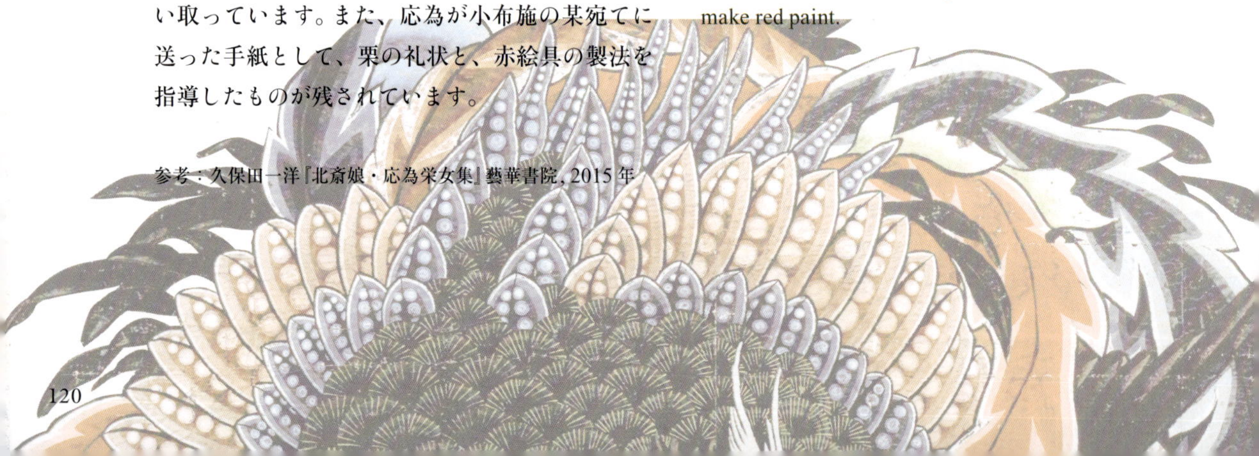

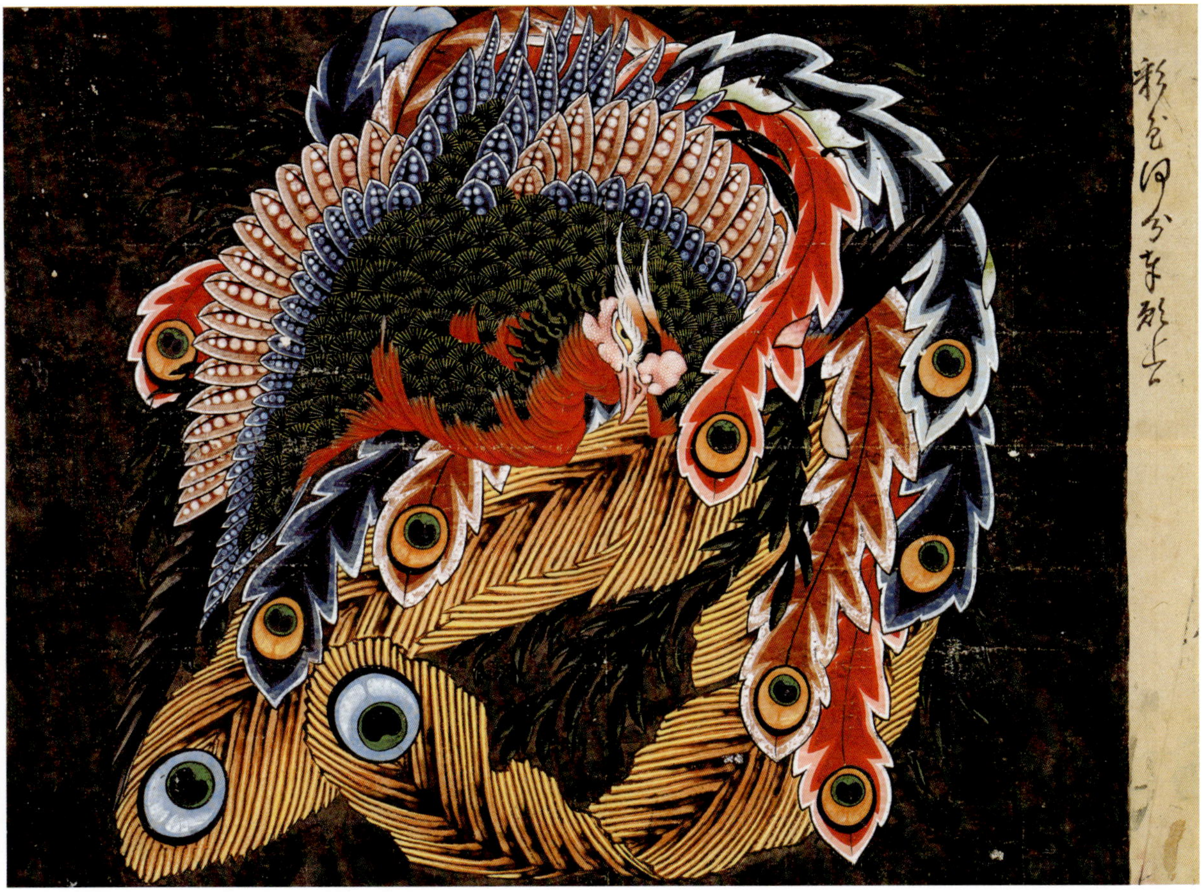

43-1 葛飾北斎 **鳳凰図天井絵彩色下絵**

弘化3年(1846)頃　紙本着色　岩松院蔵

北斎が墨の線で描いた「鳳凰図」の下絵を、高井鴻山が礬水を引いた紙に写し取り、右端に「彩色何分奉願上候」と添えて、江戸にいる北斎の元へ送りました。これに丁寧な彩色をして鴻山の元へ送り返したのが本図です。

43-1 Katsushika Hokusai

***Phoenix*, Underdrawing for Ganshō-in Temple Ceiling**

c. 1846, color on paper, Ganshō-in

Hokusai did an underdrawing for a ceiling painting of a phoenix in *sumi* ink. Takai Kōzan transferred this onto a sized sheet of paper adding the message, "Please give me instructions for the coloring," on the right edge and sent it to Hokusai in Edo. This is the sheet Hokusai colored with great care and sent back to Kōzan.

43-2 **本堂大間と鳳凰図**

弘化4年(1847)頃　板絵着色　岩松院蔵

本堂の天井に描かれた、畳21畳分の大きさとなる巨大な鳳凰図です。

43-2

The Large Room in the Main Temple and *Phoenix*

c. 1847, color on board, Ganshō-in

This is the huge phoenix, the size of twenty-one *tatami* mats, painted on the ceiling of the main temple.

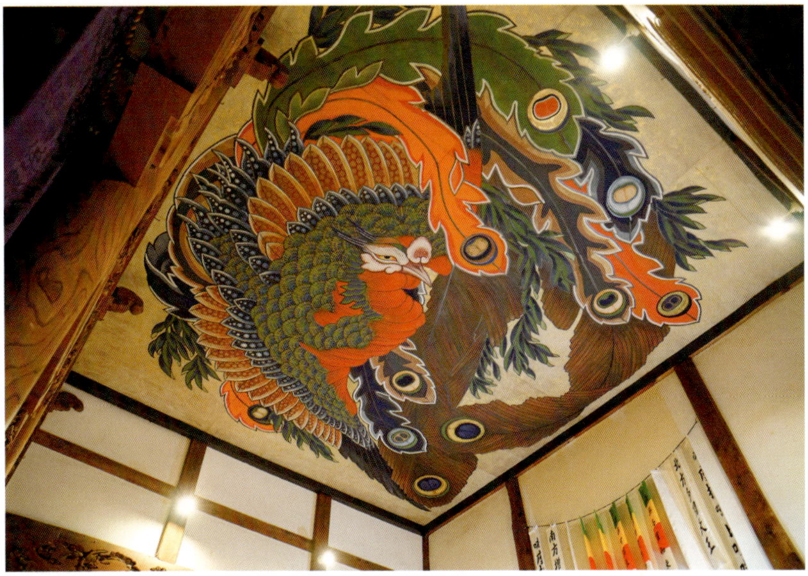

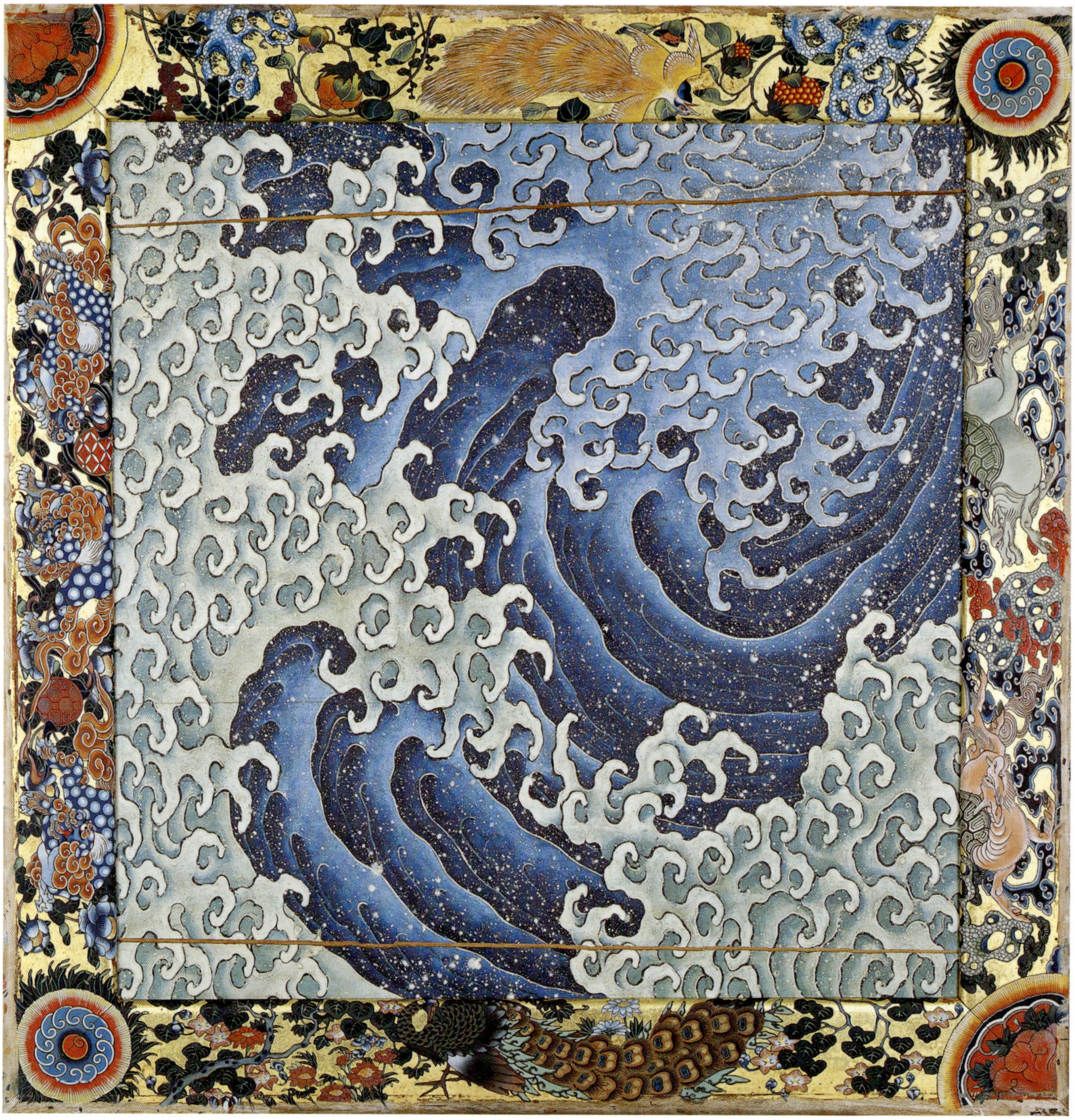

43-3 葛飾北斎 **男浪図**

弘化2年(1845) 板絵着色 小布施町上町自治会蔵(北斎館寄託)

118.0㎝×118.5㎝の大画面に、渦を巻く荒々しい波が描かれています。意匠化された波でありながら、まるでひとつの生命体としてうごめいているかのような生々しさを感じさせます。波を生涯のテーマとしていた(→10頁参照)北斎にしかたどり着くことのできない、最晩年の集大成となっています。

43-3 Katsushika Hokusai

Masculine Waves

1845, color on board, Obuse-machi Kanmachi Residents' Association
(on deposit with Hokusai Museum)

Rough whirling waves cover a huge area measuring 118.0 cm by 118.5 cm. Despite having been stylized, the vivid design gives an impression that the waves are wriggling as a single life form. This is a compilation of Hokusai's lifelong pursuit of the theme of waves (see p. 10) in his final years and an accomplishment that only Hokusai could have achieved.

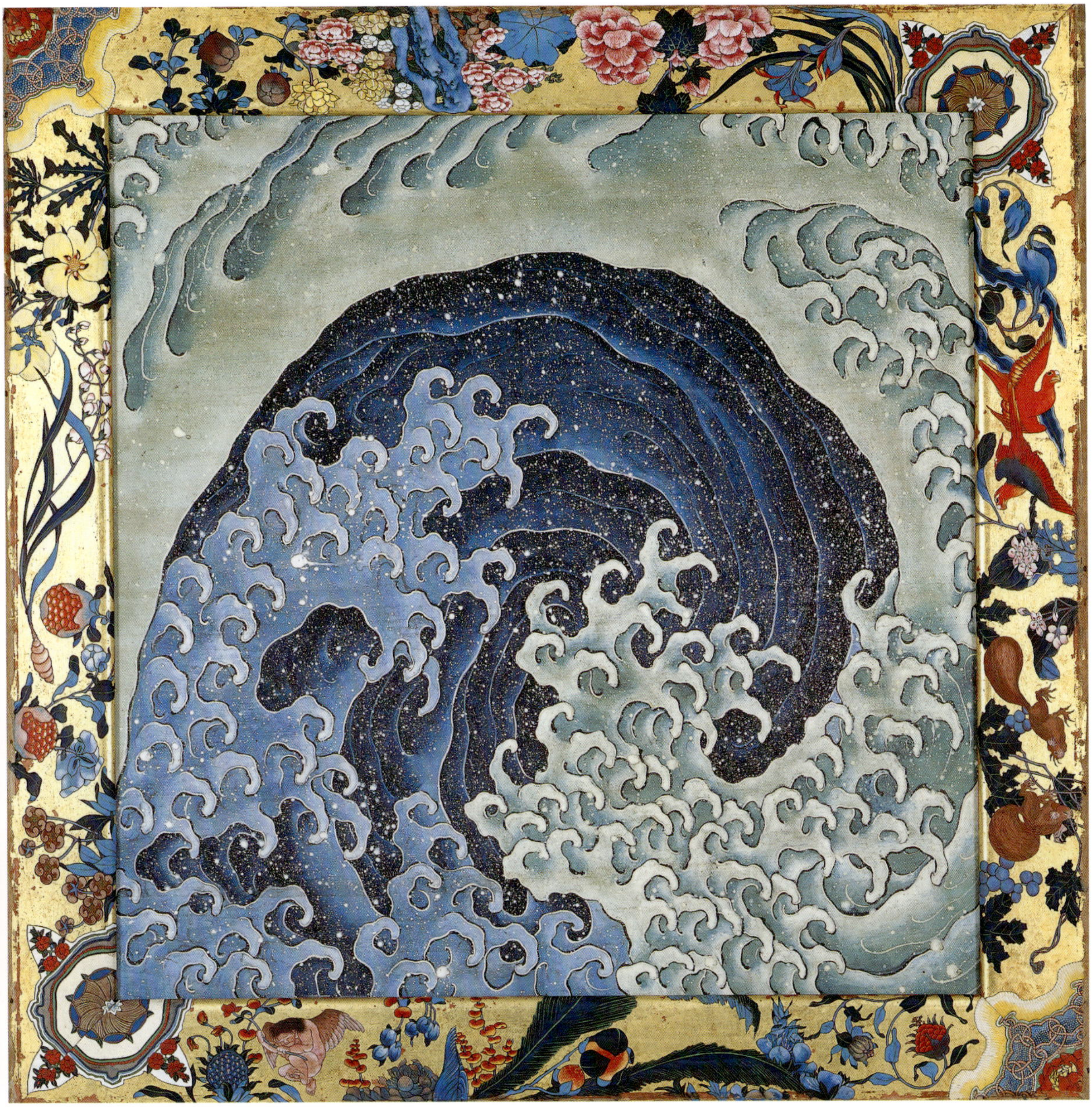

43-4 葛飾北斎 **女浪図**
弘化2年（1845） 板絵着色 小布施町上町自治会蔵（北斎館寄託）

「男浪図」の周囲を彩る金色の縁絵には、極楽鳥や犀、唐獅子、孔雀といった異国の動物たちが描かれています。一方、こちらの「女浪図」の縁絵には、異国風の花や鳥、栗鼠、そして翼のある天使の姿が描かれています。

43-4 Katsushika Hokusai
Feminine Waves
1845, color on board, Obuse-machi Kanmachi Residents' Association (on deposit with Hokusai Museum)

The golden borders of *Masculine Waves* are decorated with foreign animals such as a paradise bird, rhinoceroses, Chinese lions, or a peacock. Meanwhile, the borders of this version, *Feminine Waves*, are painted with exotic flowers and birds, squirrels, and a winged angel.

The History of Studies on Hokusai and Museums Where Hokusai's Works Can Be Seen

北斎研究の歴史と北斎に出会える美術館

北斎研究の歴史を語る上で、まず挙げなければならない書物が、明治26年（1893）に刊行された飯島虚心の『葛飾北斎伝』（蓬枢閣）です。北斎単独の伝記を体系的にまとめた最初の試みということだけでなく、北斎と面識のあった人たちによる貴重な証言を数多く収録していることが大きな特徴となっています。本書においても、北斎の人となりや画業を紹介する上で、頻繁に引用しました。

昭和に入ると、趣味的なものであった浮世絵が、学術的な研究対象になっていきます。北斎の画業を美術史学の視点から体系的にまとめた大著が、昭和19年（1944）に刊行された楢崎宗重の『北斎論』（アトリエ社）です。これ以降、鈴木重三の『人間北斎』（緑園書房、1963年）や安田剛蔵の『画狂北斎』（有光書房、1971年）など、国内外のさまざまな研究者やコレクターたちの力によって、北斎に関する研究は蓄積されていきました。

近年では、永田生慈の業績を忘れることはできません。永田は、北斎に関する多数の書籍や画集、そして雑誌『北斎研究』を刊行しました。また、国内のみならず海外でも北斎の展覧会をいくつも監修することで、北斎の顕彰に努めました。さらに、自身でも北斎の作品を膨大に収集しており、平成２年（1990）、島根県鹿足郡津和野町に葛飾北斎美術館を設立（現在は閉館）、没後は島根県立美術館に全点を寄贈しています。

日本国内には、北斎のコレクションを所蔵する美術館が数多くあります。中でも、北斎が晩年に訪れた小布施にある北斎館と、北斎の生誕の地である墨田区にあるすみだ北斎美術館は、北斎を専門に扱っている美術館として重要です。また、太田記念美術館は浮世絵全般を専門とする美術館ですが、北斎の作品も多数所蔵しています。

The foremost book to be cited in discussing the history of studies on Hokusai would be *Katsushika Hokusai-den* (A biography of Katsushika Hokusai) written by Iijima Kyoshin and published by Hōsūkaku in 1893. Not only was this the first attempt to compile a systematic biography of Hokusai as an individual, but it features numerous valuable testimonies given by people who actually knew the artist. It is frequently quoted to introduce Hokusai's character and artistic achievements in this book, too.

Ukiyo-e used to be regarded a hobby-like genre, but in the Showa era (1926-1989), it became a subject of academic research. *Hokusai-ron* (A study on Hokusai) written by Narazaki Muneshige and published by Atorie-sha in 1944 is a great work systematically compiling Hokusai's artistic achievements from an art historical point of view. Thereafter, studies on Hokusai have been accumulated through the efforts of a variety of scholars and collectors in Japan and abroad including Suzuki Jūzō, *Ningen Hokusai* (Hokusai the man, Ryokuen Shobō, 1963); Yasuda Gōzō, *Gakyō Hokusai* (Hokusai, the man mad about drawing, Yūkō Shobō, 1971); etc.

In recent years, the achievements of Nagata Seiji are unforgettable. He published many books on Hokusai and the magazine *Hokusai kenkyū*. By supervising countless exhibitions of Hokusai's works not only in Japan but also abroad, he strived to make the artist known to the public. He also amassed a substantial collection of works by Hokusai, and established the Katsushika Hokusai Museum of Art in Tsuwano-cho, Kanoashi-gun, Shimane in 1990 (now closed). After Nagata passed away, the entire collection was donated to Shimane Art Museum .

There are many museums in Japan that have a collection of works by Hokusai. Among them, there are two notable museums which specialize in Hokusai. Hokusai Museum is located in Obuse, a town Hokusai visited in his later years, and The Sumida Hokusai Museum is located in Sumida-ku, Tokyo, where Hokusai was born. While Ōta Memorial Museum of Art specializes in *ukiyo-e* in general, its collection includes a large number of works by Hokusai.

Museums in Japan with Major Collections of Works by Hokusai

北斎の作品を所蔵する主な日本の美術館

島根県立美術館

所在地	〒690-0049 島根県松江市袖師町1-5
TEL	0852-55-4700
開館時間	【10月～2月】10:00～18:30 （展示室への入場は18:00まで） 【3月～9月】10:00～日没後30分 （展示室への入場は日没時刻まで）
休館日	毎週火曜日　年末年始（12月28日～1月1日） ※企画展の開催日程等にあわせて休館日を変更する場合があります。
ウェブサイト	https://www.shimane-art-museum.jp

Shimane Art Museum

LOCATION	1-5 Sodeshi-cho, Matsue-shi, Shimane 690-0049
TEL	0852-55-4700
HOURS	[Oct–Feb] 10:00–18:30 (Last admission 18:00) [Mar–Sept] 10:00–30 mins. after sunset (Last admission at sunset)
CLOSED	Tuesdays, Year-end and New Year holidays (Dec 28–Jan 1) *Closures may be altered for special exhibitions.
WEBSITE	https://www.shimane-art-museum.jp

北斎館

所在地	〒381-0201 長野県上高井郡小布施町大字小布施485
TEL	026-247-5206
開館時間	9:00～17:00 （入館は16：30まで） ※1月1日は時間短縮開館10:00～15:00
休館日	12月31日
ウェブサイト	https://hokusai-kan.com

Hokusai Museum

LOCATION	485 Obuse, Obuse-machi, Kamitakai-gun, Nagano 381-0201
TEL	026-247-6206
HOURS	9:00–17:00 (Last admission 16:30)
CLOSED	Dec 31　*Open 10:00-15:00 on Jan 1.
WEBSITE	https://hokusai-kan.com

すみだ北斎美術館

所在地	〒130-0014 東京都墨田区亀沢2-7-2
TEL	03-6658-8936
開館時間	9:30～17:30（入館は17:00まで）
休館日	毎週月曜日（祝日の場合は開館、翌日休館） 年末年始（12月29日～1月1日） ※上記以外にも臨時休館する場合があります。
ウェブサイト	https://hokusai-museum.jp

The Sumida Hokusai Museum

LOCATION	2-7-2 Kamezawa, Sumida-ku, Tokyo 130-0014
TEL	03-6658-8936
HOURS	9:30–17:30 (Last admission 17:00)
CLOSED	Mondays (Open on national holidays and closed the following day.) Year-end and New Year holidays (Dec 29–Jan 1) *There may be additional temporary closures.
WEBSITE	https://hokusai-museum.jp

太田記念美術館

所在地	〒150-0001　東京都渋谷区神宮前1-10-10
TEL	TEL：050-5541-8600（ハローダイヤル）
開館時間	10：30～17：30 （入館は17：00まで）
休館日	毎週月曜日（祝日の場合は開館、翌日休館） 展示替え期間、年末年始
ウェブサイト	http://www.ukiyoe-ota-muse.jp

Ōta Memorial Museum of Art

LOCATION	1-10-10 Jingumae, Shibuya-ku, Tokyo 150-0001
TEL	050-5541-8600（Hello Dial）
HOURS	10:30–17:30 (Last admission 17:00)
CLOSED	Mondays (Open on national holidays and closed the following day.) For rehanging of displays, Year-end and New Year holidays
WEBSITE	http://www.ukiyoe-ota-muse.jp

・情報は2024年5月現在のものです。
・葛飾北斎の作品は常に展示されているとは限りません。
・情報は変更になる場合がありますので、事前に各施設にお問い合わせください。

*The above information is valid as of July 2023.
*Please note that Hokusai's works are not always on view.
*Please check with each venue as there may be changes to the information provided above.

List of Works
作品リスト

◎重要文化財　Important Cultural Property

【葛飾北斎】作品名五十音順
in the order of the Japanese syllabary

【葛飾北斎以外の作品】作家名五十音順

List of Works by Artists Other than Katsushika Hokusai

【著者】
日野原健司（ひのはら・けんじ）

1974年千葉県生まれ。慶應義塾大学大学院文学研究科前期博士課程修了。太田記念美術館主席学芸員、慶應義塾大学非常勤講師。江戸から明治にかけての浮世絵史、ならびに出版文化史を研究。太田記念美術館にて、「北斎と暁斎ー奇想の漫画」、「北斎漫画ー森羅万象のスケッチ」、「葛飾北斎 冨嶽三十六景ー奇想のカラクリ」、「没後170年記念　北斎ー富士への道」などの展覧会を担当。著書に『ようこそ浮世絵の世界へ　英訳付』（東京美術、2015年）、『かわいい浮世絵』（東京美術、2016年）、『北斎 富嶽三十六景』（岩波文庫、2019年）など多数。

Text by Hinohara Kenji

Born in Chiba Prefecture in 1974, Hinohara completed the master's degree program in the Graduate School of Letters at Keio University. He is Chief Curator at the Ōta Memorial Museum of Art and an adjunct professor at Keio University. His research fields include the history of *ukiyo-e* from the Edo through the Meiji periods and the cultural history of publishing, and he has been responsible for curating many Ōta Memorial Museum of Art exhibitions featuring Katsushika Hokusai.
He has also written many books including *An Introduction to Ukiyo-e, in English and Japanese* (Tokyo Bijutsu, 2015).

写真提供・協力一覧
（敬称略・五十音順）

氏家浮世絵コレクション／MOA美術館／大阪市立美術館／太田記念美術館／岡田美術館／小布施町上町自治会／岩松院／木更津市教育委員会／ギメ美術館／九州国立博物館／宮内庁三の丸尚蔵館／慶應義塾大学／国際日本文化研究センター／国文学研究資料館／国立国会図書館／島根県立美術館／角匠／すみだ北斎美術館／誓教寺／大英博物館／千葉市美術館／DNPアートコミュニケーションズ／東京国立博物館／中右コレクション／名古屋市蓬左文庫／名古屋市博物館／西新井大師總持寺／阪急文化財団 池田文庫／日枝神社／PPS通信社／北斎館／ボストン美術館／ミカエル・フォーニッツコレクション／メトロポリタン美術館／メナード美術館／茂木本家美術館／山口県立萩美術館・浦上記念館／山梨県立博物館／ライデン国立民族学博物館／早稲田大学図書館

企画編集：遊佐典枝（東京美術）
編集協力：関橋眞理（オフィスKai）
ブックデザイン：佐々木由美、岩橋香月（株式会社 designfolio）
翻訳：小川紀久子　Translation：Ogawa Kikuko

ようこそ**北斎**の世界へ　英訳付
An Introduction to Hokusai (in English and Japanese)
Anecdotes about the Renowned *Ukiyo-e* Artist

2020年8月31日　初版第1刷発行
2024年6月30日　初版第3刷発行

著　者　日野原健司
発行者　大河内雅彦
発行所　株式会社東京美術
〒170-0011
東京都豊島区池袋本町3-31-15
電 話 (03) 5391-9031
FAX (03) 3982-3295
https://www.tokyo-bijutsu.co.jp
印刷・製本　大日本印刷株式会社

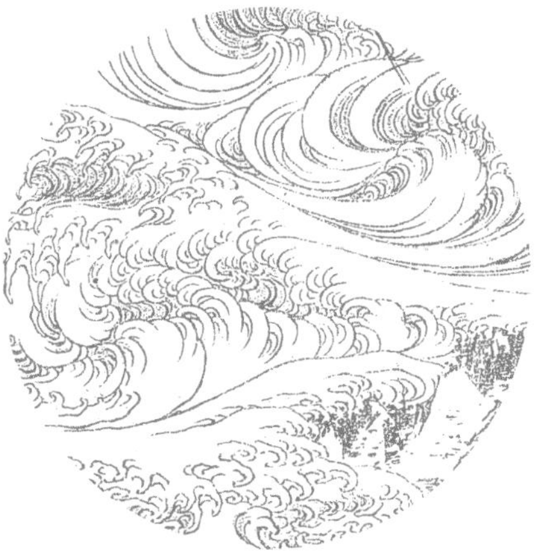

※葛飾北斎『北斎漫画』七編（国立国会図書館蔵）より作成。
From *Hokusai's Sketches*, part 7 (National Diet Library, Japan)

ISBN978-4-8087-1151-1 C0071

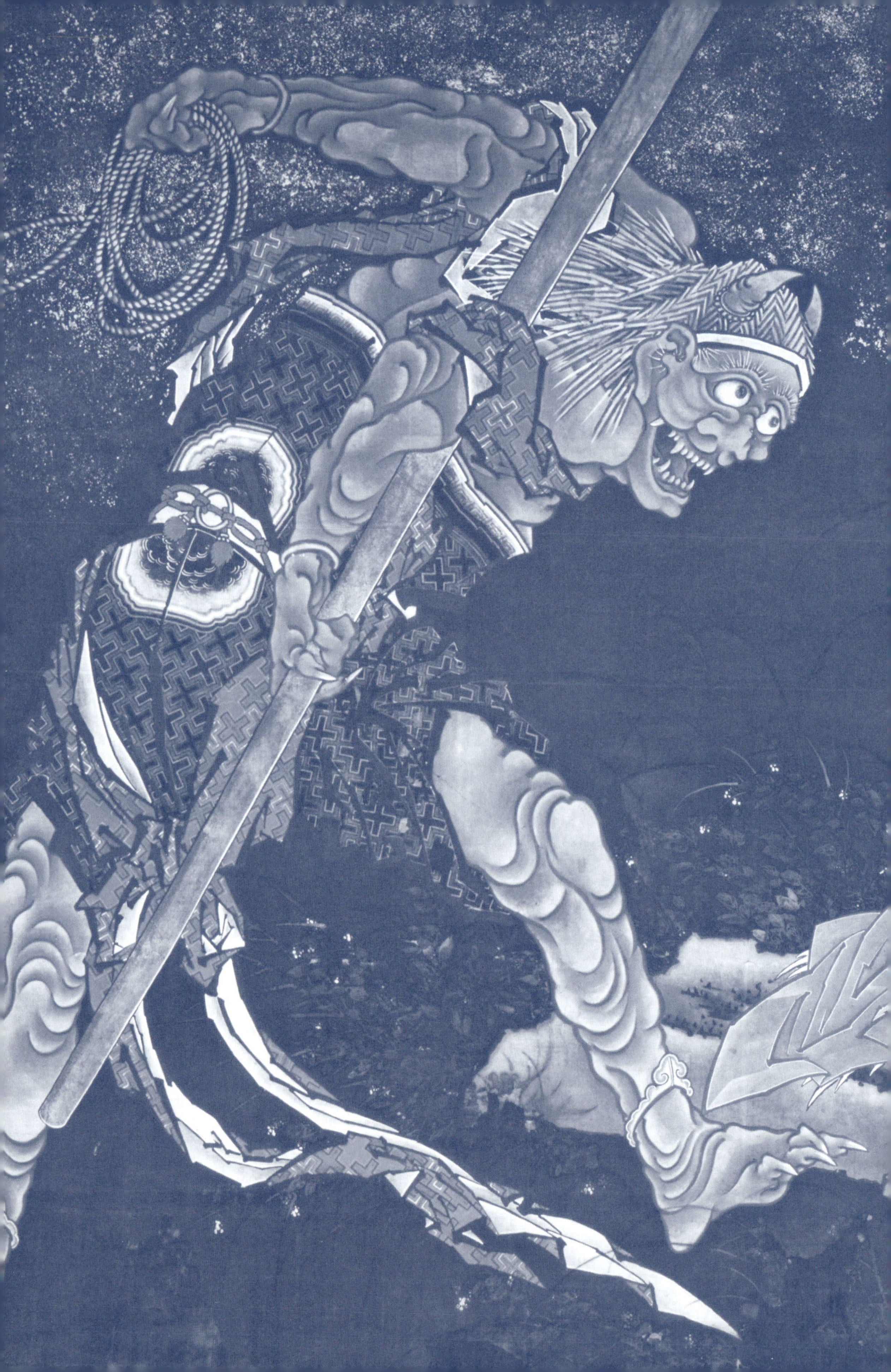